ELITE FORCES

An Encyclopedia of the World's Most Formidable Secret Armies

ELITE FORCES
An Encyclopedia of the World's Most Formidable Secret Armies

Richard M. Bennett

First published in Great Britain in 2003 by
Virgin Books Ltd
Thames Wharf Studios
Rainville Road
London W6 9HA

A catalogue record for this book is available
from the British Library.

ISBN 1 85227 974 5

Typeset by Phoenix Photosetting, Chatham, Kent

Printed and bound by
CPD, Wales

*To my mother Florence, who joyously flouted
convention all her long life; my father Harry, who
rode the hills of Northern India and sailed the South
China Seas; my daughter Katie, who makes it all so
very worthwhile; and my editor, Paul Copperwaite
without whom this book would never have happened.*

FOREWORD

Over the past 50 years the threat of terrorism has grown to the point where it has almost replaced conventional warfare. While most wars are static and territorial, terrorism remains a scattered form of violence which can strike anywhere, at anytime. Against both these threats stand the bastions of today's freedom, the Elite Special Forces. For the most part these units operate under a veil of secrecy, their deeds unsung, their deaths denied. Yet any soldier, policeman or civilian, who submit themselves to intensive training in order to complete perilous tasks in war, or combat terrorism, deserves the title 'Elite'.

Many of these units started out as little more than a private army, almost all were controversial. Often they are to be found operating behind the enemy lines in a myriad of small wars. More recently they have learnt new skills in order to take on the role of countering terrorism. And, while they remain controversial, few would argue that today's Elite Force have not earned their place in the history books.

This intensely researched and authoritative book alphabetically identifies all the major military and civilian Special Forces units in the world. The author tells in comprehensible words the amazing exploits these units have accomplished, while describing the 'nuts and bolts' which make such operations possible. The effectiveness of Special Forces is further exemplified by the fascinating description of equipment and operational procedures.

The author has analysed every aspect of the worlds most Elite Forces and conveys, in his writing, the élan with which they operate. It is a comprehensive work on the world's Elite Forces from their beginning to the present day. I have no reservations in recommending this book as an indispensable record in the study of Elite Forces for all those interested in military history.

Barry Davies BEM
November 2002.

'A' TEAM – US SPECIAL FORCES

The US Special Forces Operational Detachment-A, or A-Team, is the fundamental building block for all the Special Forces Groups. There are six A detachments in each Special Forces company. A captain leads the twelve-man team. Second in command is a warrant officer. Two non-commissioned officers, or NCOs, trained in each of the five SF functional areas: weapons, engineering and demolitions, medicine, communications, and operations and intelligence comprise the remainder of the team. All team members are SF qualified and cross-trained in different skills as well as being multi-lingual.

In the SF company, one of the six A-teams is trained in combat diving and one is trained in military free-fall parachuting. Both are used as methods of infiltration. A-teams are equipped with high-powered communications systems such as tactical satellite communications, burst transmission devices, high-frequency radios and global positioning systems. Medical kits include, among other things, field surgical kits, laboratory and dental instruments and supplies, sterilisers, resuscitator-aspirators, water-testing kits and veterinary equipment. Other key equipment includes individual and perimeter defence weapons as well as night-vision devices, and electric and non-electric demolitions, which varies according to the nature of the mission. For underwater or waterborne infiltration, SCUBA (self-contained underwater breathing apparatus) teams are equipped with open-circuit twin-80s SCUBA tanks, closed-circuit Dragger (rebreather) Lar-V, Zodiac boat and Klepper kayaks. Military free-fall HAHO/HALO parachuting teams use ram-air parachutes and oxygen systems.

ABU DHABI – UAE (UNITED ARAB EMIRATES)

EMIRATE OF ABU DHABI POLICE SPECIAL UNIT

This unit has been heavily influenced by the British SAS, and is believed to be tasked with providing CT capabilities to all Emirates within the UAE who do not already have such a team in place. This unit is 40-men strong and is based at the Abu Dhabi Airport.

ACCURACY INTERNATIONAL PM

The PM is a bolt-action 7.62mm sniper's rifle with a free-floating stainless steel barrel. It is unusual in having a fully interchangeable and adjustable trigger system which can be switched between rifles. The bolt is cleverly designed so that the head does not have to move during its operation, allowing continuous observation of the target – this continues through the recoil cycle as well. Equipped with a bipod and a retractable spike on the rear of the butt, this effectively creates a tripod effect for use during long hours of surveillance. This is considered to be of great value by the SAS SP (Special Project) teams. It has a box magazine holding twelve rounds and, with scopes such as the Schmidt & Bender 6x42, has a lethal range in excess of 700yds (640m). The 7.62mm PM or Counter-Terrorist (L96A1) can also be found chambered in .300 Winchester Magnum and 7mm Remington Magnum.

ACHILLE LAURO – HIJACK ON THE HIGH SEAS

Four heavily armed Palestinian terrorists from the Abu Nidal group in October 1977 hijacked the Italian cruise ship *Achille Lauro*, carrying more than 400 passengers and crew, off Egypt. The hijackers demanded that Israel free 50 Palestinian prisoners. The terrorists killed an elderly American tourist, Leon Klinghoffer, and threw his body overboard along with his wheelchair. After a two-day drama, the hijackers surrendered in exchange for a pledge of safe passage. However, when an Egyptian jet tried to fly the hijackers to freedom, US Navy F-14 fighters intercepted it and forced it to land in Sicily. The terrorists were taken into custody by Italian authorities. Counter-terrorist units from the US responded, including elements of Delta Force and SEAL Team Six, but the situation was resolved before an assault became necessary.

ADOO

Arabic for 'enemy' – a term often used by SAS veterans of Middle Eastern operations, in particular those who served in Oman and South Arabia.

AFGHANISTAN – 1979 SOVIET INVASION

The full-scale invasion of Afghanistan began on 27 December 1979 with an attack by Soviet Airborne Special Forces units on Kabul Airport. This was quickly followed by a lightning assault on the Presidential Palace of Hafez Amin. This was carried out by the elite Al'fa special action group and led by a full general. Having disposed of the Afghan Guards, the Soviet general, with a small number of picked men, moved through the building in a classic room-clearing operation, killing every man, woman and child they found – no witnesses to the murder of the Afghan President were to survive.

The remaining Soviet Special Forces secured the perimeter with strict instructions to shoot anyone trying to leave the building, unfortunately this included the Soviet general, who was 'accidentally shot and killed' in the latter part of the operation. Though portrayed later as a hero who died for his country, the death of the general was fortuitous, in that it removed a potential political embarrassment if the overall Soviet invasion had failed. It can be suggested that his death may therefore not have been an accident and that the life of even such a senior Special Forces officer was entirely expendable if it benefited the Soviet Communist Party.

ALAMO SCOUTS

Lieutenant General Walter Krueger established a small elite force in the Pacific combat zone, naming them the Alamo Scouts after his native San Antonio. In perhaps their greatest feat, the Scouts led US Rangers and Filipino guerrillas in an attack on a Japanese prison camp at Cabantuan, freeing all 511 Allied prisoners there. Never numbering more than 70 volunteers, the Alamo Scouts earned 44 Silver Stars, 33 Bronze Stars and four Soldier's Medals by the end of the war. In nearly 80 hazardous missions, they never lost a man in action. An elite formation that very much laid the foundation for later Special Forces units.

ALBANIA

MILITARY SPECIAL FORCES

Commando Brigade   The Albanian Army's elite Commando Brigade is based at Zall-Herr in Tirana. They are trained by US Special Forces and Turkish commandos and provide security for the port of Durres, and at several joint CIA-NSA US Intelligence Listening Sites where they serve as a 'military security force'.

Naval Commandos   The Albanian Navy maintains a small commando unit as well, and it has been reported that the training of this unit does involve a Counter-Terrorist mission.

CIVILIAN SPECIAL FORCES

Reparti i Eleminimit dhe Neutralizimit te Elementit te Armatosur (RENEA) Albania's primary Counter-Terrorist unit, RENEA, was founded in November 1991 under the code name '88' and remains under the control of the Ministry of the Interior. It has two platoon-sized units, which are trained by the regular Italian police, but not the elite NOCS unit. It is armed with TT33, Makarov PM and Beretta 92 pistols, 5.56mm M16AI and 7.62mm AK47 assault rifles and equipped with Israeli body-armour and possibly 9mm Uzi SMG. RENEA are reported to be one of the busiest CT units in Europe.

Reparti i Operacioneve Speciale (ROS)   ROS is another Counter-Terrorist unit, which has been trained by British SAS instructors. Founded in February 2000 and code-named '77', this unit also falls under the Ministry of the Interior and is based in Durres. It has intelligence duties and is used primarily against 'enemies of the state'. They use a mix of Western and Warsaw Pact weapons and its trainees undergo a particularly rigorous selection programme.

Shqiponjat – 'The Eagles' There is a new police anti-terrorist, rapid intervention group called 'Shqiponjat' ('The Eagles'). Weapons in use include Makarov PM, Tokarev TT pistols, Chinese 7.62mm Type 56 (Kalashnikov) assault rifles, 7.62mm H&K PSG and Dragunov sniper rifles.

ALGERIA

MILITARY SPECIAL FORCES
One Special Forces/Airborne Divisional HQ with
Four Airborne Regiments
Ministry of National Defence
'The Ninjas' 18th Régiment Parachutiste Commando (Special Force Airborne Regiment) trained and formed at the Special Troops Implementation School at Biskra, 330km SE of Algiers. The Ninjas have a reputation for toughness, not to say brutality in the treatment of anti-government groups. However, the problems they face in dealing with a countrywide insurgency by Islamic groups who slaughter innocent men, women and children with impunity has largely precluded the opportunity to develop the finer points of prisoner care and attention to legal niceties.

Saaykaa (Commando) Sometimes participating in CT operations in co-ordination with other types of special units. These units are based at Boughar, Medea Wilaya, 75km SW of Algiers.

Naval Units (Marine Nationale) The Navy's Special Forces include 1) the so-called Marine Fusiliers and 2) the Offensive (Combat) Divers. Both are trained at the school of Jiel, 250km E of Algiers.

CIVILIAN SPECIAL FORCES
Ministry of the Interior
URS, Unités Républicaines de Sécurité – Republican Security Units These are units initially tasked with duties of public order enforcement and the protection of sensitive sites. Because of the terrorist threat, they were forced to adapt and to transform themselves into rapid intervention and CT units. Before 1992–93, there were no units effectively specialised in CT missions. The URS main complex and command centre is situated at the El Hamiz barracks in Algiers. The URS count approximately 45 operational units; one operational unit for most of the geographical departments (wilaya). Each unit is organised into four Intervention and one Command and Support Sections.

URS Command has also the responsibility over the SCAP – Central Service for Pyrotechnical Activities (EOD or bomb squad) whose mission is to dispose of terrorist explosive devices and mines.

In the course of the years, and with the experience gained in fighting terrorism, such missions were passed to other police services, especially created for that purpose. These are:

DRS (Research and Security Directorate)   The DRS is the main Intelligence agency, tasked with internal security, counter-intelligence, military security and intelligence gathering missions. It maintains at least one Special Forces unit known as the Special Unit of the Service Action, tasked with sensitive missions, anti-terrorist and hostage rescue operations.

GIS, Groupe d'Intervention Spécial – Special Intervention Group   Created at the end of the 1970s, its existence was kept secret for a long time, until a second lieutenant of this unit killed President Boudiaf at Annaba, on 29 June 1992, where the GIS was backing-up the presidential security unit, the Brigade Spéciale. It is known that the GIS participates in many CT-missions, especially in Algiers, where it is based. There is also a facility at Blida, 50km from Algiers.

Assault and Rapid Intervention unit. Brigade Spéciale or 'Brigade 127'   of the Garde Républicaine. Elite corps of the Gendarmerie, responsible among other duties for the protection of the President.

ALGIERS AIRCRAFT HIJACKING – GIGN

Four terrorists of the AIG, the extremist faction of an Islamic fundamentalist coalition waging a bloody civil war against the military-backed government of Algeria, had managed to board an Air France airbus disguised as airport security men. As the aircraft readied for take-off at 11.15, the terrorists produced miniature AK-47s with collapsible stocks, and within minutes the aircraft was under their control and all of the 257 passengers and crew taken hostage. The terrorists demanded to be flown to Paris, and to emphasise their point they took an Algerian policeman and a Vietnamese diplomat to the front of the aircraft, shot both in the back of the head and dumped their bodies on the runway. A GIGN team, which by that evening had driven on to the military airfield of Neuilly, boarded an Air France airbus identical to the hijacked plane. Special arrangements had been made so that they could completely familiarise themselves with the aircraft's workings, and so plan and practice the counter-hijack operation, while flying south to their destination. But clearance to land at Algiers' Boumedienne airport had not been received as the team took off shortly before 20.00. Advice from two French military advisers at Boumedienne airport was ignored, and permission for the GIGN team to land continued to be refused. The GIGN team were forced to wait on board their airbus at the nearby Spanish airport of Palma de Mallorca.The Algerians tried to reassure the French government that the terrorists were bluffing, but shortly after 22.00 the French cook onboard the aircraft was murdered and his corpse thrown down the mobile stairway. Discussions between key French negotiators and high-ranking Algerian military commanders failed to produce action, and only following direct orders from the Algerian Prime Minister and senior army commanders, did the 'Ninja' Special Forces colonel agree to withdraw the stairway, allowing the aircraft to take-off at 00.02 on 26 December 1994, bound for Marseilles, where the French government had cleared it to land. The GIGN team was already in place, having touched down just twenty minutes earlier on board their airbus at an airstrip adjacent to the main airport. GIGN snipers had taken up positions around the control tower and were camouflaged among the tall grass lining the runway, closely observing the hijacked plane, Flight 8969, taxiing to a halt at Marseilles-Marignane. From that moment onwards the hijack crisis negotiations were entirely under the control of the GIGN. Problems arose when it was discovered that the terrorists had placed two ten-stick packs of dynamite in the cockpit and beneath a row of passenger seats fused by one detonator during the flight from Algeria. The amount of fuel the hijackers were demanding was three times what was needed to fly to Paris. Its real purpose, the GIGN speculated, was to create an exploding fireball somewhere above the Eiffel Tower. The GIGN spun out the negotiations still further, offering to provide the hijackers with food and to service the aircraft, cleaning it and emptying the blocked toilets, which were creating a terrible smell. Surprisingly, they agreed. Disguised among the stewards and service crew, who were allowed to board the aircraft, GIGN operatives inserted minuscule eavesdropping devices. Tiny infrared closed-circuit cameras and cannon microphones were placed by windows along the exterior of the fuselage. It was now possible to monitor closely what was happening in the aircraft. By 16.00 the GIGN were in position at the bottom of their respective mobile stairways and fully prepared. After putting their Kevlar helmets with yellowish Plexiglas visors over their heads, already hooded with ski masks, and strapping bullet-proof vests over fire-retardant suits, they armed themselves with .357 Magnum revolvers and 9mm MP-5 sub-machine guns. Snipers positioned on the top of the control tower trained their rifles' telescopic sights on the cockpit, where two of the terrorists guarded the pilot and flight crew. Just before 17.00, under cover of the distraction provided by the searing noise of accelerating jet engines coming from an airbus parked some 400 yards away, it started to move. The GIGN played for time, reassuring the frightened terrorists while the assault teams repositioned themselves, adjusting their angles of approach. The airbus got to within 30 yards of the control tower and at 17.08 a gun protruded from the cockpit's window, and shots were fired by a terrorist.

The GIGN started their assault immediately, the trailer engines of three mobile stairways started simultaneously. The group of eight commandos positioned on each climbed the steps in double file as the stairways drew nearer to the aircraft. A sniper on the control tower with a silenced .50 rifle fired six shots that smashed through the cockpit's right-hand windscreen. The heavy rounds were fired high, as it was very difficult to determine who was terrorist and who was air crew inside the cramped cabin, everyone ducking for cover as the half-inch bullets crashed inside, but this move succeeded in distracting the terrorists as the stairway came up to the right-hand door of the aircraft. The hatch-doors were wrenched open and stun grenades thrown inside the aircraft; the detonation was quickly followed by the first pair of CQQB-trained GIGN commandos. They caught two shocked hijackers along the hallway, making for the cockpit. A single .357 bullet diagonally through his forehead killed the first terrorist, but in the next half a second a barrage of automatic fire from two more hijackers barricaded with the flight crew hit the commandos, one of whom was hit by seven AK rounds. Three 7.62mm bullets perforated his exposed right arm, shooting off three fingers curled around the MP-5's handgrip, which was also shot to pieces. Other bullets hit his shoulder and chest, shredding the black vinyl fabric and denting the steel ceramic plates of his bullet-proof vest. Another round ricocheted off the Kevlar helmet as he reeled backwards, collapsing on to the carpeted hallway. More grenades were then thrown into the cockpit. The front left-hand door of the aircraft now slid open, as the eight gendarmes in the second assault wave stormed into the aircraft. A terrorist shooting from the cockpit's side window sprayed them with a burst of sub-machinegun fire before they were even inside, and several rounds hit the side of the sliding door as it moved towards the cockpit. One of the GIGN was hit in the lower legs. Falling backwards, he had to be pulled away under covering fire by other commandos, who began evacuating their most severely wounded comrades. GIGN men were simultaneously moving through the rear of the aircraft from the tail doors. Having opened emergency exits, they evacuated the 159 passengers, who came sliding out on escape chutes as the gun battle raged at the front of the aircraft. Stray bullets flew into the main seating section but no passengers were wounded by gunfire and only thirteen were treated for light injuries, mostly cuts and bruises, after the full evacuation had been completed in twenty minutes.

The ferocious battle continued for another ten minutes as two more commandos from the second wave were wounded. They continued to pour a withering fire at the cockpit, painfully aware that it still contained the flight crew. Finally they heard the pilot's voice from inside, screaming, 'Stop shooting!' The GIGN found the bullet-riddled bodies of three dead terrorists lying on top of both pilots, who were, remarkably, unscathed amid the blood, wreckage and piles of spent shell cases. They could see the package of dynamite tucked beneath the pilot's seat. It was fused to a detonator but the terrorists had died before they finally had a chance to destroy the aircraft. The GIGN action at Marseilles was one of the most difficult and successful hostage rescue operations since the SAS action in 1980 at the Iranian Embassy.

ALPHA

Alpha or Alfa. Soviet, now Russian, Special Forces group operating under the control of the KGB/SVR Foreign Intelligence Services. The nearest equivalent to the SAS and Delta Force.

AMMUNITION

Enhanced capability ammunition is produced for a number of different types of small arms regularly used by Special Forces. High-penetration rounds are produced to deal with terrorists equipped with protective body-armour, such as the KTW-round for very high velocity made of bronze alloy and Teflon-covered. The Glaser-round is filled with shot in a copper case sealed with Teflon and designed to penetrate plaster walls or wooden partitions, then fragment to cause devastating flesh wounds to the target. An advantage of this type of round is that there is little chance of a ricochet injuring a member of the assault team or, for that matter, an innocent bystander. However, in a potential aircraft hijacking that takes place in flight, a skymarshall or Special Forces team placed on the aircraft having obtained hard intelligence of the likelihood of terrorist action would use weapons equipped with special low-velocity rounds that would, hopefully, kill or disable the targets without puncturing the metal skin of the fuselage, with the possibility of a massive and probably fatal depressurisation of the aircraft at high altitude.

ANGOLA

MILITARY SPECIAL FORCES
A small Presidential Guard anti-terrorist detachment based in Luanda. The present state of this war-torn country will almost certainly prevent the establishment of a true Special Forces capability and suitable training facilities for the foreseeable future.

AO

Area of Operations.

ARGENTINA

MILITARY SPECIAL FORCES

Army Command level.

Cía. de Comandos 601–601st Special Forces Company – Campo de Mayo, Buenos Aires. This unit was deployed to the Falkland Islands in 1982 and was involved in tough combat with elements of the SAS on the slopes of Mount Kent, a strategic hill overlooking the capital Port Stanley.

Brigada Especial de Operaciones Halcón-8 (Falcon-8 Special Operations Brigade) Argentina did not possess a viable Counter-Terrorist capability until 1978, when the nation hosted the World Cup Soccer championships. At that time, the government accepted the possibility that such a widely televised event was a likely forum for a terrorist incident. The result was the formation of the Special Counter-Terrorist Team, also known as 'Brigada Halcon'. Today, the unit is made up of 75 commandos, subdivided into fifteen-man tactical teams. Each team has two snipers, one medic, one negotiator, an EOD (Explosive Ordinance Demolition) expert, a communications specialist, an intelligence specialist and eight assault riflemen. Initial training is divided into three two-month stages. Topics such as combat shooting, heliborne insertion, parachuting (HALO), explosives, sniping, intelligence-gathering and offensive driving are covered in this period. The unit also works as VIP protection, anti-hijacking of aircraft and is trained in hostage rescue (HRU). While many current members are veterans of the Argentinian Army, Halcon is under the operational control of the national police and under the direct command of the Buenos Aires (Bonsara) police department.

All Argentinian Special Force units only accept volunteers, who must pass through a tough three-day selection course, which is followed by three months' training in CQB, jungle and urban warfare at the Campo de Mayo Infantry School. Parachute training takes place at the Catamarca Airborne School and, finally, specialist training relating to the unit the successful recruits actually join. This unit has been provided with state-of-the-art equipment including image intensifiers, communications and laser sights for sniper rifles. Argentina's Security and Special Forces have a long history of human rights abuse and close connections with right-wing, even fascist death squads. In 1973 they became involved with the Alianza Anti-Comunista Argentina (AAA) who were responsible for at least 29 political assassinations and the Comando Libertadores de America (CLA), a murder squad with close links to serving military personnel. Torture and illegal executions were to form a staple part of the Special Forces tactics and at least 5,000 civilians, abducted by the security apparatus between 1975 and 1981 alone, have never been seen again. There is little evidence that the situation improved until after the fall of the military regime in the aftermath of

Argentina's defeat in the Falklands War with Britain. Though the level of human rights abuse has dropped, it has not ended completely, and even in 2002 there were reports of beatings and torture by certain Special Forces units.

Marines
COMANDOS ANFIBIOS (*Argentine amphibious special forces*)   This unit is trained and equipped to carry out operations similar to those of the USMC Recons.

Navy
BUZOS TACTICOS (*Navy's combat swimmers and demolition experts*)   This 100-man combat diver unit, based at Mar del Plata Naval Base, is organised into six platoons and is responsible for the resolution of terrorist hijackings of vessels at sea. Were involved in action against British Royal Marines during the invasion of the Falkland Islands in April 1982.

Air Force
Grupo de Operaciones Especiales – GOE (*Air Force Elite Unit*)   The Argentine Air Force maintains a small company-sized Special Operations unit known as GOE. The unit traces its history back to 1947, when the air force formed the country's first parachute school and airborne unit. The unit was originally known as the 13th Parachute Regiment and operated under army control until an official army airborne unit was raised. Over the years the air force's airborne unit was gradually relegated to a secondary role, with the army's Special Forces Group becoming the country's primary force. The 13th Parachute Regiment was reduced in size and was eventually renamed the GOE. All personnel are qualified HALO parachutists and specialise in conducting LRRP missions. Since its formation the unit has steadily expanded its capabilities, receiving training from US Army Special Forces Mobile Training Teams (MTT), the US Army School of the Americas, and the former US Army Jungle Operations Training Centre (JOTC) in Panama. Individual unit members have also trained at Fort Bragg, NC. This 100-man unit, headquartered at Moron Air Base in Buenos Aires, is responsible for resolving aircraft hijacking issues. Members are drawn primarily from the Argentine Air Force military police.

CIVILIAN SPECIAL FORCES
GEOF (*Grupo Especial de Operaciones Federales*)   Recently formed elite police unit. Highly trained in crime-busting and anti-terrorist operations.

This unit uses the following equipment: 9mm Glock 17 pistol, 9mm H&K MP5A3 sub-machine gun, 5.56mm H&K HK33A2 assault rifle, 5.56mm H&K HK33SG1 sniper rifle and 18.5mmR (12-gauge) Franchi SPAS-12 shotgun.

ARMALITE – COLT

The AR15 and AR18 series achieved substantial commercial success and some notoriety as a favourite weapon of terrorist groups and in particular the IRA. It is the US military version of the AR15, the M16 series that has become one of the world's premier combat weapons and certainly ranks alongside the Kalashnikov as one of the most widely used. The original design by Eugene Stoner for Armalite and manufactured by Colt entered service in 1961, but the best known version, the M16A1, was only introduced in 1966 after field experience in Vietnam. The M16A1 is a gas-operated rifle which fires the 5.56mm rounds from 20- or 30-round box magazines in either single shot or fully automatic mode with a cyclic rate of up to 200rpm. To avoid gross ammunition wastage a selector was eventually fitted, allowing a three-shot burst. The later M16A2 had a heavier barrel, which allows the use of the more powerful NATO SS109 5.56mm round, increasing the effective range from 340yds (310m) to 550yds (500m). The M16A3 is simply an M16A2 with a removable carrying handle, which leaves a more substantial mounting for the larger and more advanced scopes. All M16 variants can be fitted with the M203 40mm grenade launcher beneath the barrel, allowing the use of a range of fragmentation or smoke grenades. The M16 series are often fitted with laser-sights, telescopic sights or passive light intensifiers. A further variation, the M15 Colt Commando, had a shorter barrel and retractable butt and was designed for combat in restricted space, whether in jungle or urban warfare. Its range, however, was limited to around 200yds (180m). Originally manufactured by Colt exclusively for Navy SEAL team 6, the AR-23 is designed to function perfectly and accurately even under extreme conditions such as prolonged immersion in water, mud, sand and other substances (even corrosive ones). The design of this assault carbine is somewhere between an assault rifle and a SMG, resembling a short, bullpup configured M16. The AR-23 features Colt's new Advanced Loading System (ALS) which uses a special 'self-sealing' magazine that can be loaded in various conditions, even while still underwater. Other features of the AR-23 include a full-spectrum electronic sight, an integral silencer/flash suppresser, a collapsing stock, and even ergonomic rubber grips for extra control.

ARMENIA

MILITARY SPECIAL FORCES

There is a Special Operations Airborne Battalion based in Yerevan. This unit has an anti-terrorist role with a limited HRU capability. The military authorities have expressed a considerable interest in building a genuine Special Forces capability, and in consequence are seeking US and European advisers and finance to build suitable facilities and begin recruitment

CIVILIAN SPECIAL FORCES
The Ministry of the Interior
Small dedicated 40-strong SWAT-style unit which acts as a national HRU as well.

AUSTRALIA

MILITARY SPECIAL FORCES
The threat of a terrorist outrage during the run-up to the 2000 Sydney Summer Olympics was taken very seriously indeed by the Australian authorities. Every possible action that could be taken by the Special Air Service, in co-operation with the counter-terrorist branch of the ASIO Internal Security Service was rehearsed and refined in the weeks leading up to the Games. The Tactical Assault Group (TAG) of the Australian Special Air Service Regiment and its helicopter support unit had been training in the city area, to familiarise themselves with local operating conditions from road traffic flow, to mapping the sewers. This level of training is more important than ever now since the threat of international terrorism has grown. While the Special Forces have long been a prime source of covert intelligence gathering and recruits for both the ASIS and ASIO, its role as the executive arm of the intelligence community in 2002 has been confirmed. The Tactical Assault Group has been Australia's primary Counter-Terrorist Force since 1996, when some $45 million was spent on upgrading the unit's weapon, communications and command systems to considerably enhance its overall capabilities. The Tactical Assault Group is to have its role as a rapidly deployable counter-terrorist group, further extended in 2002–03 with more personnel and an infusion of advanced new equipment and indeed will also benefit from a even closer relationship with the US Army's Delta Force. The Australian Special Air Service, to whom the Tactical Assault Group belongs, was formed in July 1957 as a squadron or company-sized unit. By the time of Australia's involvement in the Borneo Campaign and Vietnam War, both in the mid-1960s, two further squadrons had been raised and, along with Signal and Headquarters units, formed the new 1st SAS Regiment. The SAS had earned a high reputation by the time it ceased operations in Vietnam, racking up an amazing record and firmly establishing itself as a major player in the Special Operations Field. The SAS had a confirmed kill rate of 500-to-1 and had won the highest possible honours for gallantry with four Victoria Crosses (equivalent of the Congressional Medal of Honour) to confirm its reputation. Australia had never felt the power of terrorism until 12.40 on 13 February 1978, when a powerful bomb exploded in the entrance to the Hilton Hotel in central Sydney. Ten days later, the newly formed 1st squadron of the Australian Special Air Service Regiment, or SASR, was designated Australia's CT force. Soon thereafter, a new unit was formed: the

Tactical Assault Group (TAG). As 'B' squadron of the SASR, members of TAG undergo the same selection and training that members of the 'regular' SASR have to complete. The selection phase is three weeks long. Those who pass undergo nearly a year of training before they can wear the coveted sand-coloured beret. TAG's training facilities include advanced outdoor close-quarters battle ranges, an urban CT complex, aircraft mock-ups, and snipers' ranges. An offshoot of the TAG group is Offshore Assault Team (OAT). Initially, twenty divers from the Royal Australian Navy Clearance Diving Teams switched branches to the SASR to help man the new unit. OAT, as the name suggests, specialises in maritime assaults, including ships, ferries and oil rigs. OAT is considered a separate but equal element of TAG. This extra responsibility has placed considerable strain on the limited manpower available to the Australian Special Air Service. All TAG/OAT personnel are HALO/HAHO qualified, and are proficient at heliborne insertions as well. Cross training with other countries is not uncommon; Australian officers are permanently assigned to both the Delta homebase at Fort Bragg and Little Creek, NAB, home of Navy SEAL Counter-Terrorist activities.

The present organisation of the 1st Special Air Service regiment includes the 1st, 2nd and 3rd Squadrons, 152nd Signal Squadron and Headquarters Squadron Group. The weapons used include the 9mm FN-Browning HP-35 pistol, 9mm H&K USP pistol, 10mm (.40 S&W) H&K USP pistol (not authorised for the counter-terrorist team), 11.43mm (.45 ACP) H&K USP Tactical pistol with suppresser (not authorised for the counter-terrorist team), 9mm H&K MP5KA4 sub-machine gun, 9mm H&K MP5SD4 sub-machine gun, 5.56mm Colt CAR-15A3 Model 977 assault carbine (known locally as the M4A5), 5.56mm LSAF F88C assault carbine (licence-made Steyr AUG A1), 5.56mm LSAF F88 assault rifle and 5.56mm ADI F88SA1 assault rifle (with 3.4× scope). The 5.56mm ADI F88GL assault rifle consists of a F88S rifle, fitted with a special barrel to accept the 40mmSR R/M Equipment M203PI underbarrel grenade launcher. It also mounts a KAC quadrant reflex sight. The SASR replaced most of the F88s with CAR-15A3s in the late 1990s. Support weapons include the 5.56mm LSAF F89A1 light machine gun (licence-made FN MINIMI with 3.4× or night-vision scope), 7.62mm Accuracy International F98 bolt-action sniper rifle (modified AW), 18.5mmR (12-gauge) Beretta RS-202P pump-action shotgun, 40mmSR R/M Equipment M203PI underbarrel grenade launcher (under M4A5and F88GL) and 84mm Bofors M3 Carl Gustaf recoilless rifle. The Australian Defence Organisation confirmed in late 2002 that it had formed a new counter-terrorist unit to respond to national security threats, which have become more evident since 9-11. A 300-strong Incident Response Regiment will be able to respond to nuclear, biological and chemical threats both within national territory and in support of Australian forces deployed overseas.

CIVILIAN SPECIAL FORCES

Australian Protective Service (APS) and VIP Protection and the Australian Federal Police HRU (Hostage Rescue Unit) all have a degree of Special Forces training and are effective SWAT-type units.

AUSTRIA

MILITARY SPECIAL FORCES

Jagdkommando (Rangers) Gebirgsjaegerbattalions (Mountain Warfare) Volunteers for the Jagdkommando must pass a series of tough personal and physical examinations and be prepared to do an additional six months in uniform before they are accepted. The training then consists of 22 weeks of instruction on survival techniques, including severe winter weather conditions in the mountains, sabotage and demolitions, parachuting (including both HAHO and HALO) CQB and combat shooting, marksmanship, unarmed combat, combat swimming, first aid and communications skills. Works closely with GEK Cobra and the German GSG-9 on HRU and intelligence tasks, while they also exercise regularly with the US Delta Force. Commando Training Centre and depot is in Wiener Neustadt, south of Vienna. This Ranger-type unit has the following weapons in use: 9mm Glock P 80 pistol (Glock 17), 9mm Steyr MPi 69 sub-machine gun, 9mm Steyr MPi 69SD suppressed sub-machine gun, 5.56mm Steyr StG 77K assault carbine (AUG A1), 5.56mm Steyr StG 77 assault rifle (AUG A1), 5.56mm Steyr StG 77SD suppressed assault rifle (AUG A1), 7.62mm Steyr SSG 69 bolt-action sniper rifle, 7.62mm Steyr SSG 69SD suppressed bolt-action sniper rifle and 18.5mmR (12-gauge) Remington Model 870P shotgun. The Kampfschwimmer (combat divers) of this unit also have 11.43mm (.45 ACP) Glock 21 pistols with sound suppressors and 9mm Steyr TMP machine pistols

CIVILIAN SPECIAL FORCES

Gendarmerieeinsatzkommando (GEK) Cobra has a history that dates back to 1973, when the unit Gendarmeriekommando Bad Voslau was formed in response to Palestinian terrorists opposed to further Jewish immigration to Israel and the use of Austria as a staging area. Following Israel's rescue operation at Entebbe and the German GSG-9 Mogadishu airliner assault which demonstrated clearly the need for a properly trained and equipped team to deal with the terrorist threat, the GKBV or Gendarmeriekommando Bad Voslau, was overhauled and Cobra was formed in 1978. It quickly developed close ties with some of the leading foreign units, GIGN, GSG-9 and Israel's Sayeret Matkal. GEK has continued to train with different SF groups, and is now considered to be one of the leading CT units. The 200-man Gendarmerie Einsatz Kommando (GEK) draws its members from the National Police Force-Gendarmerie. GEK personnel can also be called on to serve as bodyguards for visiting dignitaries and other VIPs. The unit is based in Wiener Neustadt, Austria (approximately 25 miles south of Vienna). GEK are particularly skilled in helicopter insertion and rappelling, with an extra emphasis on breaching techniques and CQB.

Weapons in use include, 357 MR 73 Magnum revolver, 9mm Glock P 80 pistol (Glock 17), 9mm Steyr TMP machine pistol, 5.56mm Steyr StG 77K assault carbine (AUG A1), 5.56mm Steyr StG 77 assault rifle (AUG A1), 5.56mm Steyr StG 77A2 assault rifle (AUG A2), 7.62mm Steyr SSG 69 bolt-action sniper rifle, 7.62mm Steyr SSG-PIV suppressed bolt-action sniper rifle, 18.5mmR (12-gauge) H&K HK512 semi-automatic shotgun, 18.5mmR (12-gauge) Franchi SPAS-15 semi-automatic shotgun and 40mmSR H&K MZP1 grenade launcher.

Mobile Einsatz Kommando (MEK) Scorpions. The National Police are supported for special operations by the MEK (Mobiles Einsatz Kommando – mobile SWAT team). The highly mobile MEK teams will usually be first to respond to a terrorist incident, with the more specialist GEK teams arriving from their main base only after the situation has been assessed and perhaps contained by MEK.

There is one exception to this, however. MEK Vienna and known as *WEGA* (Wiener Einsatz Gruppe Alarmabteilung – Vienna Swat Team) is as well trained as the GEK. WEGA snipers also won the sniper world championship for the third time in April 1999 at Camp Shelby and it is one of the world's best counter-terror teams.

AZERBAIJAN

MILITARY SPECIAL FORCES
Two Special Forces Airborne Companies based in Baku. This small nation has a potentially grave security situation, with openly hostile neighbours and considerable internal unrest. Its present Special Forces capability is inadequate for its future needs and it is expected that a full battalion will be raised by 2004. As finance permits, a small dedicated Special Operations and border patrol helicopter unit will be created.

CIVILIAN SPECIAL FORCES
Ministry of Internal Affairs
There is a 30-strong national HRU formation under the control of the Border Guards.

BADGED

Accepted for initial entry into the SAS after successfully completing the SELECTION and CONTINUATION courses (see separate entries).

BAHAMAS

MILITARY SPECIAL FORCES
Marine Internal Security Platoon which provides anti-smuggling and coastal patrols. Has a limited hostage rescue capability.

BAHRAIN

MILITARY SPECIAL FORCES
Made up of approximately 350 personnel, the Bahraini Special Forces Battalion at Manama is still not a true SO-capable unit. Training deficiencies hinder the development of this group into a viable special ops apparatus (despite the fact that it has trained with Britain's 22 SAS and US Special Forces on numerous occasions). BSF is organised as follows: Headquarters Company, Support Company, two Ranger Companies, Special Forces Company and a Counter-Terrorist Company. Weapons used include H&K MP5 sub-machine guns, H&K 91 assault rifles, Remington 700 sniper rifles and FN MAG machine guns.

CIVILIAN SPECIAL FORCES
U-Group of the Public Security Force The U-Group has provided Counter-Terrorist duties for the Bahranian government since the early 1980s and was established and trained by the SAS. While many of its officers are ex-SAS it is interesting to note that many of the non-commissioned personnel are contracted from Pakistan's Special Service Group (SSG). All members are airborne and SCUBA-qualified and receive additional training in CQB, breaching techniques and covert operations. It has at least two 25-man squadrons and a small Special Boat Section. U-Group is based on Muharraq Island and is under the operational control of Bahrain's Security and Intelligence Service (BSIS). It regularly conducts extensive exercises with the SAS, Delta Force and GSG-9 and is rated one of the better HRU/SF units in the Middle East.

BALKANS – US SPECIAL FORCES INVOLVEMENT 1990s

An unusual shipment arrived at the US base in Tuzla, Bosnia, in late 1997. Inside the hull of a C-17 cargo jet were several eight-foot-high metal containers – modern-day Trojan horses filled with a total of 65 commandos from the Navy's premier Counter-Terrorism unit, SEAL Team 6. Handlers whisked the human payload into a nearby hangar to avoid notice by Russian, Polish and other little-trusted allied troops on the base. Once the SEALs had been unpacked in secrecy and joined by others who drove in from Germany, they headed to CIA-run safe houses in the surrounding countryside. Their mission: to apprehend five PIFWCs, which stands for 'persons indicted for war crimes', in northern Bosnia. For a year and a half following the signing of the Dayton Peace Accords in December 1995, US leaders insisted that arresting people indicted for war crimes in Bosnia was not the responsibility of the allied peacekeeping forces there. That stance began to shift last summer, when NATO troops made their first arrests of suspected war criminals. US Special Operations task force conducted one of the broadest covert operations since the Vietnam War, gathering intelligence on PIFWCs and helping to seize them in a series of raids. The results, however, have been very limited, because the secret operations have been stymied by security problems, distrust among allies, a lack of useful intelligence, and disagreements among senior officials over how much to risk in the attempt to nab PIFWCs. For instance, after the SEAL Team 6 members had been deployed to their OPs, General Clark held a video conference with General Eric Shinseki, the commander of all peace-keeping troops in Bosnia. Shinseki argued there was not enough 'actionable', or specific, intelligence to guarantee the success of their planned raid. He asked for further details on the principal target – a high-ranking Bosnian Serb official named Blagoje Simic, who oversaw a Bosnian Serb police squad that allegedly murdered one man and beat and abused several others in 1992. Shinseki wanted to know how many Serbian special police lived in Simic's apartment building and might fight to defend him? How many dogs lived there? What were the staircases made of? One intelligence official thought the requests were so excessive that he walked out of the room in frustration, according to a source familiar with the conference.

Pulling the plug, Shinseki ultimately gave the intelligence staffers 72 hours to come up with the information. However, the next day, a hard-line Bosnian Serb official told a US soldier that he knew Special Operations forces were planning a raid. When word reached Shinseki, he cancelled the mission, fearing its security had been blown. The SEALs flew home. Despite an investigation, the mission's leaders never determined how the Serbs learned of their plan. Even though that raid never went forward, the presence of dozens of US commandos in Bosnia reflected the intense interest among some of America's top decision-makers in the Clinton administration in rounding up the people responsible for the Bosnian war's most gruesome events, including mass executions, systematic rapes, organised sniping at civilians, torture of prisoners, and establishment of concentration camps.

BANGLADESH

MILITARY SPECIAL FORCES

1st Para-Commando Battalion This single Special Forces unit at present handles both anti-terrorist operations and acts as the national HRU.

Bangladesh has a requirement for additional Special Forces and a portion of the defence budget is to be earmarked to provide for a second SF Battalion and improved training facilities.

BARRETT – LONG-RANGE DEATH

The Barrett M82A1/2 and other similar highly accurate heavyweight rifles have revolutionised the art of sniping since its introduction in 1983. Not only is this type of weapon capable of killing an enemy normally considered relatively safe in a lightly armoured vehicle or strongpoint, but it also has a lethal range against a soldier in the open of 1,000m (1,100yds), and in some cases distances of 1,600 and even 2,000m have been reported. These weapons are immensely powerful and quite capable of cutting a man nearly in half, even if he is wearing body-armour. The 12.7mm round is capable of bringing down a helicopter and, paired with modern telescopic sights and image intensifiers, these weapons provide static snipers with an enormously enhanced capability. The drawbacks are restricted to its length of some 1.4m and a weight of 12.24kg. The Barrett M82A2 has a box magazine holding eleven rounds and is semi-automatic only. It is widely used by the SAS and many other Special Forces, as well as the IRA and numerous other terrorist groups.

BASHA

Originally an improvised or temporary waterproof shelter made from a poncho or cape and any other materials to hand. Has since become the SAS expression for barracks or any accommodation

BDA

Bomb Damage Assessment. An important aspect of modern warfare is the necessity to inspect the damage done to 'enemy' facilities on the ground with clandestine observation, rather than relying solely upon aerial reconnaissance or satellite surveillance. Techniques for obscuring the real significance of bomb damage from aerial or space-based photography have improved immeasurably and often the only way to discover the true measure of the effectiveness of a bombing campaign is the insertion of Bomb Damage Assessment teams, despite the real danger involved.

BECKWITH, LT. COL CHARLES

While serving with the 7th Special Forces Group in June 1962, Beckwith was seconded to serve with the 22nd SAS in Hereford for one year. For the future founder of Delta Force, his time with the SAS was something of a life-changing experience after the formality and 'red-tape' of Fort Bragg. The SAS had little of the harsh discipline or rigid divide between officers and other ranks which tend to be important distinctions to the usually narrow-minded world of the conventional soldier. Unlike the US Special Forces of the time, the more informal attitude of the SAS, with regular drinking sessions between the officers invited down to the Sergeants' mess on a Saturday night, which led to a free and often very frank exchange of views, experience and ideas, was a revelation to Beckwith. The SAS is an NCOs' Regiment, with the senior sergeants effectively in charge of training, tactics and operations as career SAS personnel, while the officers or 'Ruperts' on secondment to the regiment for three-year tours merely relayed orders from above and protected the interests, traditions and high standards of the unit. Beckwith quickly became a convert to the 'British-way' and on returning to the United States lobbied his Commander at the Special Warfare Centre (SWC), General William P. Yarborough, to create an American equivalent, but without success. In Beckwith's own words 'I felt the US Army needed. . . . to be able to go out in small patrols and blow up bridges and dams and railroad lines, to take out an enemy commander, say, like Rommel, to collect information for air strikes or for attacks made by conventional forces. The American Army not only needed a Special Forces capability but an SAS one; not only a force of teachers, but a force of doers.' Indeed, Beckwith became so impassioned that he added 'The SAS had a very broad definition of what it does and remained flexible. The American Army was quite the opposite. We would go to a great deal of trouble to frame a field manual. . . . If it doesn't happen to be in the FM, no matter how good an idea it is, it won't get done. All our demolition recipes are spelled out. The Brits would never do that. They kept everything in their heads. If you aren't smart enough to keep it up there, they felt, you get your hat and go somewhere else to work.'

Beckwith's personal crusade to create a genuine US Special Forces capability to complement the elite infantry and commando tactics of the Green Berets was interrupted by the Vietnam war. However, on his return to Fort Bragg in 1974 he found an ally in General Bob Kingston, the commander of the renamed John F. Kennedy SWC. Another attempt to launch his new concept unit resulted in two years of debate and the development of the structure for a small counter-terrorist unit that would fill a niche between the responsibilities adopted by the Rangers, Green Berets and the SEALs. On 2 June 1977 Beckwith was given preliminary authority to form 1st Special Forces Operations Detachment–Delta. The original plan called for a unit 1,200-strong and divided into sixteen-man 'troops' split into four four-man or two eight-man patrols. It was intended to have the same recruitment and training methods as the SAS. However, the new unit ran into immediate problems from the established Special Forces units who feared the poaching of their best personnel, and as diplomacy was not 'Chargin' Charlie's' strong point he soon alienated both senior officers and colleagues in other units alike. The successful use of a Federal German GSG-9 hostage rescue team with the assistance of four SAS specialists to end the aircraft hijacking at Mogadishu airport in 1977 led to President Carter inquiring whether the United States had a similar capability. Beckwith was quickly given full authority to activate Delta as an operational national anti-terrorist and hostage rescue unit in November 1977. Hostility among both conventional and Special Forces units towards Delta continued. In fact the commander of the 5th Special Forces Group, Col Bob Mountel, actually formed a rival unit 'Operation Blue Light', and this force trained in similar techniques for nearly a year before senior officers discovered its unauthorised existence and ordered its disbandment. Though Beckwith now had the authority to recruit, train and plan operations, he had not managed to create the vital simple chain of command for emergencies. The SAS can ultimately refer directly to the Prime Minister, the GSG-9 to the German Federal Chancellor, while in best American military bureaucratic tradition it was proposed that the rapid reaction capabilities of Delta should be hog-tied by the requirement to first report to HQ Special Forces at Fort Bragg, then to XVIII Airborne Corps, then to Forces Command (FORSCOM), then to the Department of the Army, then to the Joint Chiefs of Staff and finally to the White House. This cumbersome route threatened to undermine the whole purpose behind creating Delta Force, though finally the lower report stages were removed and Delta was at least able to go directly to the Department of the Army. This administrative compromise was still flawed, as many of Delta's numerous disasters have highlighted. Beckwith had achieved an enormous breakthrough in a United States Army that was hidebound by administration, senseless red-tape, traditions, division between the ranks, stultifying discipline and a reluctance to accept new and unconventional ideas. Even in 2002 the US Special Forces as a whole, though greatly improved in technique and tactics over the last 25 years, are still restricted by a lack of operational independence and a commitment to a rather macho image that brings little of value to real Special Operations. Too many US recruits still appear to be picked as superb physical specimens, both brave and patriotic, rather than placing the emphasis on intellect and guile as important additions to sufficient fitness, fearlessness and loyalty. It used to be said that if you wanted to spot a member of the SAS look out for a rather thin, wiry man, sitting quietly in the corner, smartly dressed and reading *The Times*. Unfortunately the SAS has slowly drifted more towards the US recruitment pattern, with up to 60 per cent of its soldiers being drawn from the Parachute Regiment. The consequence is a reduction of intellectual capability in favour of physical prowess. However, for all the doubts about recruitment, training, operational success rates and the chain of command,

Beckwith has achieved the establishment of a major new capability for the US Army. Delta Force, as part of the USSOCOM, is now one of the premier anti-terrorist and hostage rescue units in the world, and likely to remain one of the busiest units for the foreseeable future.

BELARUS

MILITARY SPECIAL FORCES

5th Special Forces (SPETSNAZ) Airborne Brigade – Marina Gora. The two active battalions are well equipped and trained. It still co-operates closely with Russian SPETSNAZ units and has received significant amounts of advanced surveillance, intelligence and combat equipment from Russia in the last two years.

CIVILIAN SPECIAL FORCES

Ministry of the Interior
Has under its control a number of small anti-terrorist units.

BELGIUM

MILITARY SPECIAL FORCES

1st Special Reconnaissance Company This elite LRRP unit comprises 80 men and is based in Flawinne, Namen (Namur). The new training centre has a sniping range and CQB house. It operates in six-man teams, and their mission is comparable to that of Pathfinders within the US military. The organisation and training closely resembles the British SAS in many ways, and it has already been deployed abroad during the US Operation Restore Hope in Somalia.

The Para-Commando Brigade with headquarters at Heverlee, operates closely with the 15th Transportation Wing of the Belgian Air Force and has a high level of readiness. It is one of the Belgian contributions to NATO and is prepared to participate both in the Immediate and Rapid Reaction Force (ARRC). Besides the defence of Belgian territory, the Brigade is also charged with operations to protect or evacuate its citizens abroad. It has a strength of 3,000 in peacetime and three para-commando infantry battalions with the Command and Headquarters Company, Signal Detachment, A Team, B Team, C Team and E Team all based at Herverlee.

1st Paratroopers Battalion Diest
Staff Company, A Company, B Company and C Company Diest
2nd Commando Battalion Flawinne
Staff Company, A Company, B Company and C Company Flawinne
3rd Paratroopers Battalion Tielen
Staff Company, A Company, B Company and C Company Tielen

3rd Lanciers-Parachutists Battalion (Reconnaissance) Flawinne

Headquarters and Services Squadron, Reconnaissance Squadron and Special Forces Company Flawinne

The 35th Para-Commando Field Artillery Battery Brasschaat

Five 105mm guns, Liaison and Observation detachment and Command post.

There is also a small Combat Frogman section. It is a highly secretive unit, but is known to be about platoon-sized and is similar to the British SBS.

During the Second World War the Parachute unit was formed in Great Britain in May 1942 and served as part of the British 6th Airborne Division. In 1944 it transferred to the SAS Brigade, serving in France, Belgium and, in particular, the Ardennes. While the Commando unit was formed in 1940, it took part in British operations in Norway, Madagascar, the Bruneval, St Nazaire and Dieppe raids. Finally it became part of the 'International' No-10 Commando, seeing more action in the Far East, Sicily, Italy, Greece and NW Europe. In 1952 the 1st Parachute Regiment SAS and the Army Commando Regiment were brought together in a Para-Commando Regiment. In November 1991 the Para-Commando Regiment became a brigade by adding new support units, and in peacetime is about 3,000 strong.

From December 1992 to November 1993 the brigade took part in UN peace support operations. All candidates to serve with the brigade are volunteers. The are subjected to a thorough medical examination and follow, no matter what rank or branch, a five-month course at the Commando Training Centre of Marche-les-Dames before attending the one month parachutist course at the Parachutist Training Centre of Schaffen. At the end of this training, the candidates are fully qualified para-commandos. They then join their units, where they carry on with their specialised and collective training. It is continuous up to brigade level and includes the different methods of brigade deployment: parachuting, assault landing, air and helicopter transportation. This unit training is based on a three-year cycle, though specific para-commando exercises are continuous. These exercises are held in Belgium as well as abroad.

ESR (Equioes Spécialisées de Reconnaissance – Specialised Reconnaissance Teams) or *GVP Gespecialiseerde Verkennings Ploegen* dates back to 1960, when it was formed to give the 1st Belgium Corps a long range reconnaissance (LRRP) capability. They were specialised in deep reconnaissance missions behind enemy lines. Their primary task was to gather intelligence data and transmit it back to their own headquarters. ESR men were Belgium's 'Warriors of the Shadows', for the Belgian government has on several occasions denied the existence of the ESR. One of the most famous incidents was when twelve ESRs defended the Belgian Embassy in Kinshasa in Zaire from local rebels. However, officially they were never there. ESR had also been deployed in Sarajevo, Somali and Rwanda. In Sarajevo their mission was close protection to the Belgian

General Briquemont, CINC for the UN 'Blue Helmets'. Twenty-eight ESRs were deployed in Somali to discreetly monitor the partisans and keep track of their chieftains, particularly General Muhammad Said Hersi. In Rwanda the ERSs took part in operation 'Silver Back' to rescue Europeans out of the country. The ESR was officially disbanded in June 1994, but some of the members are based with the Belgian para-commandos to provide training for the 1st SRC/LRRP team. At one time stationed at Spich, Knesselaere Quater, Germany.

CIVILIAN SPECIAL FORCES

SIE/ESI Speciaal Interventie Eskadron/Escadron Special d'Intervention (Special Intervention Esquadron – Gendarmerie Royal) The 200-strong ESI was created in the aftermath of the 1972 Olympic terrorist outrage. Originally called Le Group Diane, ESI's cadre was created with a small group of highly rated Special Forces personnel and weapons-trained police officers. Although the name was changed to ESI in 1974, the name Diane is still used by the Belgian press. ESI is the prime national CT unit. The selection process lasts two weeks and has an attrition rate of nearly 50 per cent. Those who pass the selection phase face another three months of training before they become fully qualified operators. ESI are trained in defensive driving, combat shooting, CQB, martial arts, climbing, rappelling and hostage rescue techniques. They train with GIGN and GSG-9 in particular, and receive additional parachuting, commando, combat swimming and mountain warfare training in many cases. Weapons in service include the 9mmR (.38 Special) S&W Model 649 Bodyguard revolver, 5.7mm FN Fiveseven pistol, 9mm Glock 17 pistol, 5.7mm FN P90 sub-machine gun, 9mm H&K MP5A3 and MP5SD silenced sub-machine gun, 9mm H&K model 94 sub-machine gun, 7.62mm Sako TRG-21 bolt-action and Steyr SSG sniper rifle, 18.5mmR (12-gauge) Mossberg Model 500 ATP8 and 18.5×70mmR (12-gauge) Remington Model 870 pump-action shotgun used for room clearing.

BELIZE

MILITARY SPECIAL FORCES

Small anti-terrorist and HRU Detachment attached to one of the three infantry battalions.

BERETTA

One of the most famous names in small-arms design and manufacture, the present weapon from Beretta most widely used by Special Forces is the 9mm M12 sub-machine gun (SMG). First produced in 1959, it has undergone a continual programme of enhancement, with the addition of a selector switch allowing single-shot, three-shot bursts and full automatic fire. Additionally, for use by amphibious Special Forces, the interior of the M12 is coated with epoxy resin to prevent rusting. Very compact with a folding stock, it is actually smaller than either the MP5 or Uzi SMG. The M12 is fitted with a 20-, 32- or 40-round box magazine and has a cyclic rate of 550rpm, with an effective killing range of 110yds (100m). Despite the fact that it has not achieved the commercial success of its German and Israeli rivals, the M12 is in fact an excellent weapon, accurate for an SMG and, above all, reliable. The design of the magazine receiver prevents mud or dirt clogging the mechanism and this weapon also has a reputation of very rarely jamming in combat.

BERGEN – PART OF THE SAS COMBAT KIT

A backpack used by all British Special Forces on active service. The SAS Operational Research Unit developed this specialist backpack with a metal frame and detachable heavy duty fabric bag after experience gained during the 1958 campaign in Oman, when standard equipment proved inadequate for Special Forces operations. The Bergen Rucksack became known as the SAS-PARA after the Airborne forces adopted it in the 1960s. The SAS soldier, in addition to his personnel weapon – usually the 5.56mm M16AI/M203 combined assault rifle and 40mm grenade launcher or 9mm MP5/10mm MP201 sub-machine gun – additional equipment such as M18A Claymore anti-personnel mines, FIM92A Stinger surface-to-air missile, Milan anti-tank missile, 66mm M72 LAW; PRC-319 HF/VHF Radios, PRC-30 Patrol Radio or MIL/UST-1 SAT (SatCom), will be expected to carry up to 100kg in his Bergen. This will include clothing (woollen hat, spare socks, gloves and windproof smock); rubber kit-mat or arctic and desert sleeping bags; NBC (Nuclear Biological Chemical) protection kit; plastic bags – large to act as emergency sleeping bags or waterproof linings for the Bergen, with small bags to store rubbish and human waste; maps; prismatic compass (backup to the GPS); wire for trip-wires, string/twine for making temporary shelters; torch with red-filter; additional batteries; 'escape' belt used if the Bergen needs to be abandoned in an emergency (which contains food, spare ammunition, charges water bottle, weapon cleaning gear and a survival kit with wire snares, fishing line, matches, button compass and water purification tablets. Heliograph; SARBE; shaped/sabotage blocks of PE4/PETN explosives; escape map, foreign currency, survival chocolate and cooker); survival knife; medical pack containing a suture kit, painkillers, rehydrates, antibiotics, scalpel blades and two syrettes of morphine; water bottle; two weeks of dehydrated rations; additional ammunition; Nite-Site binoculars and OTIS Thermal-imaging night-vision scopes in waterproof pouches; field dressing taped to webbing, camouflage face paint and a camouflaged face veil used as a scarf. Most other Special Forces around the world will carry similar amounts, with a varying and individual load appropriate to the operation.

BG – BODYGUARD

One of the many skills provided by Special Forces. Diplomatic and VIP protection is increasingly important with the rise of international terrorism. However, many former Special Forces personnel become involved in private enterprise bodyguard activities for major business personalities, sporting and entertainment celebrities and for the staff of major multinationals regularly travelling to parts of the world where kidnapping has become endemic. The SAS formed its Bodyguard Training Team in 1962, not only to improve its own skills but also also those of the protective units of the rulers of British Commonwealth countries, clients and allies. The Royalty Protection Group and the Royal Military Police were first among British organisations to benefit from SAS training. In many ways the SAS invented modern body-guarding techniques and tactics. They effectively wrote the rule-book now largely used throughout the world, including the USA where, only a year later, slack and badly organised protection was to result in the assassination of President Kennedy – or at least that's the accepted version of events. Protecting a head of state requires armed close protec-tion (ACP); an outer cordon of armed guards/police and roaming external surveillance teams (EST). Static security at all vulnerable posi-tions, roof tops and windows on the route where a good shot is offered or where a motorcade may have to slow down; searching every bridge, sewer, tunnel or culvert along the route; searching every building likely to be used by the VIP; checking the background of every member of staff, outside contractor or anyone with access to any building used by the VIP for up to one month before the visit and obtaining up-to-date intelligence on every person ever known to have uttered a serious threat of violence; terrorist groups and political opponents who may be in the area at the time; and intensive checking and surveillance to detect anyone not already on the watch list. Above all, good intelligence is paramount and can allow an effective bodyguard operation to be conducted successfully with the minimum of visible security. The US tactic of throwing vast sums of money and personnel at the problem has not always been completely successful and the large numbers of opera-tives and different security organisations allowed to become involved can result in serious communication problems, with the end result that overall security is compromised.

BERM

A defensive wall of earth, usually thrown up quickly to give some protection to a temporary observation post or advanced fire support site.

BIGOT

This strange US weapon is a combination of a finned projectile fired from a modified .45 automatic pistol. It produced no muzzle flash and was lethal at a range of up to 15ft (5m). The original version produced during the Second World War for the OSS was a convenient and deadly night-fighting silent killer. The later 'Dart Gun' fired a single .03 calibre mass-stabilised projectile. The tip of the 0.8-inch long-dart is made of iron particles and usually carried the tranquilliser M99 or similar agent to use against guard dogs; however, it was more than conceivable that this weapon could be used against human targets, particularly as the impact of the dart caused no greater sensation than an insect bite. Advanced versions now use sub-miniature darts with much improved range and are still available to a number of Special Forces around the world. Tipped with a deadly fast-acting poison, these make an ideal assassination weapon and are believed to have been used in this role on a number of occasions.

BIRD

An aircraft, usually a helicopter.

BLACK BIRD

Low-observability or stealth USAF aircraft used for Special Operations, named after black paint job.

BLACK HAWK DOWN – DELTA FORCE

The disastrous events in Mogadishu, Somalia of 3–4 October 1993 will forever haunt the reputation of America's premier Special Operations unit, Delta Force. A badly planned and poorly executed operation to arrest a leading Somali Islamic militant quickly went wrong in the confused maze of streets around the target area. Some 99 elite soldiers were trapped by paramilitary gunmen and, in a failed attempt to rescue them by air, a UH60 Black Hawk helicopter was shot down. The US forces eventually shot their way out to safety, but only with a disgraceful disregard for civilian casualties. The true death toll is not known for certain, but is unlikely to be less than 600. Many were women and children caught in the deadly fire from vehicle-mounted automatic weapons which the US soldiers indiscriminately used to clear an escape path through the narrow, crowded streets.

The Somali tragedy was ignored as the appalling sight of dead American servicemen being dragged around the dusty streets of Mogadishu by screaming mobs traumatised the United States. However, in the light of the terrorist attacks of 11 September, history has been rewritten by Hollywood in the recent film *Black Hawk Down*. It has even been reported that, in return for covert US government funding, the first twenty minutes of an almost finished film were supposedly re-shot to turn the failed US operation into a heroic attempt to rescue an aid convoy from fanatical Islamic militants, completely obscuring the real lessons to be learned from the Mogadishu operation: that even a highly sophisticated military machine can prove remarkably vulnerable to a simple insurgency.

BLUE-ON-BLUE

SAS expression for an accidental clash between forces on the same side, often called 'Friendly Fire'. Soldiers on the receiving end of such incidents usually have a more colourful range of responses to express their true feelings.

BODY-ARMOUR

Gives limited protection from low-velocity weapons and shrapnel. Hard body-armour, made out of thick ceramic or metal plates, functions basically the same way as the iron suits worn by medieval knights: it is hard enough that a bullet or other weapon is deflected. That is, the armour material pushes out on the bullet with the same force (or nearly the same force) with which the bullet pushes in, so the armour is not penetrated. Typically, hard body-armour offers more protection than soft body-armour, but it is much more cumbersome. Police officers and military personnel may wear this sort of protection when there is a high risk of attack, but for everyday use they generally wear soft body-armour, flexible protection that you wear like an ordinary shirt or jacket. With Soft body-armour the principle at work is quite simple. A piece of bullet-proof material is just a very strong net. Each tether of the net extends from one side of the frame to the other, thereby dispersing the energy from the point of impact over a wide area. The energy is further dispersed because the tethers are interlaced. When the bullet pushes on a horizontal length of tether, that tether then pulls on every interlaced vertical tether. These tethers in turn pull on all the connected horizontal tethers. In this way, the whole net works to absorb the projectile's inertial energy, no matter where it hits. Long strands of fibre are interlaced to form a dense net. A bullet is travelling very fast so the net needs to be made from extremely strong material. The most famous material used in body-armour is DuPont's Kevlar fibre. Kevlar is lightweight, like a traditional clothing fibre, but it is five times stronger than a piece of steel of the same weight. When interwoven into a dense net, this material can absorb a great amount of energy. In addition to stopping the bullet from reaching your body, a piece of body-armour also must protect against *blunt trauma* caused by the force of the bullet. This it does largely by spreading the effect of the impact over a sufficiently wide area to avoid serious damage to the soft flesh beneath the suit. Special Forces and Hostage Rescue Units regularly use body-armour to protect the torso and head, particularly in restricted spaces and CQB situations, for although assault teams rely heavily on both speed and surprise, the possibility still exists for a determined terrorist to fire several or more shots before being killed or captured. Ballistic Helmets protect the face and skull and while the visor can protect the eyes from dust and particle caused by breaching devices and grenades, they can inhibit hearing and overall awareness. Ballistic Vests are either soft or hard with ceramic inserts added to the Kevlar layers or Load-Carrying Assault Vests for additional equipment, ammunition and weapons, often with a rappelling harness built in and limited ballistic protection.

BOLIVIA

MILITARY SPECIAL FORCES
Special Forces come under the command of the 7th Airmobile Division – DIVISION AEROTRANSPORTADA 7 – HQ Cochabamba Parachute School – BP (Esc) Batallón de Paracaidistas (Escuela) – Cochabamba Special Forces School – BFE (Esc) Batallón de Fuerzas Especiales (Escuela) or 'the Escuela de Condores' (School of Condors) – Cochabamba.

1st and 2nd Ranger Regiments   Closely connected with the US Special Forces, having been trained, equipped and advised by the 'Green Berets' since their establishment in the early 1960s. The 2nd Regiment was involved in the operation that finally destroyed the Marxist insurgency and captured Che Guevara in 1967.

Polivalente   In the early 1980s, the Army's Special Forces training centre at Cochabamba began training personnel for a new Tactical Response unit, known as the Polivalente. By 1984, the unit was manned by 40 full-time personnel who were responsible for CT and hostage rescue operations throughout the country. Initial training for this unit was provided by the United States and France. The unit was eventually split up, with elements being sent to La Paz and Cochabamba.

BOOBY-TRAPS

Explosives can be very effective in creating panic and confusion when used in a variety of booby-traps. These can range from the sophisticated, prefabricated device to the simple, hastily created opportunist variety. Pressure plates which, when trodden upon, release a catch – allowing it to spring upwards and release a firing pin – and pull-detonators attached to trip-wires are two common methods of detonating the explosive. Widely used in ambush techniques, to cover a retreat or simply left *in situ* to cause casualties, who help slow up the enemy forces at intervals long after the Special Force team has moved on. A wide range of specialist 'booby-trap' orientated equipment has been developed and a considerable amount of time and care is taken in their creation and the training of Special Forces to use them to their maximum effect – this includes the use of enemy dead as part of the trap. A dead soldier will have a pressure-activated booby-trap placed in the ground beneath his body so that even a careful colleague or paramedic will not notice; this then explodes when the body is moved, often killing or injuring vital medical personnel. A dead soldier's weapon will have a pull-detonated booby-trap attached, so that when a valuable weapon is picked up a grenade or directional fragmentation mine explodes, showering the surrounding area with thousands of metal fragments. Alternatively, the weapon itself might be booby-trapped by the addition of doctored ammunition, which explodes in the breech when fired, with the intention of blinding the user, as this means yet another enemy soldier has to be withdrawn from combat to aid him and places more strain on the often limited medical resources available.

BOSNIA

MILITARY SPECIAL FORCES

Ist Special Forces Brigade This unit received training and weapons during the Balkan conflict from Turkey, Iran and, interestingly enough, both US Special Forces and Osama Bin Laden's Al-Qa'ida organisation. Islamic fundamentalist volunteers came from many Muslim countries to fight alongside their Bosnian co-religionists.

BOTSWANA

CIVILIAN SPECIAL FORCES

Special Support Group (SSG) While the Botswana Defense Force and Police have some capability for SWAT type missions, the primary responsibility for CT actions rests with the Special Support Group. This is a paramilitary element of the Botswana Police and has a strength of approximately 200 men. They have received training from various nations, primarily South Africa.

BOUNCING BETTY

Second World War type of anti-personnel mine blown into the air before detonation to increase casualties from a massive spray of metal fragments. Similar in effect to the more sophisticated Claymore anti-personnel mines.

BRANDENBURGERS – GERMANY'S WARRIOR SPIES

The Brandenburgers were Germany's 'dirty tricks' specialists. They used their linguistic skills, repertoire of trickery and exotic equipment and uniforms to pull off all sorts of impossible feats. The Brandenburgers began modestly enough as part of the Second Department of the Abwehr (German Military Intelligence). This unit was officially founded on 15 October 1939, and was mostly made up of Ebbinghaus volunteers. It was called the Lehr und Bau Kompagnie z.b.V. 800 (Special Duty Training and Construction Company No. 800), although it was popularly known as the Brandenburg Commandos, after the city where the unit was formed.

The Brandenburgers were used to infiltrate across the border and seize key tactical objectives, usually bridges, ahead of the regular army. In fact, seizing bridges seems to have been one of their main preoccupations and, like so much of the German war machine, the Brandenburgers seem to be focused on tactical objectives rather than strategic ones.

During their operations, the Brandenburgers avoided the use of brute force. They also had a code of chivalry that might seem anachronistic to modern readers accustomed to the dirty wars of recent years. The Brandenburgers might dress up in enemy uniforms or parts of uniforms, but they would take the greatest pains to wear their own uniforms underneath. They would then hold their fire until they made their own uniforms visible. This practice also helped make the case that Brandenburgers were soldiers rather than spies. In a couple of instances, infiltrating Brandenburgers even allowed themselves to be captured rather than commit a breach of orders by firing on enemy soldiers before H-hour. Unlike other elite units of the German forces, notably the SS, the Brandenburgers did not seek out 'Aryans' for their recruitment. Because this unit would be working behind enemy lines they avoided Nordic Germans, looking instead for Slavs and other ethnic groups disliked by the Nazis and, in fact, men of Jewish descent also found a home there. The Brandenburgers were Germans first, and few if any were committed Nazis. In fact, some of the key leaders were involved in intrigues against Adolf Hitler. In their early days the Brandenburgers tended to recruit by word of mouth and personal recommendation. All members had to be thoroughly fluent in another European language, and all had to be well educated in the customs and local habits of other regions or nations. Instead of being 'racially superior' to the enemy, the Brandenburgers had to *be* the enemy, blending in and going unnoticed while performing acts of sabotage and espionage.

On 8 May 1940, the Brandenburg Commandos got their first taste of action. Wearing Dutch uniforms, a number of commandos crossed the border with Holland, their target being the bridge over the Meuse river at

Gennep. At 2 a.m. on 10 May, just as German forces were beginning to roll across the border, a Brandenburg leutnant, Wilhelm Walther, started the attack. Disguised as Dutch military police escorting a number of German prisoners, the eight Brandenburgers took the defenders of the bridge by surprise. Two guard posts were destroyed, but three commandos were wounded, and the posts on the far side of the bridge were not yet under control. Leutnant Walther advanced on these posts, and the defenders hesitated, not wanting to shoot one of their own. This proved to be a fatal error, for the posts were then destroyed and the detonators seized, just as the first armoured units arrived to consolidate the victory.

After the fall of France the Brandenburgers, now organised as a regiment, took part in many actions in the Balkans, where they were responsible for capturing the docks of Orsova, on the Danube River. But it was in August of 1941, on the Russian front, when the Brandenburg Commandos really proved their outstanding ability. Early that month, a Brandenburg unit of 62 Baltic and Sudeten Germans, led by Baron Adrian von Fölkersam, penetrated further into enemy territory than ever before. Their mission was to secure the oil fields at Maikop. Using Red Army trucks and NKVD uniforms, Fölkersam's force infiltrated the Soviet lines and moved towards their target. However, they ran into a large band of Red Army deserters. Deciding to try and use this situation to his advantage, Fölkersam persuaded the deserters to return to the Soviet cause, and thus he was able to join with them and move at will through the Russian lines. They reached Maikop, where he conferred with the city's military commander, pretending to be a NKVD major from Stalingrad. Fölkersam persuaded the Russian general to give him a personal tour of the city's defences. With a good knowledge of his target's strengths and weaknesses, Fölkersam formulated a plan for the capture of Maikop. By 8 August, with the German Army only twelve miles away, the Brandenburgers made their move. Using explosives to simulate an artillery attack, they knocked out the main communications centre. Fölkersam then went to the Russian officers and told them that a withdrawal was taking place. Having seen Fölkersam with their commander, and lacking any communications with the rest of the Red Army, the Soviets had no choice but to believe Fölkersam's story. The Russians left, and the German army entered Maikop on 9 August 1942, without a single hostile shot.

As the war in the East eventually turned in the Soviets' favour the Brandenburgers were forced to fight in a more conventional role. When the Abwehr was all but abolished, following the implication of Admiral Canaris and others in the 20 July 1944 bomb plot against Hitler, the SS special operations forces gained total domination of German Special operations and the Brandenburgers were formed into a panzergrenadier division. The history of the Brandenburg Regiment ended in late 1944, but they had earned more decorations and mentions than any other unit of similar size in the entire German army.

BRAVO TWO ZERO – SAS

The SAS aggressive patrol, codenamed Bravo Two Zero, has achieved a level of heroic failure reminiscent of Dunkirk, and without doubt the individual bravery of its members has earned them both respect and financial benefits. However, once the media hype has been removed, the real picture that emerges is of an accident waiting to happen and it was down to the high levels of training, skill and determination shown by the soldiers in the patrol that any of its members escaped or indeed survived capture. The whole operation, however, bears the hallmarks of being poorly planned, hastily committed, critically lacking vital equipment and being without accurate intelligence and the necessary support to ensure the success of the mission. The commanding officer of 'B' Squadron at the FOB (Forward Operating Base) at Al Jouf in western Saudi Arabia argued against the deployment of a Northern Road Watch Patrol (Bravo Two Zero) into Iraq in 1991, when there was inadequate preparation or local intelligence, but was overruled by senior officers aware of the political importance of Britain quickly becoming involved in military operations alongside their American allies. The SAS had been starved of funds by a succession of parsimonious governments and, when the time came, the SAS were to be found critically short of modern communications and satellite links and, crucially, night-vision devices – though some were found, too late to be issued to Bravo Two Zero, in boxes being used by the regimental sergeant major to weight down the edges of his tent. Warm clothing, absolutely essential in the bitterly cold nights regularly encountered in Iraq's Western deserts at that time of year, was left behind because of a shortage of room in the patrol's visibly overloaded Bergens. 'B' squadron arrived after the deployment of 'A' and 'D' squadrons and virtually all the available weapons and equipment had already been issued to these units. Some additional equipment was borrowed from their US allies, occasionally without the Americans being fully aware of their own generosity; however, even the British Army's traditional scrounging was unable to make up for the shortfall in effective communications. This was further complicated by a disastrous mix-up in wavelengths and codes given to the patrol. This combination of failures resulted in Bravo Two Zero being unable to contact base or call for evacuation almost as soon as they reached their operational area. The problems that were to be faced once the patrol entered Iraq had already been compounded by the SAS regiment's tradition of allowing the members of the eight-man unit involved to choose the method of insertion, the exact start-off position within the operating zone and the range of weapons to be carried. This has always been considered a vital part in instilling independence, initiative and responsibility into SAS soldiers; however, as in other much less well-publicised operations, this was to prove highly counter-productive to the chances of success. It must be considered very unlikely that any of the members of Bravo Two Zero, largely made up of NCOs as is normal in the SAS, had a profound or detailed knowledge of the operational area, terrain and habitat, environmental conditions, local population or language. Indeed the delegation of so much responsibility to the patrol led to the decision to be inserted by Chinook helicopter and to patrol on foot. A profoundly unsuitable decision in the event, as not using the regiment's stripped-down Land Rovers deprived Bravo Two Zero of the vehicle-mounted machine guns, the ability to carry additional weapons and ammunition, water and other supplies and, of course, caused them to leave behind the vital cold weather clothing. The whole SAS operation in the Gulf War was fairly chaotic at best and at times downright amateurish, but little of this was to reach the tightly controlled media. However, it directly affected the chances of evacuating Bravo Two Zero once their presence had been compromised. There appeared to be no adequate planning for this eventuality, or decisive action to mount a rescue attempt. Indeed the whole operation had been allowed to drift from the initial flawed decision to use a Chinook helicopter to insert the patrol, for this is almost certainly what actually alerted the Iraqi forces to the likely presence of an Allied Special Forces unit.

The explanation that Bravo Two Zero was only accidentally discovered by a young Arab boy herding goats simply does that equate with the fact that Iraqi forces in the area were already on alert for infiltrators, or their prompt military response. Moreover, the dramatic claims for damage inflicted by the patrol even while on the run, and suggestions that they succeeded in killing something in the region of 250 of the pursuing Iraqi soldiers, must now be treated with great care. What efforts it has so far been possible to make to verify the accounts published by 'Andy McNab', Chris Ryan and other surviving members of the patrol have so far failed to positively support any of the main claims. If anything, they confirm a fairly effective Iraqi military response that quickly put Bravo Two Zero in difficulties, and ended with seven of the eight SAS soldiers being killed or captured. Nor were Bravo Two Zero alone in failing to achieve their tactical targets, for there is no evidence that any of the other aggressive SAS patrols along the so-called 'SCUD Alley' had any greater success, though thankfully none proved so disastrous. While the SAS operations during the Gulf War were not noticeable for their military usefulness, they did succeed in achieving one highly important improvement in the regiment's future capability. The Ministry of Defence has since made available sufficient funds to hopefully ensure that a patrol like Bravo Two Zero will never again be expected to go into combat without effective communications.

The failure of Bravo Two Zero was symptomatic of a disappointing Allied Special Forces performance in the Gulf War, for despite ludicrously inflated claims to the contrary emanating from both SAS headquarters and the US

Special Operations Command, it appears on closer examination that very few, at best, and perhaps not a single Iraqi SCUD TEL (Mobile Missile Launcher) was successfully attacked and destroyed by Special Forces during the whole Gulf campaign. A number of decoys, fuel tankers and other commercial vehicles were certainly hit, but little else of military value was destroyed. While it is certainly true that such offensive patrols as Bravo Two Zero proved to have considerable nuisance value, requiring a number of major Iraqi units to be tasked to hunting them down, apart from some disruption caused to important communications networks, nothing of any real military importance was achieved, highlighting once again the confusion apparent in the combat roles allotted to the Special Forces. Specialised units such as the SAS are in reality strategic troops and, if no suitable critically important operational deployments are called for, then these units would be better held in reserve. They are not suited or trained for use just as commandos and it is unwise that their special talents should be so wantonly and so often wasted on limited tactical operations by senior battlefield commanders. The evidence that has so far emerged from the Counter-Terrorist campaigns in Afghanistan and the Philippines launched in response to 9-11 is that this situation is slowly changing. A few lessons have been learned, and although the results so far are equally disappointing, the Pentagon and Britain's Ministry of Defence may finally be getting the message.

BRAZIL

MILITARY SPECIAL FORCES
Brazil is facing new military threats for the first time in 100 years. New airborne, light cavalry and Special Forces units are to be stationed in the North East Command at Recife and Planalyo Command at Brasilia by 2003. Brazil is concerned that the growth of narco-terrorism and the civil war in Colombia will endanger the economic viability and security of its vital 'new territories' in the north.

The first truly dedicated unit was established only in 1983 as the Counter-Terrorist (CT) Detachment of Brazil's – 1st Special Forces Battalion 'Antonio Dias Cardoso', which is in turn part of the Army's Airborne Brigade based at the headquarters in Villa Mittor (Rio de Janeiro). Now some 250-strong, it was originially similar in organisation, training and tactics to the US Rangers. However, as its range of tasks has grown it has become closer to an SAS-style unit, and is now closely linked to the ABIN, the main Brazilian Intelligence Service. In 2002 a new Intelligence and Counter-Terrorist policy is likely to merge the interests of these organisations into a joint overall command structure. Only those with parachute or Special Forces background and an exemplary record are allowed to volunteer, and so many fail to get past the initial training period. According to reports, the attrition rate during the fourteen-day selection phase is as high as 90 per cent. Those lucky enough to survive go on to a thirteen-week training programme at facilities near Rio de Janeiro. Skills developed include marksmanship, combat shooting, parachuting, and heliborne insertion. However, because of Brazil's varied terrain, special emphasis is placed on long-range patrol groups and intelligence-gathering in the dense jungles and rivers of the Amazon. Further emphasis is placed on intelligence-gathering and security surveillance of the long borders with Venezuela, Colombia, Ecuador, Peru and Bolivia. The ability to track the 'narco-gangs' smuggling drugs across national borders, and the clandestine insertion of Special Forces into hostile areas are also emphasised. The unit was initially formed in 1957 as a parachute trained rescue unit, which specialised in conducting deep jungle missions in the Amazon basin. After conducting its initial selection, a US Army Special Forces Mobile Training Team (MTT) conducted the unit's first training course. The unit continued to act in its rescue role until 1968, when it was reorganised as a Special Forces detachment and placed under the control of the 'General Penha Brasil' training centre. In 1983 the unit was expanded to its current battalion strength and placed within the Airborne Brigade's organisational structure. The battalion is tasked with conducting the following missions: supporting regular and irregular forces during unconventional warfare operations. Providing mobile teams for unconventional warfare training, conducting escape, sabotage, intelligence-gathering, recon and direct action missions. Battalion troops are trained in jungle warfare at the army's CIGS jungle warfare school, amphibious operations, mountain warfare, airborne, airmobile, HAHO/HALO operations, and long-range reconnaissance operations. The unit maintains close links with the SAS, 1st SFOD-D Delta, 7th Special Forces Group and the Portugess GOE. Currently based at Guadalupe, near Rio de Janeiro, it is organised into one command and services company, two Special Forces companies, one commando company, and a company-sized Counter-Terrorism detachment. The battalion is equipped with a variety of locally produced and foreign purchased weapons including the Colt .45 and Beretta, and Imbel M-976 pistols, Belgian FN FAL rifles, US M-4 carbine, HK-53 rifles, Franchi, Remington, and Mossburg shotguns, H&K MP-5 series SMGs, Uzi SMGs licence-built Madsen model 53 SMGs, PSG-1 sniper rifles, H&K LMGs, FN MAG and US M-79 40mm grenade launchers, 57mm recoilless rifles, Imbel 60mm light mortars and Hydroar T1M1 flame throwers. Though civil liberties are better protected in Brazil today, in the period 1960–90 the situation was very different, with the Security and Special Operations units regularly abducting and torturing civilians, even children. Common among the many techniques used by the military to 'acquire' information or false confessions was the binding of a prisoner's ankles to his or her wrists, and then suspending them head-down by means of a rod passed beneath the knees, producing prolonged and excruciating muscle cramps. Death squads eliminating troublesome civil rights workers or anti-government elements were certainly not unknown, though not on the wide scale of certain other Latin American states. Human rights abuse of the native peoples of Brazil, including the Amazonian Indian population was, and occasionally still is, racist and brutal.

Força de Ação Rápida – The Fast Action Force   An elite Rapid Reaction unit closely allied to the Special Forces which has the mission to act, immediately, in any strategic area of Brazil. It is made up of the Paratrooper Infantry Brigade which is composed of one SF and three airborne infantry battalions, an airmobile artillery group, a logistic battalion, an air cavalry squadron, an airborne engineer company and a specialist intelligence and communications company at Vila Militar, Rio de Janeiro. 12th Light Infantry Brigade (Airborne) based in Caçapava, Sao Paulo, its subordinated elements are located in cities in the Paraiba valley, in the west region of Grande Sao Paulo. At Taubate, Sao Paulo, are the 1st, 2nd and 3rd army aviation squadrons, providing the brigade with its helicopter transport, while the 4th army aviation squadron is located in Manaus and is a specialist jungle warfare unit.

Navy – Marines
Batalhao de Operacoes Especiaisde – Fuzilieros Navais do Comandos Anfibios 'Tonelero' Tonelero Special Operations Battalion – COMANF   Known as the 'Fuzilieros Navais', or Naval Rifles, they are characterised by their demanding training and rigorous selection process. With a mission role adapted from the US Marine Corps, the Fuzilieros Navais form an elite amphibious force capable of acting when and where necessary in Brazil's national interests. They include the 500 highly trained troops of the elite Batalhao de Operacoes Especiais de Fuzilieros Navais do Comandos Anfibios 'Tonelero' ('Tonelero' Amphibious Commandos) or COMANF, which is a reinforced battalion originally formed in 1957, and tasked with conducting reconnaissance, raids and other special missions, and has gradually evolved into its current structure.

The battalion is currently organised into one Command and Services company, an Amphibious Reconnaissance company (RECONANF) which executes missions similar to those undertaken by USMC Force Recon units; a Reconnaissance (ground recon) company, which is known as RECONTER, specialising in conducting ground recon and LRRP missions, and two Amphibious Commando companies that execute amphibious raids, ship assaults and other direct action missions. The army provides instruction in mountaineering, parachuting and jungle warfare training at its CIGS Jungle Warfare school as well as Commando and Special Forces training, and other specialised courses. Some Tonelero personnel are sent overseas on exchange tours and to undertake specialised training courses provided by friendly Special Forces. These courses include the British All Arms Commando Course; Spain's Comando de Operaciones Especiales; the US Army Ranger School; and the USMC's Amphibious Reconnaissance Course.

Grupo Especial de Resgate (GER) – Special Rescue Group   This is a 120-man unit of the Brazilian Marines' Tonelero Battalion. All members of the unit are parachute- and diver-qualified. The unit conducts joint training exercises with the GERR/MEC Counter-Terrorist team of the navy's GRUMEC combat diver unit. Marines selected to serve in the unit undertake a period of instruction, which may last over two years, before the operator can finally be declared mission-ready. The prospective commando will have to successfully complete both the Amphibious Commando (CESCOMANF), and Special Operations Course (CESOPESP). Candidates may also be selected to undertake the Brazilian army's Free-Fall-Jump Course (CEXSAL).

Grupo de Mergulhadores de Combate-GRUMEC (Combat Divers Group) GRUMEC was formed in 1970, when small cadres were sent to the naval special operations schools in the US and France. Graduates returned to form the Brazilian Combat Diver Course. The navy's GRUMEC combat diver unit provides future COMANF commandos with instruction in a variety of insertion methods, including open- and closed-circuit diving apparatus, HALO and HAHO parachuting, explosives, and the operation of small submersibles. They are also trained in submarine lock-in lock-out procedures, infiltration from submarines and underwater demolition. The primary GRUMEC course, located at the Brazilian Navy Diving and Submarine Centre (CIAMA) in Nitieroi City, is divided into four phases. The first is a five-week course on open-circuit SCUBA, followed by another five-week section, this one emphasising rigorous physical and mental conditioning. The third phase teaches basic and advanced amphibious reconnaissance, closed-circuit (rebreather) diving operations, and attacks against enemy shipping using limpet mines and other explosives. The fourth phase is devoted to land operations, including raids, terrain orientation, riverine and jungle environment actions, SERE skills and unarmed combat. If the trainee graduates from this six-month course, he is then assigned to duty with GRUMEC, where he will be sent on to further advanced training courses, such as military intelligence, military climbing, static and free-fall airborne operations, etc. A small unit within GRUMEC, known as GERR/MEC (Retake and Rescue Special Group), has the CT and hostage rescue mission for incidents occurring on naval installations, ships and oil rigs. During wartime, GRUMEC would be tasked with operations against enemy ships, intelligence-gathering, anti-mine duties, oil-rig destruction, and other missions.

CIVILIAN SPECIAL FORCES

Comando de Operaciones Tacticas (Tactical Operations Command Team)
Following a 1988 aircraft hijacking the Brazilians found that they were not prepared for such incidents and the Federal Police quickly expanded the existing Tactical Operations Command Team (Comando de Operaciones Tacticas). They had inherited the aircraft hijacking mission from the Air Force Search and Rescue SAR units who had that duty until then, but who lacked judicial authority

Projecto Talon (Project Talon) Brazil has maintained a CT response capability since 1953, when the Ministry of Aviation formed its own unit to combat hijackings. As the number of international terrorist incidents grew the Brazilian government established Project Talon. Volunteers for this unit are carefully screened and only those who have served in airborne or Special Operations units are permitted to take part in the fourteen-day selection programme. It has been reported that this programme has an attrition rate of somewhere near 90 per cent. Those students who pass this initial phase are then sent on to a thirteen-week training evolution located at a camp outside Rio de Janeiro.

BREACHING AND ENTRY DEVICES

Breaching equipment ranges from sledgehammers and bolt cutters and high-speed thermal cutting torches to 'frame-charges' designed to blow-in the complete window or door. LINEX, a flexible and tube like explosive, can be quickly moulded to fit circumstances where it proves impossible to use ready prefabricated alternatives. Entacannon or similar are air-powered devices to shoot a heavy projectile to shatter brick walls and protected doors. Combat shotguns with enhanced ammunition are often used to blow open doors as well. Entry devices include those used for descent/rappelling/abseiling and those for ascent such as grappling irons, thrown or fired by an 'air-cannon' or lightweight-assault hooked-ladders with silent operating pads. As part of the planning a really professional Special Forces/ HRU organisation will have carried out in preparation for any eventuality, the exact heights to most commercial aircrafts' wings, cockpits and doors will be recorded and the correct length of ladder-availability ensured. This will also apply to equipment needed for commercial transport systems and most sensitive facilities likely to be terrorist targets.

BRUNEI

MILITARY SPECIAL FORCES

Special Combat Squadron, a Rapid Reaction Company, is trained in airborne and Special Forces techniques. Superbly equipped, this unit trains regularly with other Special Force units from the UK and USA. During Exercise 'Night

Crocodile' in October 1998 members of the Sultan of Brunei's elite Special Combat Squadron trained alongside the Australian Ist Commando Regiment in the sub-tropical areas of northern Queensland.

BUD/S

Basic Underwater Demolition/SEAL. Covers everything from destroying hostile naval facilities, harbours, pipelines and underwater communication cables, to sea-defences and anything that floats. A brutally tough indoctrination course, colloquially know as 'The Grinder' and designed to eliminate anyone who may be suspect, either mentally or physically, ends with 'Hell Week', which usually weeds out fifty per cent or more of those still left on the course. The instructors are looking for those who, although shattered, are physically still defiant and prepared to give that final effort that makes them suitable to become a US Navy SEAL.

BULGARIA

MILITARY SPECIAL FORCES
Special Operations Forces Command (established in 2000)
68th Special Forces (Parachute) Brigade in Plodiv   Only one of the battalions of this brigade now remains active and its equipment is still largely old and of Warsaw Pact origin. It is seeking to expand its training regime with the addition of SF advisers from the US or Western European armies.

1st Reconnaissance and Sabotage Regiment   Headquartered in Sliven. This relatively small unit carries out LRRP operations.

CIVILIAN SPECIAL FORCES
Ministry of the Interior – Security Police
Several small anti-terrorist and hostage rescue units.

BUNKER

A protective shelter can be made from any combination of materials, including earth, sandbags, wood, metal, brick or concrete. Usually now refers to a reinforced concrete underground or mainly underground defended position.

BURKINA FASO

MILITARY SPECIAL FORCES
One anti-terrorist SF detachment is believed to exist, attached to an Airborne Battalion HQ.

BURUNDI

MILITARY SPECIAL FORCES

Two independent Companies exist to protect the political leadership. Though claimed to be Special Forces, their actual training and discipline is non-existent.

CABINDA OPERATION – SOUTH AFRICAN 'RECCES'

On 13 May 1985 a South African navy strike craft carrying a Recce team as well as a back-up team left Saldanha Bay and travelled to a spot some way off the Angolan coast near its border with Zaire. The mission was to confirm the existence of ANC terrorist bases and SWAPO bases near Cabinda. The area contained oil storage installations run by the Angolans and Gulf Oil, and because of this, several large military bases were also in the vicinity. Speculative reports had mentioned US Veterans and ex-SAS guarding the installations. The Recces landed on the coast at night on 20 May following an advance scouting party sent to gather intelligence on the beach where the party would land. Under ideal cloudy skies, the Recce team's trip had been slowed by the need to launch their boats further from shore than anticipated. The longer journey, as well as rough seas, threw off the precise timing of the mission. Near shore, Captain Du Toit noticed a small fishing vessel in the area of the landing zone and that the occupants were on shore around a fire. This forced the team to wait offshore until the boat left the area. They were now three hours behind schedule, and the danger of being detected grew. Upon landing the boats were hidden and a rendezvous point set up. The men climbed a bluff and followed a route that skirted a small village and led to a road. They miscalculated the distance to the road and turned back, losing an hour of valuable time. Du Toit decided to continue and reach the 'lay over position' in a densely wooded area within the two hours prior to dawn. South African Intelligence and aerial photographs showed an uninhabited area, but in fact it was surrounded by camouflaged FAPLA bases. The hide was finally reached as day broke. This proved to be far from ideal as a hiding place, as it was not part of the jungle but an island of dense growth some distance from the jungle. The Recces hid in the undergrowth and spread into a defensive perimeter, one man at an observation post several yards to the north with a view of the course they had travelled. As dawn broke, the features of a well-hidden FAPLA base became clear some 1,000 yards from the LO-position. A few hours later, a small FAPLA patrol could be seen following the tracks they had left the night before. The team watched as the patrol withdrew, and then came back with a larger patrol which passed the hide. At 17.00 a three-man patrol followed the team's trail directly to the thicket where the Recces were hidden. They stopped short of entering the brush, and returned to their base. Meanwhile a second patrol approached the hide from the other direction, and opened up heavy fire on the hidden position. As RPG rockets struck their position Captain Du Toit ordered the withdrawal of his troops. They had no choice but to double back on the trail that brought them to this position the previous night. Two of the men were wounded as they exited the trees. FAPLA troops deployed 50 yards west of the site opened up with RPD machine guns, RPG and many AK-47s. The team turned north, pursued by FAPLA soldiers. Another group of Angolan soldiers advanced from the west, flanking the Recces so that they could only go east now. They could see a group of trees, but needed to cross 40 yards of waist-high grass to get to this cover. Du Toit took two men and made his way through the grass as the rest of the team hid in the thicket. The small team drew fire as over 30 troops moved onto the exposed position. One Recce corporal was killed as his two comrades fought on. The fighting continued for a full 45 minutes. The two men started to run out of ammunition and were both wounded, one later died and Du Toit nearly so. The contact was over and two South African soldiers were dead. While Du Toit lay on his stomach, FAPLA soldiers approached and, thinking he was also dead, stripped his equipment – only then did they realise he was alive and shot him again through the neck. He remained awake with wounds in his neck, shoulder and arm as the FAPLA soldiers began to savagely beat him. The soldiers thought that he was a mercenary, though Du Toit tried to explain that he was in fact a South African army officer. After being severely roughed up, he was finally taken to Cabinda for medical treatment then to a Luanda hospital. The remaining six Recce soldiers carefully made their way north, where they regrouped and were eventually picked up to be returned safely to South Africa. Their escape was due in part to being ignored after the Angolans captured Du Toit, who was finally to be released after some 837 days of solitary confinement in an Angolan prison in a complicated prisoner exchange arrangement.

CAMBODIA

MILITARY SPECIAL FORCES
One Airborne Special Forces Regiment.

CAMEROON

MILITARY SPECIAL FORCES
One Airborne-Commando SF Battalion.

CANADA

MILITARY SPECIAL FORCES

Joint Task Force-2 is the Armed Forces elite Counter-Terrorist and Special Operations unit and works in conjunction with the CSIS at all times. Activated in April 1993, and taking over such duties from the Royal Canadian Mounted Police (RCMP), it has three Counter-Terrorist Operational Squadrons, a Command Group and several Specialist Intelligence Detachments and is commanded by a lieutenant colonel with some 250 highly trained and motivated soldiers. Organised into specialist two- or four-man teams, they come under the operational control of a 25–30-man squadron. The Joint Task Force is very secretive and keeps much information about its size, weapons, exact roles and missions confidential. Although this unit is supposedly trained only as a Counter-Terrorist force, it is in fact a Special Operations Intelligence unit, tasked to perform the same range of missions as the Special Air Service, Delta Force, French GIGN or German GSG-9. They do in fact operate closely with those units, with cross-training and shared intelligence. In 1993 the Royal Canadian Mounted Police's (RCMP) SERT (Special Emergency Response Team) was disbanded, reportedly due to problems the officers had resolving the necessity to kill versus their desire to protect and save lives. This unit had been Canada's premier Counter-Terrorist unit. After their dissolution, the Canadian Armed Forces created a highly secretive unit in April 1993, JTF-2. With a strength of around 200–250 each member is a volunteer from one of the three services in the Canadian military. It has created a unit that is self-sufficient and able to deploy with a minimum of dependency on other units. JTF-2 was deployed to Bosnia in response to Canadian troops being taken hostage by Serb forces in early 1995. $20 million in start-up costs were earmarked for the unit in the first two years of their existence. Included in this were funds for the purchase of land and equipment JTF-2 bought from the RCMP. Based at the Dwyer Hill Training Centre in Ontario, the Counter-Terrorist facilities there include a DC-10 airliner, a range of other vehicles including a bus, a multi-storey building for hostage rescue training, a Close-Quarter Battle (CQB) building, a state-of-the-art shooting range, a gymnasium and an Olympic-sized pool. The Joint Task Force-2 has developed a fearsome reputation for its tough training and the equally difficult entry qualifications. Applicants are vetted for any and all problems. Initial selection is based on 'Cooper's Test', used primarily by both the British SAS and US Delta Force, followed by some five weeks of intensive training. It has been known for visiting, fully qualified personnel from the US Rangers and French Foreign Legion to fail this selection course. Training includes hostage rescue, marksmanship, combat shooting, combat swimming, explosives ordnance disposal, intelligence-gathering, communications, unarmed combat, strength and stamina, heliborne insertion, mountaineering, Arctic warfare, HAHO (High Altitude High Opening) and HALO (High Altitude Low Opening) parachuting. It uses a range of weapons including SIG Sauer P226/229 and Browning HP automatic pistols, Canadian C7 assault rifles, C8 carbines, Canadian C3A1, SIG Sauer-3000 and Heckler & Koch PSG-1 sniper rifles, with Heckler & Koch MP5 and Canadian C9A1 sub-machine guns, M870 Remington combat shotguns.

CANNED GOODS

The use of doctored documents or even bodies dressed in foreign uniforms inside your own borders in order to provide an excuse to attack a neighbouring country. The Germans dressed up dead Poles in appropriate uniforms and dumped them on German territory as part of the psyops preparing the ground for the eventual invasion of Poland in September 1939. The South African apartheid regime and a number of other major countries have occasionally used these techniques over the last 60 years.

CASEVAC

Casualty evacuation – usually by helicopter (see MEDIVAC/MEDEVAC).

C & C

Command and Control. Usually refers to the Command team of a Special Project or Clandestine Operation.

CENTRAL AFRICAN REPUBLIC

MILITARY SPECIAL FORCES
A small HRU unit exists, but any serious terrorist situation would certainly require assistance from the French GIGN.

CHAD

MILITARY SPECIAL FORCES
Each of the seven Military Regions has a small Rapid Reaction Anti-Terrorist/SF unit (platoon) attached to each of the local headquarters.

CHE GUEVARA – A SPECIAL FORCES SUCCESS STORY?

By the time Ernesto 'Che' Guevara was murdered in the jungles of Bolivia in October 1967, he was already a legend around the world. Though he had fought for a political belief that had a mere 23 years more to survive before it too would be relegated to history, the manner of his death was still shocking, though his crude execution at the age of 39 only enhanced his mythical stature to many. On 9 October 1967, Ernesto 'Che' Guevara was put to death by Bolivian soldiers, trained, equipped and guided by US Green Beret and CIA officers after the failure of his last campaign, in the backwoods of Bolivia, where he had hoped to ignite a revolution that would spread throughout South America. When Che Guevara was executed in La Higuera, one CIA official was present, a Cuban-American officer named Félix Rodríguez. Rodríguez, who used the codename 'Félix Ramos' in Bolivia and posed as a Bolivian military officer, had been sent to Bolivia with another Cuban-American agent, Gustavo Villoldo, to assist in the capture of Guevara and the destruction of his guerrilla band. Rodríguez and Villoldo became part of a Special Forces-CIA task force in Bolivia that included the case officer for the operation, 'Jim', yet another Cuban-American, Mario Osiris Riveron, and two agents in charge of communications in Santa Clara. Rodríguez emerged as the most important member of the group. After a lengthy interrogation of one captured guerrilla, he was instrumental in focusing the efforts of the 2nd Ranger Battalion on the Villagrande region, where he believed Guevara's rebels were operating.

On 30 September 1967 Che and his group were finally trapped by Bolivian Special Forces in a jungle canyon in Valle Serrano, south of the Grande River. By 8 October 1967 the Bolivian Special Forces had received information that there was a band of seventeen guerrillas in the Churro Ravine. On that day at around 1.30 p.m. Che Guevara's final battle commenced in Quebrada del Yuro with Simon Cuba (Willy) Sarabia, a Bolivian miner, leading the rebel group. Che was behind him and was shot in the leg several times. By 10 a.m. the next morning the Bolivian officers were faced with the question of what to do with Che Guevara. The possibility of prosecuting him was ruled out, because a trial would focus world attention on him and could generate sympathetic propaganda for Che and for Cuba. It is concluded that Che must be executed immediately, but it is agreed that the official story will be that he died from wounds received in battle. Félix Rodríguez received a call from Vallegrande and was ordered by the Bolivian Command to conduct Operation Five Hundred and Six Hundred. Five hundred being the Bolivian code for Che and six hundred the order to kill him. Rodríguez informed Colonel Zenteno of the order, but also told him that the US government had instructed him to keep Che alive at all costs. The CIA had arranged a helicopter and aircraft to take Che to Panama for interrogation. However, Colonel Zenteno repeated that he must obey his own orders and Rodríguez decided, 'to let history take its course', and to leave the matter in the hands of the Bolivian Special Forces. At 1.10 p.m. Bolivian time Che was executed by a Special Forces sergeant by being shot in the face, side, arms and legs, and then in the thorax, filling his lungs with blood. Several soldiers, also wanting to shoot Che, entered the room and fired their weapons into him. 'Willy' Sarabia had been executed minutes before Che. On 11 October 1967 Walt Rostow sent a memorandum to President Johnson stating that they 'are 99% sure that "Che" Guevara is dead'. He explained that Guevara's death carried significant implications: 'It marks the passing of another of the aggressive, romantic revolutionaries . . . In the Latin American context, it will have a strong impact in discouraging would-be guerrillas. It shows the soundness of our "preventive medicine" assistance to countries facing incipient insurgency, it was the Bolivian 2nd Ranger Battalion, trained by our Green Berets from June–September of this year, that cornered him and got him.'

CHILE

MILITARY SPECIAL FORCES
Regimiento Escuela de Paracaidistas y Fuerzas Especiales – 1st Special Forces Airborne Regiment   Formed on 2nd April 1968 and based at Peldehue. A tough selection process eliminates up to 80 per cent of recruits and the resulting highly motivated unit is rated as one of the best in South America.

The most talented go on to complete courses with the US Special Forces at Fort Benning, and in both Argentina and the Jungle Warfare School in Brazil. Directly under the control of the Army High Command, this unit played a leading part in the military overthrow of the democratically elected government of Salvadore Allende in 1973 by Chile's future dictator General Pinochet, and the deaths of thousands of civilians considered expendable or a danger by the new regime. The level of human rights abuse in Chile was on an astounding level and, indeed, should have been treated by the US and British governments in much the same way as that of the Serbians in Bosnia or Kosovo. However, the Chilean regime escaped serious problems as it was perceived to be a valuable Western ally and repaid its debt in part to Mrs Thatcher's Conservative government in Britain by providing valuable intelligence on its neighbour Argentina, and possibly playing host to British SAS operations during the Falklands War. As with so many other Latin American countries, the Special Forces and Security services operated in close co-operation with right wing paramilitary death squads, in this case the Comando de Vengadores de Los Martires (COVEMA), 'the Avengers of the Martyrs', a covert fascist group composed of serving members of the armed forces. As many as 10,000 Chilean civilians were to 'disappear', though some human rights groups have suggested the figure is closer to 20,000. General Pinochet promulgated a Decree Law on Amnesty in 1978, which granted a blanket pardon and immunity from arrest to all members of the Security and Special Forces who might have committed crimes since his accession to power. This would be taken as the basis for granting immunity to those guilty of abuse of human rights in later years, and one supposes that the immunity also applied to the good general himself.

Escuela de Paracaidistas y Fuerzas Especiales (Special Forces School of the Chilean Army)   Established with US Special Forces assistance in 1965 at Peldehue.
Other Special Forces units include:

18th Bolnas Negra Special Forces Commando (Buzos Tacticos del Ejercito) Battalion Elite Special Operations Commando unit which is used independently on anti-terrorist operations or to provide back-up for the 1st Special Forces Airborne Regiment in a crisis.

Navy
Buzos Tacticos de la Armada   (Navy Special Forces commandos). Similar in operational role to US SEALs and based at Vina del Mar and Valparaiso.

CIVILIAN SPECIAL FORCES
Unidad Anti-Terroristes (UAT) of the National Police Force ('Cobra')   Unidad Anti-Terroristes is Chile's primary Counter-Terrorist team formed in 1980. Its 120 personnel are divided into seven-man teams, each with a commanding officer. All operators have successfully completed the Chilean army's Commando Course prior to acceptance into the unit. Headquartered in Santiago near the Tobalaba Airport, this unit received training from the Israeli and South African Special Forces in Counter-Terrorist skills and, additionally, in specialist VIP and diplomatic protection duties. Weapons used include the 9mm UZI SMG and 5.56mm Galil assault rifles.

GOPE Grupo de Operaciones Policiales Especiales of the National Police (Carabineros)   GOPE was established in 1979 and became fully operational in 1980 after receiving training from the German GSG-9 and both Israeli and South African Special Forces Teams. They are primarily a Special Forces/Commando unit but are also responsible for Counter-Terrorist duties in government and diplomatic buildings. GOPE's 100-man strength is roughly divided into four 25-man teams.

Trained in airborne, SCUBA, assault tactics, CQB, breaching, rappelling and other anti-terrorist and HRU skills.

CHINA

MILITARY SPECIAL FORCES
There is a 'Kuaisu' Special Forces 'Dadui' (Regiment) Rapid Reaction Unit (RRU) attached to each of the seven Military Regions (MR) operating under

the direct command of the HQ and a 'Kuaisu' Battalion of Special Forces RRU attached to each of the eighteen PLA Ground Armies (GA) with a total strength of some 25,000 Special Forces. The total number of battalions would appear to be 32, with the fourteen attached to the 'Dadui' (Regiments). The number of SF teams within each battalion, as well as the size of the teams, varies according to the nature of the missions involved. The teams range in size from two-man units used for SR, to reinforced companies used in DA missions. Chinese SFs are equipped with the best equipment the PLA can field and, assuming they follow the pattern used by SFs of other nations, they use standard and modified versions of the equipment designed for general-purpose forces to meet their unique mission requirements. In addition, they are familiar with most foreign individual and squad weapons. Chinese SF units are known to have various types of specialised equipment, including night-vision goggles (NVGs), low-light-level television (LLLTV) systems, powered parachutes (PPCs) and unmanned aerial vehicles (UAVs). The LLLTV system can be used for day/night surveillance, target acquisition, fire control, fire adjustment, target identification and target tracking. The PPC, which the Chinese consider to be the world's lightest flying device, entered service with the SFs in 1996. It is capable of self-powered take-off and landing in very short distances, which will greatly enhance a SF unit's infiltration and exfiltration capabilities. The PPC is capable of carrying a soldier and a limited amount of gear at an approximate rate of 18–35km per hour. The air-cooled, two-stroke engine operates on unleaded gasoline and can fly for two hours on a tank of gas, for a flight range of 45km. These vehicles are capable of performing their missions for two hours out to a range of 100km. It is likely that a specialised sub-unit handles the UAVs, since they would require a considerable amount of technical and field training owing to the high-tech nature of the systems. The Chinese PLA Special Forces reportedly rely upon air force, navy and army units for air support. However, they are now developing an independent dedicated air component, with specially adapted helicopters and STOL aircraft for covert missions. Chinese SFs heavily emphasise superior physical fitness and small-arms proficiency in their soldiers. All PLA SF units are trained in a variety of martial arts and airborne operations. Elements of each unit are receiving specialised training in one or more of the following areas: UAVs, amphibious operations and SCUBA, demolitions and sabotage, communications, computers and information warfare and foreign languages. The Chinese now realise the important role of professional, well-equipped, and highly trained SFs on the modern battlefield, and even if the Chinese PLA are unable to match the West technologically for some years yet, their SFs will still surpass those of most of their neighbours and are quite capable of providing a serious challenge to Western interests. The weapons used by Chinese Special Forces are modified versions of the army's standard issues, specially designed silenced weapons and a wide variety of Russian and Western weapons, including the 7.65mm Type 64 silenced pistol, 7.62mm Type 67 silenced pistol, 7.62mm Type 81 assault rifles, 5.8mm Type 87 and 95 assault rifles, 7.62mm Type 79/85 (SVD) sniper rifles, 5.8mm Type 88 sniper rifles, 7.62mm Type 79/85 sub-machine guns and 7.62mm Type 64 silenced sub-machine guns, as well as the Twin-62mm FHJ-84 SF rocket launcher. There is some doubt over what the PLA actually considers to be Special Forces and how they compare to their Western equivalents. Such units are characterised as being technology-intensive and their members as being experts in their fields. China's SFs appear to be focused on special reconnaissance (SR) and Direct Action (DA) missions. SR missions gain strategic and tactical information of significance about enemy strength and intentions: the weather and terrain behind enemy lines, with the location of enemy command posts; reserves; weapons of mass destruction: key weapons systems; logistic sites; possible river-crossing sites; avenues of approach; and targeting data, especially for precision weapons systems of paramount importance. Chinese SFs also have reconnaissance and security force roles in airborne operations, as well as providing target illumination for airborne precision-guided munitions. While DA missions are 'short-duration strikes and other small-scale offensive activities conducted primarily by SF sabotage operations, China began developing a genuine Western-style Long-range Operations Group capable of carrying out long-range air borne operations, long-range reconnaissance (LRRP) and amphibious operations in the Guangzhou Military Region in the mid-1980s and this quickly became known as the 'Sword of Southern China'. The force received army parachute, air force and naval training and increasing supplies of modern equipment including SatCom, GPS global-positioning systems, advanced intelligence equipment, command, control, and a wide range of weapons including some specially purchased in Western Europe. Personnel were drawn from the 6th Special Warfare Group, 8th Special Warfare Group and the 12th Special Warfare Group's own Special Forces Detachments. All of the force's officers have completed military staff college and 60 per cent are said to have university degrees. Soldiers are reported to be cross-trained in various specialities, and training is supposed to encompass a range of operational environments. The force, now reported to be 4,000 strong, was fully operational in 1989 and was later joined by similar SF groups in other military regions. Five new and even more intensely trained Long-Range Operations Groups for Airborne, Reconnaissance and Amphibious warfare are aimed at being fully operational in early 2003. This new generation of Chinese Special Forces is cross-trained and multi-disciplined. The brigade-sized unit would provide the initial clandestine elements in any invasion of Taiwan, but with its multi-role capability it can be used as a mobile counter-insurgency or counter-terrorism 'fire-brigade'. The vast cities of China and a hinterland now beset by growing terrorist, ethnic and religious conflict provides the requirement for more such units. There were two primary reasons for this evolution. First, the PLA has been shifting its doctrine from the 'People's War' to fighting a 'Local War Under High-Technology Conditions'. The Chinese believe their next war will be a short, sharp conflict on their periphery rather than a protracted war of attrition on friendly terrain. Secondly, the PLA was greatly impressed by the capabilities of US and Coalition SFs during the 1991 Gulf War. The war has prompted the Chinese to accelerate the formation of modern, professional SFs capable of providing the PLA with timely anti-terrorist, reconnaissance and Direct Action (DA) capabilities.

CIVILIAN SPECIAL FORCES

The Chinese Counter-Terrorist units are known as Immediate Action Units (IAU) and are effectively an operational department of the MSS Intelligence Service. Significant terrorist activity is dealt with by a regional Immediate Action Unit and supported by the army when required. These units are not comparable with Western Special Forces, as they concentrate largely on martial arts and the 'elimination' of the threat, i.e. the intention is to kill, not to capture. Little emphasis is placed on clandestine operations, capturing terrorists, preventing incidents or indeed hostage rescue. Interestingly, China's IAU Counter-Terrorist force is largely drawn from the police force rather than the military. The name changes frequently, but as of writing in mid-2002, it is still known as the Immediate Action Unit.

CHINDITS

The nickname based on a 'Chinthe' a mythical animal and the Chindwin River, given to General Orde Wingate's Long-Range Penetration Groups in the Burma campaign during the Second World War. Wingate persuaded C in C India, General Wavell, to authorise small aggressive patrols to carry out special operations deep behind the Japanese front line. The units mainly drawn from Wingate's 77th Indian Infantry division would rely on air-drops for their supplies and reinforcements. The first operation began on 18 February 1943, when some 3,000 soldiers in several small columns crossed the Chindwin and sabotaged the Mandalay–Myitkyina railway. They then crossed the Irrawaddy in an attempt to destroy the vital Mandalay–Lashio rail link, at which point the Japanese reacted promptly and forced the Chindits to withdraw, having suffered some 1,000 casualties. A second major operation began on 4 March 1944 when Wingate deployed six Infantry Brigades, five of which landed mainly by glider in north-central Burma and blocked important Japanese supply routes at Mawlu. Wingate died in an air crash on the 25 March and his replacement, General W. D. A. Lentaigne, withdrew the Chindits westwards while suffering considerable casualties. The remaining force moved north to join General 'Vinegar Joe' Stilwell's joint

US-Chinese operations. Relations between the US and Chindits were distinctly strained at times and interfered with the best use of what was a potentially valuable co-operative effort. Despite the detractors Wingate's ideas for special operations deep behind enemy lines, carrying out sabotage and interdicting railways and other supply routes were the right ideas, at the right time, but without sufficient understanding or support from the British Command in India or their main allies. Wingate was also hampered by a chronic lack of suitably trained and equipped troops. Wingate was indeed a visionary and many of his ideas were later to be accepted and improved by the Special Forces in both the USA and UK. The modern 22nd SAS probably owes as much to Wingate and the Chindits as to David Stirling and the original fairly conventional SAS of Second World War fame.

CIVVIES

Civilian attire, at one time this referred to the clothes worn on leave or demobilisation (Demob) i.e. return to 'civvie street'. However, it is now increasingly used to denote covert/undercover operations conducted out of uniform.

CLANDESTINE WAR AGAINST IRAQ

One of the significant innovations in Operation Enduring Freedom was the initial employment of US Special Operations Command (SOCOM) as the principal operational command rather than the US Central Command (CENTCOM), which in theory remained responsible for the geographical region from its headquarters in Florida. By using a functional, rather than a geographic, command to plan the Afghan campaign, the President and the Secretary of Defence engaged in a radical and highly successful test of the 'capabilities-based' concept that is central to the current DoD re-organisation and modernisation. SOCOM is likely to play as important a role in a campaign against Iraq and the overall War on Terrorism, bringing with it the practical experience of special warfare in Afghanistan – though this appeared to be placed in some doubt when the 3rd US Army Command transferred its headquarters to Kuwait in early 2002. The US Special Forces will undoubtedly engage in information and psychological operations (PSYOPS) in support of the important softening up of Iraq before the initial combat missions get under way. Massive radio propaganda coverage will be instigated to flood Iraq with the Allies' anti-government message, and this will be backed up later with specific and tightly targeted C130 PSYOPS flights. Iraq is a country with a regime-controlled press, in which cell phones and even direct-dial long-distance calls are illegal, and the nearest Internet access is in Jordan. It is expected by US strategists that the local population will welcome a new and alternative source of information. To help ensure that Iraqi homes receive only approved transmissions the regime relies on the Al Hadi Project 858, which controls virtually all Iraqi signals, communication and electronic intelligence. Project 858 monitors the entire country for illegal communications, and reportedly can triangulate in 30 seconds. However, the regime will not be allowed to prevent transmissions from abroad such as the existing Radio Free Iraq, and among the very first targets for US 'smart weapons' and to receive the attentions of US Special Forces will therefore be the Al Hadi Projects facilities and aerial farms of Saddam's radio propaganda network. However, even more important missions for Special Forces and the Iraqi opposition groups working closely with them will be collecting information on potential targets for air and ground attacks. Saddam, having studied Western air campaigns in his own country and in Serbia, is relocating weapons-storage sites, communications centres, military and security headquarters, and similar high-value targets to schools, mosques, clinics and other types of structures normally excluded from target lists. This will make targeting more difficult and politically dangerous. Destroying the wrong mosque, or even the right one for that matter, would allow Saddam to score propaganda points in the Muslim world and with the Western press. Saddam would certainly benefit from an event similar to the bombing of the al Amiriyah Shelter during Operation Desert Storm, in which many dozens of civilians were killed. Ironically, in these days of precision-guided munitions, non-combatants are probably safer staying away from shelters that have dual-use military capabilities as al Amiriyah reportedly did, and it is notably that during the 1991 air campaign Saddam Hussein's son Uday did not go to a bomb shelter but hid out at a friend's house. It is reported that Uday later killed this particular friend, despite having been offered the protection of his home during US air attacks, in a bizarre game of 'Russian Roulette' after seducing his wife. It would be absolutely essential that, this time, the Special Forces are far more aggressive and indeed successful in the pursuit of accurate information on prime targets and the Iraqi leadership, if the United States wishes to quickly destabilise Saddam's regime. However, it has also become clear that Iraqi Special Forces, and in particular the Special Republican Guard, are far better equipped and trained than in 1991 and indeed have obtained considerable supplies of advanced electronic listening and surveillance equipment and will provide a considerable obstacle to an easy victory. Targets of opportunity for Special Forces sabotage operations may present themselves during the initial intelligence-gathering process. They may be WMD (Weapons of Mass Destruction) sites, fuel dumps, perhaps leading Baathists, high-ranking officers or even Saddam himself. It is fairly certain that the US administration will give the Special Forces considerable freedom to engage at will, assuming that any action taken does not compromise a larger operation or cause political embarrassment with potential Arab allies. The Iraqi leader reportedly uses at least two doubles, who have been surgically altered to closely resemble him. Certainly other doubles will also be dispatched around the country to divert attention, either with their appearance changed by cosmetic surgery or at least made up well enough to fool a high-flying drone or distant surveillance team. In any case, it would be useful to have 'platforms' on call to respond to these fortuitous circumstances quickly, and the new developments in missile-firing unmanned drones will be in great demand. These drones, or UAVs, may also be used to respond to requests from armed Iraqi opposition groups for their own fire support missions, particularly in the Kurdish areas where there are greater numbers of active guerrillas.

The campaign appeared to be in its preparatory stages by the late summer of 2002, with more than 1,800 US Special Forces teams operating in the North of Iraq in Kurdish territory between the Turkish border and the Iraqi cities of Mosul and Kirkuk. Supported by some 5,000 Turkish Commandos from the 1st and 2nd Brigades they were already in possession of the airfield at Bamerni and Zakhu in northern Iraq by early September. Their tasks included supporting US Army engineers in building a network of additional airfields to support the creation of an important bridgehead inside Iraq, to train Kurdish anti-government rebels and to support CIA covert action teams operating throughout northen Iraq. US Special Forces, along with the Kuwaiti SF unit and possibly SAS/SBS elements, have penetrated deep into southern Iraq and even around Basra, while additional US elite forces are preparing to operate out of Eastern Jordan by September 2002. Whenever the campaign to overthrow the Iraqi regime of Saddam Hussein finally gets completely underway, US and Allied Special Forces will undoubtedly take the dominating role in the early stages, and may indeed be paramount throughout the whole ground war. Special Forces' deep reconnaissance, target acquisition and sabotage teams will be highly important to the outcome, while these units, along with specialised revolutionary warfare teams, will be essential for mobilising, arming, training and directing the opposition groups to take over control of Iraq once, or if, Saddam Hussein has been finally overthrown or killed.

CLAYMORE

A directional mine. Claymore M18A1 mines have been used by Special Forces for more than 40 years. It is designed to kill or injure any soldier in the impact zone. Some 0.68kg of C4 explosives is used to blast around 700 small steel ball-bearings forward in an arc of 60 degrees. The projectiles are fired some 50m outward and around 1m upwards. The mine can be detonated by a trip wire or a command wire. Weighing only 1.58kg, the

Claymore is issued in large numbers to protect positions or set-up ambushes. Groups of Claymores are often used to protect an escape route for a patrol, the pursuing enemy triggering the devastating effect of numerous Claymores directed at their line of approach.

COCKLESHELL HEROES – SBS

Royal Marines Boom Patrol Detachment: the RMBPD was formed on 6 July 1942, specifically for attacking enemy shipping. It was the first small boat unit completely manned by Royal Marines, though others had served and would continue to serve in units such as the Special Boat Sections and Special Boat Squadron. Its founding commander was Major H. G. 'Blondie' Hasler, a regular officer and experienced yachtsman. The name came from the detachment's intended equipment, code-named the Boom Patrol Boat, based on a captured Italian explosive motor boat, several of which had been used against the British. This was a sixteen-foot hydroplane with a 500lb charge, which the pilot would have to abandon close to the target. In fact the BPB never saw action. The second of the two sections was to use Motor Submersible Canoes, known as 'Sleeping Beauties', single-seat 12ft 8in (4.9m) craft, powered by an electric motor. The pilot lay in them as in a modern Formula 1 car and controlled the craft by a joystick. He breathed through SCUBA gear and would have to come close to the surface to establish his whereabouts. Until these new craft were ready, the detachment, twenty-five swimmer-canoeists, trained with canoes, assault boats and surfboats.

The RMBPD's first combat action, Operation Frankton ('Cockleshell Heroes'), in which ten men in five canoes, known as Cockle Mk.IIs, were launched off the Gironde estuary in the Bay of Biscay by a submarine, was on 7 December 1942. Their mission was to paddle some 120km (75 miles) upriver to Bordeaux and attack German blockade runners, fast merchantmen used to sail to Japan. Only two canoes made it to the harbour on the night of 11/12th December and placed limpet mines on four ships. All of the men on the operation were drowned or captured and executed, except for Major Hasler and his canoe partner, Marine Billy Sparks. These two escaped to Spain after the attack and from there to the UK in April 1943. One of the ships was sunk and the others badly damaged. In February 1944 eighteen men, known as Earthworm Section, were sent out to the Middle East. Here they came under the command of the Raiding Forces (see separate entry). Their first operation was against German shipping at Portolago Bay, Leros, in mid-June. Three canoe parties were disembarked from a Royal Navy motor launch and then infiltrated the harbour, placing mines which sank three escort vessels and damaged three destroyers. All escaped successfully to the rendezvous with the ML. Other raids were carried out in the Aegean, but eventually a lack of worthwhile targets forced the section to return home in

October 1944. The RMBPD was the only small boat unit not disbanded at the end of the war, but was reduced to token strength after the discharge of most Hostilities-Only personnel.

COIN

COunter-INsurgency. Popular term used to cover guerrilla warfare, armed revolt, insurrection or rebellion and the military action taken to counter the anti-government activities. Does not refer to terrorism.

COLD WAR

Although it was a war that never happened, as far as an outbreak of fighting directly between the two super power blocks is concerned, in all other respects it was a fighting war that lasted for 45 years. A long series of bloody proxy wars fought out between the client regimes of the USA and the USSR – or indeed in a succession of civil wars, coups d'état, revolutions, rebellions, guerrilla wars and international terrorism. The Special Forces played a major part in both regional wars and counter-insurgency campaigns from Colombia to Vietnam and from Northern Ireland to Malaya. However, what is often little appreciated or reported is the use of the SAS and the US covert action teams in deep cover missions within the old Warsaw Pact countries of Eastern Europe. The SAS, in particular, used the cover provided by BRIXMIS, the British Military Mission allowed to travel around East Germany as part of the old Four Power Agreement on Berlin; the Soviets, French and US had similar teams. SAS troopers would use these missions to spot potential landing zones, observation points and generally gather intelligence to help in planning aggressive deep-penetration operations in the event of a major confrontation or outright conventional war with the Soviet Union. The SAS, and later US Special Forces, are also believed to have been involved in clandestine operations inside the Soviet Union – particularly the Baltic Republics, Central Asian and Far Eastern territories. Operations were also conducted against Soviet assets in the Middle East, Africa and during the Soviet occupation of Afghanistan. For certain highly secretive sections of the SAS, SBS and US SF the cold war was a never-ending ideal opportunity to develop and practice covert war techniques.

COLOMBIA

MILITARY SPECIAL FORCES

Agrupacion Fuerzas Especiales Anti-Terroristas Urbanas (AFEAU) – *Urban Counter-terrorist Special Forces* was formed on 8 April 1985. AFEAU is a small unit, not more than 150 soldiers drawn from all sections of the armed forces, as well as from security and police forces. AFEAU is tasked with hostage rescue and VIP protection. The need for such a unit was further highlighted by a failed assault which resulted in the deaths of not only the M-19 terrorists but many hostages as well. In November 1985, 30 heavily armed terrorists of M-19 (Movimiento 19 de Abril, or 19th of April Movement) stormed Bogota's Palace of Justice and captured some 500 hostages. Present in this group were several members of the Council of State and Supreme Court. Unprepared Colombian military units assaulted the palace and freed many of the hostages. However, in the hail of bullets and recoilless rifle fire, well over 50 hostages had been killed. Included in the death toll were eleven members of the Supreme Court. Nearly twenty of the terrorists had been killed, but eleven soldiers had also lost their lives in the process. The Colombian government considered this badly mishandled hostage rescue operation a success because all the terrorists were killed or captured, despite the deaths of over 50 hostages. In addition to the assault teams, the AFEAU has dedicated sniper teams, a crisis management team, and a hostage negotiation element. Training is carried out primarily at a facility in Facatativa, north of Bogota. Members are trained in a wide variety of disciplines, including close-quarters combat, short- and long-range marksmanship, hand-to-hand combat, and even air assault operations. Specific hostage rescue skills are developed for the major transportation scenarios, including trains, buses and a wide variety of aircraft. It is organised into six fifteen-man squads, each consisting of two officers and thirteen operators, and is under the direct command of the Commandante de las Fuerzas Armadas. After passing a rigorous seven-day selection phase, volunteers begin a six-month training phase in Facatativa, near Bogota. Training focuses on hostage rescue from buildings, aircraft, buses, ships and trains. Fast roping and rappelling skills are covered, as well as sniping, EOD (Explosive Ordinance Disposal), and heliborne assault skills. Due to their VIP protection mission, members of AFEAU are also trained in high-speed and offensive driving. Weapons include Beretta 9mm, Browning 9mm and Glock pistols, H&K MP-5 sub-machine guns, M60 7.62mm light machine guns and Galil 7.62mm and M-16A2 assault rifles.

Fuerzas Especiales (Special Forces) 'Lanceros'   The Lanceros unit was created in December 1955 in response to the 'La Violencia' civil war. Colombian army officers were sent through the US Army's Ranger school, and these officers became responsible for creating Colombia's own elite force of Special Forces/Paratroopers. At the Escuela de Lanceros School candidates are put through a ten-week course that involves forced marches, obstacle courses, marksmanship, martial arts, map reading and airborne operations. Lanceros are trained to operate in mountain environments, as well as attending a three-week jungle phase, the last phase before graduation. Their primary mission is counter-insurgency and counter-terrorism. Weapons used include 9mm FN-Browning HP-35 pistol, 9mm H&K MP5A3 sub-machine gun, 9mm H&K MP5SD3 suppressed sub-machine gun, 5.56mm Colt AR-15A2 Model 705 burst-fire rifle, 7.62mm IMI Model 339 Galil SR sniper rifle, 7.62mm Remington Model 700 sniper rifle, 5.56mm FNMI M249 light machine gun, 7.62mm Saco M60 machine gun, 18.5mmR (12-gauge) Remington Model 870 MK1 pump-action shotgun, 40mmSR Mechem MGL-6 grenade launcher and 66mm Talley M72A3 light anti-tank weapon. Considerable mobility is gained by the widespread use of helicopters, include the Bell Model 205B Huey (UH-1H) and Sikorsky S-70A (UH-60A), both types fitted with a 7.62mm Saco M60D machine gun and a 12.7mm (.50 BMG) General Electric GAU-19/A minigun.

Air Force
Grupo Anti-Secuestro de Aviones (Airborne Anti-Hijacking Group) GASDA   The mission of the Colombian Air Force's GASDA unit is directed at countering terrorist and criminal activities at all Colombian airports. The GASDA came into existence in the early 1980s and was expanded in 1985. While part of the Air Force, it is controlled operationally by the CIAES. GASDA is located at the Madrid Air Base, outside of Bogota. Organised into 25-man sections, it is believed the unit strength is somewhere between 60–90 men. Each 25-man section has three assault teams, a security team and a support element. Members are volunteers from the Air Force security police units, most are airborne-qualified, in addition to having passed the army's rigorous Lancero course.

Navy
Grupo de Comandos Anfibios (GCA) – Amphibious Commando Group   This is a SEAL-type unit established in the mid-1960s and works against drug trafficking but is also given other missions such as naval CT. The unit is based at the Cartagena Naval Base and is approximately 100-men strong. The GCA is composed of 25-man platoons, with a Training Company and a Security Company. In October 1967, soon after the unit's inception, a Mobile Training Team from the US Navy's SEAL Team 2 travelled to Cartagena to train the GCA in combat swimming, demolitions, scuba and land warfare.

CIVILIAN SPECIAL FORCES
Grupo Operational Contra Extorsion y Secuestros (GOES) Special Operations Group   This is a National Police HRU with the primary mission of rescuing kidnap victims of both terrorists and criminals. GOES came into existence in the mid-1980s and is composed of approximately 150 men. GOES operational units are composed of approximately ten men each and are assigned to Bogota, Barranquilla, Cali and Medellin. When the units are operational, they are formed into three-man teams with reserves and a

supporting sniper team. All members are volunteers who must serve a minimum of two years. The training lasts three months and includes rudimentary Special Forces tactics, breaching and CQB skills.

COMBAT TRAINING FOR SPECIAL FORCES

A Special Forces soldier is the most elite fighting man in any army. He is required to be fully trained in all areas of combat: communications, demolitions, light weaponry, medical and intelligence. Special Forces soldiers in the world's leading units are airborne-qualified, with many specialising in HALO (High Altitude Low Opening), SCUBA, STABO (extraction methods), and SERE (Survival, Evasion, Resistance, Escape). A perfect example of the standard and complexity of the combat training required by the elite units would be the 'Combatives Course' of the US Special Forces or Green Berets. Special Forces teams have high-priority missions, sometimes going weeks or months without contact with friendly units. The special Forces Combatives Course enhances the physical attributes, mental awareness, and self-confidence of the SF soldier. Also, due to the type of missions he is assigned, a thorough knowledge of combatives is often necessary to raise the Special Forces soldier's capabilities to a level whereby he will be successful. The Special Forces Combatives Course provides the medium to build a better fighting man, both physically and mentally. The SF Combatives training programme furnishes comprehensive physical development, cardiovascular and aerobic conditioning, and develops anaerobic endurance, muscular strength, flexibility and agility. A combination of these physiological factors develops a soldier who is in overall top physical condition – a requirement for the Special Forces mission. From a psychological standpoint, the Special Forces Combatives Course is also quite beneficial. The inner knowledge that, if stripped of all weapons, one still has the skills necessary to effectively defend oneself, greatly increases a soldier's self-confidence. Special Combatives training, above that of the average soldier, enhances a Green Beret's sense of identity and pride in what Special Forces stands for. The nature of the Special Forces mission means an increased possibility for close-combat encounters. Special Forces Combatives training is designed specifically for close combat and is geared for total annihilation. A soldier untrained for close combat might become wounded and/or die in such a situation and thus fail in his mission. A soldier who is properly trained in close combat will effectively neutralise his enemy and accomplish his mission.

The Special Forces Combatives Course is divided into nine basic components: physical fitness, sentry neutralisation, Filipino martial arts, kicking, punching and hand strikes, grappling and throwing, knife techniques, equipment training and mental/philosophical training.

Physical Fitness A Special Forces soldier must have outstanding endurance, strength and skill. He must be able to overcome obstacles, kill or disable the enemy in hand-to-hand combat with or without a weapon, and advance swiftly, silently and effectively. The Special Forces devotes a great deal of time and effort towards making its fighting men the best in the world.

The physical fitness programme for the Special Forces Combatives Course is geared towards achieving high fitness levels in the shortest time possible through strenuous physical exercises. This programme is divided into five 'gates' or stations: upper body, middle body, lower body, reaching and aerobics. These stations are further subdivided into variables. The variables are based on data drawn from tests and studies conducted over a number of years, as well as personal experiences of the instructors. The exercises include conventional army programmes, t'ai chi reaches, Ranger push-ups, Tiger push-ups, martial arts stretching, isometric resistance, SCUBA sit-ups and boxing reachbacks.

Sentry Neutralisation   Sentry neutralisation is taught utilising empty-hand, garrote and knife techniques. Not only are the actual killing movements taught and practised, but Green Berets also learn the philosophy of close-quarter termination, stealth, stalking, visual domination, spring power, timing, environmental control and spontaneous reactions (both of yourself and the sentry target). Realism in all situations is stressed to its highest point. Two-man sentry neutralisation techniques are presented for absolute control of an armed guard.

Filipino Martial Arts   One of the unique aspects of the Special Forces Combatives Course is the training Green Berets receive in the battle-proven Filipino martial arts, more commonly known as kali, escrima, or amis. The Filipino martial arts are often erroneously thought of as exclusively weapons arts. Although the Filipino arts do place an emphasis on weapons (mostly sticks and/or bladed weapons), they are actually a total method of fighting, utilising all ranges of combat with an integrated and sophisticated empty-hand system. Great emphasis is placed on infighting and grappling, because combat generally starts at close quarters or deteriorates to that range very quickly. The armed aspects of the Filipino martial arts are stressed in the course, however, since a bludgeoning-type weapon is most often improvised in survival situations. One can always find a stick or club, and if a Special Forces operative is forced by the situation to expend all of his ammunition, his assault rifle can make an efficient weapon even if it is empty. Personnel are taught to effectively strike with and manipulate sticks or some type of bladed weapon at long and close ranges. Apart from offensive manoeuvres, counter-offensive concepts and techniques are also essential parts of the curriculum. Unlike many martial arts and their weapons phases, individuals taught in the Filipino styles can be battlefield ready in an extremely short period of time.

Kicking   The kicking techniques imparted to the Special Forces soldier are meant for the battlefield, and thus many classical martial arts kicks are not taught – not because they are not effective techniques, but because the soldiers do not have the time necessary to put into learning them. Careful consideration of the Special Forces soldier's equipment and heavy boots dictates the kicking methods taught. He must learn effective kicks that will definitely work in a combat situation – strong, explosive kicks that will cripple and maim an enemy in a matter of seconds.

The Special Forces Combatives Course emphasises realistic training methods such as those developed by the late Bruce Lee. Full-contact training with 100 per cent commitment on air shields, heavy bags, Thai pads, and other aids, is an integral part of the kicking phase. Close-quarters kneeing, stomping, and special techniques for kicking an enemy when he is on the ground are also among the situational training presented.

Hand Techniques   In combat, one of the Special Forces soldier's most essential skills is the ability to utilise his hands and elbows in an explosively powerful way in order to effectively neutralise an enemy. Again, training methods developed by Bruce Lee and his protege, Dan Inosanto, are stressed. A finger jab, punch, slap or elbow strike can be used singly or in conjunction with kicking or grappling, depending on the situation. Focus gloves, heavy bags, and simple notebook paper are among the training apparatuses used in this portion of the programme.

Throwing/Grappling   The concepts of throwing and grappling used in the combatives course are derived from jujitsu and dumog (Filipino grappling). Such manoeuvres as the step-over, hip and circle throws are covered in the basic course. Other methods of grappling taught include leg, arm and head takedowns, neck and joint manipulations, and chokes – all in conjunction with offensive or counter-offensive attacks.

Knife Techniques   Easily carried, silent, and hard to counter, the knife can be a formidable tool when placed in the hands of a properly trained individual. Whether one is in a steamy jungle or a back alley, a knife can be a great asset in the event of close combat. Often a Special Forces soldier must rely on his knife, either to assure a quiet kill while behind enemy lines, or as an effective alternative if his primary weapons have been rendered inoperative or inappropriate for the situation.

Practitioners of the Filipino martial arts have developed knife fighting to an extremely high degree of efficiency, and Filipino methods constitute the bulk of SF knife training. Additional concepts and methods of knife fighting are also incorporated into the knife phase of the combatives course. Fluid and dynamic offensive strategies are taught to SF students for facing unarmed opponents, in addition to specific counters to be utilised when facing an enemy who is armed with a knife.

Equipment Training   Equipment training to simulate actual combative conditions, or to bring about full-power attacks, is a crucial part of the Special Forces Combatives programme. An assortment of pads, shields, and bags comprise the bulk of the training devices. Filipino martial arts weapons, improvised field weapons, and speciality weapons such as garrottes and blowguns are also used.

Mental/Philosophical Training   The philosophy behind the Special Forces Combatives Course is multifaceted. A Special Forces soldier already understands the unconventional aspects of modern warfare. He uses any and all means at his disposal in order to successfully complete his mission. A SF soldier's greatest virtue is his ability to adapt and fit into a situation. A Green Beret is a trained expert in weapons (both standard and improvised), demolitions, medicine, communications and intelligence. He can conduct his operations via land, sea or air, and can survive in all terrains and environments. Unarmed combative skills are merely another tool in the Special Forces arsenal.

In war, a soldier's job is to kill the enemy. The frame of mind that the Special Forces Combatives Course stresses is total annihilation. It is not a new concept in unarmed combat, but one that is not stressed nearly enough in the majority of conventional martial arts training. One must be able to turn on and off the killer animal dormant in all of us. Apart from this crucial mental aspect, when actually fighting in a wartime situation, the Combatives Course teaches students to understand and apply concepts of combat as opposed to learning specific techniques. Unlike many methods of unarmed combat, which specialise in one particular range of fighting, an understanding of the totality of combat is used as a base for the SF course. The Special Forces Combatives Course is presented in three phases. Phase one is a basic course designed to instruct the soldiers in fundamental fighting skills and concepts. Phase two is an advanced course, which includes more in-depth techniques combined with sensitivity training. The final phase is an instructor's qualification course. After graduating from this phase, students are authorised to instruct others in the course. As these individuals transfer to other units in the army, they will be able to perpetuate the concepts and techniques as taught in the Special Forces Combatives Course.

COMMANDOS – BRITISH ARMY

The British formed the first such unit after the fall of France and in the wake of the evacuation of the British Forces from Dunkirk. (The name 'Commando' was derived from the groups of irregular Boer soldiers who fought for independence from British rule in the South African War at the end of the nineteenth century.) 1st Commando was formed in June 1940 and saw service in Europe and Burma before being disbanded in 1946. 2nd Commando was formed in June 1940 as a parachute unit, but later retrained for an amphibious unit. It served in raids on Norway, France, the Balkans and Italy. It disbanded in 1945. 3rd Commando was formed in Plymouth in July 1940 under the command of Lieutenant Colonel John Durnford-Slater and served in France, Italy and Germany until disbanded in 1946. 4th Commando was formed in July 1940 serving in France, Netherlands and German before disbanding in July 1946. 5th Commando was formed in July 1940 and served in France, India and Burma and disbanded in Hong Kong in 1946. 6th Commando was formed in Scarborough in July 1940 and served in raids on Norway, France, North Africa, Netherlands and Germany until it was disbanded in 1946. 7th Commando was formed in August 1940 and served in Egypt and took part in the Crete disaster. Devastated as a unit, it was disbanded in the summer of 1941. 8th Commando was formed in June 1940 as part of Layforce; it served in both Crete and Tobruk, disbanding in July 1941. 9th Commando was formed in the summer of 1940; it served in France, Gibraltar, the Adriatic, Italy and Greece and disbanded in 1946. 10th (Inter-Allied) Commando was formed in January 1942, served in France, Netherlands and Germany and disbanded in 1946. 11th (Scottish) Commando was formed in December 1940, served with Layforce in Cyprus and Syria, disbanding in late 1941. 12th (Irish & Welsh) Commando was formed in early 1941, served in raids on Norway and was probably disbanded late in 1943. (13th) 14th Commando was formed in early 1943 for long-distance raids in Arctic Norway. It included a number of Canadian and Native Canadians (Red Indians) and had disbanded by late 1943. 30th Commando was formed in July 1941; a Special Engineering Unit trained as free divers for the recovery of important documents from sunken ships, and for specialist skills involved in acquiring sensitive papers and other materials from enemy facilities before they could be destroyed. Serving in France and Germany it disbanded in December 1945. There were also a further three in the Middle East numbered 50, 51 and 52 (ME), while the Royal Marines fielded nine Commandos Nos 40–48 from 1942 onwards. The commandos proved the ideal vehicle for Allied forces such as the Free French and Belgian armies in exile to re-create effective fighting forces, and a number of additional units were formed made up entirely of nationals from those countries who had escaped the German occupation. No. 10 Commando, however, was an Inter-Allied force of mixed nationalities, even including a number of anti-Nazi German volunteers serving under false identities in case of capture, while 51(ME) Commando was a mixed force of Palestinian Arabs and Jewish volunteers with British officers who served in East Africa. Some 18,000 commandos would eventually take part in the 1944 Normandy invasion and related operations. The skills the commandos were taught at their schools in Scotland and elsewhere were to influence the development of many post-war Special Forces, including those of Belgium, France and the USA. Though the British Army chose to abandon this style of unit, its tactics were maintained by both the Parachute Regiment and the Royal Marine Commandos.

COMMANDOS – FRENCH NAVY

During the Second World War the Free French government raised a number of elite and Special Operations units to strike at Nazi forces occupying Europe. One of these units was the 1ere Cie. de Fusiliers-Marins Commandos, which consisted of a group of former French naval personnel. Commanded by Commandant Philippe Kieffer, the unit was trained by British commandos to conduct raids, amphibious operations and reconnaissance missions along the European coastline. Upon completion of their training the men were assigned to the French troop of No.10 Inter-Allied (I-A) Commando. Later a second French troop, No. 8 troop, was raised and added to the Commando. The two units were used as the core of the 1er Bataillon Fusiliers Marins Commandos. Between 1945 and 1947 six Commandos were raised and given the names of former commando officers who had been killed in action. During the Indo-China war the various Marine Commandos conducted raids and amphibious operations against the Viet Minh guerrilla strongholds throughout the territory. After France's defeat by Viet Minh forces in 1953, the Commandos were redeployed. Commando Hubert was converted into a combat diver unit while Commando Treppel and De Penfentenyo were deployed to Algeria and Commando Francois was converted to a reserve unit. Upon establishing a new base of operations in Algiers and Oran, the commandos immediately commenced combat operations against communist backed guerrillas fighting for an independent Algeria. Commandos Hubert, De Penfentenyo, Jaubert, and Treppel were also deployed to support the Anglo-French assault on the Suez Canal. Following the independence of Algeria in 1962 the Commando units returned to France, where they became part of the French Special Operations Command.

COMMANDOS – ROYAL NAVY

The early amphibious raids by the commandos between 1940 and 1942 pointed up to the obvious need for better intelligence and control on the beaches. The earliest attempt at exerting some control had been by the Royal Navy manning the landing craft, but when this proved inadequate, specialised 'beach parties' were formed and were first tried during Operation Ironclad to capture the port of Diego Suarez at the northern tip of

Madagascar on 5–7 May 1942. This proved so successful that the Royal Naval Commandos (sometimes known as 'Beachhead Commandos') were formed. Their duties included: landing in or ahead of the first wave to clear the beaches, to mark limits of the beachhead, consolidate the beachhead, clearing personnel and equipment from the beachhead expeditiously, helping moor landing craft correctly, removing mines and underwater obstructions, taping the safe passage routes off the beaches for the wounded, informing subsequent waves of important intelligence about the defences and strengths of the enemy and advising how to exploit the enemies' weakness, setting up important ammunition and supply dumps, also supporting a wide variety of troops with any initial advance inland, supervising enemy prisoners of war, being available to tackle any task and act as a rearguard during any withdrawals. In August 1942, members of the Royal Navy Commands (C and D) took part in the Dieppe raid, Operation Jubilee, with a beachmaster and beach party assigned to each of the beaches. Some could not reach their assigned beach due to heavy gunfire. They suffered very heavy casualties, with many others becoming prisoners of war. Despite the problems at Dieppe a lot was learned, in particular the need for Combined Operations and within this there was an obvious need for RN Beach Parties, who would be vital in any major amphibious, as well as smaller, operations. It was clear that they needed specialised training and a school was established at Ardentinny, Scotland, to train the RN Commandos. The school at Ardentinny would accommodate between 500 and 600 men. Officers were all mixed in with the ratings, a most unusual idea for the times, and they made good use of Loch Long for amphibious landing drills, reconnaissance and gaining specialised beach skills. Other training included weapons usage, rock climbing, assault courses, embarkation and debarkation using various types of landing craft under battle conditions, route marches and field survival. The RN Commandos were expected to pass the Commando training course and receive their much-coveted Green Beret, along with the famous F-S dagger from Colonel Vaughan at a special parade. Some received additional training at Kabritt, near the Suez Canal, for duties in the Middle East, while others went to the Jungle Battle School at Chittagong for duties in South-East Asia. Others went on to complete the parachute training course and would later wear the SAS/SBS wings. Some went on to complete underwater swimming courses to qualify as 'Frogmen'. Once formed, RN Commandos were assigned letters rather than numbers. By the end of 1943 22 units had been formed. During Operation Torch in late 1942, 410 RN Commandos proved themselves in the first major Anglo-American amphibious operation of the war. Four augmented units – C (reformed after heavy losses incurred at Dieppe), E, F, G and parts of H and J – took part in the Torch landings which were carried out by three task forces (Western Task Force – Casablanca, Central Task Force – Oran and the

Eastern Task Force). The RNC landed with the first assault elements and took immediate charge of the beaches. After first eliminating snipers they dug slit trenches for protection and set up Lewis guns for use against low-flying enemy aircraft. The RNC major task was to guide ashore 29,000 troops, 2,400 vehicles and 14,000 tons of supplies on three different beaches, which was to prove vital for the forthcoming actions. Those RN Commandos working with the American assault troops wore American uniforms, since the Vichy French troops were suspicious of the British. Overall the RN Commandos worked very efficiently during Torch, despite the fact that controlling the incoming landing craft proved very difficult. It was far better than it would have been had they not been present.

Italy   The next major operation for the RN Commandos was the invasion of Sicily, Operation Husky, which involved more than 2,000 ships and landing craft. The units involved were C, E, F, G, K, M and N. They were only involved with the Eastern Task Force (British) but still had to cover 27 landing beaches. Once the assault troops were ashore the RN Commandos' job was often just getting started, since they usually had to work the beaches for weeks after directing in the supplies and reinforcements and guiding out the wounded and prisoners of war. As a sideline RN Commandos took the Island of Monte Cristo, which had an enemy radio station capable of plotting Allied shipping in the area and report back to the mainland. Also, D party took the Island of Pantelleria in June 1943.   In September of 1943, RN Commandos went in with the army assault troops and Royal Marine Commandos when the Allies landed in Italy. They were C, G, H, K, M, N and O parties, and later during the advance up the Italian coast they helped open up anchorages. At both Salerno and Anzio landing RN Commandos had to deal with minefields before they could signal the waiting landing craft to come in. At Anzio they had to use their F-S daggers to probe for wood-encased mines, which could not be located with the Royal Engineers' metal detectors. Sandbars offshore also created great difficulty during this landing but the RNC performed admirably, keeping the beachhead functioning throughout the initial landings and for months afterwards, despite almost constant German shelling. As the advance moved further up the Italian mainland they were given two additional roles: the recovery of escaped Allied prisoners of war along the Adriatic coastline; and protecting war criminals from local inhabitants long enough to get them back for Allied interrogation and preparation for war crimes trials once the war was over. RN Commandos also crossed into Yugoslavia or went down to help recapture the Greek Islands. Those who remained in Italy found themselves up against a new enemy, namely those unfortunates who were conscripted from the German-occupied countries who proved to be tough fighters, and at times suicidal, due to the fact that if they did not fight for the Germans they, or their families, would be shot. If they were captured they would have been returned to their homeland after the war and again could have been shot as traitors. Basically they had nothing to lose, so the Germans used them mainly against Allied Special Forces.

RN Commandos who specialised in jungle warfare at the training school at Chittagong included H party, which took part in the landings on the Arakan coast. These operations commenced with Screwdriver in February 1944, followed by Screwdriver II. C and E parties were active in Malaya in 1945 and helped prevent the Japanese carrying the war into India. The largest RN Commando operation of the war was Neptune, the naval portion of Overlord. Eight parties – F, J, L, P, Q, R, S, T and W (mostly Canadians) – were scheduled and trained for this, the largest amphibious operation of the war. RN Commandos went in the first wave, in order to judge whether landing craft of subsequent waves could land at the same point or had to go elsewhere. They took heavy casualties at Normandy, on some beaches having to dig in and fight off counter-attacks, but their Commando training made them very effective at dealing with the German defenders, a task they found actually less difficult than dealing with the congestion on the beaches. Wrecked landing craft and vehicles were a major problem, especially when they blocked the exits from the beachhead. Despite these difficulties they managed to clear the obstacles, organise the exits and begin bringing supplies ashore. Most of the RN Commandos on the Normandy beaches stayed for at least six weeks, helping to salvage sunken landing craft, moor Mulberry Harbours and Phoenix Piers, but most of all bringing order out of the chaos of the largest amphibious operation in the history of warfare.

Walcheren and the Rhine   The Normandy invasion was the high point of RN Commando operations, but it did not mark the end of hostilities, for they went on to take part in the capture of Walcheren and in crossing the Rhine at Arnhem with L and M parties seeing most action. RN Commandos of C, E, H, J, M, N, R and V parties were picked to deploy to the Pacific to take part in the invasion of the Japanese home islands. They were to join force X and Y from the South East Asia Command (SEAC), but fortunately it proved unnecessary as the dropping of the atomic bombs on Hiroshima and Nagasaki brought a speedy conclusion to hostilities.

COMOROS ISLANDS

CIVILIAN SPECIAL FORCES

The small Presidential Guard is the primary CT/HRU response unit for the Comoros Islands. This unit has, however, received very little training and would almost certainly rely on the French government to supply *GIGN* in the event of a significant terrorist event. This almost came to pass in October 1995 when France sent some 20 members of its elite anti-terrorist units to the Indian Ocean ahead of possible moves to oust white mercenaries who led a coup on the Comoros Islands. The commandos came from three units, including the Groupement d'Intervention de la Gendarmerie Nationale (GIGN), specialists from the Army's Special Operations Command, and the 'action' department of the French DGSE overseas espionage service.

CONGO

MILITARY SPECIAL FORCES

One Airborne-Commando Battalion. Poorly trained and equipped, the Congo would require urgent outside intervention in the event of a serious hostage rescue situation involving foreign nationals.

CONGO – DEMOCRATIC REPUBLIC

MILITARY SPECIAL FORCES

A Special Forces unit that is being formed in the Democratic Republic of Congo may be receiving training from North Korean officers. The new unit, the 10th Special Infantry Brigade, consists of several thousand troops and supposedly has a combined-arms composition – including reconnaissance, infantry and artillery elements. The unit's primary purpose will be to fight rebel forces that have been active for the last two years in a conflict that now involves several neighbouring states. A television programme featuring the graduation of 10th-brigade soldiers showed a number of North Korean officers in attendance.

CONTACT

Engagement with enemy force or a target under surveillance.

CONTINUATION

SAS course taken after SELECTION in which recruits are instructed in various SAS skills.

CORK

A drug to prevent defecation, used in the field by SF teams where the smell of human waste may give a covert operation away. Hostile security will often use sniffer dogs specially trained to detect the scent of human perspiration, urine or waste, which obviously poses a risk after a Special Forces surveillance team has been in its observation position for any length of time. This also applies to patrols deep into hostile territory, where skilled trackers or dogs/hounds may be used to follow their trail. The SAS use plastic bags to contain both urine and human waste, which is then carried in their Bergens backpacks until a suitably safe opportunity presents itself for disposal.

COSTA RICA

CIVILIAN SPECIAL FORCES
Unidad de Intervencio Especial (UIE) – Special Intervention Unit Costa Rica has no military and instead relies on the Ministry of Public Security. Within the Guardia Civil (Civil Guard) is the Special Intervention Unit. It was established in the mid-1980s and is between 60- and 80-men strong. Besides the hostage rescue mission, they are also responsible for VIP protection and conducting high-risk CT raids and arrests. The unit makes use of eleven-man assault teams, each divided into subteams of three or four men each. In addition, they have a small sniper element used for observation and fire support. The UIE is located in the 1st Civil Guard facilities in San Jose. They have received a great deal of training from a wide variety of SF sources, including Israel, Panama, USA, Argentina and Spain.

COTE D'IVOIRE

MILITARY SPECIAL FORCES
One rather well-trained Airborne-SF Company provides a reasonable anti-terrorist and HRU capability.

COVER ONE'S SIX

Watch the rear, of a patrol or convoy.

COVERT OPERATIONS – DEFINITION

Covert operations is a difficult concept to define accurately, though former Central Intelligence Agency director Stansfield Turner makes a fine attempt 'Covert action is the term that describes our efforts to influence the course of events in a foreign country without our role being known.' Turner also notes that covert action 'has always been assigned to the CIA to perform, by means of un-attributable propaganda, *sub rosa* political action, or secret paramilitary support'. However, because they are supposed to be shrouded in secrecy, one is never sure whether all the relevant data concerning their scope, origin and degree of success are available. What motivates the United States to undertake such actions, and how well the United States has been served by these measures are especially crucial issues in the light of the events of 9-11 and the so-called War on Terrorism. US covert-action policy since the Second World War has been dominated by two facts that are not always fully appreciated. First, both the scope and the scale of such operations have been enormous. Paramilitary operations, which can be more accurately described as secret wars and are the most extreme form of covert action, have resulted in countless deaths and immense destruction. Covert operations have increasingly become the instrument of choice for policymakers who wish to avoid a major confrontation or all-out war. Second, the success of US covert operations has been regularly and grossly exaggerated. Some operations, such as the one against the Soviet Union in the early post-war years and the later one against Castro, were outright fiascos. Other operations, such as the ones involving Greece and Iran, which were once acclaimed successes, left a legacy of anti-Americanism that continues to hamper the conduct of US foreign policy. Moreover, because such operations have almost always become public, with Nicaragua being an obvious example, debates over their legitimacy have fostered considerable domestic divisiveness.

A short list of the post-Second World War operations would include the overthrow of Mohammed Mossadegh in Iran in 1953, the overthrow of Jacobo Arbenz in Guatemala in 1954, the attempt to assassinate Fidel Castro in Cuba in 1963, the overthrow of Juan Bosch in the Dominican Republic in 1963, the defeat of rebel forces loyal to Patrice Lumumba in the Congo in 1964, the 1965 propaganda campaign to overthrow the Sukarno government in Indonesia, the provision of aid to overthrow George Papandreou and install George Papadopoulous in Greece in 1967 and involvement in the overthrow of Norodom Sihanouk in Cambodia in 1970. US Special Forces have also played a leading part in operations in Vietnam, Laos, Grenada, Panama, the Philippines, Somalia, Afghanistan, Pakistan, Colombia, Ecuador and Iraq. With the advent of the War on Terrorism, this list is likely to be expanded to include a number of other countries in 2002–03.

CQB

Close-Quarters Battle. In the very early 1970s the SAS clearly saw the need to greatly enhance the level of training and facilities available to train marksmen in the difficult skills required to 'take-out' terrorists or kidnappers in the close confines of a room, aircraft or vehicle without hitting the VIP or other hostages in need of rescue. The Regiment developed the Close-Quarters Battle (CQB) House, usually simply known as the 'killing house'. Countless non-military, but influential, members of the establishment have been shown around these facilities since, and with the large number of Special Forces who have shown a close interest it is hardly surprising that by 2002 it is believed that some 150–180 CQBs now exist worldwide. Special Forces personnel train in a number of hostage scenarios with suddenly appearing targets requiring instant reaction and a decision on whether it's a legitimate 'kill' or not. They are required to train in smoke, darkness and hazardous fumes, while being shot at, when exhausted or in CBW suits. An ability to handle a wide range of weapons from standard issue handguns, through silenced sub-machine guns to combat shotguns. A familiarity with unusual foreign weapons, which may be found in certain scenarios dropped by a 'dead' terrorist, and necessary to use as the soldier's own weapon will have 'jammed', is considered very important. New anti-terrorist and hostage rescue scenarios are constantly being developed to keep the most experienced soldiers from any form of complacency. In many cases live ammunition will be used and this has resulted in a number of fatalities among the trainees. Psychological aspects of the training are paramount, for the mental toughness required under stressful close combat conditions is considerable and even the best need 'reinforcement' by regular training until reactions are automatic. However, it can turn certain individuals into 'killing machines' and though screened regularly, occasionally the ethos of the Special Forces can dominate an individual conscience. The widespread abuse by Special Forces of opponents of the government of the day, and indeed against their own civilian population in countless countries around the world, has led to fears that such training and the attitudes it develops could eventually prove counter-productive in creating more terrorists and 'enemies of the state' than you can possibly kill. Despite these concerns, it is fair to say that the best are very good indeed, and considering the small scale of the operations usually undertaken, the specialist anti-terrorist and hostage rescue teams have saved a disproportionately large number of innocent lives.

CROATIA

MILITARY SPECIAL FORCES
This unit is under the direct control of the General Staff of the Croatian Army. *350. DIVERZANTSKI ODRED – 350th Diversionary Unit* It is tasked with long-range reconnaissance (LRRP) and sabotage missions. The unit consists of around 80 soldiers trained in demolitions, mountain warfare, diving and parachuting.

352. DIVERZANTSKO-RONITELJSKA BOJNA 'DELTA' – 352nd Diversionary-Diver Battalion 'Delta' is a classic naval diversionary-diver unit, similar in many respects to the US Navy SEALs. The unit numbers around 100 personnel and training for the unit lasts five months, and includes diving, parachuting, mountain warfare and other combat skills.

CIVILIAN SPECIAL FORCES
Antiteroristicka Vojna Policija (ATVP) Anti-Terrorist Military Police   A SWAT-style unit now receives considerable US assistance and training.

Anti-Teroristicka Jedinica 'Lucko' Anti-Terrorist Unit 'Lucko' Specijalna Jedinica Policije 'Alfa' (Special Police Unit 'Alpha').

CROSSBOWS

Crossbows of medieval and renaissance conflicts were relatively inefficient designs. Modern tests indicate that armour-piercing bolts, while heavier than arrows, achieved about the same velocity (130–40 fps) from a 700lb-draw crossbow as an arrow did from a 80lb-draw longbow. The initial velocity imparted to a crossbow bolt is governed by the velocity of the bow tips as the bolt and string part company. Despite their heavy draw weights, medieval laths were too massive to accelerate rapidly. This was made worse by short draw lengths, which reduced the time available for the tips to accelerate. In addition, the massive bowstrings required for such heavy draw weights robbed energy from the bolt. Balanced against these faults is the higher ballistic coefficient of the short, heavy crossbow bolt, as compared with an arrow. This meant that crossbows often could shoot further and hit harder than hand bows. Modern military crossbows are engineered to launch 500 grain bolts at initial velocities in excess of 200fps, with draw weights of about 150lbs. This provides ample kinetic energy to 'take down' a guard or lookout silently with a far lighter weapon, easier to draw and fire quietly. A longer power stroke coupled with a less massive fibreglass lath makes the difference. The modern Special Forces crossbows were developed from those used by the OSS in the Second World War, such as the 'William Tell' and 'Big Joe-5' shoulder-fired or even the 'Little Joe', a curious hand-held mini-crossbow used to eliminate sentries or guard dogs silently at close range. They are highly effective in the 10m–50m range bracket and are an important part of 'silent killing'. The Spanish and Serbian Special Forces are also known to use crossbows as an integral part of their armament.

CROW

Inexperienced soldier or 'rookie'.

CRRC

Combat Rubber Raiding Craft used by amphibious Special Forces such as the SEALs, Commando Hubert or the SBS.

CRUD

The various fungi and rashes common to soldiers in warm climates. The bane of many soldiers involved in long-range patrols in hostile environments. Part of the skill of Special Force operations is the high degree of care taken over the health of the soldiers involved. All Special Forces patrols will be as prepared as possible and have a least one highly skilled paramedic-trained soldier as part of the team.

CRW

Counter-Revolutionary Warfare. The term used by SAS to denote both Counter-Insurgency (COIN) and Anti-Terrorist operations.

CS

CS, or chlorobenzylidene malonitrile, is advertised by its manufacturers as a 'less lethal' crowd-control alternative, and despite evidence that there are indeed a number of quite severe physical and psychological after-effects, it has become the most widely used of all the incapacitating gas weapons. Although the Special Forces have access to stronger and more lasting gases, it is CS that is most often used. One particular grenade, which has been used widely by the SAS for years, combines the effects of a flash-bang grenade and a tear gas canister. The grenade goes off with a bright flash and a deafening bang (to visually disorientate and deafen for 40 seconds) while simultaneously releasing CS tear gas into the area. This grenade is often used in hostage situations, allowing the counter-terrorists to stun their target for a split second, so that the threat can be eliminated before causing any harm to the hostages. This combination of the flash-bang effect and tear gas can effectively create chaos among its targets, allowing a well-organised team to quickly and easily eliminate the threat (see separate entry for TEAR GAS).

CSAR

Combat Search and Rescue. Usually refers to the Rescue Helicopter operations that penetrate deep into hostile territory to find and rescue the crews of crashed 'friendly' aircraft. It carries highly trained paramedics to deal with the variety of injuries or wounds likely to be suffered by the rescued aircrew.

CT

Counter-Terrorism, not only a combat skill developed by Special Forces, but also the title given to many units or departments specialising in such operations. The usual term used by the US Special Forces.

CUBA

MILITARY SPECIAL FORCES

At Army level there is an Army HQ Security Regiment, a three-battalion Paratroops/Special Forces Brigade and the Comando de Missiones Especiales (CME).

Cuba's CME is a Special Forces group that specialises in jungle warfare. They have seen action in Angola and other African nations as well as some Central American countries (such as Nicaragua).

Having served all over the world, they have amassed quite an eclectic armoury. They are known to use Stechkin pistols, Colt M1911, US .30.06 Garand and Springfields rifles, 7.62mm FN FALs, newer 5.56mm FN CALs, M-16s, (some with M-203 grenade launchers and sniper scopes) and Spanish 9mm Z-84 SMGs. They also use the PM-63 RAK SMG as their main assault weapon along with the 5.45mm AKSU-74 (AKR) sub-assault rifle and have also been seen with the Polish immobilising net launchers SZO-84, or even Barnett Commando crossbows. The CME is tasked with special ops in Cuba and other countries. It is believed they received much of their training from former Soviet SPETSNAZ units.

CIVILIAN SPECIAL FORCES

General Directorate of Special Troops (DGTE) – Direccion General de Tropas Especiales (DGTE)   Special Troops are part of the official structure of the Ministry of the Interior and are the most highly trained of all Cuba's military personnel. It is estimated that there are some 2,000 divided into two battalions. Originally created to provide for the personal security of Fidel Castro, they have been involved in other important activities which include training and advising Latin American guerrilla groups and support for armed insurgencies, as well as charged with carrying out often politically sensitive 'special operations' under the direct command of Fidel Castro. Special Troops were the first Cuban personnel deployed to Angola in 1975.

CYBERWARFARE

Information warfare or command and control warfare. Either name covers the vitally important subject of providing effective communication links between friendly forces, destroying enemy communications systems and protecting friendly communications from interference. Cyberwarfare provides both the greatest opportunities for Special Forces, and indeed the greatest threats to the security of clandestine operations, as even previously rather unsophisticated military powers and terrorist groups are now quickly gaining access to a wide range of advanced technology. Computer hacking and radio scanning has moved out of the teenager's bedroom and into the world of military conflict and international terrorism. It is a threat that all military and security forces take very seriously, and spend considerable time and money on trying to harden and improve the security of their communication systems. The most simple and widely available form of military communications system is the Combat Net Radio (CNR) which comprises voice radio links between individual soldiers or units on the battlefield. Separate units can operate on different frequencies to allow information to be channelled to specific users. These are either manpack very high frequency (VHF), high frequency (HF) or ultra high frequency (UHF) radio sets or more powerful vehicle mounted radios. CNR is termed as all-informed, meaning that every station listening in can follow the progress of an operation and is the best way to ensure units respond quickly in a dynamic battlefield scenario. These small radios can be fitted with frequency hopping and encryption devices to prevent the enemy listening into friendly radio traffic. It is, of course, expensive and few armies distribute such systems below company level. However, Special Forces can expect to receive what should be totally secure radio equipment. Drawbacks include the fact that only one station can broadcast at a time, making it of little value for 'conferencing' between commanders or intelligence personnel. The armed forces are increasingly relying on Trunk Systems to provide communications for their high-brigade, divisional, corps and theatre-level headquarters, and these are best described as the equivalent to a mobile battlefield telephone network, providing voice, fax or e-mail data links. The Trunk nodes or exchanges can be moved around the battlefield by vehicle or helicopter and are linked by either UHF radio, cable or, increasingly, SatCom. These advanced systems are ideal for the real-time transmission of radar, intelligence and command information and can be customised for individual unit requirements. The digital technology means they can easily be fitted with encryption devices to protect them from hostile monitoring. Mobile systems such as the British Army's Ptarmigan or the French Army's RITA system were used in both the Gulf War and the Balkan conflicts. Indeed, in Bosnia, the systems were linked together to provide a secure alternative to the national telephone system. However, Satellite Communications are the main growth area in the military's ability to provide strategic links over long distances or to supplement terrestrial-based communications systems. Satellite telephone/fax, radio, data and e-mail communication links provide usually reliable communications over very long distances and under most circumstances. These are now considered essential for military operations such as the campaign in Afghanistan, any attempt to overthrow Saddam Hussein and of course the War on Terrorism.

In peacekeeping operations, where the local telephone and communications infrastructure has been targeted for destruction by one or both sides in a conflict, SatCom links provide a vital means to bounce communications up to a space-based platform for redirection anywhere in the world. The digital revolution brings the virtual reality battlefield ever closer, with the aim of linking every individual soldier with a suitable helmet-mounted communications system via a data link to headquarters, to allow the instant transmission of information around the battlefield. The soldier may use a form of pilot's HUD, or head-up display, reflected onto his visor to see a video display of information that will be passed around the battlefield instantly, so that soldiers will receive intelligence, orders, know the location of the enemy and their comrades and immediate threat warnings. Three-dimensional images and two-dimensional map-modelling techniques are being added into these digital communications systems, to allow the visualisation of battlefield situations. The enormous growth in new and advanced communication systems, on the modern battlefield also, however, provides a hostile military force or terrorist group with even greater opportunities to compromise the friendly C3I network, either intercepting intelligence or blocking commands at vital moments. The large numbers of radios now operating on live data links make it almost impossible to prevent hostile electronic warfare and traffic analysis teams from plotting the position of friendly forces from their radio transmissions, which is of course a huge threat to a Special Forces team engaged on a covert mission deep inside enemy territory. Using satellite links provided a degree of protection from direction-finding equipment, but this has diminished as most potential enemies of the West now have access to satellite systems. New technologies may provide both a temporary answer to this problem and a future threat as well. Laser beams can be used to move communications out of the vulnerable elements of the electromagnetic spectrum and Iraq's high command in the Gulf War protected its strategic communications from Allied eavesdropping throughout the conflict by the use of fibre-optic cables instead of radios. However, while many of the new technologies will undoubtedly be first deployed by the US and its allies, it is now quite clear that technology is severely reducing that advantage, and even relatively undeveloped third world nations with little or no industrial and manufacturing base, can develop sophisticated information warfare techniques quite capable of challenging the West's dominating military position. It is a trend that seems set fair to continue and perhaps markedly increase in the near future.

CYPRUS

MILITARY SPECIAL FORCES
Special Forces Command
One SF Regiment with three battalions.

Receives considerable assistance and training from the Greek Army's Special Forces. It is heavily equipped and trained in sabotage and stay-behind operations in the event of a serious outbreak of communal fighting leading to a Turkish invasion of Greek-Cypriot territory by regular forces based in the occupied northern sector of the island. It also has a responsibility for hostage rescue operations.

CZECH REPUBLIC

MILITARY SPECIAL FORCES
6th Rapid Reaction Brigade – Prostejov   This unit includes a single Airborne Commando Battalion with a Special Forces Company tasked for counter-terrorist operations. It is receiving considerable assistance and new equipment from the USA and a number of Western European Special Forces.

CIVILIAN SPECIAL FORCES
URNA – Utvar Rvchleho Nasazeni   Established in the early 1980s this SWAT-like unit consists of a Command section, a Special Response section with snipers and a hostage rescue capability and a 100-strong Operations section. They are well trained in many Special Forces skills including breaching techniques, anti-hijacking, SCUBA, EOD and combat shooting. As well as the usual anti-narcotics and organised crime duties, the URNA are tasked for anti-terrorist operations.

DARBY'S RANGERS

Darby's Rangers was the nickname given to the US 1st Ranger Battalion in honour of its commander, Major William O. Darby. The unit was activated on 19 June 1942, in Carrickfergus, Ireland. It fought throughout Western Europe, but achieved its greatest fame when it scaled the cliffs of Pointe du Hoc as part of the D-Day invasion of Normandy.

DE LISLE – THE SILENT KILLER

This is a very unusual weapon and was designed by Sterling Arms in 1942 for British Special Forces and SOE use. With a standard Lee-Enfield bolt-action it was none the less chambered for the US .45 pistol round and with an eight-round box magazine. A superb integral silencer runs the length of the barrel. The US .45 round is subsonic and, paired with this silencer, the De Lisle is probably the most 'silent' of all silenced weapons. The De Lisle produced no muzzle flash, even on a dark night. At any distance greater than 50m, even on a quiet night and making a sound quite unlike a firearm, it was virtually undetectable. One model had a fixed rifle butt while the second version had a folding metal butt similar to the later Sterling SMG. A very similar weapon is now made chambered in NATO 7.62mm with a Remington-700 action and known as the De Lisle Mk-4.

DELTA – DOUBTS AND DOUBLE DEALING

Delta Force, the United States primary anti-terrorist force, is an elite within an elite. However, like most such secretive elites its triumphs stay hidden, its mistakes are made in the glare of publicity.

When things went wrong it was through an excess of zeal, or because of military disasters that could not be hushed up, or when corruption encouraged by the availability of large amounts of untraceable and unaccountable funds became far too serious to be overlooked. Delta's secret role in the Grenada invasion became known largely because of scathing military criticism of its poor planning and execution of simple tasks in the field. Intending to secure the main airstrip before the arrival of the US Army Rangers, Delta arrived precisely two hours late, supposedly because planners misread Grenada's time zone. Delta Force received further unwanted exposure in October 1985 following the *Achille Lauro* liner hijack. The diversion by US Navy jets of an Egypt Air airliner carrying the hijackers, to an airfield in Sicily, had already incensed the Italian government. Delta Force seriously damaged relations by precipitating an angry armed face-off with Italian troops on the ground after the airliner had landed. Italian Prime Minister Bettino Craxi told the press a week later of the tense moment in which Italian troops were ready to fire on Delta Force troops, who had rushed out of a C-141 transport that landed right behind the Egyptian aircraft. The fiasco of Delta precipitate actions carried out with the full approval of the US government had remained hidden until then. Delta's problems were not limited to its military operations. In 1985, an army inquiry found evidence that Delta personnel had embezzled up to $500,000, with one Special Forces colonel and three associates accounting for at least $60,000. An internal army inquiry into the matter was put off in the autumn (fall) of 1985 on the grounds that it could cripple the unit's planned operations in the Mediterranean. The army ultimately announced that 80 Delta soldiers had received 'non-judicial punishments' and that seven more were facing courts-martial. Lieutenant Colonel Dale Duncan, who headed an army special operations proprietary, Business Security International (BSI), was charged with submitting a series of false invoices, including one invoice for $56,230 covering electronic equipment that had been paid for by another army intelligence unit. These were the first of what *Newsweek* called 'a growing number of investigations, prosecutions and courts-martial focusing on alleged financial impropriety by members of Delta and other super-secret units spawned by the Reagan administration.' The prosecutions that ensued brought to light some of the contradictions between covert action accounting, where the rule of thumb was to eliminate the paper trail and financial accountability. Colonel James E. Noble, an army judge on the courts-martial which acquitted Special Forces Master Sergeant Ramon Barron of charges pertaining to his work with BSI, concluded: 'The Army chose this extraordinary means to circumvent accountability for money ... By so doing they also chose to risk losing the money.' One security expert later commenting on the Delta Force's seeming disdain for standard accounting procedures, observed wryly that 'items procured for supposedly clandestine missions included a Rolls-Royce and a hot-air balloon.'

DENMARK

MILITARY SPECIAL FORCES

Jaegerkorpset (Ranger Corps) is responsible for Counter-Terrorist activities within Denmark. Jaegerkorpset is an elite Ranger Element within the Danish Army. Formed in 1961, the Jaegerkorps patterned itself after the British Special Air Service (SAS) and the US Army Rangers, but can trace its ancestry back to the Jaeger Korps formed by King Christian VII in the 1780s. Initially used as commandos, the Jaegers have over time assumed the primary role of intelligence-providers, relying on long-range reconnaissance patrols (LRRPs) to identify and monitor enemy movements. This unit is equipped with encrypted burst-transmission communications and night-vision devices. Secondary combat roles include sabotage and direct action. The Jaegers also assist the Danish police's CT unit Aktions-Styrken (Action Force) in case of terrorist attacks. The Jaegers are stationed at Air Station Aalborg in Northern Jutland and work very closely with British and German SOF. Lacking dedicated Royal Danish Air Force helicopter support, the Jaegers often use British and German helicopters. All Jaegers are qualified in high-altitude high-opening (HAHO) insertions, giving them the ability to drift up to 100km over hostile borders. One-week training sessions are conducted in this technique three to four times a year. This Ranger-type unit employs the following guns: 9mm SIG P M/49 pistol (P210), 9mm H&K Mp M/85 sub-machine gun (MP5A3), 9mm H&K Mp M/85LD suppressed sub-machine gun (MP5SD3), 5.56mm H&K Mp M/85 assault carbine (HK53A5, replaced in mid-2000 by Kb M/96OP), 5.56mm Diemaco Kb M/96OP assault carbine (C8FT), 5.56mm Diemaco Kb M/96OP assault carbine (C8SFW), 5.56mm Diemaco G M/95OP assault rifle (C7A1), 5.56mm H&K Kg M/85 assault rifle (G41 with 4× scope, replaced in mid-2000 by G M/95OP), 5.56mm H&K Mg M/85 light machine gun (HK23E, used both with belt-feed and the optional magazine adapter), 7.62mm H&K Fsg M/85 sniper rifle (PSG1), 12.7mm (.50 BMG) Barrett M82A1 sniper rifle, 40mmSR Diemaco Gk M/98 underbarrel grenade launcher (M203A1 under K M/96OP), 18.5mmR

(12-gauge) Remington Model 870PS pump-action shotgun with folding stock, 84mm Bofors Pvv M/97 light anti-tank weapon (AT4CSHP) and 84mm FFV Dykn M/85 recoilless rifle (M3 Carl Gustaf).

Navy
Froemanskorpset (Frogman corps)   Subordinate to Navy headquarters, the Froemandskorpset was created in 1957 as part of the Naval Diving School when four officers were sent to train with the US Navy SEALs and the Norwegian Froskemandskorps. It achieved independent status in 1970 with its present HQ at Kongsore Naval Base. Typical missions are shipboardings, special reconnaissance, sabotage on naval installations and direct-action combat. Peacetime assignments include assisting the Danish police in searches for missing persons, counter-narcotics, difficult diving operations and underwater demolition. Danish frogmen saw action during the Gulf War, where they helped enforce the embargo on Iraq by boarding ships in search of contraband. They are also responsible for anti-terrorist operations in ports, oilrigs and shipping. Highly trained in all aspects of combat swimming, underwater demolitions, parachuting and a multitude of special warfare skills, the personnel from this unit are highly regarded within NATO. Weapons used include the following in addition to those listed for the Jagdkommando, 9mmR (.38 Special) S&W Model 60 Chief's Special revolver (for use immediately after surfacing from a dive), 9mm H&K Mp M/85LD suppressed sub-machine gun (MP5SD3), 5.56mm Diemaco Kb M/96OP assault carbine (C8SFW), 7.62mm KAC Fsg M/99 sniper rifle (SR-25), 12.7mm McMillan Model 87 single-shot sniper rifle and 40mmSR Diemaco Gk M/98 underbarrel grenade launcher (M203A1 under K M/96OP). Some of the toughest members of Froemandskorpset are selected for dogsled-mounted, seven-month-long two-man patrols in Greenland. For hunting and against the ever-present polar bears, they are armed with 10mm Glock 20 pistols and 7.62mm (.30-06 Springfield) Winchester G M/53 bolt-action sniper rifles (Enfield-pattern M1917).

CIVILIAN SPECIAL FORCES
Aktions-Styrken (Action Force)   Danish Police Counter-Terrorist unit, a SWAT-style formation drawn from the PET (Politiets Efterretningstjeneste) or Political Intelligence Police. It has been trained by both the GSG-9 and the SAS.

DE PUNT TRAIN HIJACK 1977 - BBE

Towards the end of May 1977, 13 South Moluccan terrorists seized 80 hostages on board a train travelling between Rotterdam and Groningen,

Holland. Stopping at De Punt, the terrorists issued their demands: the Dutch government was to exert pressure on the Indonesians to grant independence to their homeland of South Molucca. In addition, several of their compatriots were to be released from Dutch jails, and a Boeing 747 jet was to be made ready at Schipol airport for their departure. To reinforce their demands, they murdered the train driver and dumped his body on the tracks.

Though negotiations were to drag on for over two weeks, the Dutch government considered a military option from the start. Dutch Marines of the BBE (Special Operations Unit) were on the scene from the beginning. Food trolleys were allowed to go to the train, but the terrorists insisted the porters – supposed to be Red Cross personnel – had to be naked to prove they were unarmed. In fact, the porters were policemen gathering primary intelligence. Intelligence can also come from released hostages, and a pregnant woman who was released was thoroughly debriefed by the authorities. Thus the Marines built up a detailed picture concerning how many terrorists there were, what weapons they carried, how many were on guard at a given time, and so on. By 10 June the negotiations had stalled and the Dutch decided to send in the Marines. Explosives had been planted in front of the train, to be used as a noisy diversion when the attack went in. At first light on 11 June, the BBE Marines prepared for action. They were formed into two bodies – one to storm the train, the other to provide covering fire. The attack platoon was equipped with highly accurate Heckler and Koch MP5 sub-machine guns and Smith and Wesson handguns. Three members of the assault party placed explosive charges on the train doors, while others placed small scaling ladders against the carriages. At zero hour, Dutch F104 Starfighter aircraft flew over the train and kicked in their afterburners. The whole train shuddered with the vibration caused by the jets and the hostages threw themselves to the floor. The charges in front of the train were detonated, and the covering group opened fire with a blistering fusillade of fire.

Interestingly, the British Special Air Service had offered the Marines a number of stun grenades to disorient the terrorists just prior to the assault, but the offer was turned down. The terrorists had no time to recover before the door was blown in and the Marines stormed inside. Ordering the hostages to get down, the Marines engaged the terrorists with accurate small-arms fire. Seven were shot and six were captured; only two hostages were killed in the firefight, which lasted less than two minutes. At zero hour plus two minutes, therefore, the train was secure and the great majority of the hostages freed.

DEROS

Acronym: Date of Expected Return from Overseas.

DESERT STORM

To Coalition military commanders it soon became increasingly obvious that their counter-Scud effort was not significantly interfering with the Iraqi mobile missile operations. Bad weather hampered aerial reconnaissance and stopped pilots spotting targets from high altitudes, while the passage of information to strike aircraft was far too slow. There was even talk of reviving the plan to airdrop the 82nd Airborne Division into western Iraq to disrupt the missile units. What were needed were forces on the ground to find where the mobile Scuds really were and then direct strike aircraft on to their targets. Before the war started the British Gulf Commander, Lieutenant General Sir Peter de la Billiere, had proposed sending in small teams of Special Air Service (SAS) to harass Iraqi troops in western Iraq, in an effort to distract their attention from the impending main attack into Kuwait. The first SAS troops were inserted into Iraq on 20 January but they were re-tasked within three days to target the mobile Scuds. At first there was no established procedure for the SAS patrols to co-operate with USAF strike aircraft patrolling the Scud boxes. SAS men had to use the emergency 'guard' radio frequency to talk to the pilots. Within a short period of time the SAS teams, roving western Iraq in heavily armed truck convoys, were almost daily calling down USAF aircraft against suspected Scud launchers. The command, control, communications and intelligence (C3I) system of the Coalition air forces worked on a 24-hour planning cycle, which was unable to respond effectively or quickly enough to new intelligence on the location of mobile Scuds. Traditional methods of planning air strikes, based on sending out aerial reconnaissance aircraft to find targets and then pre-briefing bomber aircrews on their targets, did not work when dealing with the Iraqi mobile Scuds, as they were being moved quicker than Coalition intelligence could track them. By the end of the war an improvised C3I system linking the SAS and Delta Force directly to the Coalition TACC was working effectively. It was able to integrate air and ground forces to allow a degree of real-time gathering of intelligence in the Scud boxes and enable a rapid response by strike aircraft to sightings of Scud launchers. The Scud box system enabled aircraft permanently to be in the air ready to respond to information from Special Force teams on the ground. A number of other USAF reconnaissance systems deployed to Saudi Arabia could detect Scuds in real-time, such as the Northrop Grumman E-8 JSTARS radar ground surveillance aircraft and the Lockheed Martin TR-1/U-2R with its electro-optical camera down link. The JSTARS used a radar system that could detect and, to a certain degree, identify types of vehicles for controllers in the air or in a ground station. The TR-1/U2R systems were, in effect, long-range television cameras which could then feed 'live' images to a ground station. These systems were not always available to operate over western Iraq and there were major problems in linking them into Coalition communication networks. Similar problems interfered with the passing of intelligence information from US DSP missile tracking satellites to strike aircraft operating over western Iraq. The Iraqis also proved skilful opponents and had a good idea of the capabilities of Coalition surveillance systems and were able cleverly to hide their Scud launchers. The SAS patrols also attacked Iraqi troops with anti-tank missiles and mortars. SAS liaison officers were posted to the joint US/Coalition Tactical Air Control Centre (TACC) in Riyadh and radio procedures established for the ground forces to control air strikes. The TACC was the nerve centre of the Coalition air campaign and had radio links to the AWACS aircraft that co-ordinated all air activity. Coalition aircraft were also warned of SAS patrol areas to prevent 'friendly fire' incidents. At the beginning of February the US Delta Force, along with other elements of the Joint Special Operations Task Force (JSOTF), arrived in Saudi Arabia and was soon operating alongside the SAS in western Iraq. While the SAS operated in the southern Scud box, nicknamed 'Scud Alley', around H-2 airfield, the JSOTF operated around Al Qaim, in the Northern Scud box, nicknamed 'Scud Boulevard'. By 26 January, the Iraqi Scud campaign had peaked. Scud attacks from western Iraq continued against Israel for another month but they were only able to launch single missiles at a time. The Iraqis had by then withdrawn their mobile missile units into an area close to Al Qaim to increase their protection. Scud attacks on Saudi Arabia were only brought to a halt when Coalition troops occupied southern Iraq in the final four days of February and pushed them out of range of their targets.

DET

Detachment, usually written as det. SAS term for the 14th Intelligence Company in Northern Ireland (see separate entry for 14th Intelligence Company).

DEVIL'S BRIGADE

The 1st Special Service Force, or the Devil's Brigade, was a joint Canadian-US unit that was formed initially on 9 July 1942, at Fort William Henry Harrison, Montana. Airborne-trained and adopting Special Force techniques, the Devil's Brigade saw most of its action in Italy, but also fought in France, where it was finally de-activated in 1944. Its forte was close-quarter combat against numerically superior forces, a task which it accomplished with a raw power that gave the brigade its nickname.

DIRECTION ACTION (DA)

Assaults or strikes against enemy forces and bases. A basic US Special Ops mission.

DJIBOUTI BUS HIJACK 1976 — GIGN

Shortly before 08.00 hours on 3 February 1976, four members of the Somali Coast Liberation Front (FLCS) hijacked a school bus containing 30 children as it made its way from the airbase in Djibouti to the school in the town's port area. The driver was forced to drive to within 180m of the Somali border, where a fifth hijacker boarded the bus. They issued their demands: the immediate independence of the French territory of Afars and Issas, or they would start to cut the children's throats. Negotiations between the local French commander and the terrorists began immediately, but there was concern for the children, who were on the bus in the blistering desert heat. As the talks dragged on, the government in Paris decided to despatch the crack counter-terrorist unit Groupement d'Intervention de la Gendarmerie Nationale (GIGN). This unit was highly trained and expert in a wide range of military skills, including scuba diving, parachuting, weapons training and hand-to-hand combat. Each member was superbly fit and an expert shot, and had his own FR-F1 sniper rifle and Manurhin 73 revolver. The unit as whole is equipped with a host of surveillance and detection hardware, as well as specialised pyrotechnical devices and weaponry. When they arrived in Djibouti, the GIGN men were deployed around the bus, each man in contact with their commander by means of a throat microphone. Each marksman had been assigned to watch over a particular section of the bus; it was essential that the terrorists were eliminated at the same time to avoid a general massacre of the children. To get the children out of the line of fire, a meal containing tranquillisers was sent to the bus at 14.00 hours. At 15.47 only the terrorists were visible in the snipers' sights, the children were asleep. This was the moment the GIGN Commander was waiting for, and he gave the order to fire and all four terrorists were very quickly killed. Somali border guards then opened up on the GIGN men, but were fired upon themselves by French Foreign Legionnaires covering the operation. GIGN members rushed forward and quickly began to evacuate the children. Sadly, another terrorist had got onto the bus from the Somali side and, though he was shot dead, he managed to kill a schoolgirl. Nevertheless, 29 other children had been rescued by the GIGN hostage-rescue unit.

DOMINICAN REPUBLIC

MILITARY SPECIAL FORCES
6th Mountain Rifle (Special Forces) Battalion Constanza — it has small detachments in each military zone attached to the local headquarters. Trains and exercises regularly with US Special Forces. This unit is quite competent, but with only a limited hostage rescue capability.

DONKEYS

The US Special Forces' first involvement in the Far East began before the end of 1952, when units operating behind enemy lines in Korea conducted missions with their Korean allies that remained classified for nearly 30 years. Anti-Communist guerrillas with homes in North Korea and historical ties to Seoul had joined the United Nations Partisan Forces-Korea. Known in Korean as 'fighters of liberty' the UNPFK soon became known as 'donkeys' by the Americans, who derived the nickname from the Korean word for liberty, dong-il. From tiny islands off the Korean coast, the Donkeys conducted raids, rescued downed airmen and maintained electronic facilities. Under the guidance of the US Special Forces they eventually numbered 22,000 and claimed 69,000 enemy casualties.

DOUBLE-TAP

The famous SAS/Special Forces two-shots to the head or one to the heart and one to the head. To be fired in rapid succession with a high kill probability, taking out the target before a return shot can be fired. Hours of practice on the ranges and in the CQB 'killing house' at close range enable the best anti-terrorist or hostage rescue teams to shoot accurately under a variety of stressful and difficult conditions, distinguishing between friend or foe with an almost 100 per cent success rate.

DOZIER KIDNAPPING AND RESCUE 1982 – NOCS

Operation Winter Harvest – Padua, Italy: on 17 December 1981, Red Brigade terrorists kidnapped Brigadier General James Dozier from his apartment in Verona, Italy. Dozier, the highest ranking US NATO officer in Italy, was eventually rescued in Padua by an elite Italian anti-terrorist police unit, which also effected the arrests of five of his captors. The rescue team was comprised of elements from the Nucleo Operativo Centrale di Sicurezza (NOCS) who, in January 1982, became national heroes in Italy as they carried out a lightning raid on an apartment in Padua to free General Dozier. Assaulting at just after 11.30 hours to take advantage of the bustle on the streets and the noise of a construction crew's bulldozer nearby, ten NOCS men arrived in front of the apartment building in a removal van and were dressed in civilian clothes, though they wore ballistic vests and balaclavas. One assault team member split off to seal a supermarket door near the apartment entrance so the innocent bystanders could not wander out, while the other nine men assaulted the apartment. One member of NOCS, a competitive weightlifter, took out the door quickly; another NOCS man efficiently took out a terrorist encountered in the hall with a karate blow to the forehead. As still another terrorist prepared to execute General Dozier, a NOCS man felled him with a blow from the butt of his M12. A classic hostage rescue operation which confirmed the excellent reputation as one of the world's premier anti-terrorist groups that NOCS had been building up for some time.

DRAGUNOV SVD

Partly based on the Kalashnikov, the SVD differs in using a short-stroke piston to operate the bolt carrier, more appropriate to the needs of a sniper rifle as the long stroke of the AK could affect the stability and degrade accuracy. The SVD chambered in 7.62mm Full Power was introduced in 1983 and has a ten-round box magazine. Equipped with either a PSO-1 telescopic sight or the NSPU-3 image-intensifying night sight, this Russian weapon is one of the world's most widely used Special Forces sniper rifles and is credited with an effective range of at least 1100yds (1000m).

DS

Directing Staff. In charge of SAS Training at the Hereford Depot and in the field, whether the Brecon Beacons or the Highlands of Scotland.

DUBAI – UAE (UNITED ARAB EMIRATES)

Emirate of Dubai Commando Squadron The 100-strong Commando Squadron is the primary CT unit for the Emirate. It is based on the outskirts of the city of Dubai and has received training from the British SAS. A primary responsibility is the resolution of hijacking situations at Dubai International Airport, although the existence of a combat diving section implies at least some capability in maritime operations. They are known to have a 50-man reinforcing element (SWAT-type) within the Dubai Police, which has received training, not only from the British, but the United States as well.

DUKE OF YORK BARRACKS – SAS COMMAND CENTRE

This major barracks complex in central London houses a number of military units, but arguably the most important is the 'on-call' Sabre Squadron of the SAS. This rapid reaction anti-terrorist and HRU force is maintained at near instant readiness in the capital, along with SAS Intelligence and support staff.

This rapid response anti-terrorist force is comfortable close to Buckingham Palace; the Downing Street home of the Prime Minister; the Palace of Westminster; major government offices; the Thames House headquarters of the Security Service – MI5, and over the River Thames to the Vauxhall Cross headquarters of the Secret Intelligence Service – MI6.

DZ

Dropping Zone for paratroopers or supplies to forces already in place.

EAST TIMOR 1999 – ASAS

Operation Stabilise: while not officially in East Timor, Special Forces from Australia, New Zealand and the UK have played a major role from the start of Operation Stabilise, designed to defend the lives and civil rights of the peoples of East Timor following their decision to seek independence from Indonesia in 1999. Special forces units involved in Operation Stabilise include the ASAS, NZSAS (and attached Irish Rangers), British SBS and USMC Recons. On Day One, members of the Australian and New Zealand Special Air Special Regiment were the first to arrive in East Timor, securing the main airport in Dili for the main force to arrive. As they disembarked from their C-130H, SAS troopers immediately fanned out into the scrub, taking up fire positions. During this time they met no resistance from the Indonesian Marines and Air Force Police who were tasked to secure the airport. Once the airport was secured the combined Australian, New Zealand and British Special Forces Group moved into Dili, securing Dili's port. During that time, members of the NZ SAS disarmed one member of the pro-Indonesian militia. By the second day the Australian SAS escorted a UN convoy to the jungle town of Dare. As they arrived they were met with a joyous welcome from the refugees living there. Back in Dili, the Special Forces Group were involved in the rescue of two journalists who were attacked by East Timorese members of the Indonesian Military (TNI). Facing the loss of their nation breaking away with Indonesia, the Timorese members of the TNI vented their anger towards the journalists. By the end of the first week of the operation, much of Dili had been secured. However, the rest of the country had yet to be secured, in particular the western regions along the border. Intelligence reports showed that armed militia were still terrorising the people in the townships nearest the border with the Indonesian-controlled western half of the island, and a number of further operations were required, including aggressive patrolling along and possibly across the border before the security situation was stabilised. In late October, INTERFET launched their final operation to occupy the last unsecured area of East Timor, the Oecussi enclave. As members of the 5th/7th Battalion, Royal Australian Regiment conducted their amphibious landing on the enclave, Special Forces light teams in Black Hawks provided top cover fire support for the landing. As the first wave of infantry landed, they were met on the beach by SAS recon teams that had been in the enclave weeks before the landing, observing the enemy. The operation netted 40 captured militia without a shot fired.

ECUADOR

MILITARY SPECIAL FORCES
9th Patria Special Force Brigade 'PATRIA' – Latacunga
24th Para-Commando GFE Battalion – Daule and Peripa
25th Para-Commando GFE Battalion – Quevedo
26th Para Commando GFE Battalion – Latacunga
27th Para-Commando GFE Battalion – Latacunga
9th Special Forces GEK Squadron

The Army's Special Forces are being re-equipped and enhanced in a massive programme initiated by the United States in recent years, and particularly since the terrorist attacks of 11 September as Ecuador is clearly seen as a highly important part of the War on Terrorism. Training now concentrates on parachute skills, CQB, martial arts, combat shooting and other anti-terrorist skills. Ecuador may also be used increasingly as a major base for US operations in the region, particularly as the terrorist situation in neighbouring Colombia deteriorates further.

6th Reconnaissance Battalion with 6 small LRRPS Companies. Its headquarters are in Latacunga

Puma Unit   The main HRU is this 200-strong unit. Formed in 1980, it was originally organised and trained by Israeli Special Forces advisers. Now largely trained and equipped by the Green Berets as part of the United States' growing commitment to Ecuador as its main support and anti-terrorist base in South America. The training is quite extensive, lasting up to eight months and the recruits are carefully chosen for their physical abilities and determination to reach high standards of proficiency. All will have already been well trained as members of the Special Forces or the Marines' equivalent of the SEALs.

Marine Corps
One small Commando unit trained in SEAL tactics.

CIVILIAN SPECIAL FORCES
Grupo de Operaciones Especiales (GOES – Special Operations Group) A dedicated anti-terrorist and hostage rescue unit, it receives considerable training and assistance from the United States. Weapons used include the

9mm FMAP-Browning PD pistol (Argentine-made FN-Browning HP-35), 9mm H&K MP5A3 sub-machine gun, 5.56mm Colt CAR-15A2 Model 727 assault carbine, 5.56mm Steyr AUG A1 assault rifle, 12.7mm Barrett Model 82A1 sniper rifle, 7.62mm Saco M60 machine gun, 40mmSR Colt M203 underbarrel grenade launcher and 40mmSR Hawk MM-1 grenade launcher. GOES uses the AM General M151A2 4×4 Jeep, mounting 7.62mm Saco M60 machine guns, 7.62mm General Electric M134 miniguns and 12.7mm Colt-Browning M2HB machine guns.

E & E

Escape and Evasion. Techniques taught to aircrew of aircraft penetrating hostile airspace or Special Forces involved in clandestine missions inside enemy territory. During the Second World War both SOE and later OSS developed methods, equipment and escape routes with the help of Resistance groups. Thousands of Allied aircrew in particular escaped capture because of this. The British MI9, a branch of the Secret Intelligence Service (SIS or MI6) was a dedicated E & E organisation during the Second World War. Most of its wartime duties have been taken over by the 23rd SAS Territorial Army (Reserve) Regiment.

EGYPT

MILITARY SPECIAL FORCES

Special Forces Command
There are about 15,000 fairly well trained personnel and these are acquiring large quantities of more modern weaponry and equipment. It is now receiving considerable training from US Special Forces.

The first Para-Commando unit was formed in 1959 and by 1963 was involved in the Egyptian Expeditionary force in the Yemen. By 1969 the Airborne and Commando units were combined into a Special Forces Command and the individual units were renamed Al Sai'qa (Lightning) Commandos.

They were to take part in numerous successful cross-canal attacks on Israeli forces occupying the Sinai Desert, and indeed spearheaded the major attacks against the Bar Lev defence line at the start of the October 1973 War (Yom Kippur). A dedicated anti-terrorist force, Unit-777 was created in 1978.

Task Force Unit 777 – 'Wehdat 777 Qataal'   The Egyptian Army formed Unit-777 following a dramatic growth in Islamic terrorism. It is now trained largely by US Special Forces advisers and exercises regularly with SFOD Delta Force, SEALs, GSG-9 and GIGN. Weapons include the standard range of service small arms including 7.62mm AK/AKM and 5.56mm M16 assault rifles, plus Ingram and 9mm MP5 and Israeli Uzi SMG. Egypt has a number of Special Forces units including Special Operations Troops of the Ministry of Interior's Central Security Force. They carry out VIP Protection and 'SWAT' (Special Weapons and Tactics) missions, and are often used to secure a perimeter around a terrorist incident prior to the arrival of Unit-777, while Unit-333 is a specialised Hostage Rescue Force (HRF) based in southern Cairo and consists of 120 personnel. Part of State Security since 1984, it is responsible for all such activities in Egypt. Prior to 1972, the Egyptian government played host to tens of thousands of military advisers from the Soviet Union. Thus, it came as a surprise in 1972 when then-President Anwar Sadat announced the expulsion of these forces and his intention to explore closer ties with Israel. Western intelligence provided evidence to Sadat that this event was not sitting well with several Middle Eastern terrorist organisations and that some had begun to take steps to initiate attacks against Egypt. In response, Egypt formed its own counter-terrorist unit in 1978, known as Unit-777. Soon after, they were thrust into battle unprepared in the Western desert against Libyan forces during President Sadat's determined attempt to teach his bumptious neighbour a short, but sharp lesson. They had no formal order of battle, no experience and little organisation and failed to impress a sceptical Egyptian General Staff. Initial training for the team came from the United States as far back as 1981. Yet, despite the assistance, Unit-777 was apparently not provided with sufficient advanced equipment in the early days and operational readiness suffered. In March 1978 two PFLP (Popular Front for the Liberation of Palestine) assassins had shot and killed a close associate of the Egyptian President, Anwar Sadat, in Nicosia, Cyprus.

They took 30 hostages in a nearby hotel, but were later bussed along with fifteen of the hostages to a Cypriot airliner at Larnaca airport. After fruitlessly flying around the Middle East being refused permission to land, the DC8 returned to Cyprus. By then 54 members of Unit-777 had been dispatched to Cyprus. Unfortunately, the Cypriot authorities were expecting a negotiating team not an assault force – the Egyptian Ministry of Defence having neglected to inform the Cyprus authorities of Unit-777's arrival. Despite the imminent success of negotiations, Egyptian General Shukry ordered Unit-777 to attack the aircraft, which resulted in a fierce firefight which surprised the Cypriot units on the scene. Indeed the local police and National Guard units thought the assaulting commandos were terrorist reinforcements, and in the next 80 minutes fifteen Egyptian soldiers were killed. The precipitate Egyptian action could also have cost the lives of the hostages and it resulted in a difficult period for both Unit-777 and relations between Egypt and Cyprus. Unit-777's most notorious operation, though, was the botched rescue attempt at Malta on 23 November 1985. Palestine terrorists of the Abu Nidal group, angered over Egypt's failure to protect the fleeing *Achille Lauro* terrorists, seized Egyptair flight 648, ironically, the same airplane that had been used to transport the *Achille Lauro* terrorists out of Egypt, and flew it to Luqa International Airport in Malta. This time, Egypt made sure that the foreign government knew Unit-777 was coming. The members of Unit-777, however, made several errors. First, they failed to perform any surveillance of the ground situation. Second, they failed to debrief hostages that had survived a botched execution attempt. Third, they didn't study blueprints of the Boeing 737. Fourth, they did not have stun grenades. Lastly, Unit-777 operators elected to blow a hole in the roof to gain entry to the 737. On the other hand they were under mounting pressure to act as five passengers had already been shot and that alone would normally justify action. In order to stun the terrorists and gain time for operators to enter through the hole in the roof, the explosive charge was increased beyond recommended levels. The blast was so powerful SIX rows of seats were knocked loose and nearly twenty passengers were killed. Then members who entered through the doors began throwing smoke grenades and firing indiscriminately. Snipers positioned on top of rescue vehicles began firing at fleeing civilians. In all, the botched operation killed 57 hostages. After this event, the United States refused to participate in further training with the unit, although this decision was later reversed. Understandably, Unit-777 has kept a low profile since this incident. All members are qualified in static-line airborne operations, although any skill they may have with HALO is unclear. The Egyptian Army's Unit-777 is primarily tasked with the suppression of the Muslim Brotherhood and, particularly since 11 September, Al Qa'ida and Islamic extremism. Whether Unit-777 is yet up to the task of combating the growth of Islamic terrorism is questionable. However, the United States Special Forces are now playing a major role in the restructuring of this unit to give Egypt a genuine Special Forces and Counter-Terrorist unit of quality. Egypt has begun to be a major player in the War on Terrorism, and while it is usually described as a domestic-oriented unit it has conducted both overseas and cross-border operations and is responsible for the regular protection of Egyptian embassies throughout the world. There have been rumours that Unit-777 conducted cross-border covert operations into both Libya and Sudan in the early part of 2002.

CIVILIAN SPECIAL FORCES
Special Operations Troops(CSF) The Special Operations Troops of the Central Security Forces (a branch of the Ministry of the Interior) has been used to conduct VIP protection and SWAT-type missions and could be called on to provide perimeter security in the event Unit-777 was not yet on-scene.

Unit 333 – Hostage Rescue Force (HRF) This unit, established in the 1980s, is based in southern Cairo and has approximately 100 members. Press accounts give credit to the police in their current campaign against the Islamic fundamentalists. This unit is part of State Security and run by the Ministry of the Interior. Unit-333 is responsible for all CT operations within Egypt, though reports indicate that they are superseded by Unit-777 (reasons unknown).

EL SALVADOR

MILITARY SPECIAL FORCES

Special Operations Group 1 Airborne Commando 'Atlactl' Battalion, 1 Naval Commando Battalion and a single Special Forces Company.

The Special Forces in close co-operation with the security services and various right-wing death squads created a reputation for appalling human rights abuse, so bad in fact that Archbishop Arturo Rivera y Damas was able to claim with a fair degree of certainty that some 11,723 innocent people had been murdered by the government or its paramilitary supporters in 1981 *alone*. This murderous campaign dated back to the formation in 1962 of the Organization Democratica Nacionalista (ORDEN) a neo-fascist organisation with close links to the military. The infrastructure for state-sponsored terror remains in place in 2002 and occasionally surfaces to snuff out troublesome opponents of the military. The United States Special Forces train and regularly exercise with their El Salvadorian colleagues and indeed claim a great deal of credit for creating a 55,000 strong counter-insurgency force in the country during the height of its internal problems.

Brigada Especial de Seguridad Militar – Special Brigade for Military Security (BESM) One of the results of the 16 Jan 1992 peace agreement between the government of El Salvador and the Farabundo Marti National Liberation Front (FMLN) was the creation of a new police force. As such, in March of that year, the National Guard and the Treasury Police Security Corps were disbanded. BESM is controlled directly by the Minister of Defence and is composed of four Security Police battalions, including a 456-man military police battalion. The unit is heavily influenced by the US military police and has received the majority of its training from US military advisers. One battalion is responsible for Counter-Terrorist and hostage rescue operations, while the other three battalions (475 men each) provide surveillance and counter-insurgency units to guard borders with Guatemala and Honduras. They are charged with guaranteeing national sovereignty, suppressing smuggling of drugs and other contraband, and supporting other governmental agencies in the frontier regions.

CIVILIAN SPECIAL FORCES

Grupo de Respuesta Policial (GRP) – Police Response Group   The GRP is one of a number of international police response units modelled on the US SWAT teams. They are not a Counter-Terrorist unit *per se*, but rather bear the responsibility of a national hostage rescue unit. As such, however, they would almost certainly be the first unit on-scene in the event of a terrorist incident and could be called on to effect a rescue should conditions warrant. The GRP reports directly to the General Direction of Police, which is, in turn, subordinate to the Vice-Ministry of Public Security. Unit members undergo a six-month initial training programme and must have prior police experience. The unit is currently made up of 40 officers, broken down into four sniper and two assault teams, each with four men.

EOD

Explosive Ordnance Disposal – Unexploded Bomb Disposal (UXB).

ERITREA

MILITARY SPECIAL FORCES

Eritrean Special Forces is unique among most modern special operations units in that women are permitted to operate alongside men in combat missions. This force specialises in raids and reconnaissance and has put these skills to the test in the ongoing Ethio-Eritrean War. The Ethio-Eritrean conflict began when armed Eritrean troops launched a surprise invasion of Ethiopia on 6 May 1998. Eritrea opted for war despite the fact that a Joint Border Commission was already in place to negotiate a solution to the border dispute.The Commando Division includes several Special Forces Commando Battalions.

ESTONIA

CIVILIAN SPECIAL FORCES

National Police – Special Operations Group (SOG)   This unit has a dedicated anti-terrorist role and a limited HRU capability. Its weapons include the 9mm Izhmekh PM Makarov pistol, 9mm H&K MP5K sub-machine gun, 9mm H&K MP5A3 sub-machine gun and 9mm H&K MP5SD3 sound-suppressed sub-machine gun.

ETHIOPIA

MILITARY SPECIAL FORCES
    205th Commando Brigade
    206th Commando Brigade
    Agazi Commando Division

Ethiopia has in theory a large Special Force capability, but in reality the Commando Brigades are used as elite assault infantry, while the Agazi Division is believed to field just one Special Forces Battalion which acts as an additional Presidential Security unit in a crisis, and probably has a limited hostage rescue role as well.

EXERCISE JOSHUA TREE 1978 – DELTA

This three-day exercise, held by the FBI and Delta Force, was the start of the counter-terrorist partnership between these two units/agencies. Held in 1978, one year after Delta's creation, this was one of their first training exercises. For the FBI, it was a chance to practice and refine their hostage negotiation skills. The exercise was planned and carried out at Jackass Flats on the Nevada Test Site. The terrain was desert, and it had important structures such as roads, bunkers, and an airport nearby. Actually, the airport is not specified, but Delta did assault an aircraft. The scenario for the exercise was based on Middle Eastern terrorists having seized an underground nuclear weapons site, along with several hostages (role-playing FBI agents). They demand a safe passage to their home country, along with the nuclear weapon, I suppose. At first, the FBI negotiates several hostages, in return for two buses and an airplane. The buses carry the hostages and some of the terrorists to an airplane waiting on a nearby strip. When the last terrorist boards the airplane, Delta Force operators carry out the assault. The hostages are recovered unharmed. Next, the FBI convinces the terrorists that the first group had reached the airplane safely. Now, the second group of terrorists loads up into another bus. En route to the airfield, Delta Force does a mobile assault on the bus. All terrorists are subdued and hostages rescued. The scenario ended up being so realistic, that during the assault on the last bus some of the hostages exhibited the Stockholm Syndrome and opened fire on the Delta operators. This was one of the earliest joint training exercises between Delta and the FBI, starting a partnership that would continue to this day, with the FBI's Hostage Rescue Team and Delta, who hold training exercises together. A vital part of US planning to cope with future international terrorist attacks inside the United States.

EXERCISE OLYMPIC CHARLIE 1996 – DELTA

Prior to the 1996 summer Olympic Games in Atlanta, the United States Counter-Terrorism force staged a massive exercise in what was the largest peacetime security force in the history of the Games. Present were BATF, FBI, Secret Service, local SWAT Teams, the Hostage Rescue Team, the US Army's Delta Force and even elements from SEAL units for maritime security. Even the Chemical/Biological Response Team was summoned for fear of terrorism and it developed into a specific FBI exercise dealing with the threat of chemical weapons attack. Olympic Charlie simulated a gas attack on an underground transit system and indeed Atlanta's subway service MARTA also has their own SWAT Team which, according to a company spokesman, is trained in chemical response.

EXFIL

Exfiltration, point of exit from AO.

EXPLOSIVES FOR DEMOLITION AND ASSASSINATION

The destruction of enemy targets with explosives planted by specialist clandestine forces has long played an important role in both conventional and unconventional warfare, but the activities of SAS, SOE, OSS and Soviet Partisans in the Second World War took the use of planned and well-targeted sabotage to new heights. All modern Special Operations units are taught how to use explosives to destroy buildings, bridges, aircraft, railways, power stations, communications, ships and other strategically important targets vital to an enemy's war effort. The range of explosives now available to the saboteur has increased immensely. Technology has allowed the development of advanced detonators, electric initiating caps, time fuses, delays, pressure switches so sensitive that they can be targeted to a particular person's (heavier) weight where say, for instance, two people drive the targeted car, the wife is eight stones (112lbs) while the husband is twelve stones (168lbs), radio controlled and even those detonated by a cell phone call. 'Plastique' has allowed explosives to be moulded into everyday shapes and even painted to look commonplace, for example the hotel bedside lamp doctored with a small amount of 'Plastique' that exploded when switched on, killing the target instantly. Plastic explosives are therefore the popular choice for both the assassin and sabotage missions, with the benefits of ease of use, being lightweight and having considerable power. Some of the most commonly used are known as C3 and C4 in the USA, PE2, PE3 and PE4 in the UK, T4 in Italy, Semtex in the Czech Republic, Plastit-4/5/6 in Russia or RDX, PETN, Hexagen or Cyclonite.

FAC

Acronym: Forward Air Controller. Controls air support missions for field operations. Often in the front line themselves, the FAC can call in air attacks on to troublesome hostile artillery or mortars and on advancing enemy infantry or armoured vehicles.

FASTMOVER

Usually a fighter jet.

FID

Foreign Internal Defence. Term describing US Special Forces assistance and training programmes for foreign Security and Special Forces units.

FIJI

MILITARY SPECIAL FORCES
Army First Meridian Squadron (CRW) Company.

FINLAND

MILITARY SPECIAL FORCES
Sissikomppaniat (Ranger/Guerrilla Warfare Companies) 'Kainu' Ranger Battalion
1st Ranger Company, 2nd Ranger Company and 3rd Ranger Company

In a country that revels in its martial tradition, the exploits of reconnaissance men during the Second World War have become a part of Finnish folklore. Former President Dr Mauno Koivisto (SDP 1982–94) was a member of a long-range reconnaissance company commanded by the legendary Lauri Torni, who later joined the US Army as Larry Thorne. CPT Thorne was into a second tour of Vietnam with MACV-SOG when he was killed in a helicopter crash on 18 October 1966. Considered a national hero in Finland, CPT Thorne was awarded the Mannerheim Cross, Finland's highest military award (equivalent to the US Medal of Honor) in July 1944. Present-day Finnish Army SOF are trained to collect intelligence (LRRP), conduct raids, stop border infiltrators, and prevent enemy efforts to sabotage mobilisation. The approximately 400 soldiers found in the Ranger Warfare Companies deploy and operate as small groups, transported primarily by helicopters. Conscript training for these units is approximately eleven months long; it begins at the Airborne Infantry School in Utti and combines ranger, Arctic, aquatic, air assault, and survival training.

Utti Ranger Regiment parajaegers and specialjaegers   Finnish paratroopers are guerrillas who would be dropped behind enemy lines. Some individuals are sent to the Special Forces training centre in Utti in southeastern Finland, where they receive further instruction in countering enemy saboteurs, infiltrators and guerrillas.

Navy
Laivaston Erikoistoimintayksikko (Navy Special operation unit)
1Rannikkojaakarikomppania (1st Marine commando company)

CIVILIAN SPECIAL FORCES

Osasto Karhu (Bear Force) After the Munich Olympic Massacre in 1972, the Helsinki Police Department formed a small twelve-man CT and EOD force known by the acronym ETY. Bear Force, which replaced it, was officially created in 1978 in response to the rise of European terrorism. The 40 hand-picked police officers of the Helsinki Police Department were initially trained by the GSG-9 and specialise in close-quarters battle strikes. Bear Force operators are experts in martial arts and are trained for wilderness and winter survival. All members are volunteers who must undergo a fifteen-week training course before being able to deploy with the unit. They have a small fleet of Saab 900s and Volkwagen mini-vans for cross-country movement. The Bear Force also use Frontier Guard's Agusta-Bell AB.412EP helicopters. The weapons in use include 9mm Glock 17 pistols, 9mm H&K MP5A3 sub-machine guns, H&K PSG-1 7.62mm rifle and 7.62mm Sako TRG-21 bolt-action sniper rifles and 18.5mmR (12-gauge) Remington Model 870 pump-action shotguns.

FIREBASE

A temporary artillery position, often quite isolated and established on a dominant hilltop controlling major access or supply routes. In Vietnam usually placed deep inside hostile territory and kept supplied by helicopters and airdrops.

FIREFAN

The field of fire of a gun or mortar battery. Pre-planned to cover likely routes of advance for an enemy force attacking a remote firebase or front line defensive position.

FLASH BANG

A stun grenade used by Counter-Terrorist assault teams to disorientate the terrorists or hijackers (see STUN GRENADE).

FLIGHT GA 206 HIJACKING 1981 – KOPHASANDA

On 28 March 1981, Garuda Indonesian Airlines Flight GA 206, by DC-9 'Woyla', had flown from Jakarta at 08.00 and was in transit to Palembang, and from there was scheduled to make the trip to its final destination at Medan, arrival time estimated 10.55. Once in the air, however, two passengers got up from their seats. One went to the cockpit while the other stood in the aisle. Moments later at 10.10, 'Woyla' was completely under the control of five armed hijackers. The pilot was ordered to fly to Colombo, Sri Lanka, but answered that the fuel wouldn't be sufficient to travel that distance. The plane was therefore flown to Penang, Malaysia. The terrorists were from the Jihad Commando group, Moslem radicals responsible for many acts of sabotage, raids on police stations and military bases in Indonesia from 1977–81. In an effort to familiarise themselves with the layout of the aircraft, later that evening the newly created Indonesian Special Forces, Kophasanda, borrowed another DC-9 from Garuda Airlines and used it for combat training. 'Woyla' had left Malaysia after refuelling, bound to Don Muang airfield, Thailand. The terrorists demanded the release of Jihad Commandos imprisoned by the Indonesian government, and US$1.5 million. They also demanded an aircraft be prepared for the released prisoners, for an unspecified destination. At 21.00, 29 March, 35 members of Kophasanda left Indonesia in a DC-10, all wearing civilian clothes. The Thai authorities, preferring a peaceful settlement, reluctantly agree to the storming of the aircraft. The CIA chief of station in Thailand was to meet later with the Kophasanda commandos to lend them flak jackets and breaching kits for the assault. The assault teams started to move into position at around 02.30 on 31 March and at 02.43 a Thai Special Forces commando team moved into position on the runway, to prevent the possibility of any of the terrorists escaping. At 02.43 three Kophasanda teams begin the rescue operation. Green team entered first, only to find that a terrorist was alert in the rear side of the plane. The terrorist fired, striking one assault team member in an area of his stomach unprotected by his flak jacket. The hijacker then killed himself. Blue team and Red team then entered and shot two others terrorists on sight, as the passengers took cover. The commando team shouted to the passengers to exit the aircraft. A hijacker, with grenade in hand, also ran outside and tried to throw it. But passengers pointed him out and the commando team killed him with a burst of automatic fire. By 02.45 the operation was over. All the terrorists aboard had been killed, as were the pilot of 'Woyla' and one anti-terrorist team member. A hurried and not particularly well-planned operation was carried out forcefully and succeeded beyond most expectations.

FLIR

Forward Looking Infra-Red. Fitted into the nose of aircraft or helicopters. Gives warning of heat sources.

FNG

Acronym: F****** New Guy, either a 'rookie' or simply a replacement or new member of a unit.

FOB

Forward Operating Base. An advanced temporary operating base for combat units.

FORCE-136

A British joint SOE and Special Forces unit infiltrated back into Malaya after the fall of Singapore to the Japanese in early 1942 in order to train local Malays, and in particular the Chinese Communist underground, to disrupt the Japanese Army of Occupation. Sabotage, ambush and assassination techniques were taught by British instructors parachuted in or landed by light aircraft and smal-fast-raiding craft. A highly successful campaign which, however, came back to haunt the British Colonial administration after the war, when the Chinese launched what was later known as the 'Malay Emergency' using the skills and weapons provided by the British Special Forces during the war to very good effect against the British peace-time garrison. In a strange twist of fate, this in turn helped to create the very conditions that led to the re-creation of the SAS in the 1950s as a regular formation within the British Army.

FOURTEENTH/14TH INTELLIGENCE AND SECURITY COMPANY

When the 14th Intelligence Company, simply known as 'the Detachment or det.', was formed in 1974, it was initially trained by SAS instructors. However, this small elite, unit which has operated highly successfully in Northern Ireland ever since, soon developed its own unique methodology and training programme. It has since become a world leader in the field of covert surveillance in intensely hostile environments. Both the SAS and SBS send several of their members each year to serve with the det.

Its expertise and techniques are made available to the British Intelligence and Security services, the Police Anti-Terrorist units and Special Branch, as well as Allied Counter-Terrorist units facing similar problems. In August 2002 it was reported that the 14th Intelligence Company had deployed a small covert surveillance team to operate within Spain with the knowledge of the government in Madrid. Their purpose is to monitor and gather further intelligence about the close links between the Basque terrorist group ETA and both the Provisional and Real IRA. Part of the Intelligence and Security Group, which also includes an SAS Troop and is often known as the Army Surveillance Unit (ASU).

FRANCE

MILITARY SPECIAL FORCES
Special Operations Command Formed 1992–93
The French have a very wide range of Special Forces units available from both the Armed Forces and the National Police and all of which are tasked for intelligence and counter-terrorist operations under the direction of the DGSE and DST Intelligence and Security services.

Army
The 1st Parachute Infantry & Marine Regiment (*1er Regiment Parachutiste d'Infanterie de Marine – 1er RPI Ma*) is the French army's primary Special Operations unit and based in Bayonne. The Para-Commandos are the nearest French equivalent to the SAS and indeed its origins date back to 1 August 1940 when General de Gaulle formed the Free French 1st Compaigne d'Infanterie de l'air. The 1st Para are an extremely effective and well-equipped force, with their main missions being intelligence-gathering, direct action, special operations and counter-terrorism. Training includes marksmanship, combat shooting, unarmed combat, combat swimming, desert, mountain and amphibious warfare, heliborne-insertion, para-gliding, HAHO (High Altitude High Opening), HALO (High Altitude Low Opening) and a wide range of clandestine and intelligence-gathering techniques. They are trained to use most weapons and have a stock of standard service, commercially bought and captured terrorist weapons that runs into hundreds of makes of rifles, sub-machine guns, automatic pistols, machine guns, grenades and explosives.

The operational heart of the regiment is the RAPAS (recherche et action specialiste – intelligence and special operations) squad of ten commandos (divided into a four-man command section and three two-man teams). Completely self-contained with each member of the squad expert in different disciplines.

The 1er RPIMa is part of the 11th Parachute Division. The 11th Parachute Division is similar to that of the old British 5 Airborne Brigade. It has two brigades with a total of seven battalions (Regiments).

The 1er RPIMa has developed into France's elite Special Operations unit and has now been tasked with Counter-Terrorist and Hostage Rescue missions outside and, if necessary, within France. 1er RPIMa co-operates closely with the national HRU/CT unit GIGN, regular joint training and exercises maintaining a high degree of commonality and understanding between these two elite units along with other units such as RAID, 2eme REP, and CONFUSCO. The Paras of the 1er RPIMa are also responsible for bodyguarding VIPs in conflict zones, direct action, reconnaissance, sabotage and unconventional warfare. While many of the 1er RPIMa operations remain highly secret, it is known that small units have been deployed wherever the 11th Parachute Division has been involved in a conflict and that includes Bosnia, Kosovo, Chad and Lebanon. After a recruit joins the French Army and volunteers for Airborne School at Pau, he may then be accepted into a Parachute Regiment. If he wishes to join the 1er RPIMa he will be posted to the French Commando School for additional training in Special Operations skills. Weapons used include 9mm MAS PA-MAS-G1 pistol, 5.7mm FN P90 personal defence weapon, 9mm H&K MP5A5 sub-machine gun, 9mm H&K MP5SD6 suppressed sub-machine gun, 5.56mm Colt CAR-15A2 Model 777 assault carbine, 5.56mm Colt CAR-15A3 Model 977 assault carbine, 5.56mm Colt AR-15A2 Model 701 assault rifle, 5.56mm MAS FA-MAS-F1 assault rifle, 7.62mm H&K G3A3 battle rifle, 7.62mm H&K MSG90 sniper rifle, 7.62mm MAS FR-F2 bolt-action sniper rifle, 7.62mm PGM UR Commando bolt-action sniper rifle, 12.7mm Barrett Model 82A1 sniper rifle, 12.7mm PGM Hécate II bolt-action sniper rifle, 5.56mm FN MINIMI-Para light machine gun, 7.62mm MAS AA-7.62N-F1 machine gun, 18.5mmR (12-gauge) Mossberg Model 500 pump-action shotgun, 18.5mmR (12-gauge) Benelli M3 Super 90 semi-automatic shotgun, the Remington 12-gauge pump shotgun is also used during CQB, to take down doors, 40mmSR Colt M203 underbarrel grenade launcher (under AR-15A2 Model 701), 40mmSR Colt M203A1 underbarrel grenade launcher (under CAR-15A3 Model 977), 40mmSR H&K HK79 underbarrel grenade launcher (under G3A3), 40mmSR Mechem MGL-6 grenade launcher and 40mmSR H&K GMG automatic grenade launcher. CQB kit includes a black balaclava, black nomex coveralls, non-slip boots (such as Hi-Tech), special webbing and holsters, medical kit (for team's medics), gas masks and special communications equipment.

Commandos de Renseignement et de l'Action en Profondeur – The Special Operations Team of the 2nd REP(Legion Parachute Regiment) is a particularly well-proven and effective Intelligence and Counter-Terrorist unit with a speciality in 'hard skirmishes', sabotage of hard value targets, long-range reconnaissance and patrol, POW (Prisoner of War) rescue, psychological warfare, deep clandestine penetration behind enemy lines and the elimination of terrorist targets. It operates under the control of the 11th Para Division. This Regiment is further organised into No-1 Company for urban warfare, night and helicopter commando operations; No-2 Company for mountain warfare; No-3 Company for maritime operations and No-4 Company for sabotage, demolitions and covert 'stay-behind' operations.

ALAT (Special Operations Aviation unit)   provides the 11th Para Division with air support provided by two Special Operations Squadrons, the first with Eurocopter AS552 Cougar Mk 2 CSAR and Puma helicopters and the second with Gazelle gunships. It is now part of the Special Operations Command formed in the aftermath of the Gulf War in 1991 and designed to ensure full co-operation between the various Special Force units and their parent services.

Foreign Legion
13 Demi-Brigade Legion Etrangere   The 13 RDP (13eme Regiment de Dragon Parachutistes) is currently the French Army's LRRP (Long-Range Reconnaissance Patrol) unit. Originally raised in 1676 as a cavalry unit, it continued in this role until 1963, when it acquired its current mission. The Regiment is subordinate to the BGRE (the French Army's military intelligence and electronic warfare Brigade). Although not part of COS (the French Special Operations Command), it is tasked to support COS operations and regularly conducts training with COS units. The Regiment is currently composed of seven squadrons; three 'search' or intelligence squadrons, two long-range communications squadrons and two training squadrons. The three search squadrons provide the Regiment's recon teams, while the training squadrons are responsible for providing in-house training courses and certifying new unit members. The two communications squadrons provide a secure communications link between deployed recon teams and higher headquarters. A select number of personnel, including the Regiment's GCP (Commando Parachute Group) teams, are trained in conducting HAHO and HALO operations. Other recon teams specialise in conducting vehicle-mounted patrols equipped with heavily armed P-4 Jeeps and Peugeot motorcycles. The 13e RDP conducted a number of reconnaissance missions for the Allied coalition during the Gulf War. One three-man team was captured by the Iraqis while conducting a border reconnaissance mission and was repatriated after the ceasefire agreement. The Regiment has also deployed teams to support French humanitarian and peacekeeping operations in Africa, particularly in the former colonies, and most recently deployed a squadron to support NATO combat operations in the former Republic of Yugoslavia. It is equipped with most standard French Army material, but also has access to specialised weapons and equipment. Weapons used include HK MP5SD silenced sub-machine guns, M-203 40mm grenade launcher and the Belgian produced 5.56mm Minimi LMG (US M-249 SAW). Vehicle-mounted teams may arm their selected mode of transport with a variety of heavy weapons including Browning .50 cal heavy machine guns, US MK-19 40mm automatic grenade launchers and light machine guns.

Marine Nationale (Navy)
COFUSCO – Naval Commando Command   The Naval SOF have undergone various reorganisations and name changes over the years, gaining its current

designation only in 1983. COFUSCO is based at Lorient, and operates under the direct control of the Navy Chief of Staff and consists of the following units: four active (Trepel, Jaubert, de Monfort, and Penfentenyo) assault commandos unit, a combat diver unit (Commando Hubert) and a maritime Counter Terrorism (CT) team (GCMC) and these operate under the control of COS (the French Special Operations Command). COFUSCO security units accompany French naval units deploying to overseas ports and secure French naval facilities against attack.

Commandement des Fusiliers-Marins Commandos (Assault Commando units) These four units provide the French Navy with an elite special operations strike force. The assault commandos are composed of approximately 80 men and are subdivided into four sections. Each section specialises in conducting a specific type of operation: assault, beach recon, HALO/HAHO, small-boat handling, combat diving, heavy weapons, sniping, etc. Teams from the various sections may be combined to execute a particular mission, depending on the circumstances. All aspiring commandos are drawn from volunteers serving in French naval units. The troops undergo an extensive four-month training and selection course at Lorient, on the coast of France. Upon successfully completing the basic selection course, the trainee will then undertake the French basic airborne course. Once this training is completed any survivors will receive a month of intermediate commando training. This training includes instruction in cliff assaults, rappelling, field training and intensified physical conditioning. The final stage of training consists of instruction in conducting amphibious operations and small-boat handling, while some men are selected to attend the French Combat Diver school. The commandos have participated in numerous combat operations over the past few decades. Commandos have supported French peacekeeping operations, and conducted military interventions in France's former African colonies. Weapons used include the H&K MP-5 series SMGs, the US produced M-16 family of weapons, French-produced FAMAS rifles, Swiss manufactured SG-540 assault rifles, Remington 870 shotguns, various sniper rifles, 60mm mortars, Milan anti-tank missiles, US M-203 40mm grenade launchers, and Belgian designed Minimi (US M-249) 5.56mm LMGs.

Commando D'Action Sous Marine-Commando Hubert (CASM-Underwater Action Commando) COFUSCO consists of several small and specialised units, including four naval assault commandos and one combat diver commando – Commando Hubert is a combat swimmer unit assigned to the French Navy's COFUSCO. The unit is tasked with conducting maritime special operations in support of the French Navy and intelligence services, primarily the DGSE (the French foreign intelligence directorate). The unit was initially raised during the Second World War as a commando-trained naval infantry unit. When first organised, Commando Hubert specialised in conducting amphibious operations, raids and other direct-action missions. In 1953 the unit was converted to its current combat swimmer role. At that time the unit was stationed in Algeria and was conducting combat operations against communist rebels fighting for independence from France. The unit moved its base of operations from Algeria to its current home at Toulon during the late 1950s. The unit has been heavily involved in providing support to French units in their various interventions in Africa. They have also provided support to UN peacekeeping operations. During the evacuation of the PLO from Beirut, Lebanon, Commando Hubert divers were used to clear explosives from the hull of the ship transporting PLO chairman Yasser Arafat and to search the harbour for explosives. Commando Hubert has also been involved in supporting French nuclear tests in the South Pacific. Along with men of the assault commandos, they have conducted numerous ship boardings and maritime interdictions. As part of their ongoing support for these nuclear tests, they are strongly suspected of having planted the explosives that sank the *Rainbow Warrior* in New Zealand. Commando Hubert divers have also been extremely active in testing the security of French naval facilities by conducting simulated raids on ships, submarines, and nuclear storage facilities. Currently Commando Hubert is composed of 80 men divided into two companies. The first company consists of 50 men and is subdivided into four sections designated A, B, C, and D. A section is the command and support section. It consists of the unit HQ and the units Hurricane RIBs. B section is the maritime counter terrorism (CT) section. The unit specialises in conducting underwater approaches to terrorist targets. They conduct joint operations with the Navy's GCMC and GIGN's diver section. In the event of an assault being ordered on a target at sea, B section divers would act as guides for the GIGN team. C section is the SDV section. The divers of this section receive additional training in the use of SDVs and their maintenance. D section contains the unit's snipers and heavy weapons experts. The section is responsible for performing beach reconnaissance, shipping attacks, underwater demolition operations, providing heavy fire support and testing new equipment for use by the unit. All members of D section are both HAHO and HALO qualified. There are currently plans on the board to form an E section. E section will consist of the units Hurricane RIBs, small boats, and support personnel drawn from the 2nd company. The 2nd company is a support unit made up of 30 men. Men are assigned to one of the company's teams, which specialise in communications, SDV maintenance, logistics, or small-boat operation and repair. Prospective unit members are selected from personnel currently serving in French Marine Commando units. They undergo training at the French Navy's diving school located at Saint-Mandrier, near Toulon. The school runs seventeen separate courses for armed forces personnel. Prospective Commando Hubert members attend the school's combat diver course. The first phase of combat diver training consists of attaining the basic diver qualification and is open to all French naval personnel. The second phase of training is an advanced diving course and is restricted to combat divers and ordnance clearance (EOD) personnel.

Weapons used include the 9mm MAS PA-MAS-G1 pistol, 9mmR (.357 Magnum) S&W Model 686 revolver (used in dive operations as it will function underwater), 5.7mm FN P90 personal defence weapon, 9mm H&K MP5A5 sub-machine gun, 9mm H&K MP5SD6 suppressed sub-machine gun, 5.56mm Colt CAR-15A2 Model 723 assault carbine, 5.56mm Colt CAR-15A2 Model 733 Commando assault carbine, 5.56mm SIG SG551 SWAT assault carbine, 5.56mm MAS FA-MAS-G2 assault rifle, 7.62mm H&K G3A4 battle rifle, 7.62mm H&K G3SG1 sniper rifle, 7.62mm MAS FR-G2 bolt-action sniper rifle, 7.62mm PGM UR Commando bolt-action sniper rifle, 12.7mm McMillan Model 93 sniper rifle, 14.5mm MOM M3 Gepard bolt-action sniper rifle, 5.56mm FN MINIMI-Para light machine gun, 7.62mm MAS AA-7.62N-F1 machine gun, 18.5mmR (12-gauge) Remington Model 870P pump-action shotgun and 40mm SR Colt M203A1 underbarrel grenade launcher (under CAR-15A2 Model 723). The unit's Hurricane RIBs are manufactured by Zodiac and are capable of transporting ten troops at speeds up to 50mph. Unit members are allowed a large amount of discretion in their selection of personnel equipment. Hard body-armour and Kevlar or spectra helmets are worn during CT operations. For other missions the unit prefers the light plastic Protec helmets favoured by many elite units.

CIVILIAN SPECIAL FORCES

Raid – Reaction, Assistance, Intervention, Dissauder 'The Black Panthers'   This is a highly secretive group, formed in June 1985, and appears to counter the general practice among elite counter-terrorist forces by recruiting direct, rather than from already-trained soldiers or police. The unit is currently based at Bievres on the outskirts of Paris and has a strength of 60: headquarters and support ten-strong, special task group (negotiators, EOD, etc.) ten strong and four assault teams each ten-strong. The normal operational uniform is a black coverall and mask (hence their nickname 'Black Panthers') and the operators are permitted to make personal selection of weaponry, either foreign or French. The selection tests are very severe and are followed by a nine-month training course and various other courses of instruction: for example, some become HAHO/HALO qualified or undertake maritime training with the Navy's Commandos – Marine. The training includes a fast-driving course, mountain training, an intense shooting course (each member shoots 300 cartridges per day) and close-combat (a derivative of the Israeli 'Krav Maga'). One of RAID's best known operations occurred on 15 May 1993, when a fifteen-man RAID assault force ended a two-day stand off between police and a terrorist who had strapped sixteen sticks of dynamite on his chest and taken 21 nursery school children and their teacher hostage. When microphones placed around the school by RAID members indicated that the terrorist, an Algerian named Eric Schmidt, was snoring, the unit jumped into action. One group formed a shield that began evacuating the hostages, while another raced to the location where intelligence said Eric Schmidt was holed up. Woken by the running boots and sound of escaping children, he began to move menacingly towards the approaching RAID officers. Three .357 rounds ended his extortion attempt. The entire assault had lasted 30 seconds, and none of the hostages were killed. RAID, along with other elements of the French Special Forces, and in co-operation with the Security organisations have been heavily involved in combatting Islamic terrorism in France, partly caused by the French government's support of the Algerian regime and, increasingly, since 9-11 because of the effects of the growing international War on Terrorism. RAID is lavishly equipped with the best equipment and weapons available, and although it uses many of the same weapons as GIGN, RAID officers are still permitted to select their own side-arms. Weapons used include the HK-MP5 series of sub-machine guns, SIG SG551 5.56mm rifle, the Matra-Manurhin MR-73 .357 revolver, and the Baretta 92FS pistol with the extended 20-round magazine, but personnel weapons such as the Glock 19 and Sig-Sauer family are gaining in popularity among team members.

GIGN – Groupe d'Intervention de la Gendarmerie Nationale (Intervention Group of the National Gendarmerie)   was formed in November 1973 and now has over 100 personnel. It quite quickly developed a reputation for being one of the world's busiest and finest Counter-Terrorist units.

GIGN have taken part in over 1,400 operations worldwide, and because of this they are trained to act effectively in a myriad of situations. At first it was split into GIGN-1 (Northern France) at Maisons-Alfort near Paris and GIGN-4 (Southern France) at Mont-de-Marsan. Eventually in 1976 the two units were merged and by 1984 had four twelve-strong teams of NCOs and Officers, with one team on a 30-minute standby for deployment anywhere in the world. Training includes HALO (High Altitude Low Opening) to parachuting into the sea in full SCUBA gear. To even be considered for GIGN a recruit must have five years of experience with an exemplary record, the training then takes ten months and as many as 90 per cent of volunteers fail to make the grade. They train in alpine and winter environments in addition to the urban. GIGN personnel come exclusively from the ranks of the Gendarmerie and, despite their fearsome reputation as a highly effective anti-terrorist force, the GIGN has been guilty of the planting of evidence on arrested IRA suspects in Vicennes in 1982 when it is believed a number of officers were later suspended or dismissed; the maltreatment and killing of a number of New Caledonian rebels in the South Pacific during 1988, and in 1993 evidence appeared to prove that GIGN had been illegally monitoring the phones of investigative journalists. During the regular training cycle it is not unusual for a surprise test or 'sickener' to be set at various times to evaluate the candidate's ability to think on their feet and to weed out those without sufficient 'heart' to satisfy the GIGN instructors. Weapons in use include the 9mm MAS PA-MAS-G1 pistol (licensed Beretta Mod 92G), 9mmR (.357 Magnum) Manurhin MR-73 revolver, the PA-MAS-G1, 9mm Glock 17. 9mm H&K P7M13 or 9mm SIG-Sauer P228 are universally carried as backup pistols. Sub-machine guns include the 9mm H&K MP5KA5 machine pistol, 9mm H&K MP5A5 sub-machine gun and 9mm H&K MP5SD6 suppressed sub-machine gun. The 9mm FN Uzi sub-machine gun (Belgian-made IMI Model 39) is used only by the GIGN divers. The main rifle-calibre assault weapon is the 5.56mm SIG SG551 SWAT assault carbine, but the 5.56mm GIAT FA-MAS-F1, 5.56mm H&K HK33A5 and 5.56mm SIG SG550 assault rifles are also used. Some 7.62mm H&K G3A3 automatic rifles are used for overwatch. Sniper rifles include the 7.62mm MAS FR-F1 bolt-action rifle, 7.62mm PGM UR Intervention bolt-action rifle, 7.62mm PGM UR Commando bolt-action rifle, 7.62mmB (.300 Winchester magnum) PGM UR Magnum bolt-action rifle, 8.6mm (.338 Lapua Magnum) Accuracy International AWM bolt-action rifle, 12.7mm PGM Hécate II bolt-action rifle and 12.7mm Barrett Model 82A1 semi-automatic rifle. For shotguns GIGN use the 18.5mmR (12-gauge) Remington Model 870P pump-action shotgun as well as the 18.5mmR (12-gauge) Franchi SPAS-12 semi-automatic shotgun. The 40mmSR Mechem MGL-6 grenade launcher and the 40mmSR H&K HK79 underbarrel grenade launcher (under G3A3) are used to launch non-lethal grenades

EPIGN (Counter-Terrorism) Escadron Parachutiste d'Intervention de la Gendarmerie Nationale This unit was created by ministerial decree in 1984 and soon saw service in Spain in support of regular police units operating against Basque ETA terrorists. A permanent detachment was assigned to New Caledonia, where they have operated in conjunction with French Special Forces in hostage rescue missions. EPIGN commandos assisted GIGN in July 1987 with suppressing a riot at the Fleury-Merogis prison near Paris, and later took part in the assault on the hijacked Air France airliner at Marseilles Airport. One hundred and forty officers and NCOs are subdivided into four platoons of 30–35 men each and a HALO/HAHO-qualified platoon. One of the four platoons specialises in VIP protection. EPIGN training classes are very small, averaging ten students per session (conducted twice yearly).

GABON

MILITARY SPECIAL FORCES
One Airborne-Commando Company some 60-strong with a limited anti-terrorist capability. Receives some training from French advisers as well as occasional joint exercises.

GAMBIA – PRESIDENT'S FAMILY RESCUED BY SAS

While the President of the Gambia, Sir Dawda Jawara, was attending the wedding of Prince Charles and Lady Diana Spencer in May 1981 Marxist rebels were taking over his capital of Banjul and imprisoning many of his family in a hospital in the city. France helped Senegal to prepare an expeditionary force to invade the Gambia and restore the legal government, while the US Government at first offered to deploy the Delta Force but unexpectedly reneged on the offer at a crucial moment. However, a small SAS team under Major Ian Cooke flew under civilian cover to Banjul, quickly located the president's family and, having worked out a plan for both the assault and subsequent escape, subdued the rebel guards and removed the family to the safety of the British diplomatic mission. This achieved, the SAS team set about assisting the Senegalese military operation that eventually defeated the rebellion.

GEORGIA

MILITARY SPECIAL FORCES

One Recon Battalion which carries out Special Forces and anti-terrorist activities. It is intended to raise at least one additional Special Forces Battalion with US and Russian assistance in 2002–03. In a surprising military co-operation in August–September 2002, US Special Forces are now operating within Georgia, not only to provide instructors and training but to assist Georgian and Russian Special Forces flush out Chechen rebels controlling the Pankisi Gorge in the precipitous mountains and ravines of the border area between Georgia and Chechnya. Some 2,000 Chechens and ex-Afghan Al Qa'ida and Taliban fighters have taken refuge in the Pankisi Gorge, and could be capable of striking US forces based in Georgia from the rear in the course of an Allied attack on Iraq.

GERMANY

MILITARY SPECIAL FORCES

KSK Kommando Spezialkräfte – Special Forces Command   In 1995, Germany took the initial steps to form a new military special operations unit known as Kommando Spezialkrüfte, or KSK for short. Following unification of East and West Germany it was considered necessary to establish a national rapid-reaction Special Forces unit capable of protecting German nationals and interests both within Germany and abroad. The unit would also be capable of operating under conditions that other German military forces were not accustomed to, or normally trained to operate in, such as jungle and desert climates. The impetus for forming the force was partly the experience gained during the 1994 Rwandan civil war. Belgian and French paratroopers were used to rescue eleven German nationals because no suitably trained German force was available. KSK operates under the control of the German Crisis Section, and conducts missions similar to those undertaken by US Special Forces or British SAS. When the unit was declared fully operational in 1999 it consisted of 1,000 fully trained personnel with the main combat capability provided by the Commando/Long-Range Recon Companies. Each Commando Company consists of the following: HQ Platoon; four Commando Platoons – each specialising in a different area: 1st – Land Infiltration; 2nd – Air Infiltration (HALO capable); 3rd – Amphibious Operations and 4th – Mountainous and Arctic climate operations. Each platoon consists of four teams of four men each. Each of the four men specialises in one of the following areas: communications, explosives, medical, or operations and intelligence, with one of the men acting as team leader. One of the four platoons is trained in conducting hostage rescue/CT operations. Training for KSK's initial batch of recruits lasts for a period of approximately three years, with all the unit's operational elements being both military free-fall (HALO/HAHO) and SCUBA trained. The selection process and basic training for new recruits lasts about three months and is a modified version of what the SAS, and US Army Special Forces use (the US, UK and France were all involved in the initial planning and unit set up). They are also trained in high-speed and defensive driving. Uniforms consist of basic German infantry uniforms and LBE, black Nomex coveralls and balaclavas, and Kevlar 'Fritz' style helmets. Communications equipment consists of a modified helmet-mounted SEM52/SL with throat mike. Weapons in use include the 9mm H&K P8 pistol (USP), 7.62mm H&K P11 underwater dart pistol, 11.43mm (.45 ACP) H&K P12 pistol (USP Tactical) with sound suppressor, 9mm H&K MP5KA4 machine pistol, 9mm H&K MP5A5 submachine gun, 9mm H&K MP5SD6 suppressed sub-machine gun, 5.56mm H&K G36K assault carbine, 5.56mm H&K G36 assault rifle, 7.62mmB (.300 Winchester Magnum) Accuracy International G22 bolt-action sniper rifle (AWM-F), 12.7mm (.50 BMG) McMillan Model 87R bolt-action sniper rifle, 5.56mm H&K MG36 heavy automatic rifle, 7.62mm H&K G8 heavy automatic rifle, 7.62mm Rheinmetall MG3 general-purpose machine gun and 18.5mmR (12-gauge magnum) Remington SG2 pump-action shotgun (Model 870 Special). Support weapons included the 35mm Buck DM34 HAFLA incendiary launcher, 40mmSR H&K AG1A1 grenade launcher (better known as the Granatpistole), 40mmSR H&K AG36 underbarrel grenade launcher (under G36 and G36K), 40mmSR H&K GMW1 automatic grenade launcher, 60mm Dynamit-Nobel PZF3 anti-tank rocket launcher, 60mm Dynamit-Nobel BKF1 rocket launcher and the 125mm Euromissile PAL MILAN 3 anti-tank missile.

FERNSPAHETRUPPEN Fernspaeh Kompanies (SAS-type/LRRPS) Fernspah is trained as a passive LRRP (Long-Range Reconnaissance Patrol) unit. There are three Companies whose personnel are selected from the airborne division and trained at the LRRP School in Weingarten, Germany. Stock weapons from the German Army are used. Due to the Bundeswehr's long-standing disapproval of Special Operations this unit maintains a low profile.

CIVILIAN SPECIAL FORCES

GSG-9 (Grenzschutzgruppe-9) This unit was formed in 1973 as a direct result of the humiliating failure of the German anti-terrorist groups at the 1972 Munich Olympics. The inept police response to the Black September terrorists led to the death of innocent Israeli athletes and officials. The Palestinian terrorists had been able to penetrate the Olympic compound, murder two Israeli athletes and take nine others hostage. The incident took an even worse turn when the on-scene commander ordered his men to fire on the terrorists, who were preparing to board two helicopters to effect their escape. Poor marksmanship, coupled with a number of snipers who refused to fire, led to the least desirable outcome – an open gun battle. When the smoke cleared on the Furstenfeldbruck military airfield, the nine remaining hostages and terrorists were dead. A decision was quickly made to ensure that Germany would have an effective Counter-Terrorist organisation because the German Army had again proved unwilling to create elite units. The para-military Border Guards were chosen in 1973 to host the new unit. In the aftermath of the 11 September terrorist attacks in the USA, GSG-9 has increased its operational strength and now comes under the control of the Counter-Terrorist Division of the Federal Intelligence Service, the BND. GSG-9's highly skilled personnel can conduct long-term clandestine operations and infiltrate terrorist groups, carry out intelligence surveillance and counter-terrorist operations in any environment. GSG-9 recruits only volunteers from within the Border Guards and ex-army personnel. GSG-9 is currently broken down into four primary groups; GSG-9/1 Counter-Terrorist Group, GSG-9/2 Maritime Counter-Terrorism, GSG-9/3 Airborne Special Operations and GSG-9/4 Specialist Intelligence. These units specialised according to these respective taskings: counter-terrorism, maritime CT and airborne. Each group has approximately 50 personnel organised into a command and security section and five or six SETS (Specialein-Satztrupp) each with five personnel. The SETS can function as either sniper or assault teams and are capable of reasonably independent operation. The unit is currently based at the state-of-the-art centre at Saint Augustin Centre near Bonn, where they share a medium-sized compound with the regular Federal Border Guard. They are directly linked into a national anti-terrorist computer information database which is in turn linked to similar systems in the UK, France, Italy and the USA. As previously mentioned, the troopers enjoy the full support of the government when it comes to their equipment. As such, they are issued not one, but two complete sets of combat gear. One of these sets is tailored to daytime operations, while the other is built around use at night. GSG-9, like many of the larger CT groups, also has its own aviation unit, known as Bundesgrenzschutz Grenzschutz-Fliegergruppe. Unlike numerous other CT and SO units, GSG-9 members are not compelled to leave the unit after a set period of time, instead personnel are permitted to stay for as long as they are able to maintain the group's high and inflexible standards. This policy is a logical one and has the added benefit of allowing the lessons learned by senior operators to be handed down to the newer members. The training is extremely thorough and this unit has a higher proportion of graduates than most similar organisations, due to the greater demands made on the personnel's intellectual abilities by the combination of intelligence, Special Forces and detective work. Rigorous screening still ensures that there is an 80 per cent dropout rate, however. Firearms training concentrates on handguns, SMGs and sniper rifles with three half-days and two nights per week usually devoted to shooting practice. The range scenarios include dummy aircraft, trains, ships, buses and a range of buildings similar to hospitals, embassies and government offices. A CQB/combat shooting underground range, built at the St Augustin headquarters, originally cost some $10 million in the mid-1980s and has since been updated to become a state-of-the art facility. Cross-training is conducted with other NATO elite units, and some graduates attend the international LRRP (Long-Range Reconnaissance Patrol) School at Weingarten. The GSG-9 maintains a close working relationship with the SAS, GIGN, Sayeret Matkal, Delta Force and the FBI HRT.

Training includes HALO (High Altitude Low Opening) and LALO (Low Altitude Low Opening), SCUBA diving, combat swimming, demolition and explosives disposal, mountain warfare, skiing, and heliborne insertion. Weapons used include the 9mm Glock P9M pistol (Glock 17M), which replaced the 9mm H&K P7 pistol. Other weapons include the 9mm H&K MP5KA1 sub-machine gun, 9mm H&K MP5A3 sub-machine gun, 9mm H&K MP5SD3 suppressed sub-machine gun, 5.56mm SIG G37 assault carbine (SG551 SWAT, adopted 1993), Austrian Steyr AUG assault rifles, 7.62mm H&K PSG1 sniper rifle (with ZPP low-light optics or Eltro infra-red scopes), 7.62mmB (.300 Winchester Magnum) ERMA SR 100 bolt-action sniper rifle (with 12× scope, adopted 1997, some of them in 7.62mm with sound suppressors), 7.62mm H&K G8 heavy automatic rifle (with 4× scope), 18.5mmR (12-gauge) H&K HK512 semi-automatic shotgun and 40mmSR H&K MZP1 grenade launcher. The GSG-9, when assigned for VIP protection carry a special briefcase containing an 9mm MP5K that has been constructed to allow the firing of the SMG by squeezing a lever built into the handle of the briefcase.

GHANA

MILITARY SPECIAL FORCES

1st Special Forces Battalion based in Accra. A well-trained unit that exercises regularly with the SAS; it has a limited hostage rescue capability, but would undoubtedly receive considerable assistance from its British colleagues.

GIBRALTAR – DEATH ON THE ROCK

Operation Flavius 1988. Despite the extensive security precautions taken by the IRA, two well-known members of the terrorist organisation, Sean Savage and Daniel McCann, were spotted in November 1987 in Spain by terrorist experts from Madrid's Servicios de Informacion office. After observing their movements and relaying the findings to MI6 (the British foreign intelligence agency) and SAS headquarters, it was generally agreed that the duo could only be in the region for one of two reasons – to carry out an operation against the 250,000-strong British presence on the Costa del Sol, or a British Army target in Gibraltar. This was narrowed down in the months that followed by a concentrated period of co-operation between British and Spanish intelligence and counter-terrorist experts. They soon agreed: the target would most likely be the changing of the guard outside the Governor of Gibraltar's residence. In fact it was, and although they did not know it at the time, all the IRA's secret planning had been in vain. Having arrived at this conclusion in November, a cover story was produced that would postpone the scheduled event to 8 March 1988. The story released was that the change in scheduling was due to a planned refurbishing of the guardhouse. In fact, the event was deferred in order for authorities to have more time to plan their actions against the IRA terrorists.

On 1 March the authorities documented the arrival of an Irish woman travelling under a false name, Mary Parkin, later identified as Mairead Farrell, a long-time IRA terrorist. She was to be observed closely watching the changing of the guard ceremony on numerous occasions. There appeared to be little doubt that she was providing advance reconnaissance for an IRA Active Service Unit (ASU). The following day, the decision was made by the Joint Intelligence Committee in London to accept that an attack was imminent. On 3 March a team of sixteen soldiers from the SAS Special Projects Team were dispatched to Gibraltar, all of them arriving on different flights and at different times. Their mission, code-named Operation Flavius, was to prevent the suspects from carrying out the attack. Having confirmed the target, it was up to the SAS to discover how the IRA would carry out its mission. Intelligence provided to the SAS team indicated that the terrorists were heavily armed and that the method of attack would almost certainly be via a remotely detonated bomb planted in a car, and parked next to the change of command. For this reason, the orders given to the SP Team were expanded to authorise the use of deadly force 'if those using them had reasonable grounds for believing an act was being committed or about to be committed which would endanger life or lives and if there was no other way of preventing that other than the use of firearms'. This was an important distinction, as a terrorist planning to set off a remote-controlled bomb could do so with the flick of a switch on a miniaturised detonator. This meant, to an experienced soldier, that any untoward movement – a hand moving to a pocket or bag – could indicate an attempt to detonate the bomb.

At 14.50 on 6 March the three IRA members were spotted entering the town centre. Savage had been watched earlier as he drove a white Renault 5 car into the main square and parked it next to the site where the changing of the guards would later take place. After strolling through the square for a short time, they met again in front of the Renault. Minutes later, the three left the area and began walking back towards the border to the north. Seizing the opportunity, an SAS bomb disposal expert ran to the Renault and quickly inspected it for any signs of a bomb. He reported back that while he could not see an explosive device, it was still possible that the vehicle could contain one, a fact that could not be determined with certainty without actually removing the car to a safe location and dismantling it. This, of course, was out of the question and the SAS had to assume that the Renault did in fact contain a bomb. Acting on the information, Gibraltar's police commissioner signed over authority for the arrests to the SAS. On the ground, a four-man SAS team trailing the IRA trio was given the go-ahead to neutralise the suspects and prepared to move in. Back at the operations centre, the police chief called over the radio for one of his men to return to base so that he would have a vehicle ready to transport the terrorists to jail. The officer acknowledged the call, but at the time found himself stuck in a long line of traffic. In an effort to expedite his return to base, he switched on his siren and pulled out onto the wrong side of the road. A short distance away, the sound of the siren rang out across the town square. Already tense from the days spent planning the upcoming car bombing, McCann and Farrell, who were walking together, froze. Looking around, they spotted the SAS men who were then only ten metres away. McCann then made what was deemed an 'aggressive movement' across the front of his body and the closest SAS trooper opened fire, striking him once in the back. In that instant, Farrell made a move for her handbag. Believing that the bag might contain the detonator, the trooper fired twice, killing her instantly. McCann, wounded but still believed to be a threat, was then shot five more times. A short distance away, Savage heard the gunfire and spun around directly into the two-man SAS team assigned to him. He was ordered to halt, but instead of raising his hands he put his right hand down to his jacket pocket. Again believing that a remote device could be concealed anywhere on his body, both soldiers opened fire, striking Savage between sixteen and eighteen times. Within a period of seconds, all the IRA terrorists were killed and an attack which could have killed and maimed scores of civilians was apparently prevented.

In the months that followed, a major inquiry into the incident was launched, amid accusations that the SAS had never intended to arrest the trio, but rather had been sent as part of an assassination team formed to eliminate three of the IRA's top operatives. Civilian eyewitnesses to the shootings claimed that the IRA operatives made gestures to surrender, but were shot anyway. The investigation also revealed some disturbing facts: none of the three, McCann, Farrell, or Savage, were armed at the time of the shootings. Nor did any of them have in their possession a remote detonation device. Finally, an examination of the Renault found no trace of explosives. A board of inquiry eventually acquitted the SAS soldiers. However, Operation Flavius remains a point of contention in Great Britain to this day.

GIBUSH

Israeli test period, usually a selection to get into SF units.

GOLDEN TEMPLE SEIGE – PARA COMMANDOS

On 4 June 1984, the Indian army stormed the Sikh Golden Temple in Amritsar, Punjab, in an effort to crush a two-year-old terrorist campaign by Sikh separatists. Three hundred died and hundreds were wounded in the daylong gun battle. The Sikh separatists had been using the temple as a refuge and a fortress. The Sikhs' fundamentalist leader Jarnail Singh Bhindranwale was killed. The government of Indian Prime Minister Indira Gandhi used force in its effort to keep the Indian federation together, but the action sparked a violent backlash by militant Sikhs.

GRAMS KILLING – GSG-9

In June 1994 German counter-terrorist units attempted to capture Red Army Faction leader Wolfgang Grams. In the shoot-out, Grams was killed. Later reports indicated that his death may not have occurred during the gun battle, but rather later when, it is alleged, GSG-9 troopers executed him shortly after subduing him. Retaliation followed when members of the offshoot group AIZ firebombed the home of a member of GSG-9. This alone was remarkable, as any and all personal information regarding the identities of GSG-9 members is classified top-secret. The fact that AIZ members located such a serving officer suggests RAF/AIZ may have had assistance from a 'mole' inside GSG-9 headquarters at the time.

GREASE

Slang word meaning 'To kill'.

GREECE

MILITARY SPECIAL FORCES
Army Special Forces Directorate

ETA (Ediko Tmima Alexiptotiston) or Special Airborne Unit   This is the nation's prime CT/HRU force and was formed in 1959 as an LRRP (Long-Range Reconnaissance Patrol) tasked for conducting operations similar to the British Special Air Service or the US Delta Force. It specialises in, among other techniques, intelligence-gathering, counter-terrorism, direct action raids, sabotage missions and strategic reconnaissance. This is a highly secretive unit, but it is known that they regularly carry out clandestine intelligence operations inside FYR Macedonia and other former Yugoslav Republics. ETA's main intelligence mission, however, and its prime areas of operation are the borders with Turkey, Cyprus and the disputed islands of the eastern Aegean Sea. This Greek Special Forces unit has gained a considerable reputation while on joint training exercises with other similar NATO units, apart from those of Turkey. They are considered to be an effective and hard-fighting force under most circumstances. ETA has trained with the Egyptian Unit-777 Counter-Terrorist unit and is believed to be developing considerable experience of operating in the Middle East. Its troops undergo extensive and gruelling training with an emphasis on mountain warfare. This is complemented by further courses on intelligence, surveillance, parachuting, unconventional warfare and combat swimming on the Greek Navy's MYK (underwater warfare) course and at NATO's LRRP School in Germany. ETA uses a wide variety of NATO and commercial weapons, including M16 assault rifles, M203 40mm grenade launchers and Belgian MINIMI 5.56mm light machine guns.

1st Commando Special Operations Regiment(Rangers)   Created in 1946 for specialist anti-communist operations and now a primary Counter-Insurgency unit with B Commando and D Commando in Macedonia, A Commando and E Commando in Thrace, while C Commando (Amphibious

Warfare) and 13th Commando Counter-Terrorist Regiment based in Athens. It is tasked with operations in and around the capital and for reinforcing Cyprus in the event of a Turkish invasion of Greek-Cypriot territory.

Navy
Monada Ypovrixion Kastrofon (MYK, 'Underwater Destruction Unit') This unit is the Greek Navy's special warfare unit. MYK is divided into four detachments, or OYKs (Omada Ymourhon Katastophan). MYK has four main missions: infiltration and sabotage of enemy shipping and bases; reconnaissance and pre-landing beach clearance; designation ordinance disposal; and Maritime Counter-Terrorism. Created in 1957, MYK's initial cadre consisted of two naval officers who were sent to the Little Creek Amphibious Base near Norfolk, Virginia to take the US Navy UDT/R training course (the forerunner to today's BUD/S course). Upon completion of training, the two men returned home and trained an additional dozen men. This group was assigned to the Greek Navy's amphibious operations command. In 1959 the unit established its own headquarters and training facilities at Squaramanga Naval Base, but additional training was provided by detachments of USN SEALs and UDT personnel. In 1970 the unit underwent a further reorganisation and is currently composed of 110 men divided into four operational detachments and a headquarters unit. Each detachment is composed of 25 men and specialises in a certain type of mission: OYK1 – unconventional warfare/intelligence missions; OYK2 – unconventional warfare/intelligence missions also; OYK3 – beach recon and hydrographic survey; OYK4 – EOD operations. There is also a reserve unit, OYK5, that would be activated during wartime. The MYK training course lasts approximately seven months. Training is divided into three phases, with the completion of the course consisting of a five-day-long 'hell week'. Candidates who successfully complete the course go on to attend the Greek airborne course before being assigned to their unit. During the Gulf War, two OYKs tasked with enforcing the UN embargo against Iraq managed to board and search some 217 merchant ships suspected of breaking UN sanctions on Iraq. Weapons in use include the M-16A2 and MP-11 assault rifles, the MP-5 sub-machine gun and the MG-3 7.62 light machine gun.

CIVILIAN SPECIAL FORCES
EKAM   is the police national counter-terrorist force. This 50-strong unit is based in Athens, but has several additional detachments in other major cities. Each officer is a full-time member who must have at least five years on the force before being allowed to try out. Many receive training from the Greek Army's Ranger School before going on to the police counter-terrorism school. EKAM officers are trained in shipboard and aircraft assaults as well as the normal bus and train assaults. Weapons in use include 9mm UZI and H&K MP5 SMG.

GREEN BERETS – US SPECIAL FORCES

Colonel Aaron Bank and Colonel Russell Volckmann, two OSS Officers who remained in the military after the war, worked tirelessly to convince the army to adopt the unconventional guerrilla-style force they had helped to pioneer during many Second World War covert operations. They had an ally in Brigadier General Robert McClure, who headed the Army's psychological warfare staff in the Pentagon. Bank and Volckmann convinced the army chiefs that there were areas in the world not susceptible to conventional warfare – Soviet-dominated Eastern Europe in particular – but which would make ideal targets for unconventional harassment and guerrilla fighting. It was a bold idea, one that went against the grain of traditional concepts, but by 1952 the US Army was finally ready to embark on a new era of unconventional warfare with the formal establishment of the Special Forces, a designation derived from the OSS whose operational teams in the field were given the same name in 1944.

The army allocated 2,300 personnel slots for the unit and assigned it to Fort Bragg, North Carolina. The new force recruited the best troops in the army, former OSS officers, airborne troops, ex-Ranger troops and combat veterans of the Second World War and Korea. Virtually all spoke at least two languages, had at least a sergeant's rank, and were trained in infantry and parachute skills. They were all volunteers willing to work behind enemy lines, in civilian clothes if necessary. This was important considering that if caught operating in civilian clothes, a soldier was no longer protected by the Geneva Convention and would more than likely be shot on sight if captured. The first unit was activated on 19 June 1952, at Fort Bragg. It was designated the 10th Special Forces Group, with Colonel Aaron Bank as commander, and unofficially adopted the Green Beret in honour of the British Second World War Commandos. As defined by the army, the main mission of SF unit was 'to infiltrate by land, sea or air, deep into enemy-occupied territory and organise the resistance/guerrilla potential to conduct Special Forces operations, with emphasis on guerrilla warfare'. But there were secondary missions as well. They included deep-penetration raids, intelligence missions and counter-insurgency operations. It was a tall order and one which demanded a commitment to professionalism and excellence perhaps unparalleled in American military history. Special Forces, however, were designed to spend months, even years, deep within hostile territory. They would have to be self-sustaining. They would have to speak the language of their target area. They would have to know how to survive on their own without extensive resupply from the outside.

On 11 November 1953, in the aftermath of an aborted uprising in East Germany, half of the 10th Special Forces Group was permanently deployed to Bad Tilz, West Germany. The other half remained at Fort Bragg, where they were redesignated as the 77th Special Forces Group. The split of the 10th and the 77th was the first sign that Special Forces had established themselves as an essential part of the army's basic structure. For the rest of the 1950s, Special Forces would grow slowly but consistently into a formidable organisation. On 1 April 1956, sixteen soldiers from the 77th were activated as the 14th Special Forces Operational Detachment; in June they were sent to Hawaii, and shortly thereafter to Thailand, Taiwan and Vietnam. Special Forces were now casting their sights on the Far East, departing from their previously heavy European orientation. The activation of the 14th SFOD was shortly followed by three other operational detachments, each designated for Asia and the Pacific – the 12th, 13th and 16th. These were soon combined into the 8231st Army Special Operational Detachment. On 17 June 1957 the 1st Special Forces Group was formed in Okinawa and became responsible for the Far Eastern theatre of operation. By 1958, the basic operational unit of Special Forces had emerged as a twelve-man team known as the A-detachment or A-team. Each member of the A-detachment – two officers, two operations and intelligence sergeants, two weapons sergeants, two communications sergeants, two medics and two engineers – were trained in unconventional warfare, were cross-trained in each others' specialties, and spoke at least one foreign language. This composition allowed each detachment to operate if necessary in two six-man teams, or split A-teams. By the time John F. Kennedy was inaugurated as President in January 1961, the three Special Forces groups – the 10th, the 7th (redesignated from the 77th on 6 June 1960) and the 1st—had firmly entrenched themselves as the Army's elite. In 1961, President Kennedy visited Fort Bragg. He inspected the 82nd Airborne Division and other conventional troops of the XVIII Airborne Corps and liked what he saw. But what he liked even more were the Special Forces. As a student of military affairs, President Kennedy had developed an interest in counter-insurgency – the art and method of defeating guerrilla movements. President Kennedy believed that the Special Forces gave him a unique chance to carry out US policy abroad while avoiding major military confrontations, particularly with the Communist Bloc. With the new administration firmly behind them, new Special Forces groups were rapidly established. On 21 September 1961, the 5th Group was activated followed in 1963 by the 8th Group on 1 April, the 6th on 1 May and the 3rd on 5 December. The fourteen-year-long involvement with Vietnam began in June 1956, when the original sixteen members of the 14th Special Forces Operational Detachment entered Vietnam to train a cadre of indigenous Vietnamese Special Forces teams. In that same year, on 21 October, the first American soldier died in Vietnam – Captain Harry G. Cramer Jr of the 14th SFOD. Throughout the remainder of the 1950s and early 1960s, the number of Special Forces military advisers in Vietnam steadily increased. Their responsibility was to train South

Vietnamese soldiers in the art of counter-insurgency and to mould various native tribes into a credible, anti-communist threat. During the early years, elements from the different Special Forces groups were involved in advising the South Vietnamese. But in September 1964, the first step was taken in making Vietnam the exclusive operational province of 5th Group when it set up its provisional headquarters in Nha Trang. Six months later in February, Nha Trang became the 5th's permanent headquarters. From that point, Vietnam was mainly the 5th's show, until 1971 when it returned to Fort Bragg.

Other Special Forces training teams were operating in the 1960s in Bolivia, Venezuela, Guatemala, Colombia and the Dominican Republic. Counter-insurgency forces of the 8th Special Forces Group conducted clandestine operations against guerrilla forces, carrying out some 450 missions between 1965 and 1968. In 1968, Special Forces were involved in tracking down and capturing the notorious Cuban revolutionary, Che Guevara, in south-central Bolivia. South-east Asia, however, was to remain the Special Forces' primary focus. Through their unstinting labours, Special Forces troops eventually established 254 outposts throughout Vietnam, many of them defended by a single A-team and hundreds of friendly natives. The SF were also responsible for training thousands of Vietnam's ethnic tribesmen in the techniques of guerrilla warfare. They took the Montagnards, the Nungs, the Cao Dei and others and moulded them into the 60,000-strong Civil Irregular Defence Group (CIDG). CIDG troops became the Special Forces' most valuable ally in battles fought in faraway corners of Vietnam, out of reach of conventional back-up forces. Other missions included civic-action projects, in which Special Forces troops built schools, hospitals and government buildings, provided medical care to civilians and dredged canals. This was the flip side of the vicious battles, the part of the war designed to win the hearts and minds of a distant and different people. But although the Special Forces drew the allegiance of civilians almost everywhere they went, the war as a whole was not as successful.

President Lyndon Johnson had committed the first major conventional units to the war in March 1965, when Marine battalions landed at Da Nang to provide perimeter security to its air base. Then in June, the Army's 173rd Airborne Brigade entered the country, followed in July by the 1st Air Cavalry Division. From then on, a continual stream of army and marine units flowed into Vietnam until they numbered over 500,000 by 1968. But although American conventional forces scored successes in every major battle they fought, there was still no clear end in sight to a war many Americans back home regarded as a quagmire. So in 1969, after President Richard M. Nixon took office, the United States began its withdrawal from Vietnam, a process known as Vietnamisation. Gradually the Special Forces turned over their camps to the South Vietnamese. On 5 March 1971, 5th Group returned to

Fort Bragg, although some Special Forces teams remained in Thailand from where they launched secret missions into Vietnam. But by the end of 1972, the Special Forces role in Vietnam was over.

The years immediately following Vietnam were lean ones for the Special Forces. The 3rd, 6th and 8th Special Forces groups were inactivated, and there was a general de-emphasis of Special Operations as the Army concentrated once more on conventional warfare, turning its gaze from the jungles of Asia to the well-worn tank paths of Europe. However, the SF were designed to train and fight unconventional warfare, and as President Ronald W. Reagan took office in 1981, they got that chance once again. With the advent of the Reagan presidency, defence policy received a renewed emphasis. Special Forces in particular were among the beneficiaries of this new attention. The need for Special Forces capabilities had become apparent with the rise of insurgencies as far away as Africa and Asia, and as close to home as Central America. To meet the challenges of a changing world, the army injected a revitalised esprit into the Special Forces. The Special Forces qualification course was made longer and tougher to see that only the highest-calibre soldiers joined ranks with the Green Berets. In June 1983, the army authorised a uniform tab for wear on the left shoulder solely by Special Forces troops. The army established on 1 October 1984, a separate career field for Special Forces. The warrant officer career field soon followed and, on 9 April 1987, the Army Chief of Staff established a separate branch of the army for Special Forces officers. During the 1980s, Special Forces teams were deployed to dozens of countries around the globe, facing the challenges of foreign internal defence. Missions varied from training US-allied armies to defend themselves, to offering humanitarian aid, like medical care and building construction, in remote villages of Third World countries on nearly every continent. Special Forces proved particularly successful in El Salvador and Honduras, preventing civil war in neighbouring Nicaragua from spreading beyond its border. The Special Forces train foreign units and indeed are involved in conflicts in every continent – from Colombia and Ecuador, to the Balkans, Nigeria, Pakistan to Indonesia. With the events of 9-11 affecting every aspect of the US military, the Green Berets in particular are likely to have more demands made on their manpower than perhaps any other unit. Afghanistan in 2001, Iraq in 2002 and an ever growing variety of commitments have probably been pencilled in for the next ten years at least.

GRENADES

Widely used by terrorists and insurgents, but also of great value to the Special Forces. Lightweight, easy to use and effective if properly used. Smoke to cover an approach or retreat, white-phosphorous is a highly effective anti-personnel weapon, fragmentation for house clearing operations, while 'flash-bangs' and

CS gas grenades are used in hostage rescue situations. Typical Russian grenades include the RGD-5 Fragmentation with a lethal radius of 18–20m, the F1 and the RPG series. Common US grenades include the M26 Fragmentation, reportedly made famous in Vietnam by the number of times unpopular officers had a grenade tossed into their trench by young American soldiers more interested in safely completing their tour of duty than in fighting the communist enemy, simply and appropriately known as 'fragging'. Grenades are now made in dozens of different countries and the variety that a Special Forces unit may come across is bewildering, both as hand-thrown and rifle-launched grenades.

GUATEMALA

MILITARY SPECIAL FORCES
Special Operations Units

The Agrupacion (Brigada) Kaibil based at the Centro de Adiestramiento y Operaciones Especiales at El Infierno, Peten. Kaibil meaning 'strongest men' in the Quiche language, are specialist jungle fighters considered to be the best troops in the army and consist of two operational groups, and a third as a cadre unit for training and reinforcement purposes. Each group has 162 men, with four platoons of 38, each of three or four nine-man squads. Each squad has a leader and two four-man fire teams. Further to this, five brigades and fifteen military regions each have a fifteen-man Kaibil platoon, under their direct command. Neither the parachute troops nor the Kaibils have any heavy weapons, normal weapons being MP12 SMGs, M4 carbines, M16A2 and M203 grenade launchers, MAG58 GPMGs, rifle grenades and SOLTAM 60mm Commando mortars. Black berets are worn by the paras, maroon by the Kabil.

Guatemala has for much of the last 45 years been one of the most fascist and repressive regimes in the world, and its Special Forces, trained and equipped by the United States, have been the instrument of that oppression. Once again the military operations have been closely linked to right-wing paramilitaries, such as the Ejercito Secreto Anti-Comunista (ESA) which were backed by the government in its massive campaign of abduction, torture and murder of anyone even vaguely left wing. They were in turn aided by the Mano Blanca or White Hand gangs of off-duty Special Forces and Security personnel, who were violent racists and had close links to the American Ku Klux Klan. Their death squads were to kill countless thousands of the native Indian peoples.

Air Force The Agrupacion Tactica de Seguridad (ATS) garrisoned at La Aurora Air Base. It has three counter-insurgency companies, in the airmobile rapid reaction force role. It also has a small armoured reconnaissance squadron with five light armoured vehicles called Armadillos, and an air defence battery with four M55A2 20mm guns.

Marines   organised into two battalions with a total of 700 men at the Pacific Naval Base (BANAPAC) and the Atlantic Naval Base (BANATLAN). Small detachments are assigned as reconnaissance units with army task forces operating near waterways. Trained at the Centro de Adiestramiento de Infanteria de Marina (CAIMAN), at the Sipacate Naval Base.

GUINEA

MILITARY SPECIAL FORCES
One Special Forces battalion. Receives some support in the way of weapons and training from the French Special Forces.

GUINEA-BISSAU

MILITARY SPECIAL FORCES
The single Commando Company exists to protect the President, it has little in the way of any genuine training or discipline.

GUYANA

MILITARY SPECIAL FORCES
One Special Forces anti-terrorist company which is trained and equipped with the help of the British SAS. It is intended that it should develop a genuine hostage rescue team in 2002.

H-HOUR

Scheduled time of commencement of a military operation.

HAHO

High Altitude/High Opening – 'Stand-off parachuting'. This technique allows the insertion aircraft to remain in friendly airspace with the parachutist having a long flight to the DZ or Dropping Zone after release at up to 25,000ft (8km). In free-fall for only a few seconds, the parachutist uses the advanced wing or foil canopies that provide similar aerodynamic properties to an aircraft wing. The low rate of descent and high forward speed, allied to the enhanced manoeuvrability, allows the parachutist to fly quickly to a DZ up to 35 miles (56km) inside hostile territory. A standard parachute with a low glide ratio opened at the same height would simply drift with a prevailing wind, and even the most experienced jumper would have considerable difficulty in accurately reaching a DZ more than four miles (6km) from release point and having spent a dangerously long time in the air as well.

The HAHO technique demands great skill and pinpoint accuracy. The operation is more likely to be carried out at night and the distance to the DZ may be masked by low-cloud. Therefore chest-pack navigation sets are used to monitor their exact position at any given time with GPS (Global Positioning System) using a reference to navigation satellites such as NAVSTAR. HAHO is most commonly used by the Special Forces and other intelligence-based operations.

HALO

High Altitude/Low Opening – 'Military free-fall'. This technique provides a fast, clandestine delivery of forces onto a DZ. Parachutists leaving an aircraft at over 30,000ft (10kms) and maintaining the stable ('Frog') position in free-fall for around two minutes, deploy the canopy at around 2,000ft (0.6km) spending only a further two or three minutes in flight before reaching the DZ. The problems compared to HAHO are magnified by the speed of descent, which will usually vary between 120mph (200kph) and 180mph (300kph), and the heavy rucksack (or Bergen) slung low on the back of the main parachute, and the personal weapon usually attached to the parachute harness along the length of the soldier's body.

Should an emergency occur, the resulting 14G breaking shock effect of the parachute opening at such speed could inflict severe damage on both the parachutist and his canopy. Hypoxia ('blacking out' due to oxygen deficiency) is a serious problem for free-fallers and is largely overcome by the provision of several minutes' supply of oxygen though, as an additional safety feature, barometric triggers are filled in case the parachutist is temporarily unable to deploy his parachute. The 'wind-chill' factor of a combination of speed and high altitude is overcome by the provision of specialised warm clothing and warming the oxygen supply used to prevent hypoxia. HALO-qualified soldiers need constant training and superb physical conditioning, 'Military free-fall' techniques are dangerous and hard to perfect, though they are an essential part of a Special Forces capability – it is very much a case of regular practice if not making perfect, certainly saving lives. Later US developments are believed to include the capability for automated self-steering canisters to be dropped by aircraft at up to 35,000ft (11.3km), free-falling 34,000ft and only deploying the parachute at around 1,000ft and dropping the final 800ft or so at very slow speed. The dropping time would be activated by a laser beam directed by a Special Forces team on the ground and the entire flight would be guided by on-board computerised steering with an accuracy believed to be within 30m (33 yards) on the target. It is anticipated that this will prove a highly useful method of clandestine insertion of arms and equipment, needed in Special Forces operations inside potentially hostile territories, where the personnel involved have entered openly as tourists, on business, or have been infiltrated under conditions which largely preclude the movement of heavier weapons and electronic equipment.

HARD DOG

Specially trained attack dogs, sometimes known as 'War Dogs'. Usually picked for their strength, ferocity and bravery, they are often the most feared of all opponents when on a clandestine patrol in hostile territory. A range of special silent weapons, chemical sprays and fast-acting poisons have been developed over the years to deal with guard and attack dogs.

HEAD SHED

SAS term for those 'in authority'. Can refer to officers or NCOs.

HECKLER & KOCH WEAPONS

H & K MP5 AND MP201 One of the most widely used weapons by Special Forces and an important series of MP5 sub-machine guns (MP derives from Maschinen-Pistole) have been developed since its original introduction in 1965, including the MP5A2 which has a plastic in-line butt and a pistol grip and is chambered for 9mm, with either a fifteen or thirty-round straight or curved magazine. With a cyclic rate of 800rpm (rounds per minute), a selector switch allows for single shots, a two to four round burst or fully automatic. Standard sights are calibrated to 440yds (400m), though the maximum effective killing range is less than half that. The MP5A3 used by the SAS in the Iranian Embassy Siege is identical, except that is fitted with a retractable tubular metal stock, reducing the overall length and making it more suitable for Special Operations. The main drawback to the excellent silenced versions is the perennial problem of such modifications, a substantially reduced maximum effective range. However, these are superb weapons and widely used; MP5SD1 without a stock, MP5SD2 with a fixed plastic butt and MP5SD3 with a metal stock. The MP5SD is fitted with an integral silencer. The bolt noise is absorbed by rubber buffers and when used with subsonic ammunition this weapon is virtually silent from only fifteen feet away. A covert action variation, the MP5K is miniaturised to be as easy to conceal as a pistol — no stock, a shortened barrel and an extra forward handgrip. Though it only has the range of a typical handgun, its additional accuracy and weight of fire can be vital in counter-terrorist operations. The later MP5KAI is a special version with no protrusions allowing it to be carried under clothing or in a special holster. The MP-5 series of sub-machine guns has seen more counter-terrorist action the world over than any other weapon. It is only natural that its direct descendant, the MP-2013, carries on the tradition. The MP-2013 differs little from the original MP-5 in design, except that it has been chambered for 10mm rather than 9mm. Some of the MP-2013's improvements are its compound plastic body and integral silencing. The most common model used in counter-terrorist forces is the MP-2013SD. The SD's main difference is that it includes a flash suppresser and an improved silencer (cannot be heard without cyberaudio). This makes the weapon slightly longer than normal, and also decreases the weapon's range by about 50m. The flash suppresser is a great asset to Special Ops units raiding buildings where any spark might send the structure sky high (drug labs, chemical storage dumps, bomb-making facilities, etc.). The MP-2013SD can be seen in service with the SAS, SBS and GSG9 as well as with the DEA, and SWAT teams around the world

H & K PSG1 The PSG1 is a semi-automatic 7.62mm sniper's rifle with a free-floating bull barrel and single adjustable trigger. A heavyweight weapon at around 17.5 lb (8kg) and is therefore most often used for precision kills from a fixed position. The stock has an adjustable cheek pad, while a pistol grip and butt plate all help to extend stability and the sniper's comfort zone. Equipped with a bipod and either a five-round or 20-round box magazine the PSG1 has an enviable reputation as an excellent sniper's weapon. It is equipped with a sight such as the Hensoldt Wetzler 6x42 which is adjustable from 100m to 600m, and which also has an integral battery-powered illumination unit for the cross-hairs in low-light shooting situations. This sight also is very fast in engaging multiple targets.

This famous German arms manufacturer is now British owned.

HEREFORD – SAS DEPOT

For just over 40 years this quiet English town, not far from the border with Wales, has played host to the 22nd Regiment of the SAS. After the Regiment was re-created in 1952, it served in Malaya from 1952–58 and the Jebel Akhdar campaign in Oman 1958–59. The SAS was re-established in the British Army's ORBAT (Order of Battle) in 1958 and opened its new depot and training centre at Merebrook Camp in Malvern, Worcestershire. A dilapidated former emergency military hospital, its low-lying and decaying Nissen huts regularly flooded in winter and had remained largely unused since 1945. The Regiment moved with some relief to the former Royal Artillery Boys' training unit at Bradbury Lines, Lower Bullingham, in the south-eastern suburbs of Hereford in 1960. The depot and training centre, which would eventually house the CQB 'killing house' among other sensitive facilities, was sometime later renamed 'Stirling Lines' after the founder of the SAS, Colonel David Stirling. As the town grew in size and the demands for added security for the Regiment increased, a decision was made to move the SAS to the recently vacated RAF base at Credenhill on the other side of Hereford. Rebuilding began in 1997 and the Regiment transferred to its new state-of-the-art facilities in May 1999. The base was officially opened on 30 September 2000 retaining the name 'Stirling Lines' and includes the famous clocktower, which has been re-erected on the new parade ground.

HOLLYWOOD IMAGE – GRITTY REALITY

The Special Forces Group, popularly known as the Green Berets, was created in 1952 to carry out US foreign policy largely in the Third World and to confront the communist menace in the Cold War.

The heroic image so beloved of the flag-waving patriots created by countless clean-cut film heroes of the John Wayne variety is far from the reality of the mean, murderous and often ineffectual military operations that have occupied the Green Berets, in common with most other Special Forces units, for much of the last 50 years. Though Hollywood obviously needs very little official encouragement to continue to churn out glossy pot-boilers such as *Black Hawk Down*, the majority are at best a distorted version of the truth, and at worst total fantasy, with the suspicion that some are actually based deliberately on official propaganda to obscure inconvenient or politically embarrassing facts. Much of the Green Berets' day-to-day work involves assistance to foreign countries, training and advising Special Forces from Colombia to Indonesia. The unpalatable fact is that this is entirely in keeping with an underlying and long-running US covert policy. The military assistance is provided for two main reasons: one, to use the foreign forces as surrogates, mercenaries, canon-fodder if you like in various US proxy-wars; and secondly, and if circumstances and allegiances change, to ensure that the United States knows the true capabilities of any particular force it might be called upon to fight. As any experienced Special Forces commander would probably confirm, this is a vital consideration in a world of ever changing threats and regional alliances.

HONDURAS

MILITARY SPECIAL FORCES
Special Tactical Group Tamara/Fco Morazan
2nd Airborne Infantry Battalion – Tamara
Special Forces Battalion – El Cajon
Special Night Operations Troops (Rangers) – Tamara

Special Forces School and Parachute School — Tamara
Commando de Operaciones Espaciales (COE) of the Honduras Army SF
Command

This is the National HRU, formed in 1983 with a strength of 60. Trained by US SF advisers, the recruits from the Airborne Battalions are given additional training in hostage rescue, anti-terrorist and counter-insurgency tactics. They are equipped with a variety of modern weapons including 9mm UZI SMG, 5.56mm CAR-15 and GALIL assault rifles, Remington 700 and M21 sniper rifles and the Remington 1100 shotgun.

CIVILIAN SPECIAL FORCES

'COBRAS' Political Squadron of the FUSEP (Public Security Force)   This SWAT-like unit receives limited training in HRU and Airborne Special Forces tactics.

HUMAN TORPEDOES AND COMBAT SWIMMERS – ITALY

In October 1935 two young Italian naval architects, T. Tesei and E. Toschi, submitted plans for the first human torpedo, the Siluro a lenta corsa (SLC) or 'slow course torpedo' for use by combat swimmers. A working prototype had been built and tested at La Spezia by the end of 1936 and a special department undertook research and training until Italy's entry into war on 10 June 1940. The role envisaged for the SLCs, or maiali ('pigs'), was that of clandestine Special Forces attacks on the British naval bases at Gibraltar, Malta and Alexandria, and a number of submarines were modified to carry these SLCs. The first unsuccessful attempt was made in August 1940 with a raid on Alexandria, with the Italian submarine Iride carrying the SLCs. On 22 August the Iride was spotted in the Gulf of Bomba and sunk by aircraft from the carrier HMS Eagle. But the secret of the SLCs was still intact and a double operation was planned for September, with the submarines Sciré carrying SLCs to attack Gibraltar, and Gondar similarly equipped to attack Alexandria. Sciré found no worthwhile targets at Gibraltar and returned to base. Gondar, similarly unsuccessful at Alexandria, was depth-charged and sunk on her return journey. Although the SLC crews were captured with Gondar's crew the Royal Navy still knew nothing of the SLC programme and a further attempt on Gibraltar was made in November 1940, again with Sciré. This time a rich prize was spotted in Gibraltar: the battleship HMS Barham. Two of Sciré's three SLCs broke down after launching; their crews scuttled the SLCs and escaped into Spain. The crew of the third, piloted by Lieutenant Birindelli, nearly succumbed to oxygen poisoning from their highly dangerous breathing apparatus, but not before Birindelli, on the edge of unconsciousness, dragged his SLC to within 30 yards of the battleship. On the night of 25–26 July 1941 the Italians attempted a combined attack on the naval base at Malta. It was an audacious plan, reflecting highly on the courage of the Italian volunteers. High-speed explosive motorboats were to blast breaches in the protective booms and nets, allowing two SLCs to penetrate the harbour. Radar alerted the British defences and the attack was smashed; one of the SLCs blew up but the other was salvaged and examined. Even this disaster did not lead to the abandonment of the SLC programme and on 20 September 1941 the tanker SS *Denbydale* was badly damaged in Gibraltar by an SLC charge fixed to the bilge keel. The attack was launched from the submarine *Sciré*. The most famous SLC attack of the war was also launched from *Sciré* two months later, on the British battleships HMS *Queen Elizabeth* and HMS *Valiant* in Alexandria harbour on the night of 18–19 November 1941. Three SLCs penetrated Alexandria, two of which laid their warheads correctly. The attack commander, Count Luigi de la Pene, was captured with his second in command, Bianchi, and interrogated aboard HMS *Valiant*. The prisoners were held deep within the battleship until de la Pene, knowing that nothing the British did now would be of any use, confirmed that explosives had been placed beneath both ships and were due to detonate within minutes. The Italians were back on deck when the two battleships were shaken by the violent explosions and settled in the shallow water onto the harbour bed. The Italian Navy now had the domination of the Mediterranean within its grasp, but the opportunity was wasted. Both battleships still had their upper decks well above water and were able to simulate readiness for sea by emitting funnel smoke, confusing photo-reconnaissance aircraft into believing that the ships remained undamaged. With the four men from the other two SLCs all captured ashore, it was not until months later that the Italian Navy learned what a chance they had missed. For the time being, the British had no answer to SLC attacks apart from vigilance and the formation of special diving parties to search ships' bottoms for unexploded charges.

Another method of attack tried by the Italians was by swimmers from the *Folgore*, an Italian ship interned at Algeciras, across the bay from Gibraltar. Yet another interned ship, the *Olterra*, was modified to create a special underwater compartment from which SLCs could be launched and proceed directly across to Gibraltar. The first SLC attack from the *Olterra* on 7 December 1942, failed. The three craft were spotted during the approach; one was damaged by depth charges, the second came under machine-gun fire and returned to *Olterra*, while the crew of the third was killed by explosive charges. It took until May 1943 before enough parts and personnel had been smuggled through Spain to the *Olterra* for another three-craft attack on Gibraltar. On 8 May 1943 three SLCs evaded the British patrols and fixed their charges to three merchant ships at Gibraltar, sinking one of the ships and badly damaging the other two. All three SLCs returned to *Olterra*, but as it took so long to replenish the SLC team through Spain, there was only time for one more attack, which sank two cargo ships and a 10,000-ton tanker in August 1943, just before Italy left the Axis and joined the Allies for the remainder of the war.

HUNGARY

MILITARY SPECIAL FORCES

88th Airmobile Battalion (Rapid Reaction) – Szolnok.   This unit has replaced its Warsaw Pact era equipment with a range of German, French and US weapons and surveillance gear. It now trains with Western Special Forces, is developing a genuine hostage rescue capability and is seeking to become a fully integrated member of the anti-terrorist alliance.

CIVILIAN SPECIAL FORCES

Rendöri Kulonleges Szolgalat (RKSZ – Police Special Service)   A rapid-reaction force, part of which is a dedicated anti-terrorist and hostage rescue section.

Weapons used include the 9mm IMI Model 941 Jericho pistol, 9mm FÉG P9R pistol, 7.65mmSR CZ vz.61 Skorpion machine pistol, 9mm FÉG KGP9 sub-machine gun, 9mm IMI Model 46 Mini-Uzi sub-machine gun, a few 9mm H&K MP5SD3 suppressed sub-machine guns, the 7.62mm FÉG AMD-65 assault carbine (cut-down AKMS), 7.62mm IMI Model 339 Galil SR sniper rifle, 7.62mmR Izhmash SVD sniper rifle, 7.62mm SIG-Sauer SG2000 bolt-action sniper rifle and 18.5mmR (12-gauge) Beretta RS-200P pump-action shotgun. In late 2000, the 9mm H&K USP pistol was adopted.

HUSH PUPPY

The US Navy sponsored the development of a silenced pistol for use by its SEALs teams during the Vietnam War. Nicknamed the 'Hush Puppy' because of the cover story for its intended use, that of killing guard dogs, this modified steel-framed Smith & Wesson Model-39 pistol was used for eliminating sentries and for assassinations during Project Phoenix, a CIA covert operation that ran from 1967 to 1971 and saw the assassination of up to 30,000 suspected Vietcong supporters by US and South Vietnamese forces. As the Mark 3 Mod 0, this weapon needed the insert in the silencer replaced after every sixth shot. A highly effective weapon and one that in a modified form is still available to US Special Forces and the CIA alike.

IA

Immediate Action.

INCREMENT – SAS

The Increment is a highly trained and selected group of SAS and SBS personnel specialising in intelligence-gathering and covert actions, detached from normal duties to carry out operations on behalf of the Secret Intelligence Service (SIS or MI6). The unit is made up of both serving and recently retired personnel working closely with the SIS 'paramilitary' Special Operations Directorate. The dissident SIS officer Richard Tomlinson has publicly accused this unit of being involved in SIS-sponsored plans to assassinate foreign leaders, including Serbia's Slobodan Milosevic. In 1998 Tomlinson confirmed the existence of the unit, which he described as 'a small cell of the SAS and SBS which is especially selected and trained to carry out operations exclusively for MI5/MI6,' and indeed of a written assassination plan. He claimed that the document proposed three methods of assassinating Milosevic. The first method was to train and equip a Serbian paramilitary opposition group to assassinate Milosevic in Serbia. An MI6 Officer called Fishwick argued that this method would have the advantage of deniability, but with the disadvantage that control of the operation would be low and the chances of success unpredictable. The second method was to use The Increment to infiltrate Serbia and attack Milosevic either with a bomb or in a sniper ambush. The MI6 officer argued that this plan would be the most reliable, but would be undeniable if it went wrong. The third proposal was to kill Milosevic in a staged car crash, possibly during one of his visits to the ICFY (International Conference on the Former Yugoslavia) in Geneva, Switzerland. Chillingly, the MI6 Officer even provided a suggestion about how this could be done, namely disorientating Milosevic's chauffeur using a blinding strobe light as the cavalcade passed through one of Geneva's motorway tunnels.

Whatever the truth of such stories The Increment has been used as the covert 'strong-arm' of the Intelligence Service since the downgrading of its own military capability in the 1970s. Operations against terrorist threats to Intelligence officers and facilities and providing protection for senior officers are certainly part of their remit. However, with the growth of international terrorism and the greater awareness of the threat since 9-11, this secretive but highly effective unit may eventually be absorbed into a greatly expanded SIS covert military capability.

INDIA

MILITARY SPECIAL FORCES

The Para-Commandos are now India's premier Special Forces, formed after the 1965 Indo-Pakistan war highlighted the need for a much-enhanced Special Operations capability. Since 1978–79 the Para-Commandos have been trained in advanced parachute techniques, with their trademark black jump suits, wrist altimeters, square canopy, leaf pattern parachutes, and armed with modern automatic weapons, grenades and a jack knife. This unit provides the Indian Army with a powerful and adaptable Special Force capability, tasked for a wide range of counter-insurgency and anti-terrorist missions. Their tasks include clandestine operations, sabotage and intelligence-gathering behind the enemy's front line. Their training is of the highest quality, consisting of marksmanship, combat shooting, heliborne-insertion, combat swimming, explosives ordnance disposal, mountain warfare techniques, prisoner of war rescue, surveillance and HALO and HAHO (High Altitude Low/High Opening). They regularly cross-train with Special Forces from other armies and personnel are sent abroad on specialist courses. Weapons in use include the 9mm Israeli UZI and 9mm German MP5A2/3 sub-machine guns, 5.56mm US M16A2 assault rifles, and a range of specialist sniper rifles including the 7.62 mm Mauser SP66, PSG-1/MSG-90 and the SSG-2000. They are equipped with a wide range of specialist communications and GPS. India has long maintained a number of elite airborne units. The first airborne units were formed by the British, during the Second World War. When India gained its independence in 1947, it retained a number of its former airborne units, with the remainder being transferred to the new Pakistani Army. During the 1965 Indo-Pakistani War, the Indian army authorised the formation of an *ad hoc* commando unit known as 'Meghdoot Force' and was organised by Lieutenant Colonel Megh Singh of the Brigade of Guards. The unit performed successfully in combat, and the army authorised the Parachute Regiment to form a permanent para-commando unit. The new unit was raised in June of 1966 and, designated as the 9th Battalion, was followed by the 10th Battalion formed in 1968–69. During the 1971 Indo-Pakistani War, both Para-Commando Battalions saw combat. The 9th Para-Commando Battalion was committed to the Kashmir region. The Battalion was divided into three combat groups, lettered A-C, with each group being assigned to a different infantry division. A group was primarily used in a static defence role. B group conducted operations in the Jammu-Chhamb sector. C group conducted a raid against a Pakistani artillery battery. The 10th Para-Commando Battalion, which was also divided into the lettered combat groups, operated in the Thar Desert of Rajasthan. The Battalion's A and C groups conducted raids against several Pakistani targets, including a Jeep raid conducted by C group, on the Pakistani town of Islamkot. During the late 1970s the army authorised the formation of a third para-commando battalion. The 1st Parachute Battalion (1st Punjab) in 1978 was chosen, and was soon redesignated as the 1st Para-Commando Battalion, but unlike the other two Para Commando Battalions, the 1st Para-Commando Battalion was not assigned a geographic specialty, but instead was designated as the Parachute Regiment's strategic reserve force. During this same period Indian airborne units had been experimenting with military free-fall parachuting techniques, developing a HALO/HAHO capability. In June of 1984, an 80-strong element of 1st Para-Commando Battalion was involved in Operation 'Blue Star'. Sikh separatists had fortified an area of stone buildings in Punjab known as the 'Golden Temple'. The Indian government ordered an operation to regain control of the area. After a paramilitary commando unit of the Special Frontier Forces, which was assigned the task, but failed to lift the siege, the para-commandos were ordered to take over. Tasked with leading the army's assault on the complex and neutralising Sikh machine gun positions the para-commandos suffered heavy casualities, with over half the force being killed or wounded, but they were successful in fulfilling their mission. In July of 1987 10th Para-Commando Battalion was assigned to the Indian Peacekeeping Force (IPKF) deployed to the nation of Sri Lanka. The Sri Lankan government had been conducting a counter-insurgency campaign against Tamil guerrillas. Under pressure from India, Sri Lanka allowed the deployment of the IPKF, which was supposed to arrange the disarmament of the Tamil forces. Instead it only made matters worse, with Indian forces becoming involved in a number of clashes with Tamil forces. The situation came to a head when a group of Indian commandos was kidnapped, and killed by Tamil guerrillas. In retaliation the Indian government launched Operation Pawan. On 3 November 1988, the small island nation of the Maldives was taken over by a force of Sri Lankan mercenaries. The Maldivian President requested assistance from the Indian government and a military force was dispatched to the island. Among the units that compromised this force was the 10th Para-Commando Battalion. The force was successful in regaining control of the island and spent the next several days hunting down the fleeing mercenaries. On 1 February, 1996, the latest addition to the Para-Commando family was raised. The 21st Maratha Light Infantry was redesignated 21st Para-Commando Battalion and now specialises in jungle warfare operations. The major commitment for India's Special Forces continues to be Kashmir, where units operate both in the counter-terrorist role and in preparation for aggressive operations deep into Pakistan-controlled territory to find and destroy the Islamic separatists' main training camps. The continued threat of Chinese intervention along India's long and vulnerable northern frontier, the insurgency in Nepal and continuing ethnic violence in Assam and the North-East Frontier Area also place a further strain on Special Forces manpower.

SCTU Special Counter-Terrorist Unit   of the Para-Commandos, is around 100-strong, formed in 1979 and reputed to be Asia's finest HRU. It operates as part of the Special Frontier Force based at Sarsawa airbase in Uttar Pradesh. Extremely well-trained SCTU personnel are airborne- and commando- trained before joining; they then develop a wide range of specialist HRU skills including CQB, breaching, rappelling, surveillance techniques, communications and the use of explosives.

Navy

The Marine Commando Force (MCF – MARCOS)   For many years, the Indian
Navy had wanted to establish an elite force for special maritime operations
and the Indian Marine Special Force (IMSF) was formally raised in February
1987. The IMSF first went into action a few months afterwards in Sri Lanka
to fight against the LTTE (Liberation of Tamil Tigers Eelan). During
Operation Pawan, a single battalion of the Army's 340th Independent
Brigade, raised in 1983 and trained for maritime operations, left the naval
base of Vizag for Jaffna and Batticaloa in Sri Lanka on board landing ships,
together with a detachment of the IMSF which was to provide the beach
reconnaissance party. As one of the first IPKF units to be deployed, the 340th
Brigade served until operations in the Tricomalee area were complete.
Besides leading the beach landings, the IMSF also provided security patrols
along the coastal road, west of Jaffna, until the Army's 41st Brigade was
deployed to take charge. On 21 October 1987, a Indian naval force
conducted a successful amphibious raid against a LTTE base at Guru Nagar.
In 1991, the IMSF had its name changed to the Marine Commando Force
(MCF). MCF trainees now have to complete a two-year course, the first
phase of which lasts one month. The tests are so hard that the failure rate is
about 50 per cent, but for the successful recruits there is another nine
months during which trainees are taught how to use different types of
weapons, conduct special warfare techniques and how to gather tactical
intelligence. The MCF also conducts operational reconnaissance training,
which includes a variety of environments: beach, coastal, riverine and jungle.
This part of training is conducted in co-operation with other Indian Special
Forces at the Combined Commando School at Sirsawa. They also have to
undergo a parachute-training course and a diving course at Agra and Cochin.
It has a strength of some 1,500, with three main MCF groups detached to the
three naval commands; Bombay (West), Cochin (South) and Vizag (East).
INS Abhimanyu, in Bombay, is where most of the specialised MCF training
is now done. Each of the three main MCF groups have smaller integral units
known as the Quick Reaction Section (QRS) about the size of a large platoon
and tasked for counter-terrorism and specialised warfare. Unlike standard
MCF units, which are armed with weapons like the 7.62mm assault rifle and
the Sterling Mk.4 sub-machine gun, the QRS use AK-47 assault rifles and
MP-5 sub-machine guns. Although all the MCF members are qualified
parachutists and undergo a combat divers' course, only a few manage to
complete the free-fall (HALO) parachute training, and it is these elite that are
usually selected for operations with Cosmos CE-2F/X100 two-man subs.
When the MCF's role was expanded to include attacks on harbour facilities
and the sabotage of enemy ships, the navy chose the Italian Cosmos CE-
2F/X100 as the delivery vehicle, and eleven vehicles were bought in 1990. It
has a length of seven metres, a weight of 2100kg, and a maximum

underwater combat range of 25 nautical miles. It carries two operators and is fitted with a forward compartment for carrying special equipment like heavy explosive charges or limpet anti-ship mines.

MARCOS is currently very active in Jammu and Kashmir as part of the army's counter-terrorist efforts. Their main task is to control the infiltration of terrorists from Pakistan to Jammu and Kashmir through Jhelum River and Wullar, a 65sq. km freshwater lake. Clad in wet suits or BDUs and riding on inflatable raiding craft, they interdict arms supplies and fresh militants crossing over into Indian territory.

The Special Frontier Force (SFF) was created on 14 November 1962, near the end of the Indo-China War. The Cabinet Secretariat had ordered the raising of an elite Special Forces-Commando force composed mainly of Tibetan refugees. Its main goal was to conduct covert operations behind Chinese lines in the event of another Indo-China war. The SFF made its home base at Chakrata, 100km from the city of Dehra Dun. Chakrata was home to the large Tibetan refugee population and a mountain town in the foothills of the Himalayas. Starting with a force of 12,000 men, the SFF commenced six months of training in mountain and guerrilla warfare. The RAW Intelligence agency from India and the US CIA also helped in raising the force, as it was considered a valuable potential source of information about Chinese military dispositions within Tibet. The SFF's weapons were all provided by the US and consisted mainly of M-1, M-2 carbines and M-3 sub-machine guns. In 1964 the SFF began its airborne training at Agra, later to establish its own airborne training programme at Sarasawan airbase near Saharanpur. By the late 1960s, the SFF was organised into six battalions, each consisting of six companies, and was commanded by a Tibetan lieutenant colonel, and the number of Tibetan officers and NCOs has increased markedly since. To some the SFF appears to form a Tibetan army in exile, though the chances of the Chinese ever relinquishing control of Tibet is remote. Despite this the SFF has conducted limited cross-border reconnaissance operations, as well as highly classified raids to place sensors in the Himalayas to detect Chinese nuclear and missile tests.

CIVILIAN SPECIAL FORCES

National Security Group (NSG). 'Black Cats' Commandos. Elite anti-terrorist force 12,000 strong.

The NSG is divided into two groups – the Special Action Group (SAG) and the Special Rangers Group (SRG). The SAG, which comprises 54 per cent of the force, is the elite, offensive wing with members drawn from the Indian Army. The SRG, on the other hand, has members on deputation from central police organisations like the Border Security Force (BSF), the Central Reserve Police Force (CRPF), the Indo-Tibetan Border Police (ITBP) and the

Rapid Action Force (RAF). The primary function of the SRG is to play a supportive role to the SAF, especially in isolating target areas. For maintaining the young profile of the force, troops are rotated and sent back to their parent organisations after serving in the NSG for three to five years. The basic training period at the organisation's training centre at Manesar, 50 km from New Delhi, lasts 90 days. Only those who complete the entire course successfully are inducted into the NSG and given further specialised training. Some NSG personnel have received additional training in Israel and use weapons like the 9mm Uzi sub-machine gun. The NSG's weapon of choice is the Heckler & Koch family of 9mm sub-machine guns, the 7.62mm PSG-1 sniper weapon and the H&K 512 12-gauge shotgun. They are also armed with state of the art, day and night, surveillance gadgets and other sophisticated equipment.

There is a small Special Protection Group (SPG) formed in 1984 after the assassination of Mrs Gandhi to provide VIP bodyguards and protection for both National Government and visiting foreign officials. Very little information is known about the Special Security Bureau (SSB) other than its strength, which is at two battalions' worth. Apart from being a specialised commando outfit, it also an intelligence agency, likely to be used behind enemy line operations. By 20 August 2001, over fifteen SSB platoons were deployed along the 250- kilometre-long Indo-Nepal border, as Maoist rebels from Nepal are intensifying their activities along the Indo-Nepal border in the face of an onslaught by Nepalese armed forces in their traditional influence area.

INDONESIA

MILITARY SPECIAL FORCES

Special Operations Command (KOPASSUS)   its main missions are intelligence operations, counter-insurgency and anti-subversive operations. However, KOPASSUS, often known as the Red Berets, has seen its areas of operation expanded recently to cover all the main areas of Indonesia vulnerable to foreign intervention, such as Borneo or Irian Jaya. It conducts infiltration, reconnaissance and 'militia' training behind the lines in areas liberated by anti-government insurgents, or in the case of a possible intervention by a foreign power. Its training, while of a high commando standard, falls well short of the multi-role capability expected of Western elite units. KOPASSUS receive the best of new weapons and have an interesting array available including French FNC SSIV-1, Russian AK47 & US M16 assault rifles, Belgian FN MINI light machine guns and Israeli UZI sub-machine guns. Indonesia is full of separatist movements and while most are poorly armed and trained, KOPASSUS has still been called upon to support the local territorial garrisons on many occasions, often with brutal effectiveness. In the major re-organisation of June 1996, KOPASSUS was not only increased in size with the addition of two extra battalions, but also returned to the original 'formation' of its establishment in 1952. This was done to simplify its structure and to allow the better use of manpower to ensure that at least 25 per cent are on active duty at any one time. KOPASSUS has long been considered the elite corps of the Indonesian Army and it has traditionally emphasised its compact size and rapid strike potential. It has also gained the unfortunate reputation of being very closely associated with human rights abuses and disappearances. It has also been held responsible for the arming and training of militias guilty of the mass slaughter of civilians in East Timor and elsewhere. It now has five groups and a Presidential Guard Group with around 6,000 personnel. Its headquarters is at Cijantung, Jakarta, Java with Group-1 Strike-Para Commando (three battalions) based in Western Java, Group-2 Strike-Para Commando (three battalions) based in Central Java, Group-3 Training Command based in Western Java, Group-4 Combat Intelligence Squadron-sized based in S. Jakarta, Java and Group-5 Counter-Terrorism battalion-sized based in S. Jakarta. This elite corps is trained in a wide range of hostage rescue and anti-hijack techniques. Group-Presidential Guards (PASPAMRES), battalion-sized, based in S. Jakarta, provide close protection for the President and senior government ministers. KOPASSUS operates throughout Indonesia and in clandestine intelligence operations in neighbouring countries, particularly with Group-4 CIS based in Jakarta. In early 1952, Alex Kawilarang, then commander of the 3rd Teritorium (Siliwangi), based in Bandung, West Java, established a company-sized commando unit called Kesatuan Komando Teritorium III. Soon after, Army HQ became interested, and moved this unit under direct HQ supervision. The name was changed to Kesatuan Komando Angkatan Darat, and it grew in size. The first class was held from 22 February until 19 July 1954. At that time, KKAD was commanded by Major Idjon Djambi, Captain Soepomo as XO, and Captain Marzuki Suleman as chief of staff. On 27 April 1956, KKAD became Resimen Para Komando Angkatan Darat (RPKAD), with three companies, each of 300 men and three platoons each. These companies were A (combat), M (HQ) and Z (demonstration). Later on, RPKAD became Komando Pasukan Sandi Yudha (Kopasandha), consisting of about 5,000 elite red berets, divided into four groups, i.e. two Para-Commando groups, and two Intelligence units. During the reorganisation of the army in 1996, Kopasandha shrank to about 3,000 men with yet another name change to the present one, Komando Pasukan Khusus (KOPASSUS).

In the wake of the Islamic extremist bombing of a nightclub in Bali in October 2002 which killed over 180 people, including large numbers of Australian and British tourists, the International pressure on the Indonesian Government to order its Special Forces to take tough action against Islamic groups allied to Al Qa'ida will undoubtedly force KOPASSUS into the front line of anti-terrorist operations and indeed into a new era of close co-operation with both US and Australian Special Forces.

Detachment-81 (Special Commando Team) of KOPASSUS   100-strong HRU unit organised and trained by GSG-9, it has also trained with the SAS.

Satgas Atbara (Counter-Terrorist Task Force) of the Indonesian Air Force)   Satgas Atbara is an elite unit whose members are selected from the Indonesian Air Force Rapid Reaction Strike Force (Paskuan Pemukul Reaksi Cepat or PPRC). This team specialises in hostage rescue situations involving hijacked aircraft and may also be involved in anti-terrorist security at Indonesian Air Force bases. Satgas Atbara is based at Sukarno-Hatta International Airport.

Kesatuan Gurita of the Indonesian Navy   This unit is a combat swimmer unit dedicated to Counter-Terrorist operations at naval installations and others offshore, such as hijacked shipping or oil platforms. Recruits are drawn from the Marine Corps UDT and Amphibious Reconnaissance units, and reportedly undergo limited hostage rescue training. It was established in 1982 and has a strength of over 250 men. They are organised into combat teams of 24 men each, subdivided into three teams with a leader element. Satgas Gurita is based at the port of Jakarta, Indonesia.

Komando Pasukan Katak (KOPASKA)   KOPASKA was formed on 31 March 1962 by President Sukarno to help his campaign in Irian Jaya. In that campaign they were ordered to be human torpedoes similar to Japanese 'kamikaze' troops. In doing so they rode the torpedo, guiding it until hit the enemy's ship. KOPASKA is heavily influenced by the early US Navy Underwater Demolition Teams (UDT) and the modern Navy SEAL Teams. This foundation was built when early KOPASKA members were sent to the United States for training with the UDTs. That tradition continues today as each year a few men from the unit travel to Coronado, California, and Norfolk, Virginia, to participate in SEAL training. The unit strength is approximately 300 men, divided into two groups. One is attached to western fleet, based on Jakarta, and the other one is attached to eastern fleet based at Surabaya, East Java. Their main duty is underwater demolition which consists of raiding enemy's ships and bases, destroying main underwater installations, beach reconnaissance, prisoner snatches and preparing beaches for larger naval amphibious operations. In peacetime the unit deploys seven-man teams to serve as security personnel for VIPs. Primary among these duties are the escort and personal security of the Indonesian president and vice president. They are also responsible for limited search-and-rescue duties and have deployed as part of United Nations peace forces. Recruitment for the unit is held once a year and draws exclusively on navy personnel with the maximum age of recruits being 30. The length of the initial training is seven months. After the selection the men who pass will undergo four-phase continual training. The first phase of this is one week of physical training (Hell Week), the second phase is basic underwater training, the third phase is commando training, and the fourth phase is parachute training. In the end, from up to 700 recruits each year, usually only five or six make it and become KOPASKA.

CIVILIAN SPECIAL FORCES

SATGAS GEGANA Counter-Terrorist Task Force of the National Police About 200-strong, this unit is based at Kelapa Dua, some 20km from Jakarta. Drawn from both the police and military, they are trained in combat shooting, martial arts, rappelling, entry techniques and other HRU skills. Armed with a variety of weapons including M16 and AK rifles.

INDONESIA – US ROLE IN SPECIAL FORCES TERROR

The US role in the recent catalogue of horrors in East Timor is deep and far reaching, the culmination of over three decades of nurturing the Indonesian reactionary regime. A 1994 Amnesty International Report on Indonesia stated 'Army personnel and members of elite military units, such as the Special Forces Command (KOPASSUS) . . . have been responsible for the most grave violations against suspected political opponents.' Because of the well-documented record of human rights violations by KOPASSUS and other elements of the Indonesian military, in the early 1990s the US Congress cut off funding for training of Indonesian military personnel by US forces. Indonesia was one of the prime beneficiaries of the Joint Combined Exchange Training (JCET) programme. By 2000 there had been at least 36 JCET exercises in Indonesia with fully armed US combat troops including Green Berets, Air Force Commandos and Marines. By far the main recipient of the US special training has been a force legendary for specialising in torture, disappearances and night raids on civilian homes. Of the 28 Army/Air Force exercises known to have been conducted since 1982, Pentagon documents indicate that 20 have involved the KOPASSUS Red Berets. The US exercises with KOPASSUS included Sniper Level II, Demolition and Air Operations, Close-Quarters Combat, and Advanced Sniper Techniques. In July 1998, the *Washington Post* ran a major series on JCETs. In a lead story in its 12 July edition, the *Post* claimed that in Indonesia US Special Operations forces had conducted 41 training exercises since 1991 and that most of the exercises involved Indonesia's elite KOPASSUS troops, whom US officials have accused of involvement in kidnapping and torture of anti-government activists. Less than two years later, just exactly how these lessons were adopted exploded into the world's view in the streets of Dili, East Timor's capital in September 1999. Throughout East Timor thousands were murdered, hundreds of thousands made homeless, entire cities burned to the ground. There is a strong suggestion that the US government knew this was coming and that their Indonesian colleagues would play a leading role. Following attacks by pro-Indonesia militias in Dili in April 1999, Human Rights Watch put out a report on the connections between the militias and the Indonesian military. The report stated that a known pro-Jakarta extremist, Eurico Gutteres, led 'Aitarak', the militia responsible for the attacks. The report described Gutteres as 'a leading figure in Gardapaksi' a militia/youth gang whose 'members were reported to receive military training and equipment from KOPASSUS'. With the declaration of a worldwide War on Terrorism following the terrorist attacks on New York and Washington DC in September 2001, the United States seems set fair to once again ignore the Indonesian government's 36 years of constant human rights abuse and suppression of independence movements – and the deaths of probably well in excess of 1,500,000 of its citizens. The US Special Forces are expected to re-establish their close links with KOPASSUS in the hunt for Islamic terrorists linked with Al Qa'ida.

INSERT

Insertion, point of entrance into an operational area inside potentially hostile territory. In many cases Special Forces will be inserted by HAHO or HALO parachuting, quiet STOL aircraft or stealth helicopters into remote desert or jungle airstrips, by submarine or small boats or on foot across national borders against relatively unsophisticated defences. However, when planning an operation against a developed military power the range of difficulties to be overcome are immense; from alert border patrols; guard dogs; watch towers with machine guns and searchlights; electrified fences; minefields; seismic movement and infrared sensors; battlefield and coastal surveillance radars, effective communications monitoring; air and satellite surveillance. Tight internal security and aggressive patrolling can further inhibit successful Special Forces operations, even once the border or coast defences have been breached. The planning that goes into a successful clandestine mission in the face of this level of opposition is immense. The fact that US, British and other NATO Special Forces were indeed able to carry out a number of highly successful covert operations deep inside the Soviet Union and Warsaw Pact countries throughout the Cold War is an immense credit to their professionalism and bravery, though not necessarily to the political motives behind some of the operations.

INTELL

Intelligence information. The life blood of all Special Forces operations and often in very short supply when most needed.

INTELLIGENCE AND SURVEILLANCE EQUIPMENT

The Special Forces anti-terrorist and hostage rescue units require good access to strategic and, more importantly, tactical intelligence. The latter, obtained in real-time when possible, is vital for the success of operations against hijackings and sieges where knowing the position of the hostages is paramount.

Gathering such intelligence requires advanced surveillance technology and expert technicians capable of getting the necessary information without alerting the terrorists. Today's Special Forces have a bewildering variety of devices available for use, including active and passive night vision/light enhancers; starlight or infrared sights and a range of optics similar to those used by the sniper. Closed-circuit television (CCTV) and Thermal Imagers; fibre-optic micro-camera pin-hole systems with wide angle lenses inserted to within a millimetre of the back of the plasterwork or paper in the targeted room after a silent drill has bored a suitable hole in a 'party' wall. Sophisticated listening devices such as the electronic stethoscope for listening through walls and directional microphones in open ground. Laser infrarometres, which can possibly pick up speech patterns from vibrations picked up from windows or other objects near the targeted speakers. Highly sensitive miniature or sub-miniature microphones or transmitters lowered down chimneys, disabled air-conditioning systems, ducts or lifts. Monitoring landline or mobile phones and computer systems, and indeed the whole range of SIGINT (Signals Intelligence) technology supplied by NSA and GCHQ, and even Radar Imaging, Photo Imaging and Communications Intelligence (COMINT) satellite systems can all be called upon to provide the vital mission intelligence required for success against the terrorist and safe rescue of the hostages involved.

INTERNATIONAL TERRORISM

The Special Forces of the USA, UK and their allies are now more likely to have to combat religious and ethnic insurgencies and international terrorist groups than its more traditional enemies; politically motivated revolutionary movements and regional or ethnic rebellions against a pro-Western regime. With the possible exception of Communist China, there are now no foreign governments seriously seeking to expand their influence in the Third World by covert military means. It remains true that the foundations of the modern terrorism were very definitely laid during the Second World War, when both the British SOE (Special Operations Executive) and the US OSS (Office of Strategic Services) found a ready audience among the freedom fighters/resistance groups that sprang up all over a German-occupied Europe, in Japanese-controlled Asia and, later still in the immediate post-war period, after the Red Armies had conquered Eastern Europe. SOE, OSS and later SIS and the OPC/CIA were to take often very highly motivated and politically orientated groups, train them in covert activities, the use of weapons and explosives, the techniques of assassination, sabotage and of clandestine political organisation. In fact, the West primed the terrorist pump. From the training camps in Britain and Canada, and the resistance groups throughout Europe and Asia sprang not only many of the leaders of the post-war world, but also the founders of international terrorism. They found a ready supply of arms, money, training, political advice and occasionally combat support from the Soviet Union, China and their allies – Cuba, North Korea and East Germany in particular. However, the Western allies replied in kind and very often took the initiative, with the result that many of the world's most repressive regimes claimed allegiance to the democratic ideal, while ensuring that their brutal security and Special Operations units were well armed and trained by the West's leading elite forces.

While the US Special Forces (Green Berets) in particular and to a lesser extent the SAS, GIGN and GSG-9 are still all deeply involved in training foreign Special Forces in anti-terrorist and hostage rescue operations, the limited capabilities of many of these countries are very obvious and their need for support from Western advisers and actual combat units is growing. International terrorism, and in particular Islamic terrorism, has dominated the planning and training of the West's leading Special Forces units for more than a decade. Although the events of 9-11 certainly highlighted the threat that now existed even to the continental United States, and concentrated thinking towards developing the means and tactics to fight an effective 'War on Terrorism', it was simply another brutal act in the growing terrorist campaign against Western interests and policies that has really been underway in some form or another since the mid-1950s. The Special Forces will undoubtedly be forced to constantly change their operational tactics in the fight against a determined, ruthless, cunning and shadowy enemy in the years ahead. To understand the scope of the problems now facing both the Intelligence Community and its executive arm, the Special Forces, it is only necessary to prepare a short list of just some of the leading terrorist movements of the early twenty-first century.

The Real IRA appeared on the scene in 1997 with a wealth of experience in terrorist tactics and bomb-making and though it has as yet failed to make the breakthrough into becoming a genuine international terrorist group, there can be very little doubt that is its long-term intention. Whether known as the Continuity IRA, New IRA or Volunteers of Ireland the truth is that they have to some extent finally blown away Irish Republican isolationism. It is a much less sectarian organisation which now has a number of dissident Protestants among its ranks and they are also actively recruiting among Scottish, English and European elements who have no known connection with Ireland, the 'Troubles' or the Catholic religion. These are the long-term 'moles' whose activities will be very difficult to detect. The Real IRA quickly expanded the relationship the Provisional IRA had established with the Basque revolutionary group, ETA. Together they established new arms routes from the Balkan and the Baltic States. The Real IRA went on to provide training in bomb-making techniques to both Croat and Serbian terrorists and to right-wing groups in the Baltic, particularly the Kajtselite in Estonia. Those same skills have also been offered to the Colombian FARC and the Kurdish PKK by both the Real IRA and their colleagues in the Provisionals in return for money and very probably drugs, for this latter is fast becoming the currency of international terrorism and many other such groups now either trade in drugs or protect those who do. The Real IRA has shown its ruthless nature with the car bomb attack in the centre of the small town of Omagh, Northern Ireland, on 15 August 1998, which killed 29 and injured a further 220 innocent victims. Terrorism in Northern Ireland is not however confined to the Republican or Catholic communities. In fact it might well be true that Loyalist (i.e. Loyal to Ulster remaining part of the United Kingdom) terrorism and the Protestant 'death squads' are responsible for more civilian deaths since 1969 than all the Republican groups whether Official, Provisional or Real IRA put together. With upwards of 4,000 active members the Ulster Defence Association (UDA) and its offshoot the Ulster Freedom Fighters (UFF) are the largest paramilitary grouping in Northern Ireland. Formed in 1971 as an umbrella organisation for loyalist paramilitary groups it remained a legal organisation until 1992, when the British government was finally forced to proscribe (ban) it following a growing number of terrorist bombings and murders by the UFF and its 'Red Hand Defenders' (of Ulster) terror squads.

Europe has a growing number of extremist groups both from the left and increasingly the racialist or extreme right wing. However, one the longest established is the ethnic revolutionary group ETA (Euzkadi Ta Askatasuna – Basque Fatherland and Liberty).

Basque territory is divided politically between the French and Spanish states. ETA was founded in 1959 with the aim of establishing an independent homeland based on Marxist principles in the northern Spanish Provinces of Vizcaya, Guipuzcoa, Alava, and Navarra, and the south-western French Departments of Labourd, Basse-Navarra, and Soule. Primarily involved in bombings and assassinations of Spanish officials, security and military personnel, politicians and judicial figures, ETA finances its activities through kidnappings, robberies and extortion. ETA has extended its terrorist bombing campaign in 2001–02 to popular holiday resorts along the Mediterranean coastline, threatening Spain's crucial tourist industry.

Latin America still seethes with potential revolution and insurgency and while those groups in Mexico and Central America are at present largely quiescent, the conflict in Colombia shows no sign of abating and groups in Bolivia, Brazil, Peru and Ecuador are becoming more active again. With estimates of their strength being in excess of 12,000 paramilitaries, the FARC or Revolutionary Armed Forces of Colombia (Fuerzas Armadas Revolucionarios de Colombia) established in 1964 as the military wing of the Colombian Communist Party, is Colombia's oldest, largest, most capable and best-equipped anti-government movement. Although organised along military lines they continue to adopt terrorist tactics with bombings, murder, kidnapping, extortion and hijacking occurring regularly against Colombian political, military and economic targets. In March 1999 the FARC executed three US Indian rights activists on Venezuelan territory after it kidnapped them in Colombia. Indeed foreign citizens are often targets of FARC kidnapping for ransom and it also has well-documented ties to the international drugs trade. The other main insurgent group in Colombia is the National Liberation Army (ELN), a Marxist group formed in 1965 by urban intellectuals inspired by Fidel Castro and Che Guevara. It has now largely resorted to terrorist and criminal activities with hundreds of kidnappings carried out each year for ransom, often targeting foreign employees of large corporations, especially in the petroleum industry, with hijacking, bombing, extortion and murder featuring alongside its low-key guerrilla war.

Osama Bin Laden is very much the face of the new terrorist international and with an original network of bases in Sudan and Afghanistan and an unknown number of connections to Islamic Jihad groups in the Lebanon, Palestinian West Bank, Libya, Bosnia, Kosovo, Albania, Egypt, Kashmir, Pakistan, Malaysia and Indonesia his influence was certainly considerable. However, Bin Laden is but one of a new generation of sophisticated and cosmopolitan extremists, well versed in the habits and tactics of their adversaries. The Islamic Front, effectively established in its present form in 1998, is an umbrella organisation that includes at least twelve different terrorist groups and is very much a creation of a group of hardline Egyptian extremists who can trace their past back to the Muslim Brotherhood and beyond. Osama Bin Laden had the international contacts and skills they needed and to some extent probably acted as a front man for their long-term ambitions. The terrorist attacks of 9–11 have been firmly laid at the door of Bin Laden's own group, Al Qa'ida, though the suspicion remains that other organisations including Hezbollah played a far more important role than is usually accepted. This echoes the way the destruction of Pan Am Flight-103 over Lockerbie in 1988 was blamed solely upon Libya, when again the suspicion remains that both Syria and Iran were far more responsible for the attack.

Al Qa'ida (The Base – Islamic Army for the Liberation of the Holy Places–World Islamic Front for Jihad Against Jews and Crusaders) Bin Laden's organisation, established in 1988, is multi-national, with members from numerous countries and with a worldwide presence. Senior leaders in the organisation are also senior leaders in other terrorist organisations, including those designated by the Department of State as foreign terrorist organisations, such as the Al-Gama'at al-Islamiyya and the Al-Jihad (Jihad Group – Islamic Jihad – New Jihad Group – Vanguards of Conquest–Talaa' al-Fateh) an Egyptian Islamic extremist group active since the late 1970s. Merged with Bin Laden's Al Qa'ida organisation in June 2001, the Jihad Organisation in Yemen, the Pakistani Al-Hadith group, the Lebanese Partisans' League, the Libyan Islamic Group, the Bayt al-Imam Group in Jordan, and the Islamic Group in Algeria. Al Qa'ida has worked hard to radicalise existing Islamic movements and create new radical Islamic groups where none exist. It supports Muslim fighters with arms, money and volunteers in Afghanistan, Kashmir, Pakistan, Tajikistan, Philippines, Indonesia, Bosnia, Kosovo, Chechnya, Algeria, Somalia and the Yemen – among others. It also receives considerable assistance from Iran and probably from Communist China in return for not supporting the Muslim tribal insurgents in Western China against the Beijing government. Al Qa'ida's ambition is to overthrow nearly all Muslim governments which are viewed as corrupt, to eject Western military and business assets from those countries and eventually to abolish state boundaries, creating a Pan-Arab superstate.

Bin Laden was involved in operations against the US forces in Somalia in 1993, and in 1995 Bin Laden reportedly agreed to finance a 'Gulf Battalion' organised by the Iranian Guardians of the Revolution to operate out of the Yemen and the Horn of Africa. Al Qa'ida is suspected of being responsible for the 1996 bomb attacks on US service personnel in Dhahran, Saudi Arabia, and in mid-1996 Bin Laden and a group of other leading Islamic extremists reached agreement 'to use force to confront all foreign forces stationed on Islamic land'. It resulted in the formation of international committees for long-term planning, secure finance and mobilisation of resources both of men and arms. A higher military committee was also established to oversee implementation of the plan. Bin Laden publicly issued his 'Declaration of War' against the United States in August 1996. Bin Laden's war planning has been slow and deliberate, with several peripheral groups carrying out atrocities in Saudi Arabia and Kenya for example, but no major attacks by Islamic Jihad or any of the main terrorist organisations. The events of 9-11 changed that, however, and the immediate Western perception was that it would be followed by a deluge of similar attacks. This is not Islamic Jihad's plan, however; theirs is a waiting game, to test America's nerve and to accept the damage and casualties the expected massive US response would cause, rebuild and move on to new attacks that have been in the planning stage for some years. As a number of US senior politicians have rightly predicted, the War on Terrorism will last at least a generation. Indeed in the one area where the United States has so far been able to claim some military success, Afghanistan, there are signs in late 2002 of something of a revival by Bin Laden's international force of Islamic volunteer fighters and their Taliban allies. Two new main bases have been established inside Pakistan, hundreds of miles north of where US and Pakistani troops were operating during the summer months. Al Qa'ida is reported to have regrouped under a new name Fateh Islam or Islamic Victory, together with the Taliban, Kashmiri militants and other radical Islamic groups. There are suggestions that China itself may now be involved in supporting the camps, either by tacitly allowing Islamic radicals of the ethnic Uighur minority in China's western Xinjiang Province to cross into Pakistan to join Al Qa'ida, or by covertly offering to provide them with advanced military equipment.

The Abu Sayyaf Group (ASG) is the most violent of the Islamic separatist groups operating in the southern Philippines and some of its leaders have trained in the Middle East and allegedly fought in Afghanistan during the Soviet war. The group split from the Moro National Liberation Front in the early 1990s, and although it claims that its motivation is to promote an independent Islamic state in western Mindanao and the Sulu Archipelago, areas in the southern Philippines heavily populated by Muslims, the ASG now appears to use terror mainly for financial profit, including extortion and kidnappings for ransom. The group's first large-scale action was a raid on the town of Ipil in Mindanao in April 1995, and in April of 2000, an ASG faction kidnapped 21 persons, including ten foreign tourists, from a resort in Malaysia. On 27 May 2001, the ASG kidnapped three US citizens and seventeen Filipinos from a tourist resort in Palawan, Philippines. Several of the hostages, including one of the Americans, were murdered.

The Jammu and Kashmir Liberation Front (JKLF) is one of the oldest and most widely supported terrorist groups in Kashmir. Indian security forces currently confront at least a dozen major insurgent groups of varying size and ideological orientation. The more prominent groups include the secular pro-independence Jammu and Kashmir Liberation Front (JKLF) and the radical Islamic and pro-Pakistani groups Hizb-ul-Mujahideen (HUM), Hizbollah, Harkat-ul-Ansar, and Ikhwanul Muslimeen. At present JKLF is established in all the Districts and Tehsils of Azad Kashmir, in Gilgit, Diamer and Skardu Districts of Gilgit-Baltistan and in the main cities of Pakistan. The Muslim insurgency and its terrorist attacks inside the Indian-controlled Jammu-Kashmir section of Kashmir and on India itself, including the Parliament Buildings in the capital of New Delhi, have raised tensions between Pakistan and India to a point where a war, and perhaps even a nuclear conflict, have become a distinct possibility.

Armed Islamic Group (GIA) is an Islamic extremist group, dedicated to the overthrow of the secular Algerian regime and replacing it with an Islamic state. The GIA began its violent activity in 1992 after the government refused to accept the victory by the Islamic Salvation Front (FIS), the largest Islamic opposition party in the first round of national elections in December 1991. The GIA, with other smaller Islamic extremist groups, are responsible for the brutal killings of thousands of civilians, including virtually whole remote villages where hundreds of victims have been found with their throats cut. The Al-Aqsa Martyrs Brigade comprises an unknown number of small cells of Fatah-affiliated paramilitaries that emerged at the outset of the current Intifada to attack Israeli targets. It aims to drive the Israeli military and settlers from the West Bank, Gaza Strip and Jerusalem and to establish a Palestinian state. Al-Aqsa Martyrs Brigade has carried out shootings and suicide operations against Israeli military personnel and civilians and has killed Palestinians who it believed were collaborating with Israel. Al-Aqsa operates mainly in the West Bank and has carried out a number of major attacks inside Israel and the Gaza Strip in 2001–02 and works in close co-operation with HAMAS (Islamic Resistance Movement – 'Harakat Al-Muqawama Al-Islamia') a radical Islamic fundamentalist organisation which became active in the early stages of the Intifada, operating primarily in the Gaza District but also in Judea and Samaria. Formed in late 1987 as an outgrowth of the Palestinian branch of the Muslim Brotherhood, HAMAS activists, especially those in the Izz el-Din al-Qassam Brigades, have conducted many attacks, including large-scale suicide bombings, against Israeli civilian and military targets. In the early 1990s, they also targeted Fatah rivals and began a practice of targeting suspected Palestinian collaborators, which continues. Increased operational activity in 2001 during the Intifada, claiming numerous attacks against Israeli interests. Group has not targeted US interests and continues to confine its attacks to Israelis inside Israel and the Occupied Territories.

Primarily operating the West Bank, Gaza Strip, and Israel. HIZBOLLAH (Party of God – Islamic Jihad – Islamic Jihad for the Liberation of Palestine) was formed in 1982 in response to the Israeli invasion of Lebanon, and this radical Shi'a group takes its ideological inspiration from the Iranian revolution and the teachings of the Ayatollah Khomeini. It is dedicated to the 'political elimination' of Israel. Although closely allied with and often directed by Iran, the group may have conducted operations that were not approved by Tehran. While Hizbollah does not share the Syrian regime's secular orientation, the group has been a strong tactical ally in helping Syria advance its political objectives in the region. It has been involved in numerous anti-US and anti-Israeli terrorist attacks in the period 1982–2002. It has wide international support and has been successful in building a large military infrastructure in the Beka'a Valley, Hermil, the southern suburbs of Beirut and southern Lebanon.

IRAN

MILITARY SPECIAL FORCES
Iranian Special Operations Command includes a full Special Forces Division with at least three Light Infantry Brigades. In addition the 23rd Commando

Division has raised Special Force units trained in mountain warfare, particularly along the border with Afghanistan, and contains a number of specialist assault and sabotage units whose main tasks are to destroy the oil platforms and giant tankers that crowd the narrow waters of the Arabian Gulf and the vital Straits of Hormuz. Other units would attempt an amphibious assault to occupy the southern coast of the straits in order to bring the waterway firmly under Iranian control. The Iranian Special Forces, while tough, motivated, reliable and with a considerable ability to conduct clandestine operations, lack the true Special Operations skills necessary to be considered an elite fighting force, and Iran simply does not have the infrastructure or finances to produce a true Special Force capability at the moment. Within the Revolutionary Guards Corps (Pasdaran Inqilab) are a range of small covert action units whose tasks go well beyond the normal range of Special Operations. These include maintaining Islamic purity, assassination, and the training, arming and control of Islamic terrorist groups both within the Middle East and, increasingly, throughout the world. Pasdaran-trained Special Force personnel are attached to the main Iranian Intelligence services, and often operate within Europe and the United States on clandestine intelligence-gathering and subversive missions.

IRANIAN EMBASSY SIEGE – SAS

Operation Nimrod.   The British Special Forces first dramatically gained the public's attention on 5 May 1980 when, on the sixth day of the Iranian Embassy siege, members of the on-call B Squadron's Pagoda Troop, the SP (Special Projects) alert team of 22nd SAS Regiment, stormed the building to free the remaining 25 hostages. At 19.23 hours the troopers on the roof of No. 16 Princes Gate stepped over the edge of the roof and began their rapid descent. The first two pairs made it down safely; however, one of the ropes, purchased in haste in London during the first day of the siege, succumbed to friction and twisted into a knot. The knot fouled in the gear of one of the SAS men, stranding him precariously just outside one of the second-storey windows. This development prevented the SAS pair below him from using explosives on their entry window as planned, for fear of killing the entangled trooper. Instead, they smashed the windows with sledgehammers and tossed in their stun grenades. The entangled man was soon cut free and dropped to the balcony, whereupon he rejoined the assault team. Oan, who had been responsible for killing one of the hostages, Abbas Lavasani, the Iranian press attaché, was on the phone with negotiators at the first moments of the assault, a carefully choreographed diversion designed to fix Oan in one location. The sound of breaking glass, however, caused when a member of the first team inadvertently kicked an upper-storey window while rappelling, prompted Oan to hang up and make his way to the first floor landing on his way to investigate. He looked up to see one of the SAS men preparing to break through a window and raised his weapon to fire. Police Constable Lock acted quickly, tackling the gunman and taking him to the floor. The struggle ensued for a moment longer until the trooper broke into the room and yelled, 'Trevor, leave off!' Lock rolled clear of the terrorist, who promptly levelled his weapon at the constable. The SAS man fired his MP-5, emptying the magazine and killing the terrorist leader. At 19.26 hours, two members of Pagoda Troop at the front of the embassy activated the ten-second fuse on a frame charge affixed to a window. The large explosion that followed both signalled the rappelling teams at the rear to begin their assault and provided entry to the four SAS men on the balcony. Simultaneously, electrical power to the building was cut, and tear gas canisters fired through the broken windows in an effort to contribute to the chaos being forced onto the terrorists. These teams were supported by a rarely reported team that burst through a weakened first-floor plaster wall shared by the Iranian and Ethiopian Embassy and linked up with the main assault teams. The first room to be assaulted contained neither hostages nor terrorists, and prompted the troopers to move even more quickly. The noise caused in the first few minutes alerted the three terrorists in Room Ten that an assault was under way, prompting them to open fire on their hostages, killing one and injuring two. Upon hearing the approach of the SAS men, however, they threw away their weapons and shouted in Farsi, 'Tasleem!' ('We surrender!') before diving to the floor. Seconds later, troopers burst through the door and, realising what had happened, demanded: 'Who are the terrorists?' When one of the hostages pointed them out, they were immediately shot and killed. As the hostages were being rapidly evacuated down the main stairs and out the back door, a lone terrorist brandishing a fragmentation grenade was spotted amid the group. His position among the civilians prevented the closest trooper from firing. Instead, the SAS man struck him in the back of the neck with the butt of his MP-5, sending the terrorist sprawling down the remaining stairs, away from the fleeing hostages. Two troopers at the base of the stairs immediately emptied their 30-round magazines into the would-be assassin, killing him instantly. Upon hearing the gunfire, the terrorist guarding the four female hostages threw his weapon down and attempted to hide among his hostages. When the SAS arrived, however, he was seized and quickly searched for weapons and a possible detonation trigger for the explosives Oan had sworn were planted throughout the embassy. The terrorist unwisely resisted the search and was rewarded by being unceremoniously hurled down the stairs before being dragged out of the building. He would be the only terrorist to survive the SAS assault.

Within less than ten minutes the hostages were safe and all but one of the terrorists was dead. The image of a superb Special Forces operation had been firmly established in the minds of both the media and the general public, and indeed a 'love affair' with the SAS and a deal of unwarranted attention has continued ever since. The fact that the operation was not well planned and its execution botched, with one soldier perilously trapped in ropes while abseiling down the rear of the embassy, risking giving the terrorists sufficient warning to kill their hostages; frame explosives specially designed to only blow in the windows actually setting the building on fire, hampering the rescue attempt, and that the SAS soldiers summarily executed terrorists even after they had laid down their arms and surrendered, has been deliberately ignored. Only the intervention of one of the hostages, a Metropolitan Police Constable from the Diplomatic Protection Group, prevented the one surviving terrorist from being frog-marched back into the burning embassy by SAS soldiers to be 'shot while resisting'. PC Trevor Lock was silenced by the Police Authority from fully describing the events of that day and later resigned from the Police in disgust. The fact that the so-called terrorists, though dangerous and responsible for the murder of one hostage, were not from a dedicated terrorist organisation, but were in fact political militants from the Democratic Revolutionary Movement for the Liberation of Arabistan (DRMLA), and quite out of their depth, has also been ignored. What cannot be glossed over is that the operation that raised the status of the SAS to heroic levels was only a limited success and in fact only just avoided becoming an outright failure with the deaths of many of the hostages.

IRAQ

MILITARY SPECIAL FORCES

The Iraqi Special Forces, having gained a considerable reputation during the 1980–88 war with Iran, surprisingly gave a poor performance in the 1991 Gulf War. A major re-organisation has taken place during the late 1990s to address the perceived weaknesses, and greater emphasis has been placed on intelligence, physical fitness, mental toughness and motivation with the help of a number of foreign military advisers. The problems caused by UN sanctions have been partly overcome by the widespread 'black market' smuggling of new weapons, communications and other specialist surveillance equipment, from mainly Russia and the Ukraine. Under the control of the Office of the Presidential Palace, with its Headquarters in Baghdad, there are a number of ultra-reliable Special Forces with just one major mission, the protection of Saddam Hussein. These units include the 'Green Berets' or 33rd Special Forces Brigade, and the Special Republican Guard Motorized Infantry Brigade; both are Rapid Reaction units. There are also a number of specially trained detachments for dedicated Counter-Terrorist and Hostage Rescue operations. The Special Force Brigade belonging to the 7th Adan Republican Guards Mechanized Division has a number of highly specialised units tasked for deep penetration into Kurdish territory. Similar to the concept of the NATO LRRP (Long-Range Reconnaissance Patrol), these units contain Kurdish and indeed Turkish-speaking personnel, along with an entire Special Forces Brigade within the Alabad Motorized Infantry Division who are deployed for clandestine penetration of Kurdish-held areas. Regular cross-border Special Operations have been carried out into Turkey in order to keep surveillance on Kurdish fighters and NATO operations from Turkish airbases. Carrying out acts of assassination, sabotage, intelligence-gathering and psychological warfare, these units also carry out close surveillance of the Turkish and Iranian border areas. During the Second World War, Iraqi officers suggested the possibility of establishing special-purpose forces within the Iraqi armed forces, then serving under British authority. The Iraqi officers, many of whom had served in the mountains of northern India, suggested a Special Forces organisation called light mountain forces, which would complement Regular Army formations. However, the idea did not meet with any encouragement from the British Military Mission in Iraq. In 1951, many officers and men were sent outside of Iraq to receive specialised strike/commando training. In December 1954, a select group from Army units was sent to the UK for commando training. Upon their return, a commando brigade and the first independent parachute company were formed. They were maintained until 1959, when the brigade was disbanded and the first parachute company was converted to a parachute battalion. In 1964 the idea of forming strike units in the Army was considered. Due to increased interest in these operations, commando experts were brought in from Egypt to assist in developing a training course. Training began in 1965, with the British Military Mission in Iraq administering the first training course, in conjunction with Egyptian advisers. However, as time determined, training in strike and commando operations seemed to be at cross-purposes. Since the tactics were essentially similar, it was decided to merge the two types of training and formations under the title of Special Forces or Special Forces Command. The term 'strike force' continues to be used to designate a special mission. The Special Forces Command was converted in the late 1960s to brigade-size groups, and the Special Forces Administration was formed. Acting as elite Infantry or Assault Commandos the Iraqi SOF normally have a definite tactical objective in support of division or corps mission requirements, and could probably only accomplish a limited regional strategic requirement.

The training has been expanded to include long-range reconnaissance and unconventional warfare, such as sabotage, assassination and kidnapping, with the help of former East German, Russian, Chinese and North Korean military advisers. The capability of the Iraqi Special Forces to conduct long-range special operations missions similar to those of US or British Special Forces units is considered extremely limited. A decisive factor in any Iraqi Special Forces operation is the delivery, logistical and organisational support systems that are critical to successful accomplishment of any Special Forces mission, and these three support systems are a serious weak link in any projected Iraqi Special Forces mission. In concert with these support systems, a battalion-size unit under the Special Forces Command specialises in air supply techniques. However, the effectiveness of this unit is in question, due to the US-imposed no-fly zones and sanctions.

Special Forces Command   The present Special Forces command is now believed to include the 1st Special Forces Brigade originally raised in 1964–65 and which acquitted itself well against the IDF on the Golan Heights in Syria in the 1973 Yom Kippur War, the 2nd Special Forces Brigade raised in 1973, the 3rd Special Forces Brigade and the 33rd, 65th, 66th and 68th Special Forces Brigades all raised by 1985.

IRELAND, REPUBLIC (SOUTHERN)

MILITARY SPECIAL FORCES

Sciathán Fhiannóglaigh an Airm (Army Ranger Wing)   With terrorism on the rise, the Irish government felt that it would be prudent to have members of the military receive more specialised training. After conducting a review of international hostage rescue teams/counter terrorism (HRT/ CT) units, the Irish government directed the formation of a new military special operations force. Formed in 1980, the Irish Army Ranger Wing (ARW) is the Republic of Ireland's military special operations, and Counter-Terrorist (CT) force. The unit is based at Curragh Camp, in County Kildare. The force is composed of 100–150 Ranger-qualified personnel and operates under the direct control of the Irish Army Chief of Staff. Between 1968 and 1971 a small group of Irish military personnel were selected to attend US Army Ranger training, at Fort Benning, GA. The group was drawn from senior NCOs, and officers of all branches of the Irish armed forces, and upon their successful completion of training, the group were used to establish a similar training programme in Ireland. This group formed the initial training cadre at the Irish Ranger school at Curragh Camp. Volunteers are required to pass a gruelling four-week selection course. Survivors of the selection course then advance to the six-month-long basic skills course. The course provides instruction in combat medicine; weapons and explosive handling; hostage rescue training and tactics; CQB and precision shooting survival training; mountaineering; Long-Range Patrolling; and a basic parachute course. Upon completion of initial training the Rangers may progress on to more specialised training courses conducted by the unit and other services. Rangers can receive instruction in HAHO and HALO operations; EOD; fast roping and rappelling; a combat diver course including training in small boat handling, and amphibious operations; and a sniper course, with approximately half the unit qualifying as snipers. Personnel who successfully complete the demanding course are awarded a black and gold 'Fianoglach' or Ranger tab.

The Rangers are tasked with conducting several missions. Their more conventional military tasks include: conducting raids, ambushes and sabotage operations; conducting Long-Range Recon Patrols in support of conventional units; intelligence-gathering; VIP protection; capture of key enemy personnel; counter-insurgency operations. However, 'their most important role is as the country's premier CT and hostage rescue unit, not the Garda Emergency Response Unit (ERU), although both train together and closely co-operate. The Ranger Wing also train with other SOF groups around the world, including US Army Rangers, British SAS, Australian and NZ SAS, GIGN, GSG-9, Dutch Commandos and the Swedish Special Forces. Weapons used include the 9mm SIG-Sauer P226 pistol, 9mm H&K MP5K, MP5A3 and MP5SD3 sub-machine guns, 5.56mm Steyr AUG A1 assault rifle (adopted 1988), 5.56mm H&K HK33SG1 sniper rifle, 7.62mm Accuracy International AW/AI 96 sniper rifle (adopted 1992), 18.5mmR (12-gauge) Remington Model 870 pump-action shotgun, 5.56mm Steyr AUG A1 light support weapon, 5.56mm FN MINIMI-Para light machine gun , 7.62mm FN MAG machine gun and 84mmR FFV M2 Carl Gustaf recoilless rifle.

CIVILIAN SPECIAL FORCES

Garda (police) Emergency Response Unit The ERU is the specialist response unit of An Garda Siochana and provides armed backup to the Gardai. Formed in 1978, it officially became the national HRU in 1980. The 50-strong ERU is a separate unit to the SDU or Special Detective Unit, who are primarily an investigative unit, although they too carry firearms. It trains with the Canadian RCMP, the GSG-9 and GIGN and receives training in a wide variety of Special Forces skills, including parachuting and SCUBA. Weapons used include 9mm UZI SMG and MP5 SMGs, and Remington 700 sniper rifles.

ISA

Intelligence Support activity – the activities of this highly secretive unit which drew its personnel from both the US Army's Special Forces and from the US Navy SEALs was shrouded in mystery from its inception to its supposed demise. With some 200 personnel, it is tasked to provide clandestine intelligence for Special Operations. Two years after the Delta corruption inquiry in 1985, fresh investigations revealed more information on Business Security International, which suggested that it had operated quite apart from Delta Force. BSI was described as a front for army covert actions, set up in 1983 and code-named 'Yellow Fruit', to provide security for joint army-CIA operations in the Middle East and Central America. An April 1987 CBS News report linked 'Yellow Fruit' to the covert operations of the National Security Council that were co-ordinated by Lieutenant Colonel Oliver North and retired General Richard Secord. In its reporting on the 'Iran-Contra' affair, CBS tied BSI ('Yellow Fruit') to a Swiss bank account used by North and Secord to lease a cargo ship for arms movements. The army half-heartedly disputed the bank account charge, but CBS stood by its story (the account number had been provided to CBS by a former member of the unit). 2 BSI/'Yellow Fruit' was most likely an operation run by the newest of the Pentagon's covert intelligence agencies, Intelligence Support Activity (ISA).

ISA was created as the US Army's Foreign Operations Group (FOG), in response to the crisis in Iran after the fall of the Shah. It operated over a year without the knowledge of the Secretary of Defence, the CIA, or indeed Congress. The unit was formally established in October 1980 by the US Army chief of staff General Edward C. Meyer. Initially used for covert intelligence collection to support Special Operations during the Iran crisis, ISA was subsequently employed for covert operations considered too sensitive for the army's Special Operations and Intelligence establishment. Although ISA was allegedly unknown to Congressional intelligence oversight committees until 1982, it had already engaged in major covert operations. The first hint of ISA's existence emerged in March 1983, when Lieutenant Colonel James 'Bo' Gritz testified to a Congressional subcommittee about his abortive raid into Laos early that year. Gritz said that in 1981 he had been approached by 'a special intelligence (group) referred to as "The Activity"' concerning a covert mission into Indo-China aimed at freeing any US MIAs still held there. Although neither Congress nor the Pentagon would confirm the account or therefore the existence of the ISA, by May 1983 press inquiries established that Gritz had received some support in the intelligence area from a new army agency, the ISA. The *New York Times* concluded that the ISA had co-ordinated with the Italian NOCS in the January 1982 rescue of General James Dozier from the Red Brigade kidnappers and was 'operating missions against leftist forces in El Salvador and supporting anti-government forces in Nicaragua'. Other sources credited ISA with unspecified operations concerning hostages in Lebanon.

Like Delta Force, some ISA personnel exploited its clandestine operations for personal gain. In 1985, the ISA was reportedly disbanded after FBI investigators 'discovered lavish trips being taken by some officers and their wives'. But the *Washington Post* reported that in 1986 the ISA had carried out a number of classified actions in co-ordination with the intergovernmental 'Operations Sub-Group' (OSG) set up to co-ordinate Counter-Terrorist operations. It has been suggested that the Counter-Terrorist Joint Task Force at Fort Bragg, a unit of less than twenty men, may have been 'an operational component of ISA'. Other reports place ISA operating in Bosnia in 1994 under the code name 'Torn Victor' and, indeed, in 1998 as a highly secretive component of JSOC, some 275 strong and specialising in Direct Action, SIGINT and linguistics. Operates alongside Delta and DEVGRU.

ISRAEL

MILITARY SPECIAL FORCES
Army General Staff Command (Mateh Haklali).

Sayeret MATKAL General Staff Deep Reconnaissance Unit-262 is Israel's primary Counter-Terrorism and Intelligence-gathering SF Unit, formed in 1958 and absorbing the operational experience gained by the original Israeli Special Operations Force, Unit-101, and indeed adopting its SAS-style structure. In 1974 Matkal and other Special Force units started to acquire genuine Counter-Terrorist training provided by the British SAS and the US SEAL and Delta units, and by 1980 had a high degree of both operational experience and capability. In 1985 the Israelis established a discreet Special Forces base at Mitkan Adam with a Special Training Installation (Maha-7208) and the Counter-Terrorism Warfare School (Unit-707). This now includes hostage rescue, close-quarter battle, combat shooting and other highly specialist facilities. Training, which is remarkably tough even by normal Special Force standards, includes advanced intelligence and surveillance techniques, assassination, booby-traps and specialist explosives, combat swimming, sniping, specialist parachuting (HAHO and HALO), cold weather and desert warfare techniques, heliborne insertion and sabotage. This highly capable force, which is tasked for intelligence and CT operations outside Israel, is required to provide two action-ready units at all times for counter-terrorist operations anywhere in the world. In order to be accepted into most of the IDF SF units, one must first pass a selection phase, which is known as 'Gibush'. This lasts three to five days and focuses on physical stamina and the candidates' behaviour under sleep deprivation, fatigue and intense mental and physical pressure. There are also written exams and the inevitable interview with a psychologist, which usually take place at the end of the 'Gibush'. Several hundred recruits start the 'Gibush' on each training cycle. Only 50–100 will get through and only the best 20–25 will be selected for the unit. Once the soldiers have been accepted they begin a training regime known as 'Maslul' that, in most of the IDF SF units, lasts 20 months. Unlike most foreign SF units, once qualified the soldiers are not reassigned to other already operational teams in order to fill gaps, but remain in the same team from their recruitment date throughout their IDF service and until the end of service – which is usually at the same time as the end of the mandatory service. Weapons used include the 9mm FN-Browning HP Mk 3 and 9mm SIG-Sauer P226 pistols and the 11.43mm (.45 ACP) H&K USP pistol. The 9mm IMI Model 46 Mini-Uzi machine pistol is used in urban areas. The standard weapon is now the 5.56mm M16AI, 5.56mm Colt CAR-15A2 Model 777 assault carbine and 5.56mm Colt CAR-15A1 Model 653. The sniper rifles are the 7.62mm Mauser Model 86SR (adopted 1996) and 7.62mm Remington Model 700 bolt-action weapons (main sniper rifle, adopted 1997, M24 configuration with 9× scope). The sniper support weapon is the 5.56mm Colt AR-15A2 Model 645 burst-fire rifle (M16A2, with 4× scope). The 12.7mm (.50 BMG) Barrett Model 82A1 rifle is also employed. The 5.56mm IMI Negev light machine gun is used for fire support. The 18.5mmR (12-gauge) Benelli M1 Super 90 semi-automatic shotgun is used, as is the 40mmSR R/M M203PI underbarrel grenade launcher (on the CAR-15A2 Model 777).

The Field Intelligence Corps and Military Intelligence or AMAN has a further range of dedicated SF formations such as 'unit Yachmam' for intelligence and target acquisition, unit T'zasam for special reconnaissance duties in Palestinian areas, while unit-504 handles human clandestine intelligence resources. Mistaravim Units Mistaravim is the Hebrew term for 'becoming an Arab', illustrating the units' tactic of using plainclothes men and women, acting, speaking and thinking as Arabs. Though they are heavily involved in the occupied Palestinian territories, their remit extends to Lebanon, Syria, Jordan and Egypt. Even Iraq and Saudi Arabia have been targeted successfully by these deep-cover agents in recent years and not surprisingly, these units work closely with the MOSSAD.

Sayeret Duvdevan ('Cherry' – Unit 217) IDF Central Command – Rama Army Base, Palestinian West Bank. A Mistaravim Unit for undercover and CT operations in Palestinian areas and the Sinai. Formed 1988–89 this secretive unit operates mainly on the Israeli-Egyptian border for deep-cover clandestine operations inside Egypt and are experts at merging successfully with the local population.

Sayeret Ha'Druzim Founded in the 1960s as a Druze paratroop recon unit. Operates in the Lebanon and Syria.

Sayeret Ha'Beduim Border Security unit mainly composed of Bedouins. Operates in Jordan.

The Israeli Army has highly specialist Palsar or long-range reconnaissance and patrol groups (LRRP) attached to each of the regular infantry brigades such as the Sayeret Golany Palsar-95, Sayeret Givaty Palsar-435, Sayeret Nahal Palsar-374 and the T'zanhanim (parachute) Palsar, and similar units attached to the regular armoured brigades, the Palsar-7 and 500. These units carry out clandestine reconnaissance patrols deep behind enemy lines and ensure that the parent brigade have the best possible information at all times on the potential threat.

Israel has had a long-term interest in and commitment to Special Forces from before the War of Independence in 1948 and this has further developed in the 55 years since the creation of the state of Israel. In 1948 all the Jewish resistance movements were joined together in order to form the IDF. One of the Hagana outfits, the Golany unit, was turned into the IDF first infantry brigade in February 1948. This unit was to form the first Special Reconnaissance Platoon, effectively an early Long-Range Reconnaissance Patrol (LRRP) Unit, acting as pathfinder for the infantry brigade. But unlike the other reconnaissance platoons that existed in each of the Golany brigade's battalions, the Special Reconnaissance Platoon was also responsible for Special Operations against enemy strongholds, and more complex missions such as sabotage and intelligence-gathering inside Arab territory. The Special Reconnaissance Platoon was in fact the first official Israeli SF unit, evolving into Sayeret Golany, which is considered one of the finest units in the IDF. In June 1948 the IDF formed its Paratrooper unit, the T'zanhanim Company. In 1949–51 neighbouring Arab armies and terrorist groups launched thousands of small attacks against Israel's borders, bringing a predictable response from the IDF, which retaliated strongly. However, the regular infantry units, including the T'zanhanim Paratroop unit, were found to be simply not up to the task. Therefore in 1951 the IDF formed Unit 30, a secret formation that belonged to the IDF South command and was designed to execute retaliation missions while operating in small and well-trained teams. However, Unit 30 personnel lacked sufficient and proper SF training, and performed poorly, so in 1952 the unit was disbanded. In August 1953, the IDF tried again to form a dedicated new SF unit and created Unit 101 as a SF unit designed to perform complex missions far behind Israeli borders. Unit 101 was initially composed of only 20–25 men, most of them former T'zanhanim and Unit 30 personnel. The creation of Unit 101 was a major landmark in Israeli SF history and established small-unit direct action, insertion and patrol tactics that are still utilised in 2002. Unit 101 is considered to be the unit with the most influence on the Israeli infantry-orientated units, including both Special and conventional units. It was also the first time the IDF formed a brand new SF unit from scratch, rather then modify a previously existing infantry-orientated unit, as with the Golany Brigade Special Reconnaissance Platoon. It was also the first time the IDF formed a unit that received its orders directly from the IDF General Staff (the IDF High Command – MATKAL).

However, Unit 101 only existed for five months under its aggressive commander, Ariel 'Arik' Sharon, and was disbanded after a raid in which the unit's members killed dozens of unarmed Arab citizens in an infamous and extremely brutal act of retaliation. Its personnel were transferred to the T'zanhanim company. After the merger the joint outfit turned into a brigade size unit, composed of two battalions – 869 Battalion (made out of the original T'zanhanim company personnel) and 101 Battalion (made out of former Unit 101 personnel). This merger was actually quite ironic since the T'zanhanim officers were originally opposed to the creation of Unit 101, not wanting another competitor for prestigious retaliation missions that had previously been theirs alone. Arik Sharon now became the new

CO of the T'zanhanim infantry brigade and was now able to launch full-scale covert attacks against his Arab opponents and ensure that the T'zanhanim became Israel's prime retaliatory unit for the remainder of the 1950s.

However, the IDF Command still did not believe that Sharon's unit provided them with a small, compact and secretive Special Forces capability. So in 1958 Abraham Arnan formed Sayeret MATKAL, answering directly to the IDF High Command. This unit combined the operational experience gathered by Unit 101 and the structure of the UK Special Air Service (SAS), the role model for SF units worldwide. Sayeret MATKAL was also formed one year after the IDF first helicopter squadron became operational in 1957 and close co-operation between the two allowed Sayeret MATKAL to deploy for longer and deeper inside Arab territory than any unit before. After losing the prestigious SF title, the T'zanhanim brigade formed it own SF unit, Sayeret T'zanhanim, in October 1958. In the early 1960s the IDF created Regional Sayeret in the Southern, Northern and Central Commands. These were known as the Sayeret Shaked (South Command), Sayeret Shoualey Shimshon (South Command), Sayeret Harouv (Central Command) and Sayeret Egoz (North Command). While those units were supposed to be skilled LRRP units, performing delicate intelligence-gathering missions, most of them soon became raid-units competing with Sayeret MATKAL, S'13 and Sayeret T'zanhanim. These command-level Sayerets became loose cannon units, acting as autonomous outfits, with little or no discipline whatsoever. They were to be disbanded once the IDF commands realised that they could get the same level of performance from the infantry brigade Sayeret units already in existence. However, the watershed for Israeli Special Forces was the Munich Olympic massacre in 1972 and this led to the creation of genuine Counter Terrorism and Hostage Rescue Team Capabilities. Sayeret MATKAL in particular was to be later re-organised to become a dedicated such unit with improved training, equipment and a widening connection with both long-established and newly created SF units springing up all over the world. However, it was to take yet another disaster before the changes would be finally pushed through.

In the Mahalot Massacre incident, 15 May 1974, three heavily armed terrorists took over Mahalot High School in the north of Israel, taking several dozen teachers and students hostage in the process. Sayeret MATKAL, by now the Israeli unit with the most advanced CT, was selected to carry out the rescue attempt. At the beginning of the raid, a Sayeret MATKAL sniper was suppose to take out the terrorist who was guarding the room in which most of the hostages were being held. The sniper, who was equipped with a Second World War Mauser 98, and not used to short-range headshot sniping, only wounded the target. The injured terrorist started throwing grenades and turned an automatic weapon on the hostages. More mistakes were made, both in the planning and in the execution of the assault, and although all three terrorists were eventually killed, so were 21 child and four adult hostages. Moreover, at least two civilians were killed by friendly fire since the Sayeret MATKAL entry team was under-trained in CQB close-combat shooting.

After the fiasco in Mahalot, the Israeli government, along with the IDF General Staff, made three important decisions. An all-new civilian CT Unit would be created under MAGAV, much like the German domestic CT unit – GSG9. This unit was later named Unit YAMAM. Most of Israel's SF units would now finally acquire advanced CT capabilities, with Sayeret MATKAL and S'13 on the cutting edge, forming one team in each unit that would specialise in CT scenarios. The Israeli units began a very extensive and intensive training regime including accepting help from foreign instructors mainly from Britain's SAS, the US Navy SEALs and later from the Delta Force. By 1980 Sayeret MATKAL and S'13 were fully CT-operational, and the rest of the units were not far behind. In 1985 another important step was taken when the Mitkan Adam army base housing the IDF Special Training Installation was formed. This included the IDF CT Warfare School (Unit 707) and the IDF Snipers' School. The growth of international terrorism with the threat this poses to Israel and Israeli interests and citizens abroad, the Palestinian Intifada, the suicide bombing campaign and the War on Terrorism have placed extraordinary strains on Israeli Special Forces and the Sayeret MATKAL in particular. The campaign of sabotage against Arab states and the assassination of leading Islamic militants has been largely carried out by Sayeret MATKAL and international protests aside, these operations are likely to continue and even intensify, particularly following the projected US military campaign against Iraq in 2002–03.

Heyl Hayam – IDF Navy

Shayetet 13 (S'13) – Naval Special Forces, Atlit Naval Base. A highly specialised unit that mounts deep penetration surveillance and sabotage missions along the Mediterranean coasts of Egypt, the Lebanon and Syria and in the Gulf of Aqaba and Red Sea areas.

CT and HRU situations involving merchant vessels, harbours and coastal installations, or intercepting and boarding vessels suspected of terrorism involvement or gun-running, are among their many responsibilities. S'13 has some 150 men + combat divers group (20 men). Trains with the USN SEALs. Weapons in use include 9mm FN-Browning HP Mk 3 and 9mm SIG-Sauer P226 pistols, 9mm IMI Model 46 Mini-Uzi machine pistol, 5.56mm Colt CAR-15A2 Model 777 assault carbine, 5.56mm Colt AR-15A2 Model 645 burst-fire rifle (M16A2, with 4× scope), 7.62mm Tulamash AKM assault rifle, 7.62mm Mauser Model 86SR, 7.62mm Remington Model 700 bolt-action weapons (M24 configuration with 9× scope), 12.7mm (.50 BMG) Barrett Model 82A1 rifle, 5.56mm IMI Negev light machine gun, 18.5mmR (12-gauge) Benelli M1 Super 90 semi-automatic shotgun and 40mmSR R/M M203PI underbarrel grenade launcher (beneath the CAR-15A2 Model 777).

CIVILIAN SPECIAL FORCES
Mishmar Ha'Gvul – Israëli Border Guards (Israëli Police)
Unit YA'MAS (Yechidat Ha'Mista'arvim Shel Mishmar Ha'Gvul)   Three special units for infiltration and CT undercover operations, based in Jerusalem and created in 1993 in the Gaza Strip, while those in Judea and Samaria were both created 1989. Mainly composed of Arabs and Druze.

Unit YA'MA'N (Yechida Mishartit Meyuchedet), headquarters at an intelligence base near Tel Aviv. Officially named SAMAG, which stands for Sayeret Mishmar Ha'Gvul or Border Guard SF Unit. Domestic CT and Hostage Rescue unit, created 1974 and some 200 strong. Weapons in use include 9mm Glock 17 pistol, 9mm IMI Model 49 Micro-Uzi machine pistol, 9mm IMI Para Micro-Uzi machine pistol (uses Glock magazines, with sound-suppressor, reflex sight and IR laser), 9mm IMI Model 46 Mini-Uzi sub-machine gun, 5.56mm Colt CAR-15A2 Model 733 Commando assault carbine (main weapon), 5.56mm Colt CAR-15A2 Model 777 assault carbine, 7.62mm H&K PSG1 sniper rifle (few), 7.62mm IMI Model 339 Galil SR sniper rifle (sniper support weapon), 7.62mm Mauser 86SR bolt-action sniper rifle (adopted 1996, main sniper rifle), 7.62mm Steyr SSG 69 bolt-action sniper rifle, 12.7mm (.50 BMG) Barrett Model 82A1 sniper rifle, 5.56mm IMI Negev light machine gun, 18.5mmR (12-gauge) Benelli M1 Super 90 semi-automatic shotgun and 40mmSR R/M M203PI underbarrel grenade launcher (under CAR-15A2 Model 777).

ITALY

MILITARY SPECIAL FORCES
Folgore Parachute Brigade   based at Livorno, near Pisa. The Folgore forms part of the Italian Army's Rapid Reaction force and includes the 1st Carabinnieri Parachute Regiment, but more importantly the 9th Para-Assault Regiment 'Col Moschin' (the name refers to a mountain peak, Col Moschin). This unit was created for sabotage and intelligence operations during the Cold War, but proved to be so well organised and flexible that their responsibilities were extended to cover all aspects of Special Intelligence operations and Counter-Terrorism. The regiment is based at the Vannucci barracks in Livorno. It is currently composed of a Regimental HQ, a support company, the 101st training company, and the 1st 'Incursori' Para-Raider

Battalion. The Para-Raider Battalion is composed of three operational companies. The 110th and 120th 'Incursori' companies are the battalion's two professional Special Operations units and are composed of seasoned officers and NCOs. The 111th 'Guastatori' Company is composed of log service volunteers, who have agreed to extend the length of their draft in order to serve in the unit. The 111th is assigned to ACE (Allied Command Europe) Rapid Reaction Corps (ARRC), and acts in a LRRP role. This regiment provides the Italian Army with one of the best trained, most effective and most widely experienced Special Force units found anywhere in the world today. The training programme for this regiment includes an initial eight-month period at the Piza parachute school and it is a further year before the surviving volunteers, virtually all NCOs or officers, are passed fit to join the 'Col Moschin'. Training for the regiment varies depending on which company the prospective Incursori will be assigned to. Trainees for the Guastatori Company undertake a 32-week training course within the 101st Training Company. During the course trainees receive instruction on land navigation, demolition, reconnaissance, marksmanship, field craft and patrolling. Physical fitness is stressed throughout the course, with multiple timed speed and endurance marches being the norm. The training is aimed at ensuring that each soldier has the ability to operate in any environment; they are taught survival, evasion and escape techniques, interrogation and counter-interrogation and free-fall parachuting (HALO and HAHO). Heliborne insertion, mountain, desert and underwater warfare, combat shooting and sniping, unarmed combat, clandestine intelligence operations, hostage rescue, counter-terrorism, sabotage and long-range patrol are also taught. Officers and NCOs wishing to join the regiment undergo an additional 52 weeks of training. Their course includes a month of instruction on tactical free-fall parachuting and a twelve-week block of instruction provided by the Navy's COMSUBIN at their Varigano base. During the twelve-week course students receive instruction on the use of SCUBA equipment, underwater demolition, small-boat handling and navigation. During the boat handling phase students are taught how to use Zodiac inflatable boats, Plasteco RIBs, and two-man Klepper Kayaks. They also undergo ten weeks of training at the Alpine Warfare School in Aosta. The students receive instruction in basic mountain warfare techniques and skiing. The last portion of their training is conducted in the field, under simulated combat conditions. SERE training is also included in this portion of their training.

The 9th 'Col Moschin' is a battalion-sized force, tasked with executing missions similar to those conducted by the US Army's Special Forces and 75th Ranger Regiment or the British SAS. The unit conducts seven specific types of missions: direct action missions that require unconventional warfare skills; raids against high value targets; interdiction of enemy lines of communications; LRRP operations; Strategic Reconnaissance; Counter-Terrorist/hostage rescue missions abroad and high-risk missions in support of conventional forces. The unit was originally raised in 1963 as the 9th Para Sabateur Battalion, but was redesignated as the 9th Para-Raider Battalion (Incursore) in 1980. The 'Col Moschin' regiment has taken part in Counter-Terrorist and Special Operations missions in the Alto-Adige during the late 1960s. From 1982 to 1984 the unit was deployed to Lebanon as part of a multinational peacekeeping force trying to maintain order in the country. Over the last decade the unit has increasingly found itself being deployed in support of United Nations (UN) peacekeeping/making efforts; the *Achille Lauro* hijacking of an ocean liner in 1985; in 1991 they found themselves deployed to Kurdistan in Northern Iraq during Operation Provide Comfort; in 1991 they were deployed to the former Italian colonies of Somalia and Ethiopia. In June of 1991 they evacuated 250 from the Ethiopian capital of Addis-Ababa in response to the country's civil war, and while the majority of the world was focused on developments in the Gulf, Col Moschin Incursori conducted a Non-Combatant Evacuation Operation (NEO) of Western civilians from the Somali capital in a mission dubbed 'Operation Ippocampo'. In 1992 the Incursori were once again deployed to the war- and famine-ravaged nation of Somalia. The country's former communist-backed government had completely collapsed, and the tribal clans who make up the country's population were battling for control of the resources that remained. The Italians were part of a multinational peacekeeping force. The force was supposed to help stabilise the country, and allow it to start moving towards recovery. The mission ended in failure and with the humiliating withdrawal of all UN forces in 1994. In 1994 the African nation of Rwanda began a bloody civil war. Thousands of innocent civilians were slaughtered by the various factions seeking to exterminate their rival tribes. Several Western European governments, with citizens residing in Rwanda, formed a joint evacuation force. The force would secure a safe passage for refugees, and evacuate any Western nationals. The Italian contingent was composed of Col. Incursori. The Italians, along with a company of US marines, were tasked with securing the area around the international airport at Kigali. In 1995 war erupted in the Middle Eastern nation of Yemen and the Incursori were deployed to the area after a cease-fire agreement was reached. The unit has also been heavily committed to supporting Italian operations in Bosnia and have maintained a constant presence there since 1992. The Incursori act as the Italian Brigade's reconnaissance and Quick Reaction Force. On 31 March 1996, while stationed in Sarajevo, the unit was redesignated as the 9th Reggimento D'Assalto 'Col Moschin'. Deployed in both Albania and Kosovo in 1996–2000, they are now taking a leading role in operations against Islamic terrorism in 2001–03.

Weapons in use include the 9mm Beretta M-92SB pistol, 9mmR (.357 magnum) Colt Python revolver, 9mm H&K MP5A5 sub-machine gun, 9mm

Beretta M-12 sub-machine guns, 9mm Steyr AUG-P sub-machine gun, 9mm MP5SD3 sound-suppressed sub-machine gun, 5.56mm Beretta SCS-70/90 assault carbine, 5.56mm Steyr AUG A1 assault carbine, 5.56mm Beretta SC-70/90 assault rifle, 7.62mm H&K G3SG1 sniper rifle, 7.62mm H&K MSG90 sniper rifle, 7.62mm Accuracy International AW bolt-action sniper rifle, 7.62mm Mauser 86SR bolt-action sniper rifle, 12.7mm (.50 BMG) Barrett Model 82A1 sniper rifle, 5.56mm Beretta MINIMI light machine gun (licenced from FN), 7.62mm Beretta-Motofides MG-42/59 machine gun (licence-made Rheinmetall MG1A2), 18.5mmR (12-gauge) Beretta RS-202P pump-action shotgun, 18.5mmR (12-gauge) Franchi SPAS-15 semi-automatic shotgun, 40mmSR Colt M203 underbarrel grenade launcher (under SC-70/90), 90mm Instalaza C-90 light anti-tank weapon and 90mm Dynamit Nobel Panzerfaust 3 anti-tank rocket launcher.

It can call upon a specialist squadron of the Italian Air Force from the 15th wing in the form of HH3F helicopters or from the 46th Air Brigade with G222 (US C27 Spartan) fixed wing transports for special operations. The weapons available to this unit include 9mm Beretta-92 automatic pistols, 9mm MP5 sub-machine guns, 5.56mm SCP70/90 para automatic rifle, MSG90, SP86 and Barrett M82A1 sniper rifles, Beretta RS202 combat shotguns, 5.56mm Minimi machine guns and even Milan anti-tank missiles.

Navy

Comando Subacqueo ed Incursori (COMSUBIN) – Marina Militare Italiana   The Italian Special Forces have a well deserved reputation for toughness and effectiveness, forming part of a tradition that stretches back to the Second World War when Italian combat swimmers established a reputation for excellence. The COM.SUB.IN is an elite, all-volunteer force of approximately 600 men mainly recruited from the San Marco Marine Regiment and operating under the direct command of the Navy Chief of Staff. The unit's history dates back to the Second World War when the Italians formed several different naval assault/combat swimmer units to conduct commando operations against naval targets. One of the most famous of these units was the Xa Flottiglia 'MAS' which carried out several important raids, including the sinking of two British battleships in Alexandria harbour. After the September 1943 Italian armistice, the Regia Marina's various assault units were divided into two parts, with the units in the southern part of the country ('MARIASSALTO') fighting alongside the Allies, and the units in the northern part of the country continuing to fight alongside the Germans. The 1945 Peace Treaty did not allow Italy to possess naval assault units and, as a result, the various assault units were regrouped in a new organisation called 'MARICENTROSUB'. The new unit was mainly used for harbour mine-clearing duties. The Italians had to wait for the abolition of that Treaty and their formal entry in NATO in order to reform a dedicated naval Special Operations unit which was given the designation 'Gruppo Arditi

Incursori' ('GRUPPARDIN') and based at the Varignano Naval Base, near La Spezia. Prospective unit members undertake an intensive ten-month basic training programme which is followed by an addtional 42 weeks of Airborne, Ranger, and other specialised training. The course is divided into four phases: land warfare training, naval warfare training, ranger, parachute, climbing training and amphibious warfare training. Training also includes additional instruction in hand-to-hand, silent killing, small-arms, heavy weapons, counter-terrorism, demolition, mine-clearance, communications, intelligence-gathering and survival, through the duration of the course.

GOI – Gruppo Operativo Incursori The 'Incursori' of the GOI are COM.SUB.IN's offensive arm and composed of combat diver teams. It is composed of 150–200 operators and conducts operations near the coastline and is divided into three specialised sections:

UN.I.S – Unita Interveni Speciali (Special Intervention Unit-maritime counter-terrorism) Weapons unit (which handles the units heavy weapons)

GOS – Gruppo Operativo Subacquei (Underwater Operations Group) GOS is COM.SUB.IN's diver unit. They are tasked with protecting Italian naval vessels and facilities from attack by hostile forces, ensuring that the 'Incursori' teams are properly trained to conduct undersea operations, providing support for divers onboard fleet ships, carrying out various undersea duties, conducting maritime search and rescue operations, experimenting with new equipment and developing new diving techniques.

GNS – Gruppo Navale Speciale (Special Naval Group) GNS is intended to support COM.SUB.IN operations; it operates two naval support vessels that are used to transport COM.SUB.IN personnel and equipment.

Ufficio Studi (Study and Research Centre) This is a 'research/studies group' that is tasked with continuously searching for new equipment and weapons, evaluating equipment currently available on the market, buying new equipment, modifying equipment already in service after receiving requests from operators in the field, studying new weapons, and communications systems for possible use by COM.SUB.IN. Weapons used include the 9mm Beretta M-92SB pistol, 7.62mm H&K P11 underwater dart pistol, 9mm Beretta PM-12S sub-machine gun, 9mm H&K MP5A3 and MP5SD3 sub-machine gun, 5.56mm Beretta SC-70/90 assault rifle, 5.56mm H&K G41 assault rifle, 7.62mm Mauser 86SR bolt-action sniper rifle, 12.7mm (.50 BMG) Barrett Model 82A1 sniper rifle, 5.56mm Beretta MINIMI light machine gun (licensed from FN), 7.62mm Beretta-Motofides MG-42/59 machine gun (license-made Rheinmetall MG1A2), 18.5mmR (12-gauge) Franchi SPAS-15 semi-automatic shotgun, 40mmSR H&K MZP1 grenade launcher, 40mmSR Colt M203 underbarrel grenade launcher (under SC-70/90), 40mmSR H&K HK79 underbarrel grenade launcher (under G41) and 90mm Instalaza C-90 light antitank weapon.

Marines
San Marco Battalion This 1,000-strong Marine Battalion is an amphibious task force, which was originally dedicated to intervening on NATO's southern flank in support of either Greece or Turkey in the event of war with the communist bloc. However, this all-volunteer unit now has a national anti-terrorist role and trains to intervene abroad in the event of Italian citizens or interests being directly threatened by a hostile force. They train in beach assaults, cliff climbing, parachuting and heliborne operations. The battalion is organised into an operations section comprising four assault companies supported by training and logistics sections.

CIVILIAN SPECIAL FORCES
Polizia di Stato (National Police)
NOCS – Nucleo Operativo Centrale di Sicurezza (Central Operative Security Division) known as the 'teste di cuoio' or leatherheads, because of their distinctive headgear; a paramilitary force of only 50 men which achieved lasting fame with the rescue of US General James Dozier from the terrorist Red Brigade in January 1982. NOCS trains at the Abbosanta Special Base in Sardinia, where they train intensively in many Special Forces techniques, but with a considerable concentration on night operations and the use of sophisticated electronic surveillance equipment. Like the GSG-9, the NOCS studies terrorist methods, ideology and lifestyles so that eventually they can 'think like a terrorist' in order to anticipate terrorist actions and planning. It also has a reputation for its excellent range of high-tech surveillance equipment and the way it is used operationally.

Weapons in use include the 9mm Beretta M-92S pistol, 9mm Beretta Mod 8000 Cougar pistol, 9mm Beretta PM-12S sub-machine gun, 9mm H&K MP5A5 sub-machine gun, 9mm H&K MP5SD6 suppressed sub-machine gun, 5.56mm IMI Model 365 Galil SAR assault rifle, 7.62mm H&K G3SG1 sniper rifle, 7.62mm H&K PSG1 sniper rifle, 7.62mm Mauser 66SP bolt-action sniper rifle and 40mmSR H&K MZP1 grenade launcher.

GIS – Gruppo Intervento Speciale (Special Intervention Group) The GIS has a strength of only 100 and operates with a 30-man operations section and a specialist sniper squad. It was formed in 1977 with its base near the town of Lavarno. It is made up of soldiers from the Ist Carabinnieri Parachute Regiment. It trains regularly for anti-hijack and hostage rescue missions at several major Italian airports and has a reputation for outstanding fitness and technical ability in such areas as demolition, breaching, rappelling and other entry techniques. The GIS also has its own SAS-style 'killing house' for combat shooting and hostage rescue scenarios and now operates both within and outside Italy. The GIS has rightly acquired a fearsome reputation and is considered an elite among the world's elite. This unit uses the following weapons: the 9mm Beretta M-92S pistol, 9mmR (.357 Magnum) S&W Model 28 Highway Patrolman revolver, 9mm Beretta M-93R machine pistol, 9mm Beretta PM-12S sub-machine gun, 9mm H&K MP5A5 sub-machine gun and MP5SD3 suppressed sub-machine gun, 5.56mm Beretta SC-70/90 assault rifle, 7.62mm H&K G3SG1 sniper rifle, 7.62mm H&K MSG90 sniper rifle, 7.62mm H&K PSG1 sniper rifle, 7.62mm Mauser 86SR bolt-action sniper rifle, 12.7mm (.50 BMG) Barrett Model 82A1 sniper rifle, 18.5mmR (12-gauge) Franchi PA-3 pump-action shotgun and 18.5mmR (12-gauge) Franchi SPAS-15 semi-automatic shotgun. Vehicles include black Range Rover 4×4 utility vehicles and Agusta AB412 and Agusta A119 Koala helicopters.

JAMAICA

MILITARY SPECIAL FORCES
Both the 1st and 2nd Battalions of the Jamaica Regiment have small SF trained detachments under the command of the JDF IU (Intelligence Unit). The level of organised crime and insurgency within Jamaica has placed a severe strain on these units' limited trained manpower, and there is a strong possibility that with a considerable input of US aid and advisers an additional battalion will be raised in 2003 as a dedicated Special Forces unit.

JAPAN

MILITARY SPECIAL FORCES
The Japanese Defence Ministry intend to give the land forces a genuine anti-terrorist and counter-insurgency capability and the first step was taken in 2000 to create a Special Operations warfare centre and to provide for training by personnel from the US Delta and SEAL units.

Initially, new units will be created within the existing structure of the Japanese forces Airborne Brigade. However, within five years it is intended that the Japanese with have a considerable Special Forces capability, with at least three dedicated battalion-sized units for domestic anti-terrorist and hostage rescue operations. Additionally all such units would be trained, equipped and given the important logistic and aviation support infrastructure to carry the fight against the terrorist well beyond national borders. Japanese long-term intentions include therefore the provision of a genuine International Intervention capability provided by a full Airborne Special Forces Brigade Group.

CIVILIAN SPECIAL FORCES
The Japanese intelligence services have had to deal effectively with the growing threat of extremist behaviour, such as the eight deadly attacks by

members of the Japanese Red Army on the Tokyo subway since 1972, or the Aum Shinri Kyo religious group that used Sarin nerve gas in an attack that killed 12 and injured 5,500 Tokyo subway passengers in 1995. It resulted in 26 stations and two complete lines being shut down, with the consequence that the city largely ground to a halt. The National Police, who had to commit around a third of their available manpower to the incident for several weeks, responded in April 1996 by forming a Special Assault Team. This para-military force is organised into ten platoons each of 20 personnel, and are trained to the highest possible military standards by, in particular, the French GIGN Gendarmerie Special Operations unit. At least one of these platoons is specially trained to operate at the major airports around Tokyo. They have received training from among others GSG-9, GIGN, SAS and the Sayeret Matkal. They are considered very skilled and proficient in a wide range of techniques from heliborne insertion, combat shooting, hostage rescue, counter-terrorism, anti-hijacking, with a particular interest in buses and subways, and close-quarter battle situations. There is in addition a small, and very discreet, special hostage rescue unit for highly delicate operations, and these extremely fit and well-trained personnel are known as the 'modern ninja'.

JOHN F. KENNEDY SPECIAL WARFARE CENTER

The Special Warfare Center and School began as the Psychological Warfare Division of the Army General School at Fort Riley, KS, in 1951. The school moved to Fort Bragg in 1952. Civil-affairs classes were added to the curriculum when the Civil Affairs School moved from Fort Gordon, GA, to Fort Bragg in 1971. In 1961, the school established the Special Forces Training Group to train enlisted volunteers for assignments in Special Forces groups. The Institute for Military Assistance at Fort Bragg, NC, was, on 1 October 1983, redesignated the JFK Special Warfare Center, as a result of a Special Operations forces (SOF) realignment of that year. The JFK Special Warfare Center was in essence a branch school, but was categorised as a TRADOC special activity. Further SOF realignments in 1990 transferred the TRADOC School to the US Army Special Operations Command at Fort Bragg, by orders of 20 June. The John F. Kennedy Special Warfare Center and school's Special Forces Underwater Operations School in Key West, FL, provides Special Operations training revolving around maritime operations and infiltration techniques used to infiltrate enemy areas to avoid detection. The school offers three specific courses related to underwater operations: the Special Forces Combat Diver Qualification, the Special Forces Diving Medical Technician and the Special Forces Combat Diving Supervisor. The legendary Green Beret and the Special Forces tab are symbols of physical and mental excellence, courage, ingenuity and just plain stubbornness and these are only awarded to those who successfully pass the training at the US Army John F. Kennedy Special Warfare Center and School at Fort Bragg, NC. At the heart of Special Forces training is the 1st Special Warfare Training Group, which conducts the Special Forces Assessment and Selection Course, Special Forces Qualification Course and all advanced Cpecial Forces skills training such as language training and regional studies.

The first step for a soldier wishing to become Special Forces-qualified is Special Forces Assessment and Selection; a 24-day course designed to focus on student trainability and suitability in Special Forces. The SFAS cadre look at nearly 1,800 Special Forces volunteers each year to determine who is suitable for Special Forces training and who may be unable to adapt to the Special Forces environment. Candidates attend SFAS at Camp MacKall, NC on a temporary duty (TDY) status. Candidates who enter this course find themselves under constant evaluation starting with the day they in-process until the day they out-process. Teaching, coaching, training and mentoring are important aspects of the programme. Land navigation is used as a common medium to judge student trainability. A series of twelve attributes linked to success in the Special Forces Qualification Course (SFQC) form the basis for evaluating candidate suitability. These attributes include intelligence, physical fitness, motivation, trustworthiness, accountability, maturity, stability, judgement, decisiveness, teamwork, influence and communications. Though land navigation is an important evaluation tool, other training events such as a one-mile obstacle course, runs, road marches and rappelling are also used to evaluate students. A board of impartial senior officers and non-commissioned officers reviews the soldiers' overall performance during the course. It makes the final determination as to whether a soldier is suitable for Special Forces training and identifies the specific Special Forces military occupational speciality for which he will be trained. After successfully completing the Special Forces Assessment and Selection Course the soldier is then eligible to attend the Special Forces Qualification Course.

The US Army's Special Operations University is responsible for Special Operations training, leader development, doctrine and personnel advocacy. The centre and school's Training Group conducts the complete spectrum of Special Operations training. In addition to its training role, the school also tests new equipment at the US Army Yuma Proving Ground (YPG) which is a general-purpose desert environmental test facility. YPG is located 26 miles north of Yuma, Arizona, on US Highway 95. This installation covers nearly 1,400 square miles and offers climate and terrain similar to major desert areas worldwide. YPG is primarily involved in developmental and operational testing of artillery weapons and ammunition, aircraft armament systems, mobility equipment and air delivery systems.

JORDAN

MILITARY SPECIAL FORCES

A Special Operations Command (SOCOM) was established on 1 October 1996 and is tasked to deal with a possible Palestinian uprising and the growth of Islamic terrorism. It also secures the borders with Syria and supports the hard-pressed police in attempting to prevent the smuggling of equipment across the border into Iraq. The Special Forces date back to the first small parachute unit in April 1963, while the first Special Forces brigade was formed in 1971.

Ist Special Forces Brigade with 71st Counter-Terrorist Battalion SOU-71. This unit includes a specialist 100 strong HRU team originally formed in 1973 and which took part in breaking the siege of the Intercontinental Hotel, Amman, in 1977.
101st Special Force Battalion.

Airborne Brigade
81st Ranger Battalion.
91st Airborne Battalion (this battalion can be tasked for external use in support of Arab allies)
    The first commander and founding influence of SOCOM, Prince Abdullah (now King Abdullah) established a close and long-lasting working relationship with both the SAS and the Parachute Regiment in Britain. Exercises take place with the French GIGN and forces from Bahrain, Egypt, and Oman. The SF Brigade has a number of electronic warfare, psyops and aviation support units with UH1Hand AH1F helicopters. Weapons in use include the 9mm FN-Browning HP-35 pistol, 9mm SIG-Sauer P226 pistol, 9mm H&K MP5K sub-machine gun, 9mm H&K MP5A3 sub-machine gun, 9mm H&K MP5SD3 suppressed sub-machine gun, 5.56mm Colt CAR-15A2 Model 733 Commando assault carbine, 5.56mm Beretta SC-70/90 assault rifle, 5.56mm Colt AR-15A2 Model 701 assault rifle (adopted 1985), 7.62mm Steyr SSG 69 bolt-action sniper rifle and 7.62mm Saco M60 machine gun.

CIVILIAN SPECIAL SERVICES

Police Public Security Groups include a Specialist Airport Anti-Hijacking unit highly trained as Sky Marshals and for HRU operations against aircraft or airport buildings. Based at Amman's Queen Alia Airport, this 500-strong unit is highly rated and, while using much the same weapons as the other Special Forces, also has suppressed low-velocity handguns for safe use aboard aircraft.

Unit-14 is a national SWAT-style unit which works closely with the Army's Special Forces.

JSOC

The major reorganisation of the US unconventional warfare capability in the wake of the failed attempt to rescue US hostages being held prisoner in Iran in 1980 led directly to the creation of the JSOC or Joint Special Operations Command. Its major aim was to co-ordinate more effectively all the various units involved in often very complicated covert operations and to avoid at all costs a repetition of the fatal confusion that developed during the planning and execution phases of a brave, but flawed, rescue operation. JSOC was activated on 15 December 1980. The joint headquarters is tasked to study special operations requirements and techniques, to ensure effective levels of co-operation and where possible equipment standardisation, to plan and conduct Special Forces operations exercises and oversee the standard of training. It also acts as a think tank to develop new or improved Special Forces operational tactics. It controls the Special Forces of the US Army, USAF and the US Navy. Traditionally the US Marine Corps has remained outside its control, but in the light of its huge increase in worldwide commitments caused by the War on Terrorism and other potential conflicts, USMC Special Units are likely to be attached to JSOC from late 2002 onwards to further enhance its overall anti-terrorist and special operations capability.

JSOSE

Joint Special Operations Support Element. Controls and develops the logistic and technical support services vital in ensuring the good management and combat effectiveness of the US Special Forces under operational conditions.

JUNGLE WARFARE

As the British were to learn from fighting the Japanese in the Second World War, the communist insurgency in Malaya in the 1950s, or the French in Indo-China and later the US Army in South-East Asia, jungle warfare has its own unique problems. The terrain; the dense, steamy climatic conditions; disease, plant, animal, insect and reptile threats which often caused more casualties than the enemy; the sheer difficulty in maintaining weapons and equipment when rust can appear in twelve hours and uniforms rot in days; and the endless nightmare of resupply of food and ammunition, made jungle warfare a technique that required highly specialist training. Jungle Warfare Schools run by the Brazilian and British Armies have been at the forefront of developing suitable techniques and new equipment. It is very difficult to walk through true jungle conditions without leaving telltale signs of your progress for a skilled tracker to follow, and the SAS often attempted to overcome this by using discernible animal tracks in an attempt to confuse an enemy. However, progress through the densest jungle or swaps could be appallingly slow, with distances of only 550yds (500m) taking a full day of painstakingly holding vegetation aside to avoid damage and then moving it carefully back into place. Constantly clambering over fallen trees, slipping and sliding down steep muddy slopes, fording swollen streams and rivers, wading through stinking swamps full of rotting vegetation and avoiding injury from a variety of natural threats such as the Nante Sikkit, a thorn tree that spreads fronds for up to 21ft (7m) in every direction. They are virtually invisible among the thick vegetation, but are as strong as steel wire and covered in vicious barbed thorns. Malaria-carrying mosquitoes, a disease usually kept at bay with Paludrine tablets; poisonous snakes and insects; infected wounds or cuts; debilitating stomach bugs; heat; exhaustion; and often both thirst and hunger make keeping a unit combat-effective extremely difficult. However, for most soldiers having served for any length of time in the jungles or swamps of South-East Asia, the biggest night-mare were the leeches. No matter how careful the soldier tried to be, he knew that at the end of a difficult and dangerous patrol he was likely to be infested with leeches clinging to his body. They crawled up the soldier's legs or dropped off vegetation and worked their way inside clothing to the softest areas of the body – ankles, wrists, neck, ears, armpits and genitals. Their saliva numbed the skin so the victim was not aware of their position. At the end of a patrol the mutual de-leeching was a vitally important but sickening daily procedure. On one occasion an SAS trooper was mortified to discover eleven blood-bloated leeches hanging 'like a bunch of grapes' from his penis. The fact that European Forces have learned to excel under such conditions is a measure of the success of jungle warfare training over the last fifty years, and of course for the well-trained soldier the jungle can be a friend, providing everything he needs: food, water, shelter, camouflage and even early-warning of an enemy's approach.

JUST IN CASE KIT

Emergency pack carried by Special Forces for use when a soldier becomes separated from his unit or left behind enemy lines. The typical 'Kit' carried by British Special Forces during the numerous campaigns in Japanese occupied territory in the Second World War included a pistol and ammunition, a small bag of gold sovereigns, a compass, knife and compact tool kit. However, the most imortant elements were a square of silk printed with a message in several local languages offering a substantial reward to anyone offering the bearer help and safety, and a poison capsule as the last defence against capture and the treatment likely to be received from the Japanese before being finally killed. These 'last resort' kits have been used in myriad variations by the British, French, American and other leading Special Forces in every theatre of war since 1945.

KALASHNIKOV

Mikhail Kalashnikov's original design, although influenced by the German assault rifles that appeared towards the close of the Second World War, became a triumph of military practicality, ease of mass production and reliability. Since the first version, the AK47, achieved widespread use in the early 1950s the design has constantly spawned new variations produced both in Russia and throughout the world. The AKM, which is of simplified design, is capable of manufacture in relatively unsophisticated industrial facilities. Both were chambered in the short Russian 7.62mm round, with 30-round curved magazines, and had a cyclic rate of 600rpm. The RPK was the squad automatic weapon variation. In 1974, a re-chambered version appeared as the new 5.45mm AK74. Lighter and with a higher cyclic rate of fire at 650rpm and an effective range of 550yds (500m), it has already appeared in a number of variations from the standard with fixed stock; the airborne/Special Forces version with folding stock; and the squad automatic weapon, RPK-74 with 40-round magazine and the AKR sub-machine gun. This later variant is very similar to the AKS-74, but with a shorter barrel and an effective range of only 110yds (100m).

KAYBAR

Broad-bladed combat knife famously used by the US Navy's elite SEAL units.

KAZAKSTAN

MILITARY SPECIAL FORCES
Spetsnaz Brigade
This is a Rapid Response Unit capable of carrying out Special Operations missions, it also includes the Aristan (Group Alpha and Service A), a unit tasked with counter-terrorism and hostage rescue. In 2001–02 Aristan received an input of new US surveillance equipment, weapons and probably training by Special Forces.

CIVILIAN SPECIAL FORCES
Ministry of the Interior
The Internal Security Troops include a small 30-strong Rapid Response HRU Team.

KENYA

MILITARY SPECIAL FORCES
D (SF)Company, 20th Parachute Battalion

CIVILIAN SPECIAL FORCES

General Service Unit (GSU) of the Kenya Police   This unit is rated as quite competent and has received considerable training from US Special Forces advisers. Links exist with the SAS and for more than twenty years with Israeli Special Forces, particularly since the GSU provided security for Israeli Air Force C-130s after the Entebbe hostage rescue operation, and continues to provide high level security for El Al aircraft at Nairobi airport.

The unit is trained in a range of anti-hijacking and HRU skills as well as COIN and anti-terrorist duties.

Weapons used include MP5, Uzi and Sterling SMGs, FN FAL and G3 rifles, FN MAG machine guns, Remington 700 sniper rifles, Remington 870 combat shotgun and the M79 40mm grenade launcher.

KIA

Acronym: Killed In Action.

KLICK

K, a kilometre, the US military uses the metric system.

KOLWEZI RESCUE OPERATION 1978 – 2 REP

On the 19–20 May 1978 the elite 2nd French Foreign Legion Parachute Regiment (2 REP) was deployed to deal with the crisis that occurred in Shaba Province in south Zaire (the Democratic Republic of Congo). The province was invaded by separatist rebels who took over the town of Kolwezi, with a population that included over 3,000 Europeans, mainly mining experts and their families, who were regarded as potential hostages by Major Mufu and his 4,000 separatist Tigers.

A drop of Zairean paratroopers into the town on 16 May was a fiasco. The Zairean leader, President Mobutu, had discussed the affair with his French counterpart to arrange foreign intervention if necessary; it now became very necessary. Colonel Philippe Erulin's 2 REP was put on standby. The first elements to leave were 1, 2 and 3 Companies, and part of the HQ Company, in five DC-8 aircraft on the night of 17/18 May. The Support and 4 Company would follow later. Flying to Kinshasa, the 500 Legionnaires were packed into four C-130s and one Transall aircraft for the drop.

It was broad daylight when the Legion paras landed near Kolwezi, but fortunately the Tigers were caught off guard. A command post was quickly established and the men began to regroup. Even before all the paras had landed, the first groups fanned out and advanced to their objectives. Although the Tigers outnumbered the paras, their discipline and morale had crumbled. As Legionnaires cleared large parts of the town, white settlers began to emerge from cover, most of them hungry, thirsty and suffering from shock. Tragically, those held in the Impala Hotel were killed before the Legionnaires reached them. Within two hours of the initial jump, the Legionnaires were in almost complete control of the town. A second wave of aircraft carrying the 4th Company, Support Company and the rest of HQ Company was ordered by Colonel Erulin to fly on to Lubumbashi to avoid a night drop.

Meanwhile, on the ground the Legionnaires continued to engage the enemy, killing many Tigers and suffering only six casualties. The second wave dropped in during the early hours of 20 May, but there was little overall fighting until the afternoon, when 4th Company ran into heavy resistance near Metal Shaba. The Tigers mounted an attack, but were stopped by the Support Company's 81mm mortars and 89mm anti-tank rockets. The Tigers fled, leaving 80 dead. This was the last major action at Kolwezi, the paras then conducted mopping-up operations. The operation confirmed the immense professionalism and effectiveness of the 2 REP, and indeed its place among the top elite Special Forces of the world.

KOREA – NORTH

MILITARY SPECIAL FORCES

8th Special Operations Corps North Korea has one of the world's largest Special Operations capabilities, with over 80,000 elite light infantry organised into 23 brigades and at least eighteen independent battalions. They are undoubtedly the best trained and have the highest morale of all North Korean ground forces. The Ministry of the People's Armed Forces controls the bulk of the Special Operations Forces through one of two commands, the Reconnaissance Bureau (RB), the Training Unit Guidance Bureau (TUGB) and the Sniper Bureau (SB). The Reconnaissance Bureau is the primary organisation within the Ministry of People's Armed Forces for the collection of strategic and tactical intelligence. It also exercises operational control over agents engaged in collecting military intelligence and in the training and dispatch of unconventional warfare teams. The RB is also the primary intelligence organisation tasked to plan SOF infiltration and reconnaissance operations in the ROK. Subordinate to the RB are nine reconnaissance battalions (including a navy and air force battalion) and a sniper brigade.

The Training Unit Guidance Bureau (TUGB) is directly subordinate to the General Staff Department while the Sniper Bureau operations are basically the same as light infantry, except they are conducted in team-sized units. The TUGB is also the central training and guidance command for all SOF units and serves as a training command and a wartime controlling authority for strategic and corps-level SOF missions. Subordinate to the TUGB are eight light infantry brigades (including three airborne), two airborne brigades, and two amphibious brigades. Under the control of the Forward Corps (1st, 2nd, 4th,

5th) are four reconnaissance battalions, three sniper brigades, and three light infantry brigades. Subordinate to mechanised corps are five reconnaissance battalions and four light infantry brigades.

The Special Operations Force (SOF) of the Korean People's Army (KPA) is tasked to conduct raids in enemy rear areas and to perform reconnaissance and intelligence operations. Trained in unconventional warfare tactics, KPA SOF units will attempt to create a second front in the Republic of Korea (ROK) rear with clandestine infiltration and harassment tactics. In addition, raids on targets outside the Korean Peninsula possibly could be conducted. Strategic SOF units develop targeting information, report ROK civilian and military actions, conduct post-strike assessments, and verify enemy intentions. Typical missions would involve the location and destruction of national-level artillery; airfields; storage facilities; air defence locations; and command, control, communication and intelligence (C3I) assets in ROK/US rear areas In addition, strategic units also may conduct operations that include the kidnap and assassination of key enemy personnel. Under limited visibility or the cover of darkness, operational- and tactical-level SOF units will attempt to infiltrate the DMZ dressed as ROK civilians or ROK military personnel. This will be done over land and through pre-constructed tunnels, led by reconnaissance teams of five to ten men. Because the DMZ is primarily mountainous, the SOF will use this terrain to provide cover, concealment, safe areas and numerous routes for escape and evasion. Lowlands will be used for their thick weeds, tall grass and woods to provide cover and concealment. Once past the main ROK defences, operational- and tactical-level units will attempt to arrive undetected at pre-selected target sites that are critical to ROK/US military operations. Typical targets include: ports, airfields, logistical points, avenues of approach, rail lines, C3I assets, and other reinforcement areas. At H-Hour, pre-positioned SOF units within ROK/US rear areas will attack targets as massive artillery and rocket attacks are initiated from north of the DMZ. Simultaneously, additional SOF units will slip through the DMZ, be inserted by air, and land on South Korean beaches.

In the 1970s, in support of overland insertion, North Korea began clandestine tunnelling operations along the entire DMZ, with two tunnels per forward division. By 1990 four tunnels dug on historical invasion routes from the north had been discovered by South Korean and United States tunnel neutralisation teams: three in the mid-1970s and the fourth in March 1990. The South Koreans suspect there will be as many as 28 tunnels by early 2003.

KOREA – SOUTH or ROK

MILITARY SPECIAL FORCES
Special Warfare Command The main Counter-Terrorist unit is the 707th Special Mission Battalion. Following the tragic events of the Arab terrorist attack on

Israeli athletes at the 1972 Munich Olympic Games, South Korea in anticipation of hosting the 1988 Games, formed the 707th battalion in 1982. The unit, based in Songham, south-east of Seoul, is organised into two companies, each with four fourteen-man operations squads and supported by specialist women-only, weapons, demolitions and intelligence teams. Counter-Terrorism training, often provided by the German GSG-9, is extremely tough, with some six months of developing advanced fitness, weapons and infantry skills. This is followed by a further six months of training in close-quarter combat skills, special warfare training, underwater warfare and parachute techniques. Mountaineering and cold weather warfare is also very important to a unit often called upon to operate in sub-zero conditions. All members of the 707th are SCUBA- and parachute-qualified. One of the more unusual training routines involves regular exercise in the snow and sub-zero temperatures and swimming in freezing lakes without any thermal protection. It is also reported that the 707th maintains a group of combat-qualified female personnel for use in situations where a woman would not be suspected of posing a risk, such as an airline hijacking where food and medicine might be allowed to be taken on board. The 707th has already seen considerable and successful action in operations mounted against North Korean infiltrators, provided security for VIPs and for key facilities during the 1986 Asian Games, the 1988 Olympics and the 2002 Soccer World Cup. At all of these events terrorist attacks were considered to be a real danger. The 707th's soldiers, distinguished by their black berets, are assigned urban counter-terrorist missions. They also constitute a quick-reaction unit for other kinds of emergencies and special-warfare requirements in wartime. There have been rumblings from certain political and military sectors that the 707th is to be disbanded or re-organised under another name in due course, but there remains a clear intention to keep both its skills and a dedicated anti-terrorist capabililty, whatever transpires with this particular unit. In addition to working with special Korean Counter-Terrorist police units, the 707th also trains with special units from the United Kingdom, United States, Israel and Australia. The 707th uses a wide variety of foreign and domestically produced weapons, including the 9mm Berretta M9, 9mm Daewoo automatic pistol, 9mm H&K MP5 sub-machine guns, 5.56mm CAR15 carbines, Daewoo K1/2 assault rifles albeit modified for assaults with the addition of forward pistol grips and in some cases low-light and night vision device, and 7.62mm PSG-1 and US M24, M-40 and RAI .50 calibre sniper rifles. Modified M-60E3s and K3 Beltfed are used for machine gun support. For rearguards Tactical a Benelli Super-90 shotgun with pistol grips is used.

Special Warfare Command (formed on 1st April 1958)
Direct Special Force unit
707th 'White Tiger' Special Mission Battalion.This battalion has two companies, each with four Operations Teams (each fourteen men),

Demolition Team and Support Team.

Airborne Brigades
1st 'Golden Eagle' Airborne Brigade – HALO/HAHO
3rd 'Flying Tiger' Airborne Brigade – Land infiltration
5th 'Flying Horse' Airborne Brigade – SCUBA and combat swimming operations
7th 'Flying Horse' Airborne Brigade – Special Operations, direct support to infantry divisions
9th 'Ghost' Airborne Brigade – Special Operations, direct support to infantry divisions
11th 'Golden Bat' Airborne Brigade – Special Operations, direct support to infantry divisions
13th 'Black Jaguar' Airborne Brigade – Special Operations, direct support to infantry divisions
Special Warfare Centre – Training

Special Assault Regiments   (Similar roles to US Rangers, one deployed with each forward corps)
701st Special Assault Regiment
702nd Special Assault Regiment
703rd Special Assault Regiment
705th Special Assault Regiment
706th Special Assault Regiment
708th Special Assault Regiment

Special Assault Brigades (counter-infiltration brigades)
201st Special Assault Brigade
203rd Special Assault Brigade
205th Special Assault Brigade Republic of Korea Marine Corps

Marines
The ROKMC created in 1949 has a considerable Special Operation capability. With Recon and LRRP units attached to each of the eight Combat Regiments. They first saw action in the Korean War when in one particular action a squad of the ROKMC wiped out an entire battalion of the North Korean invasion force. As a result to this, they were acclaimed by the foreign media and dubbed the 'Invincible Marines'. The Marines were deployed during the Vietnam War and were stationed in Danang. Operating alongside the USMC and the US Navy SEALs, their most notable operations were 'Operation Van Buren' and the Battle of Hoi An, where they acquitted themselves exceptionally well against regular North Vietnamese units.

CIVILIAN SPECIAL FORCES
Tae-t'ero-Tukkong-Tae Counter-Terrorist Special Attack Unit of the National Police

Mainly made up of recruits from the Combat Police, an elite Border Patrol unit. It consists of around 100 personnel and has received training from both the GSG-9 and US Special Forces.

It carries out VIP protection duties as well as HRU tasks. It has its HQ at Yongin with a well-equipped training facility having a CQB house, and specialises in martial arts. Armed with a range of modern weapons including the MP5 SMG and M21 sniper rifle. This unit played a significant role in providing protection for major sporting events, including the 2002 Soccer World Cup.

KRAV MAGA

The Israeli Special Forces are unusual in having developed their own unique martial art technique known as 'Krav Maga', Hebrew for 'Contact Combat'. The technique was first introduced in 1972 and subjected to continued refinement throughout the rest of the 1970s; it has since been adopted by many foreign Special Forces including the French GIGN. Unlike other commonly used martial arts Krav Maga is not based upon an oriental technique or any form of harmony philosophy. Instead is a straightforward, brutal and highly effective form of unarmed combat that combines all the most effective killing methods found in other martial arts, but combined with a positive focus on aggressiveness, decisiveness and the use of unpredictable moves. The trained personnel using Krav Maga must have but one goal in mind, and that is to quickly disarm, incapacitate or kill the enemy by the use of any and all means available.

There are highly intensive courses in Krav Maga run for the Israel Defence Forces (IDF) at both the Counter-Terror Warfare School in the Mitkan Adam army base and the Combat Physical Training School at the Wingate army base, which is now responsible for the continued development of 'Contact Combat' and for training courses for Krav Maga instructors.

KUWAIT

MILITARY SPECIAL FORCES
Army
10th Al Tahrir Commando Battalion – guards Falayka Island and Kuwait International Airport

Special Forces – Kuwaiti Special Forces were dealt a severe blow during the Iraqi invasion in 1990. Yet, despite initial losses during the primary assault, it has been reported that Kuwaiti SF troopers regrouped and conducted limited military operations with the assistance of Coalition Special Operations personnel. The 500-man force is geared primarily towards

Counter-Terrorism and hostage rescue operations. Within the Special Forces are three primary units, the first being a CT element, the second a riot control unit, and the third a VIP protection unit. Headquartered on the outskirts of Kuwait City, this unit enjoys a close relationship with the Special Operations Forces of many Western nations, especially the US Army's 5th Special Forces Group (SFG).

Navy
Fast Attack Unit – coastal patrol and maritime interdiction and combat swimmer unit.

KWANGJU MASSACRE – 1980

The US Special Forces stationed in South Korea and working alongside Korea's own Special Warfare Command, along with the DIA, CIA and the Carter administration have all been accused of being implicated in the so-called 'Kwangju Massacre'. By reason of their obvious foreknowledge and the tacit support they showed when following General Chun Doo Hwan's seizure of control of the country on 17 May 1980, the ROK Special Warfare Command (SWC) deployed large numbers of Special Forces ('Black Berets') units, including the 7th SWC Brigade to Kwangju, to suppress some 30,000 rioting students protesting at the military coup. Many hundreds of students are believed to have been killed by the Special Forces in a Tiananmen Square-style operation, and the soldiers' actions led to such local resentment that two years later the 11th and 13th SWC Brigades were still having to cope with considerable anti-government violence in the Kwangju area.

KYRGYZSTAN

MILITARY SPECIAL FORCES

Two understrength Special Forces Battalions which are trained and equipped in a similar way to the Russian SPETSNAZ.

The 'Scorpion' a 250-strong Special Operations company based in Bishkek provides the primary anti-terrorist and hostage rescue capability.

LAHORE AND ISLAMABAD HIJACKINGS – SSG

The SSG was mostly used in border and covert operations, until 1985, when a PANAM airliner was hijacked by four anonymous terrorists. Disguised as members of the ASF (Airport Security Force), with concealed Russian AKSU SMGs and TT33 pistols, the terrorists succeeded in boarding the aircraft.

Fortunately, an air hostess had discovered the fact just as the pilot was preparing for take-off, and rushed to the cockpit to warn the pilot. The crew considered it wise to leave the plane through the emergency hatch in the cockpit without drawing the attention of the hijackers.

Government officials later offered to negotiate a peaceful end to the hijacking but the hijackers were reluctant to negotiate and threatened instead to shoot the passengers if they were not allowed to leave unharmed. The SSG was put on stand-by and soon given the go-ahead. That night the SSG, armed with automatic weapons and wearing black uniforms and light body-armour, entered the plane by breaching the doors of the plane. The hijackers, who were expecting an operation, resisted and opened fire on the commandos. Unfortunately, the passengers who were not prepared for the assault panicked when the lights of the plane were suddenly cut. SSG were still not fully trained for such combat in confined conditions and due to this many of the passengers were caught in the deadly firefight and heavy casualties ensued. Although all the terrorists were killed and the hijack ended, it was not without at least ten civilian casualties. It was suggested that the cause for the failure of the operation was the use of inappropriate weapons and tactics. It is certainly true that the SSG had not been trained to handle CQBs (Close-Quarters Battles) at that time. Between this operation and its second major test, the SSG had honed and perfected its CQB capabilities, so when, in 1994, terrorists hijacked a school bus in Islamabad carrying more than 35 primary school children, as well as two teachers and a driver, they were far better prepared. It was quickly learned that the kidnappers were six Afghan militants who were now holding their hostages in a building. The terrorists had drawn all the curtains so there was virtually no contact. Clandestine contact was made with some of the hostages the next day, telling them that an operation would be carried out at sunset aimed at killing all the terrorists on the spot, therefore the hostages had to be prepared for the sudden attack. The hostages had to shift themselves on the floor or under any furniture just one minute before the assault. Any confusion or carelessness could result in severe casualties. The news quietly spread between the hostages during mealtime. The next day, at the given time the hostages moved to the appropriate locations and a volley of gas and smoke grenades was fired through the windows. After an interval of three or four seconds SSG's commandos of the 'Zarrar Jareeh', the main assault team of the Musa CT Company, began entering through windows and doors armed with MP5 sub-machine guns. Also carried were laser-aimed Glock and Beretta pistols and spare gas grenades. They were wearing camouflage uniforms, Kevlar vests and gas masks, and in less than two minutes all six terrorists were dead, with no serious injuries to the hostages.

LAOS

MILITARY SPECIAL FORCES

Five independent anti-terrorist Infantry Companies carry out limited special operations. Equipment and training is woefully inadequate for these units, and there appears little opportunity for this to improve in the near future.

LATIN AMERICA – US SPECIAL FORCES INVOLVEMENT

There is a long history of US Special Forces involvement in Latin America, and units of the US military remained very active throughout the entire region in 2002. They are present in nearly every country in the hemisphere, taking part in counter-narcotics operations, training missions, and other activities. Special Operations Forces (SOF) are specialised military units designed to confront a wide variety of situations ranging from peacetime threats to open warfare. They are most frequently employed in three settings: 'crises and conflicts below the threshold of war, such as terrorism, insurgency, and sabotage'; in major conflicts, where they serve as 'force multipliers . . . increasing the effectiveness and efficiency of the US military effort', and in 'situations requiring regional orientation and cultural and political sensitivity, including military-to-military contacts and non-combatant missions like humanitarian assistance, security assistance, and peacekeeping operations.'

Special Operations Command South (SOCSOUTH), based at Roosevelt Roads Naval Air Station in Puerto Rico, is the Special Forces component of the US Southern Command (Southcom), the regional military command for Latin America. SOCSOUTH co-ordinates most Special Forces activity in Latin America and the Caribbean. Training with foreign security forces accounts for a great deal of Special Forces activity in Latin America and the Caribbean. Special Forces teams deploy over 100 times each year for joint training in nearly every country in the hemisphere. The vast majority of these SOF training deployments fall into two categories: Joint Combined Exchange Training (JCET) and counter-narcotics training. Special Forces deploy to Latin America and the Caribbean dozens of times each year under the Joint Combined Exchange Training (JCET) programme, which involves sending small SOF teams overseas to work with, or to train with, foreign militaries. The average JCET group is comprised of 10 to 40 troops, though groups can include as many as 100. After operating in 101 countries worldwide in 1997, and about 95 countries in 1998, the JCET programme has declined somewhat, with deployments to 62 countries in 1999. This markedly increased in 2000–01, and even more so following the events of

9–11 and the growth of conflict and instability in Latin America. JCET deployments are usually funded through Major Force Program 11, the SOF operating budget. The JCET programme, according to a Defence Department spokesman, 'is not designed to train the forces of other countries. It's designed to train our Special Forces in how forces of other countries operate.' This statement may come as a surprise to the countries involved.

Counter-narcotics missions account for much SOF activity in Latin America and the Caribbean today. Army Special Forces, according to a Southern Command publication, are well represented on 'an interconnecting network of military teams' that provide 'intelligence, planning and training to countries actively engaged in countering cocaine cartels'. Special Forces' counter-narcotics mission involves extensive contact with the region's militaries and police, much of it through training. Special Forces teams deploy frequently to Latin America to train foreign units in counter-narcotics, often through joint training activities that can resemble JCETs. When the subject matter is drug-related, training the US personnel need not be the activity's primary purpose – which allows US Special Forces to legally take an active role in operations.

LATVIA

MILITARY SPECIAL FORCES
Specialo Uzdevumu Vieniba (SUV)   SF 'Green Beret' Team. A company-sized and well-trained unit capable of limited anti-terrorist and hostage rescue operations.

Izlukdesanto Bataljons (IDB)   Recce 'Red Beret' Team. A capable and well-equipped LRRP unit.

LEBANON

MILITARY SPECIAL FORCES
The origins of the Special Forces date back to the French-Lebanese para-military unit, the Troups Speciales du Levant formed in 1922. The first commando battalion was formed in 1951; however, during the civil war of the 1970s and Israeli invasion of 1982, the Special Forces, in common with most of the army, split along religious lines as the country disintegrated. A new Special Forces command was established in 1983 and greatly expanded following the Taif agreement in 1989 that restructured the entire Lebanese Armed Forces. It was responsible for counter-terrorist and special operations.

The Lebanese Special Forces are increasingly well trained and equipped by the US as Rangers with a limited HRU capability, and can probably be expected to take some part in any serious attempt by Israel and the US to rid

Southern Lebanon of the pro-Iranian Hizbollah fighters stationed in large numbers in the Beka'a Valley. Weapons used include Star 9mm and Kassnar 9mm pistols, SIG M540 5.56mm assault rifles, Remington 700 sniper rifles and Remington 870 combat shotguns.

The Special Operations command now has five Special Forces Regiments, 1 Commando Regiment, 1 Airborne Regiment (Red Beret) and a Marine Commando Company (Light Blue Berets).

CIVILIAN SPECIAL FORCES
Tactical Strike Force of the Kiwa al Amn al Daakhili or ISF Internal Security Force
Has an enhanced HRU capability, including training in urban warfare, assault tactics, breaching methods, CQB and other skills taught by US Special Forces advisers. The weapons used include Swiss SIG M540 assault rifles and Remington 700 snipers' rifles.

LIBYA

MILITARY SPECIAL FORCES
Special Forces Command
The nineteen or twenty Battalions reportedly in existence probably play a bigger role in supporting the regime of Colonel Gaddafi and causing trouble in neighbouring countries than in providing a genuine Special Forces or HRU capability. The five Republican Guard Brigades also have a limited Special Forces role. Libya has recently been buying Western equipment to supplement its ageing stock of Russian weapons.

LIC

Low Intensity Conflict. Insurgency, rebellion or a long-running conflict that never quite spills over into a full-scale guerrilla war.

LICENCE TO KILL

In 2002 President Bush signed an intelligence order authorising the CIA and related Special Forces to overthrow, capture or indeed kill the leader of a foreign country. The fact alone that the President of a sovereign nation can be targeted in such a way by the 'leading democratic defender of international law' is surprising enough. The fact that the last US President to be so rash as to openly target a major foreign leader was to die in a well-planned assassination in November 1963, which many expert observers still believe to have been directly linked to CIA attempts to murder Fidel Castro, should have been sufficient to cause a greater degree of caution in the White House. By agreeing to allow the use of lethal force against President Saddam Hussein and the terrorist leader Osama Bin Laden, strangely both former close allies of the United States, President Bush has opened the floodgates of possible retaliation in kind against himself, his direct family, close colleagues and every member of the US political community, both in the United States and around the world. Nor will the American business community, sports and entertainment celebrities and ordinary tourists be immune from revenge. Targeted assassination has, thankfully, remained a rarity in the international 'great game' and with few exceptions, such as the British-sponsored assassination of Heydrich and the US killing of Admiral Yamamoto during the Second World War, leaders such as Churchill, Roosevelt and Truman fought shy of attempting to assassinate Adolf Hitler or, later, Stalin. This was for the very sensible reason that retaliation was certain. The lesson of a weakness for executive action possibly leading to a monumental 'blowback' has obviously not been fully understood. President Saddam Hussein, or his successors, will undoubtedly retaliate and, following recent clandestine meetings of the regional operational commanders of Islamic Jihad in Algeria and Austria, it is becoming increasing clear that Al Qa'ida in particular may now directly target the US leadership, as well as other high-profile personalities. In a largely free society, despite the recent security clampdown, it will prove impossible to guarantee that President Bush or his successors will not suffer a similar fate to the Kennedy brothers.

The question of morality or even the legality of planning the assassination of a foreign national, let alone the leadership, has been easily and quickly forgotten in the aftermath of 9–11. However, the effects of this decision by the US President will probably directly influence global Special Forces operations, worsen security problems and hinder the work of the diplomatic community long after George W. Bush is consigned to history. For once assassination becomes a matter of state policy, as it already appears to be in Israel, then the normal interflow of negotiation and trust between sovereign states, or even with dissident and warring groups, will become nigh on impossible. The damage that will do to the chances of a long-term improvement in international relations is quite incalculable.

L DETACHMENT – SAS

L Detachment and R Troop, also part of the Territorial Army but separate from 21st and 23rd SAS L Detachment, is actually part of 22nd SAS and used to be known as R Squadron. Its new name honours David Stirling's 'originals' of 1941/42. All members of L Det. are ex-22 SAS or former regulars from other units. Those who are not already qualified operators must complete regular SAS selection. Their wartime role is to reinforce 22nd SAS, and fifteen reservists did so during the Gulf War being attached to A and D Squadrons. The 50 members of L Det/R Troop do a similar job for 264 (SAS) Signal Squadron.

LIMA EMBASSY SIEGE

Operation Chavin de Huantar

On 22 April 1997, a composite force of Peruvian Special Forces carried out a hostage rescue operation that many thought impossible for Peru to organise successfully. The troops stormed the Japanese ambassador's residence where, for more than four months, fourteen members of the Tupac Amaru Revolutionary Movement (Movimiento Revolucionario Tupac Amaru– MRTA) had been holding 72 hostages. The MRTA had conducted a daring assault on the ambassador's residence on 17 December 1996, during a celebration of the Japanese Emperor's birthday. Initially, the MRTA had taken more than 500 hostages, but had released all but 72 during the period leading up to the assault by Peruvian forces. The rescue operation lasted only 22 minutes. There were only twelve 'friendly' casualties: one hostage and two soldiers dead, and nine wounded. All fourteen MRTA terrorists were killed. Peru's determination to end the crisis without giving in to the terrorists' demands elevated its reputation around the world to unprecedented levels. In the end, however, the success was due more to the terrorists' own mistakes and boredom than to any unusual capabilities of the Peruvian Counter-Terrorist forces. From the outset, the Peruvian government refused the terrorists' demands and adopted a stand-off strategy. While the government led the terrorists into protracted negotiations and the task force prepared and trained, policemen guarding the residence conducted a series of harassing activities, including sudden loud noises, constant music and other distractions as part of the 'wearing down' psyops process. The night before the final assault, half of the task force assembled close to the residence and slowly began to take up their positions. Seventy policemen stationed themselves around the perimeter of the house. Eight sharpshooters took positions on the surrounding rooftops. The remaining personnel of the assault force had been divided into three groups. At 15.17 (Lima time) President Fujimori issued the order for the task force to assault the Japanese ambassador's residence. Six minutes later, the residence's main living room and kitchen floors exploded, killing several terrorists who were playing soccer in the living room. The explosions were caused by charges that had been carefully placed in a series of tunnels dug under the house and grounds. At the same time, the three assault groups converged on the house, conducting a rapid and violent assault against the MRTA members. One group emerged from the underground tunnel into the side of the residence, attacked the service areas, and climbed to the second floor. A second group, which had breached the western gate of the compound, assaulted the residence's main door, and the north and south sides of the building. The third group scaled the northern outer perimeter wall. Breaching charges were used to open up the residence and rescue the hostages. At 15.24, one minute after the first explosion, commandos were already entering the residence itself.

Rescue of all 72 hostages took only 28 minutes, and by 16.00 the operation was completed. The assault force employed a variety of light automatic weapons, AK-47s, AKMs, P-90s, UZIs, mini-UZIs and MP-5s as well as various handguns. Sniper teams were equipped with FN-FAL rifles with optical scopes. All assault task force members wore the army's SF uniform: olive utilities uniform, olive armoured vest and combat boots. The 70 members of the National Police, which secured the perimeter of the facility, were dressed in berets, black or olive armoured vests, dark T-shirts, utility trousers and combat boots. Armed primarily with AK-47s and AKMs, the force also included several armoured vehicles used to secure the cordon. The Special Forces task force considered the underground tunnel an absolute necessity for a successful operation and, for weeks after the assault, there were reports that miners experienced in digging through sandy soil had been brought from southern Peru to build the tunnel. The Special Forces carried only light weapons into the residence and a five-to-one ratio in manpower gave the assault units the overwhelming advantage. The surprise effect of the explosion coming from inside the residence contributed to stunning the terrorists and may have saved the lives of many hostages. While the operation had a certain degree of both tactical and political risk it was planned and conducted in a very professional manner.

LITHUANIA

MILITARY SPECIAL FORCES
One Jaeger – Special Forces Battalion A Ranger-LRRP style unit some 350 strong. A tough and capable unit, now increasingly well equipped.

CIVILIAN SPECIAL FORCES
ARAS Special Police Task Force This anti-terrorist and hostage rescue unit is armed with the 9mm CZ75 pistol, 9mm H&K MP5A5 sub-machine gun and 5.56mm Steyr AUG A1 assault carbine.

LITTLE BIRD

The two Special Operations versions of the OH-6A are the 'Little Bird' AH-6C armed variant, and the MH-6B transport/utility version, which can carry up to six personnel for quick insertion and extraction missions and is the only light assault helicopter in the army inventory. It can be armed with a combination of guns and folding fin aerial rockets and, with an un-refuelled range of 250 nautical miles, it provides a potent capability for small-scale operations. The AH-6 Little Bird Gun, a light attack helicopter, has been tested and proven in combat. Armed with guns, Hellfire missiles, and 2.75-inch FFAR, it provides fire support to both ground and air Special

Operations. The un-refuelled range of the AH-6 is 250 nautical miles. These versions were all powered by a single Allison T-63 252 SHP engine. Later versions are based on the successful Boeing (McDonnell Douglas) MD-500/MD-530 series helicopters. The AH-6J attack helicopter, armed with two seven-tube 2.75-inch rocket launchers and two 7.62mm M134 'miniguns' or a combination of 50 Cal. machine guns, MK19 40mm grenade machine gun, Hellfire missiles and Air-to-Air Stinger (ATAS) missiles, and the MH-6J insertion and extraction transport are both based on the MD-530F with a more powerful engine and improved avionics, including an embedded GPS/inertial navigation system and forward-looking infrared (FLIR).

LONG-RANGE DESERT GROUP (LRDG)

The Long-Range Desert Group (LRDG) was Britain's original Special Force in North Africa, long before the creation of the SAS. With its unrivalled mastery of the Western Desert, in its long-range and heavily armed trucks, the LRDG even earned the praise of Rommel for their skilful reconnaissance, punishing raids and powers of evasion. The LRDG later ferried David Stirling's SAS raiders on their early missions to destroy aircraft on enemy airfields far behind the lines following the debacle of the SAS's very first parachute raid, when a ferocious gale scattered the raiders all over the desert. Hand-picked members of the LRDG came from the Guards, Yeomanry cavalry units and other specialist units, and from the New Zealand and Rhodesian forces. In one of their most outstanding feats in early 1942, the LRDG made a round trip of 1,500 miles in nineteen days, much of it through completely featureless terrain. Its troops navigated the vast and inhospitable sand seas in Egypt's Western Desert and the Libya Deserts with the help of the stars and a sun compass. They also knew how to negotiate treacherous surfaces, and to conserve water with special condensers, but above all they learned to read tracks so that they could tell how many vehicles, men or camels had gone in various directions. Reconnaissance always remained the primary purpose of the LRDG. They did not seek confrontation, but when there was no alternative often inflicted just as much damage as the SAS. The LRDG was very much like a 'private army', formed to meet the particular conditions of desert warfare. The standard 'platoon' truck was the Canadian-built Chevrolet 15cwt truck chassis of the Egyptian Army, fitted with desert tyres and with an open body big enough to hold the stores and equipment needed for long trips into the desert. For desert operations with a very heavy load, they had extra leaves inserted into the springs, desert type tyres, wireless, and a condenser fitted on the running board and connected to the radiator to conserve cooling water. Doors and door pillars were removed, extra spare wheels fitted and pintle mounts were added for machine guns and anti-tank rifles. The load carried might be up to two tons, consisting of food, fuel, ammunition, water and explosives for demolition work. Sand-mats of

Firework display: a Royal Air Force Chinook helicopter deploys anti-missile flares in a low-level flight over Afghanistan in support of 45 Commando Royal Marines deployed on Operation Jacana. American and British special forces began training Northern Alliance fighters in October 2001, and the first major deployment of coalition forces occurred on 26 November 2001. Chinooks were used to ferry SAS troops into action. (Helen Mudd/DPL)

Above British Marine Commandos patrol in Afghanistan, 2002. (Graham Meggit/DPL)

Top right US Marines disembark from their CH-53E helicopter as Coalition Forces push towards Kandahar, Afghanistan, 10 December 2001. (Graham Meggit/DPL)

Bottom right A US Marines Cobra attack helicopter flies low over the ruins of Shawack, 13 March 2002, in support of soldiers from the 10th Mountain Division searching for Taliban and Al-Queda fighters. (Popperfoto)

Boys toys? US special forces dune buggy during the Gulf War (*above left*), July 1990–March 1991, Australian SAS patrol (*above right*) in Afghanistan, 2002, and a British SAS machine-gun patrol in Freetown, Sierra Leone (*right*). Having the right gear can be a matter of life and death – or escape and capture – for special forces, as the members of SAS aggressive Gulf War patrol Bravo Two Zero can testify. The decision to insert them by Chinook perhaps led to their detection by the Iraqis, and deprived them of useful equipment that could have been transported by Land Rover. (Khalid Moud/Andrew Chittock/DPL)

The more things change ... British Marine Commando and civilian, Afghanistan 2002 (*left*). (Graham Meggit/DPL)
Russian soldiers (*below*) repair one of their cars in a Kabul suburb as Afghan civilians pass by, 1 December 1980. (Popperfoto)

Right Urban fashions: a Special Forces sniper pictured in Pristina, Kosovo. He wears a blue sniper suit for camouflage and has a number two who can be seen just behind him. (Dil Banerjee/DPL)

Below Nerves on edge, a US Marine secures the US Embassy in Mogadishu, Somalia, 12 October 1992, just before the commencement of Operation Restore Hope. On 3–4 October 1993, a disastrous arrest attempt undermined the worthwhile relief effort already accomplished and resulted in shocking news footage of dead Marines being dragged through the streets. The six hundred-odd fatal Somali casualties that had earlier resulted when Delta Force members shot their way to safety did not have a place in the Ridley Scott movie of the episode, *Black Hawk Down*. (Popperfoto)

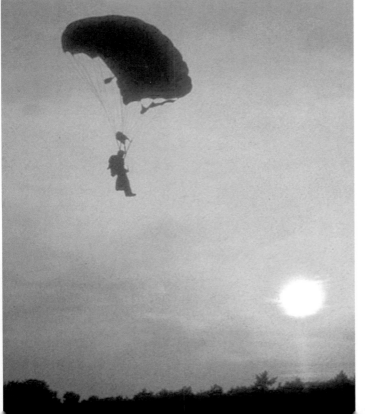

Above GI Jane: female soldier serving with US Special Forces. A number of women are believed to have served with Britain's SAS, and Israeli and Russian special forces have deployed them for years. Their numbers are set to increase as new technologies make disparities in typical physical strength between women and men less relevant. (Marc Clare/DPL)

Left An SAS soldier dropping by steerable freefall canopy. (Max Delaney/DPL)

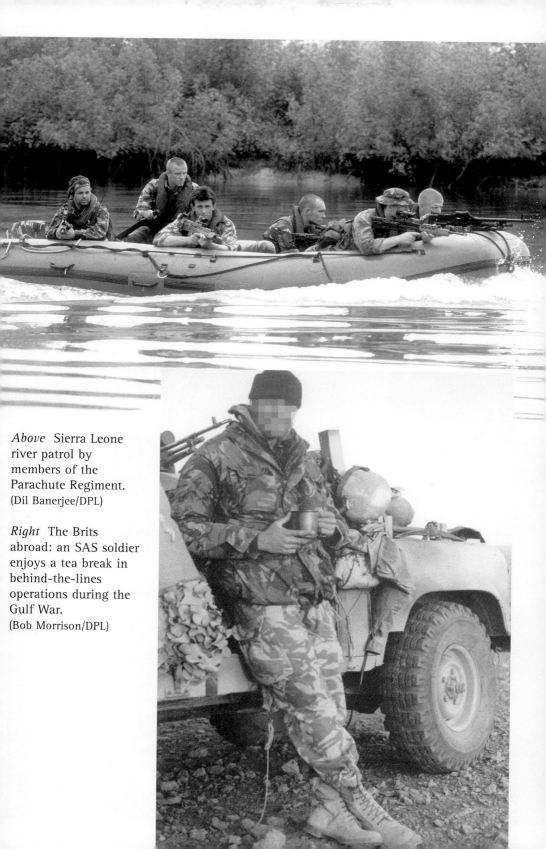

Above Sierra Leone river patrol by members of the Parachute Regiment. (Dil Banerjee/DPL)

Right The Brits abroad: an SAS soldier enjoys a tea break in behind-the-lines operations during the Gulf War. (Bob Morrison/DPL)

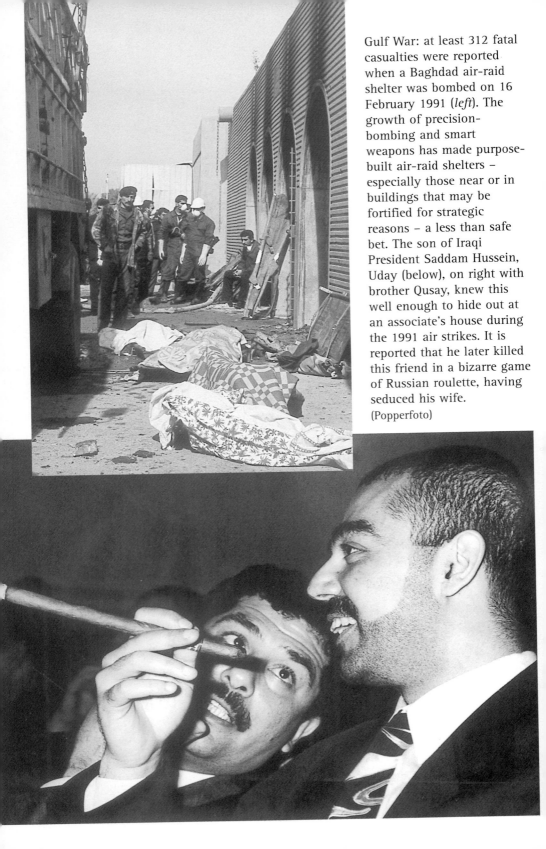

Gulf War: at least 312 fatal casualties were reported when a Baghdad air-raid shelter was bombed on 16 February 1991 (*left*). The growth of precision-bombing and smart weapons has made purpose-built air-raid shelters – especially those near or in buildings that may be fortified for strategic reasons – a less than safe bet. The son of Iraqi President Saddam Hussein, Uday (below), on right with brother Qusay, knew this well enough to hide out at an associate's house during the 1991 air strikes. It is reported that he later killed this friend in a bizarre game of Russian roulette, having seduced his wife.
(Popperfoto)

Right Turkish special forces hang tough during a NATO exercise. They are armed with M60 and AR16 weapons. The country has a strong elite forces tradition, dating from the days of Ataturk in the 1920s. (Andrew Chittock/DPL)

Below Turkish commandos return from a territorial dispute with Greece, 31 January 1996. Turkey's border with Iraq, together with experience gained during ethnic rebellions by Armenians and Kurds, may make it a crucial player in George Bush's War on Terrorism. (Popperfoto)

Above No longer on its way to highlight unilateral French nuclear testing in the South Pacific, Greenpeace ship the *Rainbow Warrior* sinks in Auckland harbour, New Zealand, 7 July 1985, with the loss of one life. (Popperfoto)

Below Major Alain Mafart (*left*) and Captain Dominique Prieur (right), French special forces members assigned to the DGSE, were each jailed for ten years for the fatal sinking of the *Rainbow Warrior*, which caused major international embarrassment for the French government. (Popperfoto)

Right The Avenue of Eternal Peace? Many of the more than 5000 students massacred in Tiananmen Square, Beijing, in June 1989 had recently completed their own military service with the local Beijing garrison of the people's Liberation Army, the 38th. Though not normally associated with special forces, the event was only brought to a close by the 27th, a Praetorian Guard for Chinese President Yang Shangkun, together with China's 15th airborne corps. (Popperfoto)

Right Tourist trap: a passer-by points out the spot where two of three IRA terrorists were shot dead by SAS operatives in Gibraltar on 6 March 1988. Though Operation Flavius remains controversial, it undoubtedly prevented a major terrorist action aimed at British troops stationed on the island. (Popperfoto)

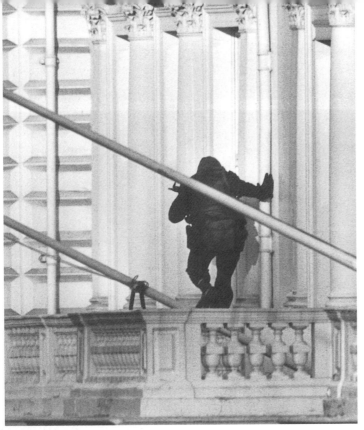

Pictures familiar to all Britons of a certain age: an SAS member (*left*) storms London's Iranian Embassy on 5 May 1980 in a highly successful operation to free twenty hostages. Police Constable Trevor Locke (*below left*), holding his uniform hat before him for identification, exits the building. PC Locke has since said that the life of the surviving Iranian fundamentalist was preserved only because he had placed the man under arrest as the assault commenced. (Popperfoto)

The people's poster-boy: Che Guevara (right) and (below) dead at 39 on a laundry-room sink in the Vallegrande Hospital, Bolivia, 9 October 1967. Bolivia's 2nd Ranger Battalion, who captured Guevara in a firefight south of the Grande River, had been trained by United States Green Berets. His execution, made to look like injuries sustained in the field, spared Bolivia the problem of a trial but denied America's CIA the opportunity to interrogate him. (Popperfoto)

Founding Father: Lt. Col. 'Chargin'' Charles Beckwith (*left*), who served in Vietnam and led the aborted rescue attempt of American hostages at the US Embassy in Tehran in April 1980, is the maverick creator of America's Delta Force, one of the world's premier anti-terror and hostage-rescue units, and set to remain one of the busiest! (Popperfoto)

Man of Guile: Maj. Gen. Orde Wingate (*right*) was a tactical visionary who organised daring raids on Japanese forces during the Burma campaign of 1942. Today's 22nd SAS owes much to Wingate and his Chindits. (Popperfoto)

canvas and steel channels were carried to assist vehicles through the many shifting sands and dunes. A sun compass was usually carried in the dashboard and theodolites and sextants were used to fix positions. The Long-Range Desert Group's task for most of the time was watching, waiting, recording enemy movements and getting the information quickly back to HQ. They were physically tough and determined, indeed on one occasion nine men walked 200 miles back to base, fortified by a single packet of biscuits and a few mouthfuls of water. Later in the war, they went on to achieve further success in the Aegean, Adriatic, Italy and Yugoslavia, fighting alongside local partisans and also using their considerable expertise and reconnaissance skills to help the RAF and Royal Navy sink more than 100 enemy naval and merchant vessels. The LRDG was eventually disbanded in June 1945.

LONG-RANGE RECONNAISSANCE PATROL (LRRP)

In 1958 the first LRRP units were formed by the US 7th Army in West Germany and assigned to V and VII Corps. The units were designated as the 3779 and 3780 US Army LRRP Companies. Initial volunteers could be selected from throughout the 7th Army, but were in the end primarily drawn from airborne units of the 8th Infantry Division. Each unit consisted of a small HQ, a communications platoon, and two patrol platoons. The patrol platoons consisted of eight four-man patrols. Both units were capable of conducting airborne and airmobile operations; surviving for long periods of time, with little or no outside support; and were highly skilled in long-range communications skills. What was generally unknown at the time was that unit members were also secretly trained in deploying Special Atomic Demolition Munitions (SADM). In 1965 both units were redesigned and moved to the Continental US. As the US increased its commitment to the war in Vietnam, it began to deploy large numbers of combat troops. The need for highly trained and motivated soldiers capable of making long-range patrols deep into enemy territory under difficult conditions and in secrecy became quickly apparent soon after the US Army became fully involved in the region. This gave rise to the formation of small reconnaissance units of platoon size which were responsible to the Brigade or Divisional Commander. Two of the earliest examples of these 'provisional' units were formed by the 196th Infantry Brigade and the 173rd Airborne Brigade. They were designated as Long-Range Reconnaissance Patrols or 'LRRP'. Eventually larger combat units were granted the authority to form permanent LRRP units. Divisions were authorised LRRP companies, and independent brigades, smaller LRRP detachments. Personnel were initially drawn from the divisional or brigade cavalry, scout or anti-tank units. Many of the personnel selected were graduates of the Ranger School, or the Jungle

Warfare School in Panama, but most received their training 'in unit' or from the MAC/V RECONDO School. Rapidly expanding operations caused some LRRP units to field members who had not attended school, however, and in some cases teams were sent to the field with one or two members who had never patrolled in the jungle before – which resulted in a number of avoidable casualties in early operations.

The MAC/V RECONDO (Reconnaissance Commando) School was formed at the request of General Westmoreland, the commander of US Troops in Vietnam. Based at Nha Trang and officially opened on 15 September 1966, the school was staffed by members of the 5th SFG (Airborne) and many of the instructors had also attended the British Jungle Warfare School in Malaysia. Students included troops from the USMC, US Army, RTMC, RT Army SF, ROK Recon Marines, Vietnamese SF and Rangers. As a final graduation exercise students were required to conduct an actual combat patrol under the supervision of instructors. The three-week reconnaissance-commando course was with a maximum school capacity of 120 students, with classes of 60 students being trained every two weeks. The training programme consisted of a one-week airborne course for reconnaissance-commando students, and included mandatory instruction on escape and evasion, and survival. A one-week long-range reconnaissance patrol course was for troops assigned to projects Delta, Sigma and Omega. There was also special training as required, such as HALO (High Altitude Low Opening) parachute training, and SCUBA training. Emphasis was placed on physical training and fitness, with this part of the programme constantly being upgraded. The worst of the physical programme was the notorious Recondo sandbag runs, in which the student either carried one 30-pound sandbag for four miles or, worse still, two 30-pound sandbags for ten miles. Students who did not complete the sandbag runs or failed tests on subjects such as communications, intelligence or map reading, were automatically dropped from the school. The LRRP usually operated in four- to eight-man patrols. The LRRP units provided ground force commanders with intelligence on the tactical situation in their areas of responsibility (AOR). LRRP units were also tasked with a number of direct action (DA) missions. Units attacked Viet Cong (VC) supply areas, tracked enemy units, directed air strikes, and harassed the VC. During the course of the war, all LRRP units in Vietnam were redesigned as rangers, and made separate companies of the 75 Infantry Regiment. With the US withdrawal from the conflict in Vietnam most of the LRRP/Ranger units were disbanded. By the end of the war, only two ranger units remained on active duty.

The last Recondo class was taken in 1970. Project Delta had officially ceased its operations and departed RVN on 30 June 1970, with the Recondo School officially closing on 31 December 1970. During its operational time the MACV-RECONDO school graduated 3,357 troops from a total of 5,395 who attended its courses. On 1 January 1969 the LRRPs officially became

Rangers when the 75th Infantry Regiment was reactivated. This was intended to strengthen and centralise the long-range patrol assets in Vietnam. Although now termed Rangers, only those men of the 75th Infantry who had completed the Fort Benning Ranger course could wear the Ranger tab. During the course of the war LRRPs conducted around 23,000 long-range patrols, of these two-thirds resulted in enemy sightings. LRRPs are also reported to have accounted for some 10,000 enemy KIA through ambushes, sniping, air strikes and calling in artillery bombardments. The primary mission of the LRRP is intelligence-gathering, although the LRRP are assigned a whole myriad of tasks which include locating enemy reserves, combat patrols, conducting ambushes, bomb damage assessments, the locating of enemy command posts and other key facilities, locating targets for air/artillery/ground attack, prisoner snatches, reconnoitring LZs for airmobile operations, and the placing of sensors along known enemy infiltration routes. Once on the ground the LRRP team would normally try to avoid contact with the enemy, that is unless they were on a hunter/killer or 'snatch' mission. If enemy troops were spotted the team would try to remain hidden, relying on helicopter gunships, artillery fire, or jets, to deliver their ordnance onto the enemy positions. If it did come down to a firefight then the team would try to hit hard and fast, and then try to exit the area as quickly as possible. Communication was by hand signal, if it did become necessary to speak, then a whisper direct into the ear was used. Radio communication was kept to a bare minimum, and was often via coded clicks on the handset button rather than actual voice transmission. The LRRP idea has been adopted as a standard Special Forces technique, and most developed military forces now have LRRP units, either attached to more conventionally trained units or as special units in their own right. NATO's major LRRP School is at Weingarten in Germany and now trains SF soldiers from across the world.

LONG-RANGE SURVEILLANCE UNITS (LRSU)

The Long-Range Surveillance Units (LRSU) trace their origin to the US Army's Long-Range Reconnaissance Units (LRRP). During the early 1980s, the US Army once again found itself lacking a deep reconnaissance unit. After conducting a brief study, it was decided that the re-activation of an LRRP type unit would best meet the army's needs. While debating the structure of the new units, senior army officers felt that the name LRRP was too closely associated with the conflict in Vietnam. After a short debate the designation of Long-Range Surveillance Units was chosen.

The LRSU perform passive intelligence-gathering missions, and are not equipped for offensive combat operations. LRSUs take great pains to avoid being detected and provide US Army divisions and Corps with the ability to deploy covert reconnaissance patrols deep into the enemy's rear. Operating as six-man teams, LRSU teams are trained extensively in long-range communications, survival, covert observation and various infiltration techniques. Many LRSU unit members are qualified in HALO/HAHO and combat diving skills. In certain situations they may also engage in stay behind operations. Units are capable of being infiltrated on foot, by aircraft, parachute or small boats. Units may be deployed up to 150 miles behind enemy lines. They are expected to operate on their own, for up to 30 days. Team members are capable of providing bomb damage assessments; directing artillery fire; targeting emery anti-aircraft systems for destruction; and locating enemy troop concentrations. Each Army Corps is authorised a Long-Range Surveillance Company (LRSC) and each Division a Long-Range Surveillance Detachment (LRSD). LRSC have a large headquarters platoon, a communications platoon, and two patrol platoons, while the LRSD have a smaller number of teams authorised per patrol platoon. Active Army LRSU are assigned to their parent military intelligence (MI) unit, and LRSU, or units with similar type missions, have been deployed during most major combat operations since their inception during the early 1980s. The 82nd Airborne Division 2/17 Cavalry deployed a LRS type unit, during Operation Urgent Fury, while Operation Desert Storm allowed a number of LRS units the opportunity to deploy for their first combat missions. LRS teams from various LRSU assigned to VII Corps and XVIII Airborne Corps were infiltrated deep into Iraqi territory. The teams reported on Iraqi troop movements, weather conditions on the ground and any other information deemed pertinent. An LRSU from the 101st Airmobile Division narrowly avoided being captured by Iraqi troops. The team had been directing Allied aircraft onto Iraqi troop positions with increasing accuracy and eventually the Iraqis became suspicious. They deployed patrols to the area they suspected of containing US ground troops. As the Iraqis closed in on their position, the teams commander called for an immediate extraction and US transport helicopters and Apache gunships arrived on the scene just as the Iraqis were climbing up the hill to where the team had their OP, allowing the team to be safely returned to their Saudi base. Another LRS team, assigned to the 24th Mechanized Division, was able to avoid detection by Iraqi patrols that came within feet of its position. LRS teams from the 10th Mountain Division deployed to Somalia, and operated throughout the country.

European and US-based LRS teams have also been active throughout Bosnia in the last few years, and in April of 2000 the Secretary of Defence ordered the deployment of an LRS unit to Kosovo to support ongoing NATO peacekeeping efforts in the Serbian province. The US Army runs a Long-Range Surveillance Leaders Course (LRSLC) for LRSU team leaders and officers, and Allied troops and members of other services may attend on a space-available basis. The course is run by Co.D, 4th Ranger Training Bn. co-located with the US Army Ranger School, at Fort Benning, GA, the school's cadre providing instruction in a wide range of skills. The course includes instruction in techniques for constructing underground hide sites; escape and evasion methods; identifying threat equipment, aircraft and personnel even while camouflaged; improvised long-range communications; basic and advanced field craft, and various other skills. All of this topped off by a realistic field training exercise (FTX). Many LRSU members are also graduates of the International Long-Range Reconnaissance Patrol School. Based in Germany, the school is jointly funded, and staffed by personnel from the UK, Germany, the US and the Netherlands. US LRSUs conduct training exercises and exchange programmes with various US allies. In recent years these exercises have included deployments to the UK, Germany and Italy. Joint training exercises have involved units from British TA SAS, France's 13th RDP, Belgium's ESR, Italy's 9th Para Assault Regiment and Germany's Long-Range Scout Companies.

LOUGHALL AMBUSH – SAS

Beginning in late 1986, the Provisional Irish Republican Army (IRA) had turned its attention to driving out the security forces based in Northern Ireland. In response, the British government stepped up action to monitor the movements of IRA members, in an effort to head off further incidents. As part of this escalation, the SAS began regular rotations of its soldiers into Northern Ireland to work with the Royal Ulster Constabulary (RUC) and elements of the UK MI5 intelligence organisation. The IRA, however, had been at war with the British government for over 60 years and had adapted well to the presence of the growing anti-terrorist apparatus. In fact, by early 1987 the Republican terrorists had carried out no fewer than 22 separate attacks on police stations alone. And while some incidents had been prevented, at the time there seemed no end in sight to the ongoing urban war. A series of related events that occurred during this time, however, would soon bring about a dramatic reduction in the IRA campaign. In 1986, an IRA team had used a similar heavy vehicle in an earlier attack by means of a large explosive device placed in the JCB's steel bucket. The vehicle was then driven through the closed main gates of the Royal Ulster Constabulary (RUC) station at the Birches, County Armagh, and the device detonated, causing major damage. For this reason, authorities were on the alert specifically for thefts of similar heavy equipment. When just such a vehicle was reported stolen in April 1987, RUC security initiated an immediate investigation. Following the theft of a JCB mechanical digger/tractor from a construction site in East Tyrone, an alert went up throughout the intelligence networks of the security forces. The digger was soon discovered, parked near a disused farm just 16km from the RUC station at Loughall. Suspecting an attack was soon to follow, security forces contacted the SAS. In short order, surveillance teams from the RUC's E4A unit monitored IRA terrorists transporting explosives to a disued barn. On 8 May, the RUC intercepted a phone call between two of the group's members: the IRA was ready to strike. Immediately, a joint RUC/SAS team moved in around the Loughall Police station, which had been quickly but quietly evacuated. RUC snipers took up position while SAS troopers spread out through the compound and nearby countryside (to prevent the escape of any IRA members following the attack). The intercepted call had also provided the SAS with ample time to establish a box-type ambush, centred on the most likely approach route. At approximately 19.20 an eight-man IRA unit (actually two active service units or ASU operating in tandem) approached the RUC station in a stolen blue Toyota van, followed closely by the JCB, laden with beer kegs filled with 500 pounds of explosives in its bucket. Following their plan, five gunmen exited the van and opened fire on the compound, effectively preventing security forces from intercepting the JCB as it smashed through the main gate and made its way into the courtyard. The three terrorists (the driver and two armed guards) jumped from the tractor and ran towards the safety of the getaway van.

The RUC and SAS, however, had anticipated this and as the terrorists entered the pre-established kill zone, they opened fire. Seconds later, the bomb was detonated and in the massive explosion that followed, a large section of the closest RUC building was demolished, as was as another structure some 50 feet away. Chunks of plaster, steel and wood were sprayed in all directions; however, the design of the JCB's bucket directed the majority of the blast toward the RUC station. In the aftermath, all eight terrorists were killed while, in a tragic development, two civilians with no connection to the IRA appeared in a white Citroen car, unknowingly driving directly into the ambush zone. Thinking that the car belonged to an unexpected IRA team, the SAS opened fire, killing the driver and seriously wounding the passenger. According to standard procedure in counter-terrorist operations designed to retain anonymity, British army helicopters soon arrived to extract the SAS team and deliver them to a secure area. For a period of time following the failed Loughall operation, the IRA reportedly suffered from significant disruption of the group involved. Elements of the IRA leadership suspected that a mole had revealed the details of the operation to the Security Forces. This theory caused the group's internal security to be reviewed and revised. However, the IRA search for a mole proved fruitless and it was gradually accepted that the Security Forces were wholly responsible for uncovering the plan through good Intelligence work.

LTD

Laser Target Designator. Used by Special Forces to 'illuminate' a target difficult to find from the air.

The 'scatter' effect of the laser striking the target is picked up by detectors on-board the attacking aircraft and 'smart' munitions are immediately launched, often considerable distances from the target, which then home in on the 'illuminated' target, usually with great accuracy.

LUP

Laying Up Position. A secure resting-place used during a Special Forces operation behind enemy lines.

LUXEMBOURG

CIVILIAN SPECIAL FORCES
There is a small Mobile Response Group (MRG) of the Gendarmerie responsible for surveillance and rapid intervention in the event of a riot or hostage rescue situation. Help would be quickly available to the Luxembourg authorities from the Belgian ESI, French GIGN or German GSG-9 in the event of a serious terrorist incident. Weapons used by the MRG include the 7.62mm FAL rifles and the 9mm UZI and H&K MP5 SMGs.

LZ

Landing Zone, a temporary or hastily prepared site for a helicopter or aircraft to land.

MACEDONIA

MILITARY SPECIAL FORCES
Special Task Force Brigade
Special Forces Battalion VOLCI (WOLVES) The Volci are the nation's prime Special Operations and Anti-Terrorist unit and are usually held on a three-hour standby. The 550-strong 'Wolves' have been deployed throughout northern Macedonia to deal with the Albanian insurgency in that part of the country. Prior to the outbreak of hostilities, uniforms consisted of black uniforms and Kevlar helmets, but currently there seems to be no standard uniform and soldiers are given a great deal of freedom. Equipment and weaponry is primarily Yugoslavian in origin, and consists of M95A rifles, and CZ-99 pistols. In addition the German MP5 and even crossbows are also used.

Commando Battalion SKORPII (SCORPIONS) The Skorpii, with an HQ in Stip, were originally formed with the specific purpose of participating in NATO-led peacekeeping operations and thus the training is designed to meet NATO standards. This initially consisted of convoy escort duties and checkpoint control. However, the 'Scorpions' are reported to have also trained with Italian Special Forces units and participated in the Partnership for Peace military exercises along with Italian, Austrian and Slovakian SF units in 1997. The 'Skorpii' use standard armament of the Macedonian army, which includes M-70/80 assault rifles, M-76 and M-79 sniper rifles and similar weapons.

A third Special forces unit is being established 2002–03 with personnel drawn from both the army and police and may be similar to GSG-9, parachute-trained and 700 strong. They will have sophisticated weaponry and equipment, such as satellite communications, night-vision goggles and laser range finders at their disposal.

CIVILIAN SPECIAL FORCES
MINISTERSTVO ZA VNATRESHNI RABOTI (MVR) Ministry of Interior Affairs
SPECIAL POLICE UNIT 'LIONS'   The 'Lions' are a rapid reaction force which is widely believed to have been established by the Macedonian Ministry of Internal Affairs for a 'final assault' on the Albanian National Liberation Army (NLA) after NATO finished the Operation Essential Harvest in 2001. The Lions are equipped with modern equipment, wear a red beret and use Yugoslav army type uniform with full body-armour. They also wear the US/NATO standard Kevlar helmets. Weapons include 7.62mm M-80A assault rifles.

SPECIAL POLICE UNIT TIGRI (TIGERS)   The premier police counter-terrorist unit are the Tigers. The unit is under the control of the Interior Ministry and was set up in 1995 in response to the growing ethnic Albanian violence in the Tetevo uprising. The 'Tigers' are modelled on the Serbian SAJ. During the height of the Albanian insurgency in the north-west of the country, the Tigers participated in the heaviest battles alongside its army counterpart, the Wolves. Weapons consist of CV-99 9mm pistols, Croatian HS-2000 9mm pistols, M80 5.56mm assault rifles, M86 7.62mm LMGs, M76 and G3SG/1 sniper rifles and H&K MP5.

MALAWI

MILITARY SPECIAL FORCES
The Independent Parachute Battalion has one 50-strong Special Forces trained detachment with a very limited hostage rescue capability.

MALAYAN EMERGENCY – SAS

The Malaya Emergency was in fact a full-scale insurgency by communist guerrillas of Chinese origin from 1950–59. The resurgence of the SAS was far from easy when an expert in guerrilla warfare, 'Mad' Mike Calvert, was enlisted to study the Malaya problem, and implement a solution. Calvert went on patrol in Malaya to discover the depth of the problem personally, covering over 1500 miles of enemy-infested territory. Calvert and the Director of Operations General Sir Harold Briggs decided to implement what became known as the 'Briggs Plan'. The idea was to uproot whole indigenous populations, moving them to fortified villages, while undertaking to deny the CTs a steady food supply.

Calvert was instructed to raise a force of soldiers who would live in the jungle, taking the battle to the terrorists on their own ground. Creating the Malayan Scouts (SAS) was the step. The recruits consisted of veterans from SOE, SAS, Ferret Force and Force 136, as well as men dissatisfied with their regular units. Calvert went as far as Rhodesia, recruiting well over 100 volunteers to form what would eventually become C Squadron. His Intelligence staff was made up of Chinese interpreters from Hong Kong while other soldiers came from 21st SAS, the Reserves and Territorial Army, some of whom had served under David Stirling. While conflicts with the enemy were few, the Malayan Scouts quickly relearned some vital lessons about jungle warfare. When Calvert was invalided back to Britain, his replacement shipped off many of the unit's more troublesome members and instituted a new measure of discipline. A number of officers returned to England to start a selection process that would become infamous for its toughness. In Malaya, a new tactic of parachuting into the high trees ('Tree Hopping') which covered the landscape was instituted, and although there were frequent casualties, it continued until the end of the war. The Scouts would stay in the bush for weeks at a time, mounting far-ranging patrols, doing reconnaissance and engaging the enemy, while being resupplied by air drops.

A new policy was authorised by General Sir Gerald Templar, the Military High Commissioner, which coined the phrase 'winning the hearts and minds of the Malayan people'. Soldiers went into villages and assisted the inhabitants with medical aid and protection from terrorists, gaining their trust and assistance in intelligence-gathering. This tactic of influencing the local population worked well, toughening their resolve to stay free. It was an accomplishment of great importance as Malaya eventually achieved a peaceful route to independence. One of the most famous soldiers to serve in Malaya, and typical of the new breed of SAS soldiers, was Sergeant Bob Turnbull, an amazing tracker and incredible jungle fighter. His favourite weapon was a 12-gauge pump-action shotgun, perfectly suited for devastating effect at close quarters. At one point, Turnbull tracked a group of four communist terrorists to their hideout in a small hut deep in the jungle. He waited patiently, and watched as the sentry went inside to stay dry when it began to rain. At this point he approached quietly and opened up, killing all four.

MALAYSIA

MILITARY SPECIAL FORCES
SPECIAL SERVICE GROUP HEADQUARTERS
The role of the Special Service Group is to provide facilities and equipment to carry out special missions including parachute operations and maritime operations. These operations can be carried out either covertly, or jointly with other regular forces in enemy-held territory.

GGK-Grup Gerak Khas This is the largest SOF element in Malaysia. The mission of the GGK is to provide a squadron to locate, report, harass and disrupt the enemy through long-range infiltration, as well as operating in close collaboration with guerrilla or partisan forces. GGK will also plan, prepare for and, when directed, deploy to conduct unconventional warfare, internal defence, special reconnaissance and direct actions etc. in support of government policy objectives within designated areas of responsibility. GGK continually train to conduct unconventional warfare in any of its forms, including escape and evasion, subversion and sabotage, counter-terrorist, counter-insurgency and their most highly regarded expertise, jungle warfare. It developed an excellent reputation in operations against the communist terrorists and has also seen action in Cambodia, Somalia, Western Sahara, Namibia and Bosnia among others. Currently, there are three Special Forces regiments:

    11th Special Forces Regiment
    21st Special Services Group
    22nd Commando Group

SPECIAL WARFARE TRAINING CENTRE (SWTC)
The role of SWTC is to provide specialised courses and training for personnel from all the services.

The Special Forces use the following weapons; the 9mm H&K P9S pistol, 5.56mm Colt CAR-15A1 Model 653 assault carbine, 5.56mm Colt AR-15A1 Model 613 assault rifle, 5.56mm SME AUG assault rifle (licensed from Steyr), 7.62mm Accuracy International PM bolt-action sniper rifle, 12.7mm (.50 BMG) Robar 50 bolt-action sniper rifle, 7.62mm H&K HK11A1 light machine gun, 7.62mm FN MAG general-purpose machine gun, 7.62mm Vektor SS-77 general-purpose machine gun and 40mmSR Colt M203 underbarrel grenade launcher (under AR-15A1).

NAVY
History of Paskal or Pasukan Khas Laut began in 1975, when the Royal Malaysian Navy saw a need for a security regiment trained in modern maritime warfare. Its main purpose is to protect naval bases all over Malaysia. At that time, the RMN main base was still at KD Malaya

(Woodlands, Singapore). The first batch of 30 officers and men were sent to Surabaya, Indonesia, and they were initially trained by instructors from KOPASKA (Indonesian Navy Underwater Combat Unit).

On 1 October 1980, Paskal was officially established when the government started to enforce the EEZ (Exclusive Economic Zone) on Malaysian waters. Other than that, there was also a requirement to protect Malaysian offshore stations near the disputed Spratly islands, and Paskal was actually the first team sent to occupy Layang-Layang atoll on behalf of Malaysia.

CIVILIAN SPECIAL FORCES

The Pasukan Gerakan Khas (PGK) During the communist insurgency, the Royal Malaysian Police had a paramilitary arm called Pasukan Polis Hutan (PPH). By 1969 this included the elite 69th Commando Battalion or VAT 69. There was also a purely civilian force known as Unit Tindakan Khas (UTK). UTK had a SWAT-like function as well as close protection roles. After the last remaining communist terrorists finally laid down their arms in 1989 both units were in limbo. In December 1997, the PPH was renamed as Pasukan Gerakan Am (PGA) while UTK and VAT 69 were formally disbanded and merged to become the *Pasukan Gerakan Khas (PGK)*. This unit has some 1,600 personnel and is trained at Fort Kemar, located deep in the jungle of Perak, where transportation is limited to helicopter and small aircraft only. The training is supervised by a group of instructors from British SAS (Special Air Service) and NZSAS.

MALDIVE CRISIS – IMSF

When, in November 1988, mercenaries of the People's Liberation Organization of Tamil Eelan (PLOTE), an organisation used by India to counter the LTTE (Tamil Tigers), attempted to stage a coup in the Maldives, the Indian Armed Forces quickly launched an operation to re-establish the former government. Under the codename Operation Cactus, Indian paratroopers assaulted the capital on 4 November 1988; however, 46 mercenaries with 27 hostages, including the Maldivian Minister of Education, managed to escape on board a merchant ship. The next day the vessel was detected by an Indian Il-38 May MR aircraft and was then tracked by a Tu-142M Bear-F, another maritime recon aircraft, until two Indian naval vessels were able to intercept the ship. Two Sea King Mk.42 helicopters from one of the naval vessels, dropped depth charges to deter further resistance. Finally on the morning of 6 November 1988, IMSF commandos boarded the vessel and took control without any resistance from the mercenaries.

MALI

MILITARY SPECIAL FORCES

One Airborne Commando and one Special Forces Battalion based in Bamako. Equipped and trained by the French Special Forces, it would probably quickly receive additional support from French Foreign Legion units or the GIGN in the event of a major hostage rescue situation involving VIPs or foreign nationals.

MARTIAL ARTS

Widespread use by Special Forces (see UNARMED COMBAT).

MASSACRE AT GAGGENAU – SAS RETRIBUTION

In the chaos of the immediate post-war Europe, a freelance six-man team of SAS soldiers set out to hunt down those responsible for a mass grave discovered at Gaggenau near Baden-Baden. It had contained the bodies of 28 captured SAS men, who had been tortured and murdered by the Gestapo following Hitler's infamous 'Commando Order' earmarking all such captured allied Special Forces for death. It soon became depressingly clear that the allied governments of Clement Attlee in Britain and Harry S. Truman in the USA were less than keen to carry on with the search for the large numbers of Nazis still at large. It has been said that the main reason for this was that the Allies preferred to recruit its former Nazi enemies to fight the new Soviet threat, than to prosecute them for war crimes. SAS Lieutenant Colonel Brian Franks decided to take the law into his own hands and, using a 'phantom' signals network, operated under the nose of the British military authorities, who did everything possible to prevent the freelance team from operating within its area of occupied Germany. The unit, under Major Eric Barkworth, continued to successfully hunt down Gestapo officers held responsible for the massacre of their colleagues long after the SAS had been officially disbanded. It has been suggested that certain elements of SOE, before it was disbanded, and later SIS, the British Intelligence Service, provided the SAS team with valuable information and helped cover for them. It has also been suggested, in certain more lurid versions of the story, that a number of the Nazi officers failed to make it to court, the SAS men preferring a slightly more direct and appropriate form of retribution.

MAU

Marine Amphibious Unit – USMC. An operational combat group deployed in specialist amphibious support ships with a variety of landing craft and assault helicopters. An MAU may often be found in company with a US Naval Carrier Battle Group for major operations such as Operation Enduring Freedom, when several such powerful US Fleets were deployed in the Persian Gulf and Arabian Sea.

MAURITANIA

MILITARY SPECIAL FORCES

One Para-Commando Special Operations Battalion based in Nouakchott. This 600-strong unit has seen considerable action against the Polisario guerrillas fighting both Mauritania and Morocco for the independence of the Western Sahara. The unit is largely equipped and trained by the French Special Forces.

MAUSER SP66

Widely used dedicated sniper rifle chambered in 7.62mm and uses the Mauser short-bolt action, introduced in 1976. The large stock has adjustable cheek pad and butt plate, a thumb-hole and pistol grip. A flash hider/muzzle brake is fitted to the barrel. The magazine only holds three rounds, but this is not considered a major drawback for what is usually considered a very accurate weapon. The rifle is usually fitted with a Zeiss Diavari ZA 1.5-6x variable telescopic sight or one of the later night-vision optics.

MECCA SIEGE – GIGN

The GIGN had dealt with the deadly fanaticism of Islamic terrorists before, but in 1979 a captain and two sub-officers were to be dispatched on an urgent mission to Saudi Arabia to help dislodge several hundred armed Muslim extremists who had taken over the Sacred Mosque in Mecca.

Thousands of pilgrims on their annual 'hajj' to Mecca were being held hostage in a labyrinth of underground passages beneath the mosque. The very survival of the Saudi monarchy probably hung in the balance as Captain Paul Barril presented the Saudi National Guard with his plan to use paralysing gas to flush out the insurgents from an underground area of 60 square kilometres. The GIGN advisers trained hand-picked teams of Saudi soldiers in demolitions and room-clearing techniques to conduct the assault, which resulted in 2,000 dead after an entire day of close-quarters battle.

MEDIVAC (MEDEVAC)

Medical evacuation, of injured personnel.

MERRILL'S MARAUDERS

Merrill's Marauders, a Ranger type outfit, came into existence as a result of the Quebec Conference of August 1943. During this conference, President Franklin D. Roosevelt, Prime Minister Winston Churchill of England, and other Allied leaders conceived the idea of having an American ground unit spearhead the Chinese Army with a Long-Range Penetration Mission behind enemy lines in Burma. Its goal would be the destruction of Japanese communications and supply lines, and generally to play havoc with enemy forces, while an attempt was made to reopen the Burma Road. A presidential call for volunteers for 'A Dangerous and Hazardous Mission' was issued and approximately 2,900 US soldiers responded to the call. Officially designated as the 5307th Composite Unit (Provisional) code name 'GALAHAD' the unit later became popularly known as MERRILL'S MARAUDERS, named after its CO, Brigadier General Frank Merrill. Organised into combat teams, two to each battalion, the Marauder volunteers came from a variety of theatres of operation, including some from US-based units and the jungles of Panama, while the remainder were battle-scarred veterans of Guadalcanal, New Georgia and New Guinea campaigns. In India some Signal Corps and Air Corps personnel were added, as well as pack troops with mules. After preliminary training operations undertaken in great secrecy in the jungles of India, about 600 men were detached as a rear echelon headquarters to remain in India to handle the vital air-drop supply operation for the six Marauder combat teams (400 to a team). Colour-coded Red, White, Blue, Green, Orange and Khaki, these teams began their march up the Ledo Road and over the outlying ranges of the Himalayan Mountains into Burma. The Marauders, with no tanks or heavy artillery to support them, walked over 1,000 miles throughout extremely dense and almost impenetrable jungles and in five major and 30 minor engagements, they defeated the veteran soldiers of the Japanese 18th Division (conquerors of Singapore and Malaya) who vastly outnumbered them. Always moving to the rear of the main forces of the Japanese, they completely disrupted enemy supply and communication lines, and climaxed their behind-the-lines operations with the capture of Myitkina Airfield, the only all-weather airfield in Burma. For their accomplishments in Burma, the Marauders were awarded the Distinguished Unit Citation in July 1944. The unit was consolidated with the 475th Infantry on 10 August 1944. On 21 June 1954, the 475th was redesignated the 75th Infantry. It is from this redesignation of Merrill's Marauders that the modern-day 75th Ranger Regiment traces its name.

MEXICO

MILITARY SPECIAL FORCES
GAFE-Grupo Aerotransportado de Fuerzas Especiales (Airborne Group of Special

Forces) There are a number of company-sized air-mobile Special Forces units (GAFEs) with the intention being that each of the twelve Military Zones should contain at least one such unit. The massacre of 45 unarmed civilians in Chiapas by SF death squads on 22 December 1997 brought the brutal fury of Mexico's low intensity warfare in southern Mexico to the world's attention, as well as to a lesser extent, the significant part the US Special Forces have played in the training of Mexican and other Latin American Special Forces. It is without a shadow of doubt true that the majority of those who take part in the death squads and other acts of human rights abuse, both in Mexico and throughout South and Central America, have been trained by the US Special Warfare schools, and in all probability armed and financed by the United States directly or indirectly. In October 1995 William Perry, the US Secretary of Defence, met with his Mexican counterpart, General Enrique Cervantes Aguirre, and agreed to increase the levels of co-operation between the two countries. Within months a first group of young Mexican officers were training in Special Forces and anti-drug operations at Fort Bragg, NC. Equipment supplied included 73 Huey helicopters as well as high-tech intelligence hardware, rifles, grenades and flame-throwers. The January 1996 issue of the Fort Bragg magazine *Special Warfare* discussed the training of Mexican Special Forces and stressed that 'Grupo Aerotransportado de Fuerzas Especiales (Airborne Group of Special Forces) or GAFE' was an important component of the development of Mexican Special Forces. It went on to state that, 'particularly heavy emphasis is being placed on those forces that will be located in the states of Chiapas and Guerrero, where "special airborne forces" will be set up'. The 4,000 or so Mexican soldiers trained at Fort Bragg can also draw on the vast experiences of the 7th Special Forces Group, experts in low intensity warfare and counter-insurgency whose global responsibility and field of action is Latin America. During the early 1980s the unit 'drafted the initial plan for US Military trainers in El Salvador' and 'played a critical role in helping the Salvadoran military grow . . . to a counter-insurgency force of 55,000 men under arms'. In addition, the 7th SFG 'played a very important role in preparing the Honduran Military to resist and defeat an invasion from Nicaragua' and 'also assisted the Honduran forces in conducting their own counter-insurgency operations and ultimately defeating the Honduran communist-supported insurgency'. Later in the 1980s the 7th 'became involved in counter-narcotics operations in the Andean Ridge countries of Venezuela, Colombia, Ecuador, Peru and Bolivia', then 'participated in Operation "Just Cause" to restore democracy in Panama'. Its official history added 'Today we are continuously engaged in Foreign Internal Defence throughout Central and South America.'

CIVILIAN SPECIAL FORCES

Force F 'Zorros' was created in 1983 as a force equipped to fight organised crime and narco-terrorism. It has since evolved and taken on additional missions requiring dedicated counter-insurgency and anti-terrorists units. Force F, better known as the 'Zorros', is a 350-man unit based just north of Mexico City. They are organised into three main groups: urban commando squads, emergency ordinance disposal squads and sniper and marksmanship squads. Weapons used include Beretta 9mm pistols, 5.56mm M-16A2s, CAR-15s, and HK33 assault rifles. The ever-present H&K MP5 sub-machine guns and Smith and Wesson 12-gauge shotguns are used in building assaults.

The GAT Gruppa Antiterrorist /UCIDGAT   This unit integrates the activities of the various security agencies. Weekly inter-agency meetings assessed strategic threats around the country, especially to key infrastructure targets from bombs and other terrorist attacks. As it grew and assumed new responsibilities, such as kidnappings, arms trafficking and organised crime, the GAT eventually became the Inter-Institutional Co-ordination Unit-GAT or UCIDGAT and in 1999 became the core of the PFP's subversive, terrorist and criminal intelligence effort.

MIA

Acronym: Missing In Action.

MINE COUNTER-MEASURES

Mines are used for defence in very large numbers, either in fixed fields to protect sensitive facilities, sown across possible infiltration routes and as simple area denial weapons. The Special Forces have developed the standard techniques used to deal with such obstacles to conducting a successful reconnaissance or sabotage mission. These include the simple, but time- consuming and danger-ous, *Probing the ground* with a stick or bayonet, the use of trained dogs which can sniff out the vapours coming from the explosive ingredients inside the landmines and modern lightweight versions of the metal detector – now increasingly lim-ited in their ability to find mines as many are made of plastic with only a tiny bit of metal. A new Ground-Penetrating Radar (GPR) has been developed to locate and disarm landmines. This new device can locate mines with little or no metal con-tent, as it is the explosive agents that have electrical properties that make them detectable to the right technology, such as GPR. A GPR device focuses radar energy just below the ground and just a few feet in front of the user, ignoring sig-nals that bounce back from the surface, and uses specially designed software to make buried objects shine brighter in the radar image. Once a landmine is detected, the GPR device shoots two chemical agents into the ground to deacti-vate it. One agent solidifies the triggering mechanism along with surrounding soil, allowing soldiers to cross the ground. The second chemical agent then solidifies the mine and soil permanently. The mine can then be lifted and destroyed or simply ignored. With some 250 million anti-personnel mines stockpiled throughout the world, a further 110 million already in the ground, often in unmarked fields or sown randomly, and in excess of three million additional mines laid each year, it is hardly surprising that over a million people, mainly civilians, have been killed by these deadly weapons in the last 25 years. They will continue to be a grave threat to Special Forces operations, and conversely a highly useful addition to their armoury, for the foreseeable future.

MINES

Anti-Personnel Mines (APM) are widely used by Special Forces to protect exposed positions, to cover lines of retreat, to stage ambushes and for sabotage operations. There is a huge and comprehensive range of such lethal weapons available for Special Operations. The Russians have the OZM-72 AP jumping mine, MON-50 AP directional mine, PMN-1/2/3 APM and MS1/2/3 booby-trap mines and POZM2/2M Fragmentation AP staked-mine, while the most commonly used US mines are the M14, a pressure-operated blast mine, the M16 bounding-fragmentation mine, the M18A1 Claymore and a number of Special Forces variations. Serbian MRUD (Claymore-type), PROM-1 jumping AP Mine and TMA-2 plastic APM, a myriad of Italian made APM include the VAR-40/100 series, EPR series, the V69 and indeed the Chinese Type-72A/B blast APM and Type-69 jumping Fragmentation APM are all found in worldwide use. The three main types of anti-personnel mines are the Blast, the most common type of mine, buried no deeper than a few centimetres and generally triggered by someone stepping on a plate needing only to apply about 5 to 16kg (11 to 35.3lbs) of pressure. These mines are designed to destroy an object in close proximity, such as a foot or leg, breaking the targeted object into fragments, which can cause secondary damage such as infection and amputation.

Bounding – Fragmentation, usually buried with only a small part of the igniter protruding from the ground, these mines are pressure or trip-wire activated. When activated, the igniter sets off a propelling charge, lifting the mine about 1-2m (3-6ft) into the air. The mine then detonates the main charge, showering a wide area with lethal shards of white hot metal, causing injury to the head and chest. Fragmentation, these mines release fragments in all directions, or can be arranged to send fragments in one direction as directional fragmentation mines such as the Claymore. The fragments used in the mines are either metal or glass. The most effective APM are the jumping or bounding fragmentation or directional fragmentation weapons, both of which can have a lethal area extending up to 50m from the initial explosion, causing severe injuries at up to 200m. Planted in groups, they can create deadly killing zones to catch enemy forces in an ambush or while in pursuit.

MINI-POUNDER

A small radar transmitter used to mark locations on the ground for radar-carrying aircraft.

MINI-SUBMARINES

Small submarines have been used by numerous countries for clandestine intelligence-gathering and surveillance. Japan, Soviet Union/Russia, Italy and the United States have all used them to some effect. North Korea, however, has developed these vessels for the insertion of groups of Special Forces. In June 1998 the South Korean Navy captured a North Korean 70-ton Yugo-class submarine that had become entangled in fishing nets off the eastern coast 11.5 miles (18.5km) off the port of Sokcho. The four or five crewmen managed to escape. However, in the same region in September 1996, another North Korean mini-submarine ran aground in Kangnung, leading to the death of all 24 of its crew and the Special Forces on board. Five South Korean soldiers and three civilians were killed in firefights during the hunt for the infiltrators. One of the latest in a long line of submersibles for use by the US Special Forces is the Mark-XII ASD. This is a submersible that carries combat swimmers and their cargo inside a fully flooded compartment. The vehicles launch and return to dry-deck shelters installed on host submarines. Inside the submersible, the pilot can jack in to the standard cyber-linkage system and can take advantage of a variety of sensors, including sonar, IR, UV and thermal imaging. Navigation is provided by the MUGR, a Miniature Underwater GPS Receiver. The Mark-XII is used by all Navy SEAL teams as well as by the British SBS, the French GIGN/Commandant Hubert and covert teams around the world. However, as the Swedish Armed Forces were to discover in the 1980s, the Soviet Special Forces also approached the problem of mini-submarine operations in shallow coastal waters from a different angle as well. The first proof of long-term Soviet activity arrived with a 'Whiskey' W-Class Soviet submarine stranded on rocks outside the Swedish naval base of Karlskrona in October 1981. A year later another sighting of an unidentified submarine led to the eventual use of depth charges on 5 October 1982, to try to force the vessel to the surface. Air bubbles and an oil slick was seen, but nothing else. As a result of close examination of sonar evidence and a search of the seabed by naval divers, the Swedish Ministry of Defence was convinced that up to three Soviet 'mother' submarines and three small submarines had been involved. At least two different types of mini-subs were used; one had two propellers and a reinforced keel, while the other appeared to be a hybrid with a single propeller and twin caterpillar tracks to crawl along the seabed in areas of strong tides, and at least one of the mini-subs actually penetrated Stockholm harbour. Dozens of other similar sightings were later made in the Baltic, while similar tracks were discovered on the seabed off both the Japanese and Scottish coastlines. Soviet and now Russian Naval SPETSNAZ are known to have developed a considerable capability to carry out intelligence-gathering, surveillance and Special Forces combat missions in harbours, river estuaries and along coastlines.

MISSION STATEMENT – US SPECIAL FORCES

Unconventional Warfare (UW)

A broad spectrum of military and paramilitary operations conducted in enemy-held, enemy-controlled or politically sensitive territory. UW includes, but is not limited to, the interrelated fields of guerrilla warfare, evasion and escape, subversion, sabotage and other operations of a low visibility, covert or clandestine nature. Conduct a broad spectrum of military and paramilitary operations.

Long-duration, indirect activities including guerrilla warfare and other offensive, low visibility or clandestine operations. Mostly conducted by indigenous forces organised, trained, equipped, supported and directed in varying degrees by Special Operations Forces. Direct Action (DA): Either overt or covert action against an enemy force. Seize, damage or destroy a target; capture or recover personnel or material in support of strategic/operational objectives or conventional forces. Short-duration, small-scale offensive actions. May require raids, ambushes, direct assault tactics; emplace mines and other munitions; conduct stand-off attacks by firing from air, ground or maritime platforms; designate or illuminate targets for precision-guided munitions; support for cover and deception operations; or conduct independent sabotage normally inside enemy-held territory. Special Reconnaissance (SR): Special Forces teams are infiltrated behind enemy lines to provide the theatre commander with intelligence on the enemy or to gather information on the terrain, local populace etc. of an area. Verify, through observation or other collection methods, information concerning enemy capabilities, intentions and activities in support of strategic/operational objectives or conventional forces. Reconnaissance and surveillance actions conducted at strategic or operational levels to complement national and theatre-level collection efforts. Collects meteorological, hydrographic, geographic and demographic data; provide target acquisition, area assessment and post-strike reconnaissance data. Foreign Internal Defence (FID): FID operations are designed to help friendly developing nations by working with host country military and police forces to improve their technical skills, understanding of human rights issues and to help with humanitarian and civic action projects. FID missions assist another government in any action programme taken to free and protect its society from subversion, lawlessness and insurgency. US government inter-agency activity to foster internal development of economic, social, political and military segments of a nations structure. Train, advise and assist host-nation military and paramilitary forces. Counter Terrorism (CT): Offensive measures taken to prevent, deter and respond to terrorism. Pre-empt or resolve terrorist incidents. Inter-agency activity using highly specialised capabilities. Psychological Operations (PSYOP): Induce or reinforce foreign attitudes and behaviour favourable to US objectives. Influence emotions, motives and behaviour of foreign governments, organisations, groups and individuals. Civil Affairs (CA): Establish, maintain, influence, or exploit relations among military forces, civil authorities, and civilian populations to facilitate military operations. May be conducted as stand-alone operations or in support of a larger force. May include military forces assuming functions normally the responsibility of the local government. Coalition Warfare/Support: Ensures the ability of a wide variety of foreign troops to work together effectively, in a wide variety of military exercises or operations such as Operation Desert Storm. Draws upon the SOF soldier's maturity, military skills, language skills and cultural awareness. Humanitarian and Civic Action (HCA): SOF soldiers' diversified military skills, language capabilities and cultural training make them a natural choice for supporting humanitarian action operations.

MO

Modus Operandi. Method of operation, often used in conjunction with a known terrorist when referring to his techniques and habits.

MOLDOVA

MILITARY SPECIAL FORCES
One understrength Special Forces (SPETSNAZ) battalion, based in Chisinau.

MINISTRY OF THE INTERIOR
OPON – Rapid Reaction Police has a small HRU response and anti-terrorist Special Forces team.

MONGOLIA

MILITARY SPECIAL FORCES
One Airborne Battalion with a single Special Forces (SPETSNAZ) Company. This unit provides the only anti-terrorist and hostage rescue response team available to the Mongolian authorities.

MOROCCO

MILITARY SPECIAL FORCES

Para-Commando Battalions The Moroccan Special Forces have gained considerable experience in foreign operations. A battalion fought under Syrian command in the 1973 war against Israel, while in 1976 several battalions were in action against Mauritanian forces supporting the Polisario guerrillas in the Western Sahara, and in April 1977 three battalions were deployed in a multinational force in Zaire. Since then the Moroccan Special Forces have been kept busy dealing with the Polisario still fighting for the independence of the Western Sahara and the rise of Islamic extremism. There are now at least seven Para-Commando Battalions in existence, all of which are receiving new equipment and advanced training in anti-terrorist and counter-insurgency operations from both the US and French Special Forces.

CIVILIAN SPECIAL FORCES

Gruppe Intervention Gendarme Nationale (GIGN) Established in 1980 it was organised and trained by the French GIGN as an HRU team. This 50-strong unit also receives assistance from both the SAS and GSG-9 and is usually rated quite highly for its fighting skills and in particular unarmed combat, mostly due to the presence of South Korean Special Forces martial arts instructors permanently attached to GIGN. Weapons used include MP5 and Uzi SMG, AK and M16 assault rifles.

MOSBY'S RAIDERS

During the US Civil War, Colonel John Singleton Mosby of Virginia formed a band of Confederate raiders that became a great problem for the Union generals. Operating from the outskirts of Washington, the 'enemy' capital, Mosby and 300 select volunteers cut off communications and supplies, wrecked railroads and raided headquarters behind Union lines. Because of his stealth and uncanny ability to avoid capture, Mosby came to be known as the 'Gray Ghost'. Well trained and well disciplined, Mosby and his men set a model for guerrilla warfare and very effectively anticipated many of the techniques that would be developed for the modern Special Forces. Mosby tied down a disproportionately large Union force, attempting to restrict his area operations and counter his raiding activities.

MOSCOW THEATRE SIEGE – ALPHA (AL'FA)

Heavily armed Chechen rebels stormed the Palace of Culture Theatre on Melnikov Street no more than 3 miles (5 kms) from the Kremlin on the evening of Wednesdy 23 October 2002 and took over 700 members of the audience, staff and performers from the musical *Nord-Ost* hostage. Their demands included the withdrawal of Russian Forces involved in the heavy fighting against the separatist movement in Chechnya. After three days of fruitless attempts at negotiation and the carrying out of the terrorists' threat to start executing their hostages, Russian Special Forces, including large numbers of the elite Alpha force and the FSB Security Service, stormed the building at around 05:30 Moscow time on Saturday 26 October. In the ensuing fighting some 50 Chechen terrorists including at least 18 women and the group's leader, Movsar Barayev, were killed and a number of accomplices arrested. Some 120 or more of the hostages were either murdered by the Chechens or killed by the gas, probably similar to the US developed 'BZ', which was used by the Russian Special Forces as they succeeded in preventing the Chechens from killing many more of the hostages. Indeed well over 700 civilians were rescued including a number of foreign nationals.

A major part of the overall success of this highly risky operation had depended on the Special Forces' clever use of the tunnels and sewers under the theatre. This allowed them to monitor the Chechens through high technology electronic surveillance equipment, to identify as far as possible the exact locations of the hostages and the Chechen gunmen and, in the moments before the actual rescue operation, to pump large quantities of the powerful incapacitating gas into the building. This significantly slowed down the reaction time of many of the terrorists and gained valuable time for the Alpha/FSB force to both take out the Chechens and, more importantly, to prevent the detonation of some thirty explosive devices, which would undoubtely have caused a massive loss of life both to the hostages and their Special Force rescuers. With little or no time to plan a suitable response, and under the huge pressure of the Chechens beginning to execute their hostages, the Russian rescue operation was an overall success in spite of the tragically high loss of innocent lives. However, it must now be beyond doubt that Russia has a huge internal terrorist problem and a significant increase in Special Force capability will be high on President Putin's list of priorities for 2003.

MOZAMBIQUE

MILITARY SPECIAL FORCES

The three Special Forces Commando battalions are poorly equipped but well trained, experienced and highly motivated after some 30 years of continual conflict. This former Portuguese colony has now joined the British Commonwealth and has begun to receive limited military training and some new equipment for its conventional forces. Still faced with severe internal problems and continued anti-government insurgencies, it is expected that the Special Forces units will benefit from some form of co-operation with the SAS.

MSR

Main Supply Route. Used when referring to an enemy supply route and in particular a potential target.

M21

This is a sniper version of the US M14 7.62mm rifle. The semi-automatic M21 is constructed of specially selected and highly tuned components. This is a widely used and very accurate rifle, particularly when paired with a high quality scope, such as the Leatherwood variable telescopic sight.

MUNICH MASSACRE – ISRAEL'S REVENGE

In the aftermath of the massacre of Israeli athletes and officials at the Munich Games by Palestinian terrorists belonging to 'Black September' the decision was taken, following a series of emergency security and Cabinet meetings in Jerusalem, that Israel's Special Forces would take the ultimate revenge on the perpetrators of this outrage. Secretive military units such as the Sayeret Matkal, effectively Israel's nearest equivalent to the SAS or Delta Force would, in close co-operation with Mossad, the intelligence service, hunt down and eliminate all those concerned. Mossad already had a close relationship with the national airline and additional officers were quickly dispatched to El Al offices worldwide, both to help monitor the international airports for suspects and to provide covert intelligence support for future Special Forces activity. Israel has never had a serious problem with the use of assassination as a matter of state policy, indeed many high-ranking military and political leaders have openly advocated the assassination of top members of the Palestinian leadership as the most effective deterrent to anti-Israeli terrorism. Ariel 'Arik' Sharon, the present Prime Minister and founder of Israel's first Special Forces formation, Unit-101 some 45 years ago, went so far as to argue for the formation of a special military command under direct General Staff control to totally eradicate Palestinian terrorism worldwide 'once and for all'. As an apparent firm believer in a form of Israeli 'Final Solution' for the Palestinian problem, it came as little surprise that he would later be accused by Israel's own Kahan Commission, of negligence in allowing serious war crimes to be committed following the invasion of the Lebanon in 1982 – which resulted in the massacre of up to 1,500 Palestinian civilians at refugee camps in Beirut by Lebanese Christian Falange militiamen working under the direct control of Israeli Special Forces. Premier Golda Meir was to give the Special Forces almost complete independence to plan the assassinations of the terrorists, but the personal 'go-ahead' of the Prime Minister would still be required before the killing could be sanctioned. Meir was also responsible for creating the hitherto unprecedented position of 'Special Adviser for Terrorist Matters' to be filled by the vastly experienced Special Forces and Intelligence chief Major-General Aharon Yariv, to both oversee the operations and to distance the other members of her government from actual foreknowledge of the revenge killings. Yariv and the Mossad Chief, Major-General Tzvi Zamir, agreed not to pursue the top political leadership of the PLO, parent organisation for 'Black September, but to eliminate the operational planners and activists. It was these men who most threatened Israel with further carnage. Exhaustive personal dossiers on the potential targets were compiled by Mossad from their comprehensive intelligence files and from new information that poured in from Mossad officers abroad and their many contacts in friendly foreign security services. There followed the creation of numerous Special Forces 'hit teams' or, more correctly, assassination squads who roamed the Middle East and Europe hunting leading operational members of 'Black September'. These teams were to be variously known as Black June, Wrath of God or simply WOG, The Avengers and even Squad-101 in direct recognition of Ariel Sharon's famous Unit-101. Israel has long remained tight-lipped about the true breadth and nature of its European War on Terrorism, but enough information has surfaced to provide a considerable insight into certain events. Assassination squads were organised into ALEPH or 'A' Teams to carry out the killings, while BET or 'B' Teams were to create diversions and to ensure a clean escape. Israel's embassies, the Zim Shipping offices, the El Al airline and Jewish organisations worldwide provided cover identities, safe houses and even arms caches when needed.

The first known victim of Israel's revenge killings was Wael Zwaiter, a seemingly innocent and unimportant translator at the Libyan Embassy in Rome. However, in reality he was a former high-ranking RAZD official in 'Black September's' intelligence organisation and their Operations Chief in Italy. He is believed to have masterminded several failed attempts to destroy El Al airliners in mid-air. On 16 October 1972 two men standing unobtrusively in the lobby of his apartment block fired twelve special .22 half-powder rounds from a Beretta into Zwaiter as he returned home. Virtually silent, but still deadly at close range the shots were unheard by the neighbours most of whom were apparently watching the first showing of Fellini's 8½ on TV. The assassins fled in a red Fiat 125 driven by a blonde woman. It was not unusual for Israeli Special Forces to include women as members of the 'hit teams', for believable couples were considered an advantage in clandestine foreign operations. However, in this case it appears that it was a male officer in drag. This was also a common practice and, indeed, during Operation Aviv Ne'urim (Spring of Youth) a joint Mossad-

Special Forces commando raid against 'Black September' facilities in Beirut in April 1972, the commander of the General Staff Reconnaissance Unit or Sayeret Matkal, Lieutenant-Colonel Ehud Barak, a future Prime Minister, had been disguised as a woman. The authorised killings were to continue for a number of years until the great majority of those 'Black September' terrorists actively involved in either carrying out or planning the Munich Olympic Games massacre had been killed. The killings were also to set a precedent for future Israeli Special Forces operations, many of which would be considered highly unorthodox by most democratic societies at best, and straightforwardly immoral and in total breach of international law and national sovereignty at worst. It is clear that Israel has regularly and quite deliberately used state-sponsored assassination as an official policy of its government in the fight against Arab terrorism and for the best part of its existence as an independent nation. It must now also be quite obvious that this policy has proved to be a catastrophic failure for the people of Israel, as the widespread Intifada of 2000–02 and the increasingly large numbers of deaths due to terrorist suicide attacks will most definitely and clearly confirm.

MYANMAR – BURMA

MILITARY SPECIAL FORCES
Fourteen Anti-Terrorist Commando Battalions and one Anti-Hijacking/HRU Battalion in Rangoon. These units have acquired large quantities of modern Chinese and commercially available surveillance and intelligence equipment, as well as weapons, in recent years. They have a reputation for brutality towards the civilian population in the areas of insurgency, the torture and murder of prisoners and tactics not far removed from genocide or the ethnic cleansing of the recent Balkan wars. The total strength is now probably around 15,000, including several small Special Forces units dedicated to the protection of senior Government figures.

NAMIBIA

MILITARY SPECIAL FORCES
One Special Forces Company. Well trained and highly capable, with a genuine hostage rescue capability.

NCO

Non-Commissioned Officer. Regimental sergeant major, company sergeant major, colour sergeant, master sergeant, staff sergeant, corporal, lance corporal and all such variations. It is a truism that the best Special Forces, and for that matter, the best armed forces are those with a large number of well-trained, resourceful and responsible NCOs.

NEPAL

MILITARY SPECIAL FORCES
Special Forces Brigade Kathmandu
1st Airborne Battalion
1st Special Forces Company
2nd Special Forces Company
1st Cavalry Squadron
The large-scale Maoist insurgency, particularly in Western Nepal, has seen a major growth in funding for the Special Forces and these units have developed both a considerable expertise in anti-terrorist operations in difficult mountainous terrain and a ruthless reputation for their treatment of captured insurgents and villagers suspected of co-operating with the anti-government forces.

NET

Usually written as net. – Special Forces Radio network – links Command with individual units as well as providing unit-to-unit communication.

NETHERLANDS

MILITARY SPECIAL FORCES
KCT (Korps Commando Troepen)   The Korps Kommando Tropen, or Army Commando Troops Corps, is the Dutch Army's Special Operations Force. Organised along the same lines as the British SAS, KCT is tasked with conducting various missions such as direct action, long-range reconnaissance, and intelligence gathering.

Currently, KCT is composed of one active and two reserve units; but there are plans to reorganise KCT's structure, which would lead to the activation of both reserve formations and their integration into the active force. Upon completion of this reorganisation KCT would be composed of three Special Operation Companies, one HQ and support Company, and one training Company. Currently KCT is organised as follows:

104th Waarnemings-en Verkennings Companie (104th Recon and Observation Co.): The 104th R&S Co. was formally an active unit, transferred to the reserves when the 108th SOC was activated. Tasked to act as the Dutch Army's Long-Range Recon Patrol (LRRP) unit. Unit members are trained in HAHO/ HALO parachuting techniques, and covert observation skills. Under the current plans 104th Recon and Observation Co. will be activated, and its name changed to 104th SOC.

105th Waarnemings-en Verkennings Companie (105th Recon and Observation Co.): The 105th is the second reserve formation within KCT. Current plans also call for this unit to be activated, and redesignated as the 105th SOC.

108 Korps Commando Troepen (KCT-Korps Commandotroepen), reformed 1 January 1993 as the active Commando-Special Operations unit. Tasked with conducting DA (Direct Action), sabotage and reconnaissance missions. Troops are skilled in airborne, airmobile, amphibious, Arctic and mountain operations. Some troops have also undergone training in the use of powered hang-gliders. The unit has recently seen action in Bosnia, apprehending several war crimes suspects. This SAS-type unit uses the following weapons: 9mm Glock 17 pistol, 5.56mm Diemaco C8FT assault carbine, 5.56mm Diemaco C7A1 assault rifle, 8.6mm (.338 Lapua Magnum) Accuracy International AWM bolt-action sniper rifle, 12.7mm (.50 BMG) Barrett Model 82A1 sniper rifle, 5.56mm Diemaco C7LSW automatic rifle, 7.62mm FN MAG machine gun, 40mmSR Diemaco M203 underbarrel grenade launcher (under C7A1) and 66mm Raufoss M72A3 light anti-tank weapon.

Bijzondere Bijstandseenheid Krijgsmacht: The BBEK (Armed Forces Special Assistance Unit) is the Royal Netherlands Military Police's SWAT team. This unit is tasked with responding to terrorist attacks on Dutch military installations.

Royal Netherlands Marine Corps: The RNLMC contains a number of Special Operations units, with many of them trained and organised to operate with or under the direct control of their British counterparts during war.

7 Netherlands Special Boat Squadron (7NL SBS): HQ/Staff are based at Doorn (SE of Utrecht). Known as 'Whiskey Company' it has a complement of 110 men and three officers and is organised, equipped and operates in a fashion similar to the British SBS. When conducting operations alongside the British SBS, the unit is simply known as C Squadron, SBS. The members of this highly trained combat swimmer unit are expert in parachuting, SCUBA and demolition. During wartime the 7 NL SBS would be utilised for intelligence gathering as well as sabotage missions and is also responsible for the security of Dutch passenger liners, ferries and oil-rigs. Equipment such as rigid raider craft, Klepper canoes, and closed-circuit breathing gear is used for covert infiltration. The following weapons are used: 9mmR (.357 Magnum) Colt Lawman revolver, 9mm Glock 17M pistol, 7.62mm H&K P11 underwater dart pistol, 9mm Uzi, 9mm H&K MP5A3 sub-machine gun, 5.56mm Steyr AUG A1 assault rifle and 7.62mm Steyr SSG 69 sniper rifle.

Marine Close Combat Unit: as the HRU is known, conducted its first operation during the Schevengingen jail riot by Palestinian prisoners in

October 1974. At 03.40 when the rioters were off guard, the Marine CCU assaulted the jail using stun grenades and burning through one particular door with a thermic lance. The marines fired into the ceilings and subdued the rioters in hand-to-hand combat. This unit has, by the standards of some other national HRU and anti-terrorist units, a marked reluctance to kill; however, in this case that was not a hindrance and the operation was successful and all the rioters survived, if a little bruised by the experience.

Mountain Leader Platoon: A relatively new unit within the RNLMC, the unit was formed in 1997 by consolidating all the Mountain Leaders (ML) within one unit. The platoon is organised and operates in a fashion similar to the British Brigade ML Patrol Troop (formally the Mountain and Arctic Warfare Cadre – M&AW Cadre). The platoon's MLs act as the 1st Amphibious Combat Group's rapid reaction and reconnaissance unit when deployed. They are trained in mountain, Arctic, small boat, and parachute operations, with all of the platoon's members having successfully completed the British Royal Marines ML course. During a war, involving NATO, the unit would come under the control of the British 3rd Commando Brigade.

CIVILIAN SPECIAL FORCES
Bijzondere Bijstands Eenhid (BBE): This Special Intervention joint Civilian and Military Force is the Netherlands' national Counter-Terrorist unit. Answering to the Ministry of the Interior, this unit of approximately 100 personnel is considered to be one of the best such units in the world. It consists largely of Police and Military marksmen and a Marine Close Combat Unit. Tasked with conducting Counter-Terrorist, Direct Action and various other covert missions, they are trained as expert snipers, in EOD, communications and CQB.

Brigade Speciale Beveiligingsopdrachten (BSB, Special Protection Unit): The BSB is an elite force of around 40 specially trained and selected police created in 1975. The unit is tasked with providing bodyguards for Dutch VIPs and acting as a police SWAT team. Unit members also perform covert intelligence-gathering and act as observation teams, as well as providing security at the major airports.

NEW ZEALAND

MILITARY SPECIAL FORCES
NZSAS (New Zealand Special Air Service Regiment) consists of a headquarters support wing at Papakura, a training wing and two squadrons, each with three troop specialities: boat, air and mountain. However, one of their major skills is tracking, and NZSAS trackers are much sought after as instructors for 22nd SAS, SASR and US Special Forces. The staff are regu-

larly moved between the two squadrons, one of which is trained and equipped for counter-terrorist operations and the other for commando-style `special warfare' operations. Each squadron is divided into small groups, which are trained to operate independently with teams of four to six soldiers, led by a captain or sergeant, as the basic operational elements of the NZSAS. Formed in 1955, its first overseas deployment was in Malaya in 1955–57 where the NZSAS was attached to the British 22nd SAS Regiment and spent long periods in the jungle fighting the communist ASAL insurgency. In two thirteen-week operations in the Fort Brooke area they killed ASAL leader Ah Ming and his deputy, and in the mountainous Negri Sembilan area they killed resistance leader Li Hak Chi. The NZSAS was disbanded when it returned from Malaya, but was re-established in 1959 to operate under South-East Asian conditions with the emphasis placed on long-range small-party offensive operations behind enemy lines, communications and tactical reconnaissance. The NZSAS was sent to Borneo in 1965 and worked with the British SAS and Special Boat Section of the Royal Marines. In late 1968 the first 26 NZSAS soldiers, from the '1st Ranger Squadron' arrived in Vietnam. They were based south-east of Saigon with other Australian and New Zealand army units at Nui Dat. For the next two and a half years the NZSAS operated with the Australian SAS, doing what they called 'recce-ambush patrols'. During 26 months in Vietnam the NZSAS conducted some 155 of these patrols, each usually lasting for ten days, after being dropped into an area by helicopter. Their primary task was intelligence collecting: searching for Vietnamese military positions and watching military movements from hidden observation points. The NZSAS also conducted operations with United States Special Forces in other parts of Vietnam. Some NZSAS members served with the British SAS in Oman in 1974–76, in Northern Ireland, as part of the May 1980 SAS storming of the Iranian embassy in London, fought beside Philippine forces against insurgent groups and helped to train foreign forces and operated throughout South-East Asia. Personnel were also detached for service in the Balkans and to Afghanistan in 2001. The NZSAS has provided support to the Sultan of Oman with personnel attached to the parachute training school in 1990–92. Training includes unarmed combat (karate), small weapons, heavy weapons, underwater operations (with and without tanks for beach landings), jungle operations, snow operations, parachuting and helicopter insertions. Weapons used include the 9mm SIG-Sauer P226 pistol, 9mm H&K MP5A3 sub-machine gun, 5.56mm LSAF F88 assault rifle (Australian-made Steyr AUG A1), 5.56mm ADI F88SA1 assault rifle (Australian-made Steyr AUG A1), 7.62mm Parker-Hale Model 82 sniper rifle, 5.56mm Diemaco C9 light machine gun (Canadian-made FN MINIMI) and 40mmSR R/M Equipment M203PI underbarrel grenade launcher (under F88SA1).

CIVILIAN SPECIAL FORCES
New Zealand Police Special Tactics Group (formerly the Anti-Terrorist Squad).

NICARAGUA

MILITARY SPECIAL FORCES
The Special Forces Brigade (Prefectura de Unidades de Fuerzas Especiales, or *PUFE),* is based at Sandino Airport, Managua. and comprises three units, the 1st Special Forces Battalion, 2nd Special Forces Battalion and 3rd Special Forces Battalion. These battalions are trained as an anti-terrorist force, deep reconnaissance force (LRRP) and as beach reconnaissance commandos.

NIGER

MILITARY SPECIAL FORCES
Two Airborne Special Forces Companies. Trained and equipped by the French Special Forces.

They can rely on the intervention by GIGN or Legion units in the event of a major crisis.

NIGERIA

MILITARY SPECIAL FORCES
One Airborne Brigade believed to include a Special Forces Battalion. One Independent Airborne Battalion. As part of a joint US-Nigerian programme to enhance the Nigerian Army's combat and Special Forces capability some 260 members of the 3rd Battalion of the US Army 3rd Special Forces Group (Airborne) trained some 2,000 personnel from Nigerian units in Special Forces skills in 2001 for service in war-torn Sierra Leone. These units included the 20th Mechanized Battalion (23rd Armoured Brigade), the 26th and 195th Motorized Infantry Battalions. The 1st, 65th and 73rd Infantry Battalions received similar training in 2002. The Nigerian Special Forces have an appalling reputation for human rights abuse dating back to the Biafran war and aftermath in 1969–71, and there appears to be little interest in the army in doing anything to significantly change this image.

NORWAY

MILITARY SPECIAL FORCES
Army
Fallskjermjegerkommandoen (Parachute Ranger Commandoes) 7th Jaeger (Ranger)
The Finnmark Regiment has a special guerrilla force known as the 7th Jaeger

Company whose mission is to stay behind enemy lines and disrupt their forces and operations. The 7th Jaeger Company is broken down into four platoons (Tropps), a command/Mortar tropp and three rifleman tropps, with each tropp broken down further into three eight-man teams. These teams are designed to be highly mobile and Jaeger personnel move around the snow-covered region on white Yamaha snowmobiles or cross-country skis, carrying a wide assortment of weapons. Soldiers in the unit are trained to not only survive in the snow and cold, but to fight effectively. Personnel are experts in weapons and supplies caching techniques and each unit is expected to be able to fight for two weeks without resupply. In the event a resupply or relocation is needed the 7th Jaegers call upon the Bell 412 helicopters of the Royal Norwegian Air Force. Weapons used include the 9mm Glock P 80 pistol, 9mm Kongsberg MP5A3N sub-machine gun (licence-made H&K MP5A3), 7.62mm Kongsberg AG3 battle rifle (licence-made H&K G3A3), H&K G-3 assault rifle is carried with a specially mounted 40mm grenade launcher, 7.62mm Kongsberg AG3-F1 battle rifle (licence-made H&K G3A4), 7.62mm Våpensmia NM149A1 bolt-action sniper rifle, 12.7mm (.50 BMG) Barrett M82A1NG sniper rifle, 7.62mm MKE MG3 machine gun (Rheinmetall MG3 made in Turkey) and 40mmSR H&K HK79 underbarrel grenade launcher (under AG3 and AG3-F1). In 1999, the 9mm H&K USP Tactical pistol with detachable sound suppresser was adopted, while the 5.56mm Diemaco C8SFW assault carbine with 3.4× scope and 40mmSR Diemaco M203A1 underbarrel grenade launcher replaced the AG3-F1 and HK79 in 1998.

Navy

Marinejegerkommando (Naval Ranger Command)   Marinejegertroppen FKN (Naval Commando Troop – North Norway) can be compared to the British SBS (Special Boat Squadron) and US Navy SEALs. Their primary missions are deep-penetration reconnaissance and sabotage of enemy naval installations. They use closed-circuit diving apparatus, kayaks or parachutes as methods of insertion. The initial 22-week training course for Marine Jagerne personnel occurs at the Diver and Frogman School at Haakonsvern Naval Station outside Bergen. After that they go to Ramsund Naval Station which is also their home base, for further training. Every second year elements of the unit train with the US Navy SEALs. Although it is officially denied, Norwegian SP were reported to have worked with Kosovo Liberation Army (UCK) forces to conduct intensive surveillance of Serbian forces' movements and positions two days prior to NATO's entry into Kosovo.

Weapons used include the 9mm Glock P 80 pistol (Glock 17), 7.62mm H&K P11 underwater dart pistol, 9mm Kongsberg MP5A3N sub-machine gun (licence-made H&K MP5A3), 7.62mm Kongsberg AG3-F1 battle rifle (licence-made H&K G3A4), 7.62mm Accuracy International AW-F sniper rifle, 12.7mm (.50 BMG) Barrett M82A1NG sniper rifle, 7.62mm MKE MG3 machine gun and 40mmSR H&K HK79 underbarrel grenade launcher (under AG3 and AG3-F1).

Marinejegerlaget FKS (Naval Commando Team – S. Norway) This is a reserve unit and although well trained is now cadre only.

CIVILIAN SPECIAL SERVICES
Beredskaptrop (Readiness Troop) of the National Police Counter-Terrorist group formed in 1975 and based in Oslo. This 50-strong unit receives considerable Special Forces training including parachuting and HALO at the Trandum Airborne Ranger School, SCUBA, amphibious and helicopter insertion. The basic operational unit is twelve-strong and broken down into two-man teams. Weapons in use include the H & K MP5 SMG.

NVG

Night-Vision Goggles (see entry on SPECIAL OPTICS).

OC

Officer Commanding – the officer delegated to temporarily command a unit at any given time or for a special operation. Not to be confused with CO – Commanding Officer, who is the officer appointed to command a military formation on a regular basis.

OMAN

MILITARY SPECIAL FORCES
Sultan's Special Force of the Royal Guards Brigade of Oman The prime national HRU unit, which was formed in 1977 as a COIN Battalion, it has since added the duties of counter-terrorism. This 500-strong unit has been commanded by former SAS or Rhodesian SAS officers for most of its existence and is usually considered to be a highly competent fighting force. It is well equipped, with a range of modern weapons including the ubiquitous MP5.

Omani Combat Swimmer Section This 40-strong unit has been trained by the SAS and SBS and is tasked in part to be responsible for dealing with the possible hijacking of an oil tanker in Omani territorial waters.

CIVILIAN SPECIAL FORCES
Special Task Force of the Royal Omani Police Force A limited capability HRU team about 300-strong which uses the Steyr AUG assault rifle as primary weapon.

OP (oP)

Operation. Any Special Forces, Intelligence or Military mission.

OP

Acronym: Observation Post. Usually refers to a temporary position behind enemy lines or in a well-placed defensive position.

OPERATION AZALEE – FRENCH SPECIAL FORCES

The Comoros Islands had been a French colony until July of 1975, when they gained their independence. On 28 September 1995 Bob Denard and 33 mercenaries took control of the Comoros Islands in a coup code-named operation 'Kaskar' by the mercenaries. The French President, Jacques Chirac, requested that the Minister of Defence and the Army Chief of Staff begin drafting plans for the retaking of the Comoros Islands. Intelligence was gathered and the COS (the French Special Operations Command) assets were placed on alert. Teams from GIGN, DRM and DGSE began discreetly deploying to the area around the Indian Ocean. On 3 October the French government gave Operation Azalee the green light. Bob Denard began to create a civilian government in an effort to stave off the impending invasion, and a new presidential guard was created from loyal members of the old guard that Denard himself had trained. Strategic strong points, armed with heavy machine guns, were set up around the island, particularly covering the island's two airports. By this time, more than 200 members of COS and DRM were on their way to the islands aboard a frigate and two patrol boats. Members of GIGN and Commandos Jaubert, as well as several Puma helicopters, were also in the area. The French ultimately deployed 600 Special Forces against a force of 33 mercenaries and a 300-strong dissident force. The operation started off at 23.00 on 3 October when members of Commandos Jaubert explored the beaches near the island's two airports at Hahaya and Iconi. At 02.30 three Pumas delivered members of 1erRPIMa and 13eRDP to the tarmac of the Hahaya airport. Initially taking fire from the insurrectionists' heavy machine guns, the French troopers used their night vision gear and the cover of darkness to secure the airport and local area. Twenty Comoran soldiers were captured in the process. By 03.00 members of Commandos Jaubert had secured the Iconi airport. Elements of 5eRIAOM, 2eRAMa and 2eRPIMa were flown in by C-160 Transals to hold the airfield while Commandos Jaubert headed for the main Kandani barracks. Another 30 Comoran soldiers were taken into custody while fifteen members of

GIGN flew in to liberate the French Embassy in Moroni. Another team of Jaubert commandos seized the *Vulcain* the ship used by Denard and his mercenaries to reach Comoros. The main air assault began at 05.00, when two C-160 Transalls landed elements of the Foreign Legion at Hahaya. Thirty minutes later they were joined by members of 2ea, RIAOM Marines, and 2e, RAMa artillery. By 05.50 the airport was secure and a defence zone had been established around it. French units began moving towards the capital of Moroni and by 06.30 French units were racing to reach the barracks at Kandani before Bob Denard and his mercenaries could break out. By 15.00 the next day Bob Denard and his mercenaries had surrendered. He was taken to the Iconi airport by the GIGN, flown to France, later to be convicted and jailed. France had acted decisively and used their Special Forces to move rapidly and achieve tactical surprise, using the right combination of paratroopers and Special Forces teams, French units were able to completely retake the island in less than 48 hours.

OPERATION EAGLE CLAW – DELTA FORCE

On 4 November 1979, a mob in Iran stormed the US Embassy and took the staff and USMC security contingent hostage. In all, 52 Americans were captured and were being held by the Iranian Revolutionary Guard, and it was unclear whether they were being tortured or readied for execution. Within hours, the newly certified US Army Special Forces Operational Detachment-Delta (Airborne) was on full alert and plans were being drawn up for a rescue. Delta's commander, Colonel Charles Beckwith, was intimately involved with the rescue attempt. The US faced a daunting task. Tehran is well inside Iran and far away from friendly countries. The hostages were not held at an airport as in Israel's earlier Entebbe raid. Good intelligence was hard to come by about forces inside the embassy and in Tehran. All the planning and training had to be carried out in complete secrecy.

What was ultimately decided on was an audacious plan involving all four services, eight USMC RH-53s helicopters, plus twelve USAF fixed-wing aircraft; four MC-130s, three EC-130s, three AC-130s, and two C-141s, and numerous Special Forces infiltrated into Tehran ahead of the actual assault. The basic plan was to infiltrate the covert teams into the country the night before the assault and get them to Tehran. The first night, three MC-130s were to fly to a barren spot in Iran and offload the Delta Force men, combat controllers, and translators/truck drivers. Three EC-130s following the Combat Talons would then land and prepare to refuel the Marine RH-53s flying in from the US carrier *Nimitz*. Once the helicopters were refuelled, they would fly the task force to a spot near the outskirts of Tehran and meet up with agents already in-country, who would lead the operators to a safe house to await the assault the next night. The helicopters would fly to another site in-country and hide until called by the Delta operators. On the second night, the MC-130s and EC-130s would again fly into the country, this time with 100 Rangers, and head for Manzariyeh Airfield. The Rangers were to assault the field and hold it so that the two C-141s could land to ferry the hostages back home. The three AC-130s would be used to suppress any attempts at action by the Iranian Air Force from nearby Mehrabad Airbase. Delta would assault the embassy and free the hostages, then rendezvous with the helicopters in a nearby football stadium. They and the hostages would be flown to Manzariyeh Airfield and the waiting C-141s and then be flown out of the country. All the aircraft except for the eight helicopters would be flown back; the helicopters would be destroyed before leaving. What actually occurred highlights very effectively the old military saying that 'even well thought out plans rarely survive the first contact with reality'. A month before the assault, a CIA Twin Otter had flown into the first landing area, known as Desert One. A USAF Combat Controller had ridden around the landing area on a light motorbike and planted landing lights to help guide the force in. That insertion went well and the pilots reported that their sensors had picked up some radar signals at 3,000 feet but nothing below that. Despite these findings, the helicopter pilots were told to fly at or below 200 feet to avoid radar. This limitation caused them to run into a haboob, or dust storm, that they could not fly over without breaking the 200-foot limit. Two helicopters lost sight of the task force and landed. Another had landed earlier when a warning light had come on. Their crew had been picked up but the aircraft that had stopped to retrieve them was now 20 minutes behind the rest of the formation. Battling dust storms and heavy winds, the RH-53s continued to make their way to Desert One. After receiving word that the EC-130s and fuel had arrived, the two aircraft that had landed earlier started up again and resumed their flight to the rendezvous. Another helicopter had a malfunction and the pilot and marine commander decided to turn back, halfway to the site. The task force was down to six helicopters, the bare minimum needed to pull off the rescue. The first group of three helicopters arrived at Desert One an hour late, with the rest appearing fifteen minutes later. The rescue attempt was dealt its final blow when it was learned that one of the aircraft had lost its primary hydraulic system and was unsafe to use fully loaded for the assault. Only five aircraft were serviceable and six needed, so the mission was aborted. The situation further deteriorated when one of the helicopters moving to another position, drifted into one of the parked EC-130s. Immediately both the C-130 and RH-53 burst into flames. The C-130 was quickly evacuated and the order came to blow up the aircraft and terminate the operation. However, in the dust and confusion the order never reached the people who should have destroyed the aircraft. There were wounded and dying men to be taken care of and the aircraft had to be moved to avoid having the burning debris start another fire. Because of this failure to destroy the helicopters, top secret plans fell into the hands of the Iranians the next day and the agents waiting in-country to help the Delta operators were almost captured while several groups of pro-American activists were rounded up. All told five USAF and three USMC personnel lost their lives and dozens more were injured. The Iranians scattered the hostages around the country afterwards, making any further rescue attempts impossible. They would be released much later, after diplomatic negotiations with the US government.

OPERATION ENDURING FREEDOM

The first Special Forces, US Delta Force Commandos and British 22nd SAS Regiment, arrived in countries bordering Afghanistan within 72 hours of the terrorist outrages in the United States. These elite soldiers, quickly reinforced by the USN SEAL-6 team, USMC 'Recons' and the Royal Marine SBS, later entered Afghanistan to identify important targets, in some cases 'illuminating' them for the first waves of strike aircraft when the air campaign finally began. Additional small teams of CIA field operatives and Delta Force commandos had slipped into northern Afghanistan before the end of September and established a 'semi-permanent' base there, to track down Osama Bin Laden. It is in this area that the CIA-NSA also maintains a joint intelligence listening post. MH-60K Black Hawk helicopters, which can operate under pitch-dark conditions and in adverse weather, ferried supporting combat teams from the 5th Special Forces Group (Green Berets) and large quantities of specialist electronic warfare equipment to the camp from their base at Khanabad near Qarshi in neighbouring Uzbekistan. This large former Soviet base also housed two battalions of the 10th Mountain Division, in reality a light infantry unit rather than a specialist mountain force. Moving usually by moonlight, lying low in caves and covered foxholes by day, the first waves of three- and four-man Special Forces teams combed Afghanistan's hostile countryside, searching for targets imperceptible to satellites. Above them, USAF TR1 (U2), RAF Canberra PR9 and Nimrod R1 surveillance aircraft and Predator unmanned drones (UAV), one of which had already crashed or been shot down, gave them an unparalleled view of the inhospitable terrain. Special Forces, elite fighters trained as much in information-gathering as anti-terrorist tactics, were once again at the sharp edge of the Allied intelligence community. The use on 16 October 2001 of the elderly, but still deadly, AC-130 Spectre gunships for attacks on Taliban forces surrounding Kandahar, and the increasing attacks on tanks and artillery positions around the northern city of Mazar-i-Sharif, covered the early insertion of far greater numbers of Special Forces. Those already on the ground were to be reinforced by the Green Berets, 75th Ranger Regiment and other LRRP trained units. These units were supported by elements of the three battalions of the 160th Aviation Regiment, the famed 'Night Stalkers', the only major US specialist aviation unit trained to operate at night and under adverse weather conditions and equipped with a range of exotic stealth helicopters. Based at the McChord Air Force Base in Lakewood, Washington, was the secretive USAF 22nd Special Tactics Squadron, one of six Special Operations groups that provide combat air controllers, para-rescuemen and combat weathermen and probably the best-trained, best-equipped soldiers in the US military. Their eventual role was to include identifying not only Al Qa'ida's hideouts in Afghanistan but also Hezbollah and Islamic Jihad's terrorist training camps in Iran, Syria, Algeria, Lebanon, Libya, Sudan and Yemen. A wide range of specialist psyops, electronic warfare and counter-terrorist units were soon to be deployed along with high-tech and exotic surveillance equipment and weapons. Afghanistan was to prove once again both the real value and the limitations of Special Forces. Their effectiveness is more often governed by whether the theatre command understands their true role and capabilities, and orders them to perform those duties they are actually trained and fitted to carry out. Operation Enduring Freedom contained distinct pointers that this particular message was finally getting through to the Pentagon.

OPERATION JONATHAN – SAYERET MATKAL

At approximately 12.30 on Sunday 27 June 1976, Air France flight number AF 139 was hijacked by four terrorists. The plane, of which nearly one-third of the passengers were Jewish, was flown to Benghazi. After a six and a half hour delay, the plane took off again and began flying east. It changed course and began flying south-east, and by 03.00 the next morning it had arrived at Entebbe, Uganda.

Upon arrival, the four terrorists (two of whom were members of the German Baader-Meinhof gang) were joined by three others, bringing the total up to seven. The passengers were kept on the aircraft until 12.00, at which point they were transported to the airfield's old terminal building.

When the President of Uganda, Idi Amin, visited the hostages in the terminal he claimed to be working to achieve their release and stated that Ugandan soldiers would remain at the terminal to ensure their safety. The next day at 15.30 the leader of the terrorists, a Palestine nicknamed 'the Peruvian', released specific demands. Fifty-three terrorists – thirteen held in prisons in France, West Germany, Kenya and Switzerland – and 40 in Israeli prisons, were to be released. If they were not, hostages would be executed starting at 14.00 on 1 July.

Sayeret Matkal was placed on alert shortly after the Israeli government learned about the hijacking. Members of the unit assembled at Lod Airport, while separately from Sayeret Matkal, Lieutenant Colonel Joshua Shani of the Israeli Air Force's only C-130 squadron began conducting basic flight planning for his aircraft to fly to and back from Uganda. Throughout Wednesday 30 June intelligence information began to filter in that Idi Amin was not seeking the release of the hostages and was actually collaborating with the PFLP. This made an earlier plan requiring marine commandos to rescue the hostages and then surrender to Ugandan soldiers unworkable. Earlier that day, the PFLP terrorists had released 100 passengers, leaving only the Jewish passengers and the flight crew as hostages. Jonathan Netanyahu, commander of Sayeret Matkal, was briefed on the roles and missions of the units in the plan that was then under development. It called for three ground elements: Sayeret Matkal, members of the Elite Golani Infantry and paratroopers. Netanyahu and others argued for a smaller, more flexible force and eventually Brigadier General Dan Shomron, who would ultimately command the raid, decided to go with Netanyahu's recommendation. The members of Sayeret Matkal participating in the assault met at Lod Airport at 11.30 on Saturday 3 July some six days after the terrorists had hijacked the aircraft. At 13.20 the aircraft took off and headed south at low levels to avoid detection by Soviet warships and Egyptian radar. The timing of the assault was critical; in order to slip their large C-130 transports into the airport undetected by radar the force was to land closely behind a British Airways flight that was scheduled to land for refuelling. The aircraft made a brief stop at Sharm-a-Sheikh to top off their fuel tanks and feed the troops, before the four aircraft formation headed south on their 7.5 hour flight to Entebbe. By 22.30 the aircraft had reached Lake Victoria, just a short distance from Entebbe by air. The last three C-130s broke formation and circled as the lead aircraft made its approach. At 23.00 on 23 July (Israeli time) the lead aircraft touched down. As the aircraft slowed, ten members from the elite Golani Infantry jumped out and set up landing beacons for the remaining aircraft, and as the aircraft turned onto the taxiway leading to the old terminal, the rear cargo ramp was lowered and a black Mercedes and two Land Rovers drove out. Ugandan flags flew from the Mercedes and all 35 commandos were dressed in Ugandan uniforms. The three-vehicle convoy proceeded towards the old terminal with their lights on at a steady 40mph (64kph). The vehicles drove towards the terminal for a full minute before being challenged by two Ugandan sentries. Lieutenant Colonel Netanyahu slowed the vehicles as if to stop and, when the sentries were within range, the Israeli commandos opened fire with silenced Berettas, killing one sentry and missing another; who stumbled backwards and began to raise his rifle. An Israeli commando quickly opened fire, killing the sentry with his AK-47, but also alerting the Ugandan forces. Realising that the element of surprise was lost, Netanyahu immediately ordered the drivers to head for the old terminal at full speed. As they approached, several soldiers and a terrorist could be seen milling about outside in confusion. The vehicles quickly parked by the control tower adjacent to the old terminal and the commandos jumped out and began their attack. During the initial phase of the assault, Muki Betser's (the second in command) element ran into a problem when a door that had been included in the plans was not there. Netanyahu ran past him and resumed the assault, while Betser's group found other entry to the building. A Ugandan guard jumped up from behind some wooden crates and began to fire but was cut down. Another fired from within the terminal but he too was killed by Matkal commandos now entering the building. Within three minutes of landing, four of the seven terrorists had been killed. Though the Israeli Special Forces continued to clear the building, some confusion in the difficult conditions was not unexpected and two passengers who stood up were badly wounded before it was realised that they were not terrorists. The team assigned to assault the VIP lounge in the terminal found the outside door locked. One of them threw a grenade at the door; it bounced off and exploded, slightly wounding one Israeli soldier. When they finally gained entry two men stood up and began moving towards the commandos, hands raised. Unsure as to the two men's intentions, the commandos withheld their fire until one noticed a grenade belt around the waist of one of the men. Their commands to halt unheeded, they opened fire and killed the two men. As they did, one of the terrorists dropped a grenade he had been hiding in his hand. All the terrorists were now dead. Only the Ugandan soldiers stood in the way of a safe escape. Several soldiers were holed up in the tower next to the old terminal and were firing at the Matkal soldiers remaining in the Land Rovers. The second C-130 landed six minutes after the first and two armoured personnel carriers offloaded and headed to the secured terminal, silencing the Ugandan fire quickly. Two more APCs then arrived on the third C-130. One split off and destroyed eight MiGs stationed at the base. Members of Sayeret Golani arrived and set up a defensive perimeter. Within fifteen minutes of the first C-130 landing, the hostages had been freed and the area secured.

Matkal commandos began evacuating the rescued civilians to a waiting C-130. They were hampered by passengers returning to the terminal to try and find lost property and darkness. Several of the passengers were also in shock or hysterical. Getting an accurate headcount was difficult in the darkened aircraft. At 23.52, less than an hour after the first Hercules landed, the C-130 with 106 rescued hostages took off. With the hostages safe, the rest of the force began to withdraw to their aircraft. Their movements were covered by smoke and timed explosives devices. The last C-130 left Entebbe at 24.29, 99 minutes after the first one had landed. The cost, one commando killed (the CO, Netanyahu) and one hostage dead (she had been moved to a local hospital after a choking incident and was not present during the rescue. She was subsequently executed in retribution for the raid).

The rescue at Entebbe is a classic example of a successful Special Forces operation. The Israelis used surprise and superior training to overcome their enemies and gain their objectives with a minimum loss of life. It was a logistically difficult mission and the use of a Kenyan air base for the C-130 was absolutely crucial for the overall success of the mission. Thirty-five commandos in two Land Rovers and a Mercedes with four APCs for firepower had to be transported over 2,200 miles and back again with over 100 hostages.

OPERATION JUST CAUSE – SEALS

In 1989 the United States invaded Panama. During the invasion, the US Navy SEALs were tasked with two missions. The first, to disable a boat General Noriega might use to escape, was successful (it was 'disabled' by putting so much explosive under the hull that one engine was never found!). The second was not, to the tune of four SEALs killed and eight seriously wounded. It is this second incident we will focus on. The failure of this mission started during the planning process. The original plan called for army units to be airlifted into key areas. But the Navy command was unhappy that none of their units got to share in the action, so SEAL Team 4 was given two missions, one of which probably should have been assigned to the Army Rangers. The second mission SEALs were tasked with was disabling Manuel Noriega's Learjet at Patilla Field, to prevent him from escaping in it. The plan called for 48 SEALs in two platoons to be towed near the cliffs at the end of the runway. The SEALs would then move the 3,500ft length of the airfield up to the hangar where the Lear was kept. One squad would disable the Lear, while another would pull small aircraft onto the airstrip to prevent it from being used. The others would be used to provide security at the north and south end of the fields. H-hour for the invasion was set for 01.00. The PBR from SBU-26, with CRRCs in tow, left the dock at Rodman 2000 hours on 19 December 1989. The SEALs were armed with an impressive array of weapons. Not only were pistols and M-16/203 combos carried, but also several team members had the then-new M-249 Saw or M-60 machine gun. Rounding out their arsenal were fragmentation grenades, Claymore mines, and AT-4 anti-tank rockets. At 00.45, the mission commander was notified that H-hour had been moved forward fifteen minutes (fighting had broken out early between Panamanian and American forces). The element of surprise lost, the SEALs continued towards their objective. A second problem was that the USAF Combat Controllers attached to the SEALs had not been able to raise the AC-130 Spectre assigned to provide supporting fire if needed. Other problems began to crop up as they reached the shore and assembled on the edge of the runway. There was no cover. The runway was well lit by landing lights and backscatter from the city. Worse still, the administration building and hangar itself were well lit, and fire from the nearby city began waking up houseguards in buildings surrounding the field. On the positive side, a SEAL surveillance team had occupied a rented apartment across from the field earlier in the day and could give them real-time intelligence about troop and vehicle movements.

Bravo Platoon had disarmed several guards and had begun to drag light aircraft onto the runway. As they did, the two squads of Golf Platoon made their way up the field. Radio calls came in; one reporting that a helicopter had left Colon heading for Patilla, possibly carrying Noriega. The second relayed that several PDF armoured cars mounting 90mm cannon were possibly heading to the north end of the field. About this time, the houseguards in the buildings surrounding the airfield noticed members of Golf Platoon's unprotected dash up the field. Using portable radios, they notified guards in the hangar and then took aim on the SEALs below. The hangar guards took up defensive positions in the hangar. The two squads took up position, the first within 100 feet of the hangar, the second slightly behind and to the side of the first. A call came out from the hangar for the SEALs to surrender. A SEAL responded by demanding the Panamanians surrender to the SEALs. Realising they were in a bad position on a brightly lit field, the first squad tried to relocate. Then several long bursts of fire came out from the hangar. In the initial volley of fire, all but one of the SEALs were wounded. The houseguards across the airfield also began to fire upon the SEALs, putting them in a deadly cross-fire. Four SEALs were now dead and eight seriously wounded, and those that weren't were having a hard time dealing with their wounds and getting out of the heavy rucks they'd brought with them. The second squad of Golf Platoon began to attempt to lay down a protective cover as Bravo Platoon and members of the command and control element rushed to the hangar. The USAF Combat Controllers had just made contact with the gunship, but they had been kept with the command and control element of the SEALs and were too far away to provide assistance. Surviving members began to drag the casualties away, several becoming casualties themselves in the process. Lieutenant Phillips from Golf's second squad ordered the Learjet to be taken out by rocket. The AT-4 hit the aircraft cleanly, destroying any chance of it being used to escape. The tragedy of the SEAL operation once again highlights the misuse of specialist forces by senior commanders steeped in conventional tactics. The SEALs were simply sent on a mission that would have been more suited to the Rangers. The waste of life and the talents of the SEALs must remain a severe criticism of the overall US command of the invasion of Panama.

OPERATION ROOSTER – ISRAELI SF

26–27 December 1969. The War of Attrition raged along the Suez Canal from the end of the Six Days' War in 1967 until a cease-fire agreement in

1970. The Egyptian military effort was supported by Soviet shipments of military equipment, which was of great interest to Israeli intelligence. The IDF had used equipment captured during the Six Days' War to better deal with enemy threats, using captured radars to learn the weaknesses of the Egyptian air defence and to develop electronic warfare methods. The acquired knowledge was of great value and gave the IAF the edge over enemy air defences, yet by 1969 it was becoming apparent that electronic warfare and other methods used to trick Egyptian radars were becoming less effective, and that Israeli operations were being hampered by earlier detection of incoming aircraft. Newer radars had obviously arrived in Egypt and an effort was under way to learn how to deal with this new threat. The break came after an air defence array – destroyed during a September 1969 armour raid using captured Soviet tanks and armoured personnel carriers to operate for an entire day inside Egyptian territory – eventually came back on line with a different electronic configuration which was much harder to defeat. Reconnaissance missions were quickly launched to photograph the new air defence array and soon enough a new P-12 Soviet radar was located on the beach of Ras-Arab. The immediate response was to destroy the new radar station with an aerial strike, but the attacking aircraft were stopped shortly before takeoff when an idea to capture the entire installation came up. Nicknamed 'Rooster-53', the operation was planned in just a few days, beginning on 24 December. After getting approval from the IDF chain of command, the details and mechanics of the operation were soon ironed out and the forces involved began their training on radars captured during the Six Days' War. The helicopters selected to carry the radar station to Israeli territory were the new Sikorsky CH-53 Yasur, which had only arrived in Israel shortly before. These were the only helicopters deemed capable of carrying the entire radar station, estimated at seven tons. The operation was finally launched at 21.00 on the eve of 26 December 1969. A-4 Skyhawks and F-4 Phantoms began attacking Egyptian forces along the western bank of the Suez Canal and Red Sea. Hidden by the noise of the attacking jets, three Aerospatiale Super Frelons carrying Israeli Special Forces, technicians and paratroopers made their way west towards their target. Making their approach carefully in order not to be spotted beforehand, the troops surprised the light security contingent at the radar installation and quickly took control of the site. By 02.00 on 27 December, when the raiding force had taken apart the radar station and prepared the various parts for the CH-53s, the two Yasurs were called in from across the Red Sea. One CH-53 carried the communications caravan and the radar antenna, while the other took the heavier, four-ton radar itself. The two helicopters started making their way back across the Red Sea to Israeli-controlled territory. The four-ton radar caravan was actually heavier than the CH-53 was designed to carry and soon endangered the safe completion of the operation. The cables connecting the radar to the helicopter were stretching the ribs of the aircraft, which in turn caused a hydraulic pipeline to rupture. Faced with either releasing the radar or losing control of the aircraft and crashing, the captain of the helicopter managed to cross the water line into Israel. With the last of its hydraulic pressure, the helicopter set down the radar and landed beside it. The second CH-53, which had already arrived with its lighter load, was sent back to retrieve the radar from the crash landing site. Once again the heavy load almost caused the helicopter to crash, but the radar was finally delivered to the designated point, into the hands of awaiting intelligence specialists. Although an attempt was made to conceal the mission and its success, the operation was made public a week after it took place following its exposure in the foreign press. The radar itself was studied thoroughly and provided the IAF with new countermeasures against the Egyptian air defences, removing a threat to Israeli air superiority over the Suez Canal. It was later handed over to the USA.

OPSEC

Operational Security. An absolute necessity and of paramount importance. More operations have been compromised and lives lost or seriously put at risk through a failure of Operational Security than for practically any other reason.

OSS

Office of Strategic Services. US Second World War Intelligence and Subversion agency which developed many of the techniques now used by the Special Forces. The OSS was the product of William Donovan, an imposing man-mountain of a visionary whose propensity for freewheeling activities earned him the nickname of 'Wild Bill'. Donovan was tough and smart, a veteran of the First World War who received the Medal of Honor for heroism on the Western Front in October 1918, and who made a fortune as a Wall Street lawyer during the 1920s and 1930s. When the Second World War finally erupted in Europe, and later threatened to engulf the United States, Donovan was able to convince President Franklin D. Roosevelt that a new type of organisation would have to be formed, one that would collect intelligence and carry out secret operations behind enemy lines. In 1941, President Roosevelt directed Donovan to form the Co-ordinator of Intelligence (COI). COI blossomed quickly, forming operational sites in the UK, North Africa, India, Burma and China. In 1942, the agency was renamed the OSS and Donovan became a major general. The primary OSS operations in Europe were the so-called Jedburgh missions. These consisted of dropping three-man teams into France, Belgium and Holland, where they trained partisan resistance movements and conducted guerrilla operations against the Germans in preparation for the D-Day invasion. Other OSS operations took place in Asia, most spectacularly in Burma, where OSS Detachment 101 organised 11,000 Kachin tribesmen into a force that eventually killed 10,000 Japanese with the loss of only 206 of its own. After the war, President Harry S. Truman disbanded the OSS, but not before it had left a legacy still felt today. From its intelligence operations came the nucleus of men and techniques that would give birth to the CIA on 18 September 1947. Indeed, the first directors of the CIA were veterans of the OSS, while from its guerrilla operations came the nucleus of the men and techniques that would give birth to the US Special Forces in June 1952.

OTR

On The Run. Usually refers to a terrorist or suspect who, for one reason or another, suddenly decides that the time has come to quickly absent themselves. Usually follows the discovery or at least strong suspicion that they are under active surveillance.

02 & BENEDRYL

Oxygen and a strong antihistamine, for hangovers.

PAKISTAN

MILITARY SPECIAL FORCES
The SSG (Special Service Group) In 1953–54 the Pakistan Army raised an elite commando formation with US Army assistance under cover of being a simple battalion in the Baluch Regiment. The Special Service Group established in 1956 was effectively the enlarged 19th Baluch Battalion and has been based at its headquarters at Cherat near Attock City for more than 45 years. In March 1964 a joint CIA Covert Action and US Special Forces training team helped set up the new SF Airborne school at Peshawar. All members of the 19th Baluch had to be airborne-qualified and the training included both basic and jumpmaster courses. Their initial training and orientation as regards tactics was based on the US Special Forces pattern with whom they co-operated closely in the Cold War years. Later Chinese training, tactics, weapons and equipment were also introduced. The SSG now has some 24 Companies, each of which has specialised units in desert, mountain, ranger, underwater warfare and intelligence-gathering operations. After a few preliminary operations on the Afghan border, the nascent SSG's first test came during the 1965 war. Around 100 officers and men were dropped on the night of 6/7 September near the Indian airbases of Adampur,

Pathankot and Halwara in an ill-conceived operation to destroy Indian combat aircraft and put the bases out of action. Badly planned, lacking any solid intelligence, and even more badly executed, the operation ended in a disaster. The SSG commandos fell easy prey to a hastily gathered Indian force and only a handful made it back to their own country. No Indian planes were damaged or casualties inflicted on Indian troops. By 1971, the SSG boasted three battalions with one permanently stationed in East Pakistan. Their performance in the 1971 war was much better, with 1st Commando Battalion making a spectacular raid on an Indian artillery regiment and disabling several of their guns besides inflicting casualties. 3rd Commando Battalion in Bangladesh performed creditably in a normal infantry role. The SSG's role in helping the Afghan resistance to the Soviet invasion was highly commendable and much of the credit for the spectacular successes of the Mujahideen against Russian forces goes to them. Likewise, they have fought well in the Siachen campaign though in one or two instances taking heavy casualties. In the preliminary stages of the 1999 Kargil Operations the SSG again performed well, infiltrating relatively deep into Indian territory undetected. Subsequently being used as stock infantry troops to hold posts/defensive positions, they took heavy casualties and suffered the mortification of their actions being 'denied' by their own country.

In recent years the SSG has helped train Sri Lanka Army Commandos for operations against the Tamil Tiger insurgents, conducted covert intelligence missions in Afghanistan on behalf of the Taliban, provided air-marshals for airliners carrying VIPs and conducted deep penetration operations within India and disputed areas of Kashmir in 2002. It is presently organised into three Special Forces Battalions, each of four companies, with two based at the Cherat headquarters and one on operations along the borders with India or at strategic locations such as nuclear research facilities or the Terbella Dam. In addition there are a further twelve independent Special Forces companies, including the enlarged MUSA company, now providing Pakistan with, in theory, an extensive dedicated genuine Counter-Terrorism capability. However, suspicion abounds that these units are used as much to teach the techniques of terrorism as to actually counter them.

In 1980, an anti-terrorist role was given to Musa Company, originally formed in 1970 as a combat diver unit. This dedicated CT company was trained by British SAS advisers in mid-1981. The course combines specialisation in assault, sniping, survival, demolitions, grenade throwing, rappelling, MG firing, FIBUA (Fighting In Built Up Areas), CQB (Close-Quarters Battle), para-jumping, stealth and espionage, marine courses, physical and psychological training as well as criminal psychology courses and many other courses. A wide range of skills are now considered necessary including heliborne insertion, combat shooting, parachute techniques including HAHO (High Altitude High Opening) and HALO

(High Altitude Low Opening). The SSG uses the latest and most advanced weapons, including the famed Heckler and Koch 9mm MP5 SMG, 9mm Uzi, Heckler and Koch 7.62mm Gewher-3 (G3/ HK91) assault rifle, China made Type-56 7.62mm autos (Chinese version of Russian AK47), 5.56mm M16A1, the new Steyr 5.56mm NATO A.U.G assault rifle. In their sniper weapons, they use scoped up G3s, Finnish Tikka bolt actions, PSG1 sniper rifles, as well as Steyr SSG 69 7.62mm (.308 win) bolt actions. The pistols in use are Austrian 9mm Glock 15, the Berretta M9 (M92F), the SIG Pro 226. The latest FN 5.7mm P90 SMG is also reserved for very high-risk applications.

Akbar Company (Frogman Unit)
In 1966 the Pakistan Navy created its own commando unit, the Naval Special Services (SSGN). Training was initially conducted by SSG in Cherat, Peshawar and Karachi bases. The SSGN currently maintains headquarters in Karachi headed by Pakistan Navy Commander. It has a strength of one company and is assigned to unconventional warfare operations in the coastal regions. In war, the SSGN would make use of the Pakistan Navy's midget submarine fleet. Parachute training is conducted by the Army's SSG while all other training of the SSGN is held at the SSGN training centre, PNS Iqbal in Karachi. Some students are sent to the US for specialist courses. Since the 1970s the SSGN holds joint exercises with the US Navy SEALs and the Iranian Navy.

PANAMA

CIVILIAN SPECIAL FORCES
One Special Force HRU unit serves as part of the National Police Force.

PAPUA NEW GUINEA

MILITARY SPECIAL FORCES
Special Forces Platoon. In the event of a serious hostage rescue situation or terrorist incident it is likely that a team from the Australian SAS Regiment would conduct the actual operation.

PARAGUAY

MILITARY SPECIAL FORCES
Comando de Tropas Especiales (Special Forces-Commandos) Headquartered at Cerrito:
Batallón de Tropas Especiales 1 (1st Special Forces Battalion)
Escuela de Tropas Especiales (Special Forces School)
Paraguay has distinct counter-insurgency problems and a number of its

infantry units are specially trained in jungle warfare; however, the 1st Special Forces Battalion is dedicated to anti-terrorist and hostage rescue operations. It is trained by US Special Forces and has received an infusion of more modern weapons and surveillance equipment in the last three years.

PATHFINDER COMPANY – SOUTH AFRICA

During Rhodesia's war with terrorist insurgents after the declaration of Unilateral Independence from Britain, thousands of foreign-born soldiers volunteered to serve the illegal racist regime. These soldiers made up one of the best armies in the world during the 1970s and inflicted losses on the enemy far outweighing their own. In the field, Rhodesian security forces often overpowered superior numbers of enemies, and usually carried the day. When Rhodesia became Zimbabwe, the country's finest military units were disbanded, as they were seen as a threat to the new government which was made up of old enemies. Most soldiers in the army were strongly anti-communist, and the new government was supported by communist regimes from around the world. Many disillusioned Rhodesian soldiers made their way south to be welcomed by the South African Defence Force. South Africa at the time had two highly covert military formations in the Recce Commandos and 32 Battalion. In 1980 both of these units snapped up the seasoned Rhodesian combat troops. Many former Selous Scouts joined 5 Recce, while there were sufficient numbers of Rhodesian SAS to form an additional Recce commando, 6 Recce. In November 1980, volunteers were required for the formation of another elite unit to be a part of 44th Parachute Brigade known as the Pathfinders. Pre-selection occurred at Mablique, on the border with Zimbabwe. The first stage of selection took place in the Drakensberg Mountains of south-eastern South Africa. This is a formidable place, and the scene of some of the coldest, wettest weather in the country. Forced marches of predetermined distances within strict time limits under stress with loads of rifle and 40lb rucksack, together with an 80lb ammunition box carried between two men for the first two days, stretched candidates to the limit. The men needed to hit checkpoints within a certain amount of time regardless of weather conditions. The men were constantly harassed by the instructors in an attempt to make them quit. If they had the right attitude and also completed the marches, they were allowed to continue. The next phase of selection focused more on individual skills, including patrolling techniques, navigation, survival, tracking, intelligence-gathering and reading, ambush and counter-ambush techniques. A 5km live fire assault course with wire obstacles, water crossings and bunkers along with a simulated SWAPO camp provided realistic training. Troopers also learned how to select drop and landing zones. Training with weapons progressed from 7.62 R1 (FN FAL design) and 5.56 R4 (Galil design) to captured AKs that were used for external operations. Final selection was accomplished by assessment of the candidates abilities in operational areas. They were deployed on military operations against SWAPO in South West Africa's Sector 10, as well as in Angola. They had to prove themselves in order to earn the designation of Pathfinder. Each member of a four-man team was trained in a speciality, while all members of the team were cross-trained in all the skills needed to ensure flexibility. The unit's mission was to find adequate drop zones for main bodies of troops and establish observation posts along routes known to be used by SWAPO for infiltration. Intelligence was then passed to Section 10 HQ which would deploy the 44th Parachute Brigade Fire Force, gunships or 32nd SF Battalion to intercept the insurgents. Pathfinders supported 32nd Battalion on numerous external operations, operating in Buffel armoured vehicles, light utility vehicles, or on foot. The first strike by Pathfinders was in southern Angola at Kamathu and they made quite an impression as they unhesitatingly swept through the enemy positions. By early 1981 the selection courses had produced sufficient personnel to man a body of customised vehicles. This mobile strike force was called Sabre Ops, and used nine Toyota Land Cruisers, Land Rovers and Mercedes Unimog Light Trucks. One of the Land Rovers was armed with a 20mm cannon while the other two mounted a Browning .50 machine gun. They each possessed a single FN MAG machine gun for the commander and twin rear-mounted FN MAGs. The Unimogs each utilised one MAG, while one was additionally fitted out with a 60mm mortar, and they all carried all the fuel, ammo, and food for the unit. Every vehicle was mounted with smoke dischargers, winches and puncture-proof tyres. Communication between vehicles was made possible by VHF radio, and communication with the base at Murrayhill was by High Frequency sets. Soon after receiving the new vehicles, the unit was deployed to the operational areas. In October 1981, a Pathfinder Company and elements of 2nd Para Battalion were parachuted into Angola for another camp attack. It was to be the unit's last action as a company. The CO was transferred out of 44th Para Brigade, when the South African government become rather more sensitive to charges that they were using mercenaries to fight their battles. The Pathfinders suddenly found themselves acting as a training unit instructing Citizen Force Paratroopers, a role few of them cared for. The Pathfinders were seen as an anomaly within the SADF – 'Foreigners' who seemed to enjoy the war – and many were seen as crazy due to their outlandish behaviour. Off-duty they often appeared to act quite strangely, the Pathfinders behaved like Philistines and the name stuck. The SADF commanders overlooked such antics for the sake of having such a good unit in the field. In January 1982, the Pathfinder Company was disbanded. The success of the unit had been out of all proportion to its size. From a military point of view they were a supremely successful Special Forces unit. From any reasonable moral or political view they were racist dinosaurs out of touch with a changing world and an anachronism that could not be allowed to survive.

PAVE HAWK

The Pave Hawk is a twin-engine medium-lift helicopter operated by the Air Force Special Operations Command, a component of the US Special Operations Command. The MH-60G's primary wartime missions are infiltration, exfiltration and resupply of Special Operations Forces in day, night or marginal weather conditions. Other missions include combat search and rescue. During Desert Storm, Pave Hawks provided combat recovery for coalition air forces in Iraq, Saudi Arabia, Kuwait and the Persian Gulf. They also provided emergency evacuation coverage for US Navy sea, air and land (SEAL) teams penetrating the Kuwait coast before the invasion. The MH-60G is equipped with an all-weather radar which enables the crew to avoid inclement weather. To extend their range, Pave Hawks are equipped with a retractable in-flight refuelling probe and internal auxiliary fuel tanks. All MH-60Gs have an automatic flight control system to stabilise the aircraft in typical flight altitudes.

MH-60K is the standard Special Operations version of the Black Hawk. It is capable of providing long-range airlifts far into hostile territory in adverse weather conditions. Modifications include two removable 230-gallon external fuel tanks, two .50 calibre machine guns, an air-to-air refuelling probe, and an external hoist. The MH-60K can also be armed with two M134 7.62mm 'miniguns'. A new avionics suite includes interactive Multi-Function Displays (MFDs), Forward-Looking Infrared (FLIR), digital map generator and terrain avoidance/terrain following multi-mode radar. Survivability equipment includes radar and missile warning systems and IR jammers. The MH-60K has full shipboard operability. It is powered by two General Electric T700-GE-701C 1843shp turboshaft engines. The HH-60G's primary wartime mission is combat search and rescue, infiltration, exfiltration and resupply of Special Operations Forces in day, night or marginal weather conditions. The HH-60G Pave Hawk provides the capability of independent rescue operations in combat areas, up to and including medium-threat environments. Recoveries are made by landing or by alternate means, such as rope ladder or hoist. Low-level tactical flight profiles are used to avoid threats. Night-Vision Goggle (NVG) and Forward Looking Infrared (FLIR) assisted low-level night operations and night water operation missions are performed by specially trained crews. The basic crew normally consists of five: pilot, co-pilot, flight engineer, and two PJs. The aircraft can also carry eight to ten troops. Pave Hawks are equipped with a rescue hoist with a 200-foot (60.7 metres) cable and 600-pound (270 kilograms) lift capacity. The helicopter hoist can recover survivors from a hover height of 200 feet above the ground or vertical landings can be accomplished into unprepared areas. The hoist can recover a Stokes litter patient or three people simultaneously on a forest penetrator.

The helicopter has limited self-protection provided by side window mounted M-60, M-240 or GAU-2B machine guns. Pave Hawk is equipped with two crew-served 7.62mm miniguns mounted in the cabin windows. In addition, two .50 calibre machine guns can be mounted in the cabin doors.

Mission systems on the HH-60H make it ideally suited for operations with special warfare units. Combat-equipped personnel can be covertly inserted and/or extracted in any terrain with precise GPS navigation accuracy. A variety of insertion and extraction techniques are available, including landing, hoisting, fastrope, rappel, paradrop, McGuire or SPIE Rig, and CRRC. Additionally, Helicopter Visit Board Search and Seizure (HVBSS) operations may be conducted using one or more of these insertion/extraction techniques. HVBSS missions are designed to take control of a ship considered to be a Contact of Interest (COI). The ability to interdict or 'take down' shipping during enforcement of a naval blockade requires precise planning and execution. Tethered Duck (T-Duck) was implemented to rapidly insert troops and a Combat Rubber Raiding Craft (CRRC) to water areas. The troops fastrope down to the CRRC after it is lowered into the water, and the motor is then lowered down to the troops to complete the procedure. Parachute operations are used for inserting troops when the helicopters are unable to land with a minumum free-fall drop altitude of 2,500 feet AGL (above ground level).

The maximum speed is 193 knots with a cruise speed of 120 to 140 knots. Unrefuelled range is 480 nautical miles (800km) with a combat load and aircraft at maximum gross weight of 22,000 lbs; the combat radius is approximately 200nm (340km). In-flight refuelling greatly extends this range. Pave Hawks are equipped with a retractable in-flight refuelling probe and internal auxiliary fuel tanks.

All HH-60Gs have an automatic flight control system to stabilise the aircraft in typical flight altitudes. They also have instrumentation and engine and rotor blade anti-ice systems for all-weather operation. The HH-60G is equipped with an all-weather radar which enables the crew to avoid inclement weather. Pave Hawks are equipped with folding rotor blades and a tail stabilator for shipboard operations and to ease air transportability. The non-retractable landing gear consists of two main landing gears and a tail wheel. Aft sliding doors on each side of the troop and cargo compartment allow rapid loading and unloading. External loads can be carried on an 8,000-pound (3,600 kilograms) capacity cargo hook. The Pave Hawk can be equipped with the external stores support system. The HH-60 is stationed throughout the world.

PERU

MILITARY SPECIAL FORCES
Airborne Division
B.I.Cdos. 19 – 19th Commando Special Forces Battalion – Callao
B.I.Cdos. 29 – 29th Commando Special Forces Battalion – Callao
B.I.Cdos. 39 – 39th Commando Special Forces Battalion – Callao
B.I.Para. 61 – 61st Para Battalion – Callao

Fuerza de Operaciones Especiales – Special Operations Force This now controls at least six Special Forces Commando Companies, including the Puma Special Forces Group based at Arequipa and tasked with a counter-insurgency and anti-terrorist role. Weapons used include AK-47, AKM, P-90, UZI, mini-UZI, MP-5, as well as FN-FAL rifles with sniper scopes.

Peru has had enormous terrorist and insurgency problems from the 'Shining Path' guerrillas to the siege of the Japanese Embassy in Lima, and the Special Forces are now receiving a considerable infusion of new surveillance equipment, weapons and logistic support, particularly as there were distinct signs towards the end of 2002 that terrorist activity was once again on the increase.

Peruvian Navy Special Forces Group Trains under JCET with USN SEALs

CIVILIAN SPECIAL FORCES
DINCOTE National Police Force – Anti-Terrorist Force HRU and Anti-Terrorist Teams – Trained by US Special Forces.

DINANDRO National Police Force – Anti-Drug Directorate Trains regularly under JCET with US Special Forces.

PETERHEAD PRISON SIEGE – SAS

One of the few known occasions on which the SAS has apparently been used within the UK in actions against British citizens was the use of an undercover unit in October 1987, when the SAS were used to end a siege at Peterhead prison in north-east Scotland. There is good reason to believe that the SAS has had a discreet section targeted for such specialist operations under the catch-all Military Aid to the Civil Authorities since 1984. The operation involved storming 'D' Block, where a seriously ill prison warder was being held hostage by the five hardcore rioters remaining out of an original group of some 50 dangerous prisoners serving sentences for, among other crimes, multiple murder, torture and rape, and who had originally seized control of the building. The hardcore prisoners were constantly threatening to cut the throat of the officer, whose condition with only one kidney and deprived of medication was, after a week of great stress, deteriorating quickly. Finally permission was given to use a four-man SAS hostage rescue team. At 5 a.m. the team slipped across a rook and through a skylight minutes later and after the use of CS gas and 'Flash-bangs', the officer was safely on his way to hospital and control of 'D' block returned to the prison authorities. A certain amount of legal niceties were exchanged with the local Scottish Police and Home Office officials and the SAS team returned to Aberdeen airport to fly back to barracks. Officially they were never there, and in fact there is no evidence that their skills have been called upon in other subsequent prison riots. However, it is more than possible that the Prison Services' own 'Mufti' riot squads have been trained and advised in storming and hostage rescue techniques by the SAS.

PHILIPPINES

MILITARY SPECIAL FORCES
The Philippine Army (PA) Special Operations Command (SOCOM) HQ Fort Magsaysay, Neuva Ecija Activated 1 June 1996, replaced the Special Warfare Brigade, which was disbanded in 1989 and controls the following units:
The Special Forces (Airborne) Regiment – Fort Magsaysay, Neuva Ecija
1st Scout Ranger Regiment Camp – Tecson, Bulacan
   A new unit under PA SOCOM and known as Alpha Two Zero (A-20) was formed along the lines of Delta Force and is responsible for CT operations. The first SF unit was established in 1958 in conjunction with the US Special Forces; however, on 1 December 1989, after a failed coup against former President Corazon Aquino, the First Scout Ranger Regiment was disbanded. It was an absence destined to be short-lived for on 16 May 1991, the Regiment was reactivated and the FSRR has since been successfully deployed in major troublespots across the country. It is now deeply involved with US Special Forces in the campaign against the MILF, and in particular the Abu Say'yaf Islamic insurgent groups in 2002. The Philippine Air Force (PAF) Aviation Security Command (AVSECOM) was disbanded, the responsibility being turned over to the Philippine National Police Aviation Security Command (PASCOM). The PASCOM handles security at the major airports. Counter-hijacking functions are the responsibility of the Special Operations Group (SOG) of the PASCOM. The SOG has trained alongside the Australian SAS and are equipped, trained and function in ASASR (TAG) aircraft counter-hijacking methods.

The Philippine Navy (PN) Special Warfare Group is trained, equipped and functions in the same manner as US Navy Special Warfare. Philippine Navy SEALs undergo their own BUDS and wear a trident similar to their US Navy counterparts, who have trained them in their own image. A joint PN SEAL and PM Recon unit operating directly under Naval Intelligence, the Special Reaction Group (SRG), is the local counterpart of SEAL Team Six (DEVGRU). The Philippine Marines (PM) Force Recon trains alongside their USMC Force Recon brothers, and operates in much the same way. Several members have received training in shipboarding and naval CQB.

CIVILIAN SPECIAL FORCES

The Presidential Security Group (PSG) which functions like the US Secret Service is actually a composite military command with police units attached to it. The PSG Special Reaction Group is the equivalent of the USSS 'Cat Squad'.

The Philippine National Police (PNP) Special Action Force (SAF) is formed along the lines of the British SAS, but has different recruitment and selection procedures. The SAF has received training from the US FBI, French RAID and the Israeli Ya'mam. The Anti-Terrorist Unit (ATU) of the PNPSAF is responsible for Police CT operations nationwide.

PLANNING

Planning a Special Forces Operation requires great skill, experience and knowledge of the potential combat zone, as well as accurate up-to-date intelligence. The information required can be fitted into the following categories: Mission – this may require rapid deployment so that consideration must be given to the most expeditious method of infiltration. However, keeping the mission and its target secret often takes precedence over speed. Enemy Capabilities – strengths, disposition and security likely to be encountered markedly affects the means selected for the mission. Heavily guarded land borders may force an airborne or seaborne infiltration means, though this in turn may be compromised by a strong air defence system. Terrain – the nature of the country affects the selection of altitudes, approach and exit routes or landing areas. Weather – seasonal conditions seriously affect infiltration and exfiltration, air cover or resupply missions. Temperature, precipitation, visibility, clouds and wind all affect operational parameters and the equipment likely to be required. Hydrography – in maritime operations this science is all-important. Foreshore conditions, offshore water depths, beach gradients, river, tide, surf, currents and sea floor conditions all affect small-boat or combat swimmer operations. The position of reefs, sandbars, type of seaweed, the presence of sharks, sea snakes or poisonous jellyfish, natural and man-made obstacles all need to be recorded. Astronomical Conditions – accurate advanced knowledge of periods of twilight, sunrise and sunset, moon phases and both moonrise and moonset are essential for clandestine operations. Distances – accurate information is needed to plan both infiltration, exfiltration and emergency escape routes. Training – ensuring that the units involved have recently received training in the skills most likely to be required on any particular mission. Equipment – essential to make absolutely sure that a mission unit takes everything likely to be required, failure to do so can result in cancellation at an early stage or making a dangerous air drop which might compromise the security of the mission.

PNG

Passive night goggles (see entry on SPECIAL OPTICS).

POINT

Point or point man – the soldier who walks first in formation and scouts the area ahead. A dangerous position, as his task is to check for mines, booby-traps and to trigger an ambush before the main part of a patrol can be trapped.

POLAND

MILITARY SPECIAL FORCES
Special Forces Command
Grupa Reagowania Operacyjno Mobilnego (GROM)   Although a new unit, created in 1991, GROM has worked hard and diligently at becoming a first-class Counter-Terrorist unit. GROM operators are drawn from other units within the Special Warfare community. It is a 270–300 strong unit that operates in four-man teams. All members of a team are fully trained as combat assault personnel, have a reputation for excellent marksmanship and usually speak at least two languages. GROM also has fully functioning support teams, ranging from technicians and analysts to EOD (Explosives Ordinance Disposal) personnel. All combat training is done with live ammunition, and such skills as SCUBA, HALO/HAHO, marksmanship, amphibious (with the US SEALs), mountain and winter warfare techniques are included. Because of their dedication and skill, particularly in VIP protection, GROM was selected in 1994 to take part in Operation Restore Democracy, the American-led invasion of Haiti. Fifty-five troopers were sent to train with members of the US 3rd Special Forces Group in Puerto Rico. There, they were educated in Haitian politics and social systems and allowed time to acclimatise to the local weather. During their deployment to Haiti, GROM operators provided security for several important VIPs, including UN General Secretary Buthros Buthros Ghali and US Secretary of Defence William Perry. One VIP, Lalhdar Brahimi, had a $150,000 bounty placed on

his head by groups who opposed Aristede's return. In one incident, GROM operators were stopped by a group of local slum-dwellers and informed that a boy had been taken hostage by a group of heavily armed gunmen. With the help of US Military Police, GROM were able to storm the building, extinguishing a fire that had started in the process, and free the boy. Because of the professionalism displayed by its members, US Major-General David C. Meade awarded Colonel Slawomir Petelicki, GROM's creator and first commander, the Army Commendation medal; the first time in American history that a foreign unit has been commended in such a manner. Fifty GROM personnel were deployed to Bosnia in support of the Polish Infantry battalion stationed there during the Balkan conflict. They successfully arrested a Bosnian national suspected of war crimes in June of 1998. Control of GROM was suddenly shifted from the Ministry of the Interior to the Ministry of Defence in October of 1999, and many of the senior officers were dismissed. The exact reasons for this remain unclear; however, it appears that some members of the Polish government were upset over the use made by GROM of certain illegally obtained electronic surveillance equipment. With the new command comes a new mission; in addition to counter-terrorism missions GROM is now tasked with performing 'stay-behind' guerrilla warfare in case large portions of Poland are ever invaded. Weapons include the 9mm CZ75, 9mm FN-Browning HP Mk 3, 9mm Glock 19 and 9mm SIG-Sauer P228, depending on the officer's preference, the 9mm H&K MP5A5 sub-machine gun, 9mm H&K MP5SD6 suppressed sub-machine gun, 5.56mm Lucznik kbk wz.96 Beryl assault carbine and 7.62mm H&K PSG1 sniper rifle. The Army Special Forces Command also has a dedicated LRRP capability provided by the 401st Paratroop Battalion and the 1st Commando Regiment'

Navy
7th Lujcyka Naval Assault Division   The Assault (Commando) Regiment at Lubliniec is a highly trained elite amphibious warfare unit.

POPSKI'S PRIVATE ARMY

Vladimir Peniakoff was born of Russian parents in Belgium in 1897. He moved to Cambridge to study at St John's College in 1914 and from then considered England to be his first country. He was a director of a sugar mill in Egypt when Germany invaded Belgium. As an Allied national he was accepted into the British Army. It was while being transported by the LRDG as part of the Libyan Arab Force that he earned his nickname Popski, as the New Zealanders of that unit were unable to pronounce his name. He was asked by General Sir John Hackett to raise his own unit. When he could not think of a name it was Hackett who suggested 'Popski's Private Army'. The unit was not formed until just before El Alamein, so took no part in the battles for Egypt and Libya, but it made contributions in Tunisia and Algeria and operated extensively in Italy and Austria right up to the end of the war.

PORTUGAL

MILITARY SPECIAL FORCES
Special Forces Command
Long-Range Reconnaissance Patrol (LRRP) – Special Forces Detachment. The unit is assigned as the Portuguese component of the Allied Command Europe (ACE) Mobile Force (Land). The 48-man Detachment was raised in 1996 and is tasked with performing missions similar to the US Army's Special Forces or British SAS. Some of these missions include conducting long-range reconnaissance patrols, raids against high value targets, locating enemy command and control centres, targeting and destruction of enemy air defence and radar systems, and POW rescue operations. The unit can be infiltrated by parachute, helicopter, small boat or by foot. The detachment is capable of operating independently behind enemy lines for a period of up to ten days. The unit is composed of a Special Operations platoon, medical section, communications section and transportation section. The Special Operations platoon is subdivided into a six-command section and four five-man patrols. The communications section provides a secure link between operational teams and headquarters. The unit has participated in a number of AMF (L) exercises, including deployments to Norway for cold weather training. Currently the detachment is equipped with weapons of Israeli and German manufacture, including the G-3 rifle and HK MP-5 SMGs, Israeli Galil rifles and Uzi SMGs. Other equipment is obtained from various manufacturers on an as-needed basis.

Marines
Destacamento do Accoes Especiais (DAE) (Fuzileiros Navais-Special Actions Detachment) The DAE combat diver unit is a relatively new force. Raised in 1985, the unit is one of the smallest special operations units with the Portuguese armed forces. It is responsible for conducting Special Operations, beach reconnaissance, CSAR, maritime CT, demolition operations, and other missions in support of Portuguese and NATO armed forces. Unit members are drawn from the ranks of experienced marines. Upon completion of the basic selection phase prospective recruits then begin the first phase of their training. Phase 1 of their training is conducted at the navy's combat diver school. Students receive instruction in: basic combat diving techniques, EOD and underwater demolitions.

Candidates who successfully complete the first phase are assigned to the DAE on a probationary status, and begin their second phase of training.

Phase 2 instruction includes courses on: escape and evasion techniques, advanced driving, mountaineering, offensive operations, and basic English. Once a trainee is permanently assigned to the DAE he will continue to receive various courses of instruction throughout his career. The unit is currently composed of approximately 28 men, led by a commander, and is subdivided into a command cell and four combat teams. The command cell contains the unit commander, his deputy (a lieutenant commander) and a small staff of two. The combat teams are composed of four men: three seamen and a commanding petty officer. The DAE conducts regular training exercises with its NATO counterparts, including the USN SEALs, British SBS, French Commando Hubert as well as the respective naval CT units. The DAE is equipped with Zodiac rubber boats and Skua fibreglass-hulled assault craft. Divers use LAR V closed-circuit breathing equipment when a stealthy underwater approach is required. The DAE also has access to the various ships and aircraft of the Portuguese Navy when long-distance transport is required. The weapons in use include 9mm SIG-Sauer P228 pistols, 5.7mm FN P90 personal defence weapons, 9mm H&K MP5A5 sub-machine guns, 5.56mm Colt CAR-15A2 Model 723 assault carbines, 5.56mm Colt AR-15A2 Model 701 assault rifles, 5.56mm Colt HBAR-15A2 Model 750 automatic rifles, M-4 carbine, 7.62mm INDEP G3A4 battle rifles (licensed from H&K), 12.7mm (.50 BMG) Barrett Model 82A1 sniper rifles, 7.62mm Rheinmetall MG3 machine guns, 40mmSR Colt M203 underbarrel grenade launchers (under AR-15A2 Model 701), 84mm Carl Gustaf M2 recoilless rifles and Barnett crossbows.

CIVILIAN SPECIAL FORCES

Grupo de Operacoes Especiais (GOE) – Special Operations Group The GOE of the Policia de Seguranca Publica (Public Security Police) has its origins in the Corpo de Intervencao (Intervention Corps) which was established in 1978. The CI arose out of the desire of the Portuguese government to establish a force capable of responding to terrorist incidents throughout the country. Within a year, however, the CI was disbanded and its resources reorganised into a well-funded new entity known as the GOE. The considerable financing that was allotted to the unit was used primarily in the construction of new facilities, which included a swimming pool, indoor and outdoor firing ranges, barracks, offices and a close-quarters battle (CQB) house for practising hostage rescue scenarios. Prospective recruits to GOE can apply for a selection that occurs only once every two years. If accepted, they must undergo a two-week initial screening process which weeds out all but the most determined applicants. From here, graduates are sent off to an eight-month advanced training course. This course teaches basic Counter-Terrorist techniques, including hostage rescue in urban environments, rappelling and long-range shooting. Other topics that are covered include assaults on buses, trains and aircraft, building clearing, and merchant vessel assaults. In addition, the last two months of their training focuses on VIP training. There are currently 150 members of GOE, who are organised into operational assault elements of 25 men each. Each of these is supported by a well-developed intelligence and planning section, along with the standard support elements. The unit maintains a strong relationship with the British SAS, which provided the unit's early training cadre, with additional expertise provided by the US Delta Force and Germany's GSG-9. GOE is sometimes deployed to provide VIP protection for visiting dignitaries, as well as its regular duties as the national police SWAT detachment. The unit was deployed in 1983 when the Turkish Embassy in Lisbon was taken over by Armenian terrorists. Unfortunately, the occupiers blew up the structure before an assault could be effected. GOE has a wide array of vehicles to ensure that any potential hot spot is quickly reachable by the GOE operators and this ranges from specially modified Range Rovers to Mercedes Benzes. Some of these vehicles have been specially modified with platforms and hoists that make egressing into aircraft and buildings faster and safer. Weapons in use include the H&K MP-5 9mm sub-machine gun, and the H&K 502 12-gauge shotgun is also utilised. GOE operators have a liberal personal weapons policy, so it is not unusual to see team members carrying pistols that range from Brownings to SIG Sauers to Glocks. They favour the H&K PSG-1 7.62mm and Walther WA2000 sniper rifle but, due to recent close ties with Israeli units, they are receiving the Galil 7.62mm sniper rifle. In a recent CT competition, GOE placed fourth out of at least nine participating teams.

PRAGUE SPRING – SOVIET WINTER

The attempt by Alexander Dubcek and a reformist group to liberalise the Czech communist regime in the early months of 1968 quickly earned the enmity of a still repressive Soviet government who saw it as a grave danger to their continued control of Eastern Europe, and on 21 August the Soviet High Command informed the Czech government of a major series of exercises that would take place along its borders. They were, of course, nothing more than a cover for the planned Soviet occupation of Czechoslovakia. At 23.00 on 20 August the control tower at Prague Airport received a distress signal from a Soviet cargo aircraft which asked for permission to make an emergency landing. Before the aircraft had even come to a halt, SPETSNAZ assault units had quickly disembarked and joined up with additional Special Forces teams dressed in civilian clothes, who had flown in earlier in the day on normal commercial flights posing as tourists, and now armed with weapons supplied by the KGB from secret arms dumps within the country, and with the connivance of the airports head of passport control who was a long time KGB asset. The SPETSNAZ teams quickly took over the control tower and secured the airport. Their transport aircraft had moved to the end of the runway and, with an onboard homing beacon and communications net, now helped to control the wave after wave of Soviet military transports that began to arrive at the airport. The first SPETSNAZ teams now commandeered every available vehicle and drove fast into the centre of Prague to join up with additional teams that had infiltrated the capital in the previous few days. Aided by the KGB and compliant Czech Intelligence teams they seized the radio and television stations, telephone exchanges, the security headquarters and other vital facilities. SPETSNAZ units also arrested the leading members of the Czech government and by the next morning the Soviet Union was in effective, if not uncontested, control with the first of some 500,000 conventional troops from the Soviet Union, East Germany, Poland, Bulgaria and Hungary, backed up by more than 5,000 battle tanks, pouring across the borders unopposed by a cowed and leaderless Czech Army. It had been a brilliant and highly effective large-scale use of Special Forces and perhaps the West must consider itself more than a little fortunate that it was never called upon to defend itself against the Soviet Special Forces capability when it was at its best as a strategic assault force in the 1960s and 1970s.

PRIVATISING SPECIAL FORCES' SKILLS

While there has been a long tradition of former Special Forces soldiers either being recruited by their own governments' Intelligence services, private security companies or the growing trend towards branching out into what is effectively a new form of mercenary organisation (the PMC or Private Military Companies, staffed with experienced military and intelligence personnel, with well maintained but discreet links to government agencies), are able to offer a wide range of services to the armed forces of countries that may otherwise be cold-shouldered for various human rights abuses by the governments of the major nations. There are a huge number of private concerns in the USA, UK, Australia and France in particular, who can provide anything from electronic monitoring equipment, to modern small arms, tanks and even missile systems. Not only that but they will provide maintenance and the personnel to operate the equipment, and indeed professional soldiers to train the local forces or whole units of former Special Forces personnel to fight a war for their new paymasters. Former Special Forces personnel can find a ready market for their skills among this burgeoning world of Private Armies, celebrity bodyguards and the training of Third World security forces. With private military companies (PMC) having proliferated since the end of the Cold War and with some five million ex-soldiers looking for work over the last ten years, the companies had the opportunity to pick the best, and therefore the numbers of Special Forces, marines, paras, Legionaires and intelligence officers employed spiralled. Companies such as the MPRI (Military Professional Resources Inc) established some fifteen years ago and now employing 800 mainly former high-level US military personnel, and drawing from a pool of over 13,000 freelance former members of the Green Berets, Rangers, SEALs, law enforcement agencies and other military personnel from around the world, has seen its business greatly increase since 9–11. However, its track record has included training both sides in a Balkan conflict; the Macedonian Army and the NLA (Albanian National Liberation Army). It had previously trained Kosovan, Croatian and Bosnian units and, while praised for doing a 'significant job' by the Croatians, other nations such as Nigeria and Colombia were less enthusiastic, with Colombian officials complaining that 'the MPRI's contributions were of little practical use'. Watchguard, the Guernsey-based company set up by David Stirling and KMS or Keeni Meeni Services, which was also set up and largely staffed by former SAS, provided weapons and experienced Special Forces personnel mainly to ex-British colonial states in Africa throughout the 1970s and supplied air crew to Lieutenant Colonel Oliver North to supplement ex-CIA Air America crews running guns to the Contra rebels in Nicaragua. Sandline International from its various offices in Guernsey, Washington and London provides what it describes as 'a company specialising in rendering military and security services of an operational, training and support nature, particularly in situations of internal conflict and only for and on behalf of recognised governments, in accord with international doctrines and in conformance with the Geneva Convention'. The deal signed on behalf of Sandline International by Tim Spicer OBE with the PNG was for some $36,000,000(US), though some sources claim $46 million, and other similar and very lucrative deals were also struck involving the provision of 'military assistance' to the authoritarian government of Valentine Strasser in Sierra Leone among others. Much of the work was subcontracted to another company, Executive Outcomes, which is notorious throughout Africa for its involvement in mercenary operations. Executive Outcomes operated for many years with the full sanction of the South African government. Many of its recruits are former members of the 32nd Battalion (Special Forces), South African army which, under the former apartheid regime, were actively involved in 'destabilisation' operations, particularly in Angola. The company was hired by the Angolan government in 1993 to fight the Unita rebels, formerly backed by the apartheid government. In return, Executive Outcomes, or its associated companies, was offered rich mineral concessions. The company was also involved in military operations to shore up the regime in Sierra Leone along with Sandline International, securing for itself important interests in a number of diamond mines. Executive Outcomes was reportedly active in more than 30 countries in Africa, including Kenya, Sudan and Uganda, and has close links with international oil, gold and diamond ventures. DynCorp is considered by many to be merely a CIA-front organisation providing military assistance on behalf of the US government in Colombia, Haiti, Kosovo and Bosnia. Aviation Development Corp flies surveillance planes for the CIA. Its involvement was revealed when, in Peru, it misidentified a civilian light plane as carrying narcotics. It was shot down by the Peruvian Air Force. The Vinnell Corp was established in the United States during the Great Depression and is currently owned by TRW. It has coached militaries, operated facilities and provided logistical support in more than 50 countries, starting in Saudi Arabia in 1975 where it won a controversial $77 million contract to train oilfield guards, while Kroll of New York and Saladin Security of London do mainly intelligence-gathering security work. Control Risks Group offers corporate security, research and intelligence solutions. It specialises in providing former SAS personnel to handle hostage situations and claims to have advised in more than 1,200 kidnappings and blackmail cases in 80 countries. Founded in 1975 as a subsidiary of the Hogg Robinson insurance group, it claims to have had 'more than 5,300 clients, including 86 of the Fortune 100 companies, in more than 130 countries'. Eighty-three per cent of the firms comprising the FTSE 100 use one or more of CRG's services. It has 400 employees in sixteen offices around the world and recently acquired Network Holdings Ltd., the UK's largest private forensic laboratory. Armor Holdings was founded in 1969 as 'American Body Armor and Equipment' and incorporated in 1996. It is a private security company. Its London-based subsidiary, Defense Systems Ltd (DSL) guards industrial and other sensitive sites, such as embassies and the headquarters of international organisations, including the UN's. DSL had originally been set up by former SAS officer Alastair Morrison. Gray Security is another private security company with clients in both Africa and among Latin American immigrants in Florida. Even the legendary Gurkhas now offer their services through Gurkha International. Smaller, *ad hoc* outfits from Ukraine, Russia, Belarus, France, the United Kingdom, Israel, Croatia, South Africa, the United States and other nations scour the earth for emerging conflicts. Such units are often infiltrated by criminals on the run, terrorists in disguise, sadistic psychopaths and intelligence officers. These 'dogs of war' have sometimes and quite justifiably become known for their disloyalty and lack of discipline. Many have committed acts of banditry, rape and an array of atrocities in the host countries. The quality of the training and assistance is often questionable, but as this is a marginal world of the 'hired-gun' the client is often an undesirable individual, the boss of a drugs cartel or a failed state riven by internal conflict and unable to persuade a major nation to commit forces in its defence. The private military companies, staffed with newly retired and highly experienced Special Forces personnel, are therefore often used to provide assistance to states that it would be politically embarrassing for countries such as Britain or the United States to openly support. In most cases these activities never reach the notice of the news media and, when they do, they can usually be safely dismissed or covered up by a plausible denial of any official involvement. The new mercenaries, closely linked to their old Special Forces colleagues, are a potential danger and a destabilising factor in many Third World countries, but while governments continue to want 'dirty work' done for them, usually discreetly and without fuss, then there will be a ready and growing market for their specialist military skills.

PSYOPS

Psychological Operations. Causing morale problems in the enemy forces and generally undermining an enemy's self-belief, significantly affecting his military effectiveness.

QATAR

MILITARY SPECIAL FORCES
The Border Guards Regt (Special Forces)
Oil Wells Guard Regt (Special Forces) Durkan and Umm Bab
Special Forces Airmobile Company at Barzan camp, Doha, this particular unit is reasonably well trained and capable, superbly equipped with state-of-the-art equipment, it now co-operates closely with the US Special Forces, and regularly conducts joint training exercises. In early October 2002, US Special Forces and CIA paramilitaries are believed to have helped Qatar Special Forces foil an attempted coup by dissident Army Officers apparently unhappy at their Government's firm support for US military activities i the Gulf.

RAIDING FORCES – ROYAL MARINES AND SBS

Small-Scale Raiding Force This unit was formed in 1941 at Poole, Dorset, and the home of the modern-day SBS. It was to conduct small raids on behalf of SOE, Britain's wartime sabotage service in charge of aiding resistance organisations in enemy-held territory. The 30 volunteers went out to West Africa in August 1941 and it was from Lagos in Nigeria that their first operation, code-named Postmaster, was launched in January 1942. The plan was to seize a German tanker and an Italian freighter interned in the harbour of the Spanish-controlled island of Fernando Po. While the ships' officers were distracted by a party thrown by an SOE agent, the raiders entered the port aboard two tugs, overpowered the crews and sailed the ships back to British territory. Back in Britain the SSRF's founders, Commando officers Gus March-Phillips and Geoffrey Appleyard, received permission to expand it. There were never more than 60 men, about half of them officers, most coming from the commandos or SOE. There were also French, Danish and Dutch members, and several Poles, Czechs and Germans, who served under British names. The alternate names of 62 Commando and 62 Special Training School reflected the SSRF's joint responsibilities to Combined Operations Headquarters and SOE. Training was done mostly around Anderson Manor near Poole, the unit's new home, but also in the Lake District of the north of England and at sea. Small raids were launched on the French coast, mostly from a fast torpedo boat known as the 'Little Pisser'. The approach to the shore was done on Goatley boats, ten-man collapsible craft and dories, 18–22ft (5.5–6.6m) wooden powerboats, both of which soon became popular with other small boat units. Canoes, now named cockles, were also used. Targets included lighthouses, observation posts and beach defences, with a general objective of taking prisoners and unsettling the Germans. Agents were also landed for SOE. All the members were parachute-trained, but no airborne operations were undertaken. At the end of the year most of the SSRF was transferred to Algeria, where they formed the nucleus of Bill Stirling's new 2nd SAS Regiment.

Special Boat Squadron/Service The original SB Section continued its raids, especially against German airfields on Sicily and Crete. However, it came increasingly under the influence of David Stirling and what was then referred to as L Detachment, SAS Brigade. Following heavy casualties, such as the Rhodes raid, when only two of the ten-man team returned, it was absorbed into the newly-formed 1st SAS Regiment in September 1942. A small party under Tommy Langton had gone on the Tobruk raid that month; this is often but erroneously credited as an SAS operation. In fact most of the troops in the land force were from No.1 Special Service Regiment, the last remnants of the Middle East Commandos. Operation Daffodil was a complete disaster, with almost all the men who drove into Tobruk or landed from the sea being killed or captured. Langton and three others who spent two months wandering the desert were the only ones to escape. Most of the SBS ended up in D Squadron of 1SAS, together with a troop from the Greek Sacred Squadron. Following Lieutenant Colonel Stirling's capture in Tunisia in January 1943, the regiment was split into two elements: the Special Raiding Squadron under Major Paddy Mayne, and the Special Boat Squadron under Major Lord George Jellicoe. The SRS fought in Sicily and Italy and later in the UK was expanded as the new 1SAS. The SBS, meanwhile, began training at Athlit, south of Haifa in Palestine. It had an initial strength of about 230, divided into three operational detachments and a base group. Each detachment, known as L, M and S after their original commanders, Captains Tommy Langton, Fitzroy Maclean and David Sutherland, had an establishment of six fighting patrols (one officer and twelve other ranks each) and a smaller HQ patrol. The SBS retained the SAS beret and wings, but did not change to the maroon Airborne Forces beret as the UK-based SAS were forced to in 1944, staying with beige. The first operation was by S Detachment, a raid by several four-man teams, one led by Anders Lassen, on German airfields in Crete. This took place in support of the Sicily landings in July 1943. L Detachment carried out an unsuccessful series of raids on Sardinia, launched by parachute and submarine. Most of those who landed were killed or captured and the detachment had to be reconstituted. The SBS first operated in the Aegean in September 1943, when men from M and S Detachments had the task of securing Simi. This was one of the Italian-held Dodecanese islands which the British were attempting to capture, with the ultimate aim of opening a new front in the Balkans. While small units moved onto some of the islands, Jellicoe parachuted onto Rhodes to try and convince the Italian commander not to give in to the Germans stationed there. He failed, and soon the British-held islands were under attack, weakly defended Cos being the first to fall. The first landing attempt on Simi in October was fought off by Major Jock Lapraik and his men together with the Italian garrison, with Lassen intimidating those of his new allies who weren't too keen on fighting. Simi was soon facing heavy air attacks and had to be abandoned. The only large British formation was an infantry brigade on Leros, and with the fall of Cos its only airfield had gone. Jellicoe and several patrols were present when the Germans assaulted Leros in November, their job being to attack paratroopers as they landed. However, the fall of the island was inevitable, but unlike most of the garrison almost all of the SBS escaped to Turkey and were sent back to Palestine.

Raiding Forces Middle East was established in October 1943 and the SBS was the major element of this formation. Other units included the Greek Sacred Squadron, the Long-Range Desert Group, now operating in the long-range reconnaissance patrol role, and the Raiding Support Regiment, which provided the heavy firepower needed for larger raids. Jellicoe's men were soon back in the Aegean, coming out of the night to shoot up German garrisons, demolish installations and generally raise havoc. In fact Raiding Forces carried out 381 operations on 70 different islands. The SBS detachments operated in rotation from a secret base, a large schooner anchored on the Turkish coast. Transport to and from targets was sometimes by Royal Navy Motor Launch, but more often by the caiques (local fishing boats) of the Levant Schooner Flotilla, crewed by the Navy and local volunteers. Most raiders carried the Thompson sub-machine guns, captured MP40 (Schmeissers), M1 carbines, Bren light machine guns and .45 Colt automatics being popular, as well as the

Italian mini-grenades known as 'Red Devils'. Landing was by canoe, Goatley boat and seven-man inflatables (Jellicoe Intruders), or sometimes directly from caiques. By now there was a standard course for new recruits, many of them soldiers bored with garrison duty or marines tired of manning warship guns which were never fired. Training in weapons, boating, swimming, high-speed marching and unarmed combat was done at Athlit, followed by a parachute course at Ramat David and ski training in Lebanon. All detachments had Greeks attached on their two-month operational tours, both officers and interpreters/guides. The Aegean raids kept six German divisions in the islands who could have been fighting elsewhere. The biggest raid, and the finale for the SBS in Raiding Forces, was on Simi in July 1944. The whole garrison, 180 strong, was killed or captured by the 200 raiders, who left a troop of the Greek Sacred Regiment in its place. The SB Squadron was now transferred to Italy for raids on the Adriatic coasts of Yugoslavia and Albania, its place being taken by the expanded Greek raiding force. The LRDG and most of the RSR had left for Italy earlier. The Adriatic raids were generally not as successful, facing tougher defences and often-uncooperative local guerrillas. In October 1944 the Germans were in the process of evacuating southern Greece and L Detachment was parachuted onto the airfield at Araxos as the leading part of a task force commanded by Lieutenant Colonel Jellicoe. This was 450-strong, with an LRDG squadron, two infantry companies and a few RM commandos, known as Bucketforce, which had the mission of clearing the Peloponnese. This they soon did, but were unable to cut off the German retreat from Athens. After liberating Athens, Jellicoe formed an expanded task force (Pompforce), with L Det, 4th Parachute Battalion, RAF regiment armoured cars and engineers and artillery. With these 950 men he was soon as far north as the Albanian border, forcing the Germans to retreat further than they had wanted, and had made contact with Sutherland, who was operating in that area. In the meantime Lassen and M Detachment had been island-hopping in the Sporadhes, but had decided to liberate Salonika. They commandeered four fire engines as transport and chased the last Germans out of the city. For the remainder of their time in Greece the SBS were caught up in the fighting between the Royalist and Communist Greek factions. Near the end of the year Jellicoe was sent off to Staff College and Lieutenant Colonel David Sutherland took over command; he was one of the few still remaining who had served under Courtney. The SB Squadron now became the Special Boat Service and the detachments were renamed squadrons. L Squadron rejoined S in Land Forces Adriatic, where the SBS operated from a semi-permanent base at Zara on the Yugoslav coast, which they shared with the patrols of the LRDG. M went to Crete to assist the guerrillas now besieging the Germans in a few enclaves. (Allied sea and air raiding meant that the enemy on Crete and other islands could not even leave.) In early April 1945 the 2nd Commando Brigade was fighting in the area around Lake Commachio in northern Italy. The 60 men of M Squadron were initially patrolling the lake while the main commando assault was launched from the south-east corner of the lake on the night of 8–9th April, with SBS men guiding in the assault boats through the few deep channels in the shallow water where they came under fire and sustained severe casualties. The thirteen survivors of the patrol managed to escape back to their boats. Major Anders Lassen, age 24 and already the holder of the Military Cross and two Bars, was posthumously awarded the Victoria Cross.

RAINBOW WARRIOR – FRENCH SPECIAL FORCES

On 7 July 1985 the *Rainbow Warrior*, flagship of the Greenpeace Organisation, an international body concerned with conservation and environmental issues, arrived in Auckland and tied up at Marsden Wharf. On the night of 10 July 1985 at shortly before midnight two high explosive devices attached to the hull of the *Rainbow Warrior* detonated within the space of a few minutes. The force of the explosions was such that a hole eight feet in size was opened below the waterline near the engine room. The vessel sank within minutes. Fernando Pereira, a crew member and the official photographer, was drowned while attempting to retrieve photographic equipment from his cabin. The later discovery of an abandoned rubber Zodiac dinghy and an outboard motor, and the sighting of a blue and white camper van, led to the interview of a French-speaking couple two days later by the New Zealand Police and their subsequent arrest on 15 July. Although initially identified as Alain Jacques Turenge and his wife Sophie Frederique Clare Turenge, inquiries revealed their true identities to be Major Alain Mafart, aged 35, and Captain Dominique Prieur, aged 36. Serving as commissioned officers in the French Special Forces, they had been detailed to assist members of the DGSE (SDECE) Intelligence Service to ensure that the much publicised voyage of the *Rainbow Warrior* to French territorial waters to disrupt the French nuclear test programme simply didn't happen. The vessel had to be so extensively damaged that repairs could not be completed in time for the voyage to begin. Though the French operation succeeded in part, it turned out to be a publicity disaster, as the Intelligence Service had failed to extract Mafart and Prieur directly after the attack, although the French intelligence officers had apparently flown out the day before the operation. When their arrest was linked with information obtained by New Zealand detectives in New Caledonia, Norfolk Island, Australia, Switzerland, France and the UK it proved without any doubt the major role played by the French Intelligence Service and Special Forces in the bombing and the subsequent death of Fernando Pereira. The positioning and successful detonation of the explosives indicated those responsible were trained and expert in underwater warfare, and it is believed that both French officers were serving members of the Commando Hubert Underwater Warfare unit.

RANGERS – HISTORY'S SPECIAL FORCES

The history of the modern Ranger did not begin with Robert Rogers and his force in 1756 alone, for the British militia units specifically designated as Rangers and using Ranger tactics were employed on the North American frontiers as early as 1670. The Rangers of Captain Benjamin Church brought the Indian Conflict known as 'King Phillip's War' to a successful conclusion in 1675. Rangers were organised in 1756 by Major Robert Rogers, a native of New Hampshire, who recruited nine companies of British colonists to fight for the King during the French and Indian War. Ranger techniques and methods of operation were an inherent characteristic of the colonial frontiersmen, though Major Rogers developed them and incorporated the best into the fighting doctrine of a permanently organised fighting force. Britain used other similar units: Butler's Rangers, the Corsican Rangers and indeed the Connaught Rangers in India.

RAPPELLING

Defined as the act of descending from a fixed height by letting oneself down on a rope.

Rappelling is used in mountaineering to negotiate dangerous terrain and is used frequently by the Special Forces during anti-terrorist and hostage rescue operations.

RECCES – SOUTH AFRICA

The first Reconnaissance Regiment was founded in Durban on 1 October 1972 as a small specialised SAS or Selous Scouts type unit capable of operating deep inside enemy territory to obtain valuable intelligence on enemy movements, positions and numbers. Colonel Jan Breytenbach commanded this new unit, designated 1 Recognizance Commando or 1 Recce. Soldiers serving in this unit went on to form the core of additional Recce groups. The Recce units consist of only a very few men termed 'operators'. These men were highly trained, avoided the spotlight of publicity and were rarely filmed or photographed. The units of the Reconnaissance Regiments were 1st Recce based at Durban in Natal Province; 2nd Recce (Citizen Force) based at Voortrekkerhoogte in the Transvaal; 4th Recce based at Langebaan in Cape Province; and 5th Recce based at Phalaborwa in the

Transvaal. Of interest is the fact that 3rd and 6th Recce were formed in 1980, at the end of the Rhodesian War, from former Rhodesian SAS and Selous Scouts. These were disbanded in 1981 and the remaining units absorbed the men. The units became the 451, 452 and 453 Parachute Battalions. The Recces were trained to act in tiny units or individually, far in the field with little support. The operators' mission was to gather strategic and tactical intelligence about the enemy behind his lines. Stealth and the ability to blend into the surrounding bush are essential elements of the operators' repertoire. They occasionally participate in special aggressive operations in the enemy's rear territory, destroying targets, harassing troops and causing small-scale havoc. Recce units usually operated in five- or six-man teams, though it is known that two-man reconnaissance teams operated inside Angola. The selection process showed distinct signs of having been greatly influenced by SAS procedures, and indeed the SADF did have close contact with the Rhodesian SAS (formerly 'C' Squadron of the 22nd Regiment, SAS). The Recce operators used highly specialised and personalised gear and uniforms, as well as both Western and Eastern bloc weapons and ordnance. The Recces utilised South-African-made copies of camo uniforms used by other countries and their allies. They are worn to blend into foreign troops when on covert operations. Recce missions are covert and highly secretive by nature, and must remain so in order to safeguard the lives of the men involved. Without a doubt the Recces produced superbly trained and motivated soldiers, easily on a par with the SAS or the Green Berets, both in their training and military skills. However, they were also used for a wide range of illegal operations that breached both the national sovereignty of foreign countries and the human rights of their peoples. The Recces killed without hesitation those who were considered a threat to a widely detested apartheid regime which was so flawed that it eventually self-destructed.

REMINGTON – COMBAT SHOTGUNS

Although such weapons as the SAS favourite, the Remington 870 12-gauge pump-action, are not new, they remain highly effective close-action weapons in house clearing and even blowing open non-armoured doors. Deadly at 44yds (40m), these combat shotguns are useful in hostage rescue operations or anti-hijacking assaults as their 'shot' tends to be localised and, unlike high-velocity rifle bullets, does not travel long distances.

RIVERINE OPERATIONS – VIETNAM WAR

By 1966 US troops had been committed in large numbers to three of the four corps areas of Vietnam. Only in IV Corps, the Mekong Delta region, were there no large numbers of US troops. This was due to three major factors.

First, though the delta was a major population and food centre, the military situation was not as critical as in the other corps areas. Second, due to the density of the population, there were no available tracts of land where a large military installation could be constructed without dislocating large numbers of people. And finally, the numerous rivers, streams and canals which dissected the delta severely restricted ground movement; US planners were reluctant to commit conventional units to such an environment until they found a way to overcome the mobility problem. However, in 1966, there was a strong desire on the part of the US Army to insert troops in the Mekong Delta to counter growing communist strength. In March of 1966 a joint planning committee of army and navy personnel drew up tentative plans for the establishment of a Mekong Delta Mobile Afloat Force (MDMAF). This proposal was further detailed during the summer, and by September plans had reached the implementation stage, On 1 September, the first administrative unit of the new organisation was commissioned at the Navy Amphibious Base in Coronado, California. Shortly after this, the unit received the designation Task Force 117 (TF-117), and was codenamed the Mobile Riverine Force (MRF). As originally envisioned, the MRF would support an infantry brigade and an artillery battalion using a variety of modified landing craft, support ships and specially designed assault boats. In essence this strike unit would be a self-contained amphibious assault force, complete with all support elements except aircraft. The ideal choice for the ground component would have been the marines, who were specialists in amphibious warfare, but unfortunately the Leathernecks were already heavily committed in I Corps. Instead, a brigade from the 9th Infantry Division was chosen as the infantry component of the Mobile Riverine Force. The Naval component of TF-117 was made up of a wide variety of ships and boats. The first unit, River Assault Squadron 9 (RAS 9), consisted of four APBs, two LSTs, 26 ATCs, five Monitors, two CCBs, one Refueller and sixteen ASPBs. An example of the operations carried out by the Riverine forces: Coronado IV 19 August to 9 September 1967, which took place south and south-west of Saigon in Long An, Co Cong, and Kien Hoa Provinces. Elements of the 506th VC Battalion were encountered and 34 of the guerrillas were killed. Numerous supply and arms caches were also discovered but contact was light. Close on the heels of this came CORONADO V, 12 September to 8 October in Dinh Tuong and Kien Hoa Provinces, southwest of the capital. Working with US and ARVN troops from the 7th Division, the MRF encountered the 263rd VC battalion and in a series of running battles the allied forces killed over 500 of the guerrillas. However, the 263rd fought hard and eighteen Riverine boats were hit by rockets, grenades and recoilless rifle fire. Though none were sunk, this was the heaviest fire that the MRF had yet come under. This underlined the ability of the boats to take a great deal of punishment, and also the need for additional armament to counter the growing number of heavy-calibre weapons being employed by the communists. During Coronado V the first ASPBs arrived and received their baptism of fire. Towards the end of the operation the first attempt to use flame-throwers took place in Kien Hoa Province near Dong Tam with satisfactory results. An M-132 flame-thrower armoured personnel carrier (APC) was placed in an ATC and tested under high wind conditions. No problems were encountered and additional M-132s were requested until a suitably modified monitor could be substituted for the ATC/APC arrangement. To help protect Vietnamese civilians during the 1967 National Elections, Coronado VII, 20–24 October was conducted. During the elections the MRF dispersed itself throughout the Can Guioc District, but very little contact resulted. Over 80 per cent of the registered voters turned out due to the tight security the riverine craft and personnel provided. The year ended on a more resounding note combat-wise, with Coronado IX 1 November to 21 January. This long operation was started in part to counter VC attacks against patrolling PBRs in the Giao Pue District. During 1968 much thought was given to turning over more of the Riverine war effort to the Vietnamese. The first step in this process came about in January of 1969 when the boats of RAD 91 were withdrawn from combat to ready them for turnover to the Vietnamese. This was done on 1 February 1969, and shortly thereafter RAD91 was officially dissolved. From these assets, along with eight ASPBs, the Vietnamese Navy formed River Assault and Interdiction Divisions (RAIDs) 70 and 71. This set the pattern for remainder of 1969 as the Riverine force prepared to hand over more of its assets to Vietnamese control. Operations continued to be carried out by the Riverine force, but as the year progressed more and more effort was concentrated on training Vietnamese personnel to handle and maintain the various boats.

ROGERS' RANGERS

Robert Rogers was a British colonial farmer recruited from New Hampshire in 1755 for service in the French and Indian War of 1754–63. He created a unit called Rogers' Rangers in 1756 (the first Rangers), and by 1758 he had been placed in charge of all colonial Ranger companies. The Rangers wore distinctive green outfits and developed tactics called 'Rogers' Ranging Rules', which the British Army considered unconventional. These tactics are still in use by Rangers today, including the Green Berets. Rogers' Rangers were most famous for their engagement with the Abenaki St Francis Indians, who lived midway between Montreal and Quebec. These Abenaki were credited with the deaths of over 600 colonists during the duration of the war. After the Indians attacked a retreating British unit under a flag of truce, Rogers led a hand-picked force of 200 Rangers to destroy the Indians' village.

Rogers' Rangers took part in General James Wolfe's expedition against Quebec and in the Montreal campaign of 1760. The Rangers were later sent by General Jeffrey Amherst to take possession of the north-western posts, including Detroit. In 1763 the Rangers were in the west again, during Pontiac's War 1763–64, and they participated in the Battle of Bloody Bridge. After the war, Rogers travelled to England to write of his accounts. In 1766 he asked King George III to fund an expedition from the Mississippi River to the Pacific. The King refused, but granted him command of the north-west post called Michilimackinac. From there, Rogers conducted his own expedition anyway. His ambition caused him to be sent to England on charges of treason, but he was acquitted. The British are often accused of treating the Rangers poorly during the French and Indian War, and in 1775 former members of Rogers' Rangers fired upon the government forces at Concord and Lexington. Rogers returned to Colonial America to join the Revolution when it started, as he believed, as did many other loyal British-Americans, that they upheld the true traditions and virtues of a Britain now sold out to a 'foreign' (House of Hanover) monarchy. George Washington refused his offer of help, because he feared that Rogers might be a loyalist spy. Outraged by this, Rogers openly joined the government forces and organised and commanded the Queen's Rangers, which saw service in areas around New York City and later created the King's Rangers. Special operations are therefore nothing new to the American soldier. The US Army was heavily reliant upon foreign 'mercenary' soldiers and those units involved in the so-called Indian Wars against the Native American peoples often used what would now be called special operations or ranger tactics. Though the end result for the Native population often approached the levels of 'ethnic cleansing' it gave the US Army a taste of unconventional warfare conducted by lightly armed and highly mobile self-sufficient units. It is a lesson that the present US Army is having to quickly relearn. Though the era that Rogers lived in was simpler, the skills necessary to become an elite soldier were the same. Rogers' Rangers fought in terrain that normal soldiers avoided. They crept up on an enemy with stealth and attacked hard with surprise on their side. 'Move fast and hit hard,' Rogers told his men, and they obeyed, thereby setting the standard for generations to follow. The tradition continued during the American Revolution with Francis Marion, the Swamp Fox, who led daring guerrilla raids on British forces in South Carolina and Georgia. His troops harassed the enemy with a success out of all proportion to their small numbers, because Marion used the element of surprise to its greatest effect.

ROMANIA

MILITARY SPECIAL FORCES

One Special Forces Battalion attached to each of the two Airborne Brigades. These units are being re-equipped with modern Western weapons and equipment, as the strained military budget allows, and have also received training from Western Special Forces instructors.

CIVILIAN SPECIAL FORCES
Ministry of the Interior
Gendarmerie Rapid Reaction Company   for anti-terrorist and HRU response.

RON

Acronym: Remain Over Night, a night-time position. A secure temporary position used during a patrol in hostile territory.

ROYAL RESCUE – SAS

The SAS quietly rescued twelve surviving members of the Ethiopian Royal Family just twelve hours before anti-government rebels seized control of Addis Ababa in May 1991. Four were children under the age of five; the rest were close adult relatives of the late Emperor Haile Selassie who had died after being held in appalling prison conditions by the Ethiopian government for fourteen years. A few days after the Marxist dictator Mengistu fled to Zimbabwe, an SAS team successfully transferred the Royal VIPs to the sanctuary of the British Embassy.

RT

Recon Team. A patrol to discover an enemy's position or strength. To gain intelligence on the terrain and general local conditions before an attack.

RTO

Radio-Telephone Operator, the soldier carrying and operating the radio.

RTU

Returned To Unit. Dreaded by all recruits and members of a Special Forces unit. Though it means ultimate failure, it is not necessarily seen as a disgrace. A soldier may be RTU'd for a wide variety of reasons from disciplinary to health or injury.

RUPERT

SAS term for an officer, usually light-hearted, it can have a mildly derogatory meaning; i.e. 'A Rupert'.

RUSSIA

MILITARY SPECIAL FORCES

SPETSNAZ Chasti Spetsial'nogo Nazncheniya Following the creation of a
Russian Ministry of Defence in April 1992 the SPETSNAZ came under the
full control of the GRU, with the later exception of an 8th SPETSNAZ
Brigade raised in 1996 by the MVD (Interior Ministry) especially for
service in Chechnya. The original seven brigades continue to be closely
involved in an intelligence support role as well as Special Operations and
Counter-Insurgency. During the Soviet period operational control of the
SPETSNAZ was firmly in the hands of the KGB, who used these tough and
highly motivated Special Forces in the invasions of Czechoslovakia in 1968
and Afghanistan in 1979. They were assigned by the KGB to storm the
Russian Parliament building early on 21st August 1991 with the intention
of arresting Boris Yeltsin. The GRU Special-Operations groups of the SPET-
SNAZ are trained to operate in three seven-man teams for intelligence-
gathering and covert action missions in enemy rear areas. They are also
assigned missions in ethnic conflict areas, and will play a prominent role
in the new Russian mobile force now being created which will made up of
airmobile, naval infantry, para-commando and transport aviation. Although
SPETSNAZ units may be used in other security roles during peacetime,
their primary combat task is to carry out strategic missions during the final
days prior to war breaking out and in war itself. These wartime tasks
would include: deep reconnaissance of strategic targets; the destruction of
strategically important command-control-and-communications (C3) facilities; the destruction of strategic weapons' delivery systems; demolition of
important bridges and transportation routes and the 'snatching' or assassination of important foreign military and political leaders. Many of these
missions would be carried out before the enemy could react, and some
even before war had actually broken out. The role of Special Forces was
often ill-defined within the old Soviet Army; deep suspicion was levelled at
any unit that developed an ethos or traditions that didn't fit within the
'norms' of the political officer and the Communist Party. In consequence
the SPETSNAZ formations created in the Second World War were simply
politically trustworthy units that could be called upon for special duties
and operated largely as an elite commando assault force. It was not to be
until the 1980s that the first Western-style Special Forces started to appear
with small, highly trained units dedicated to anti-terrorist and hostage
rescue operations. This was largely due to the fact that Soviet Russia had
long felt that there was no serious threat from external extremist movements, having been for decades a major supporter of insurgency and revolution aimed at overthrowing pro-Western governments, and indeed
having armed and trained numerous international terrorist groups. The

SPETSNAZ are now organised into seven brigades which are quite small, perhaps no more than 1,500 strong, with three small battalions, headquarters, communications, intelligence and support companies and are attached to the regional military districts. The Razvedchiki (Para-Commandos) Battalions are attached at divisional level, each made up of a company of long-range reconnaissance and patrol (LRRP) and a company for airborne operations. Rejdoviki (Guard) company-sized units are found at brigade level, while Vysotniki (Elite Special Forces) eleven-man units and trained to a far higher standard, are attached at battalion level in the 103rd, 104th and 105th Airborne Divisions. Training has been increased in both range and techniques since the collapse of the communist regime in 1991, and today includes weapons handling, familiarity with domestic and foreign arms, marksmanship, physical fitness with an emphasis on endurance, tracking, patrolling, camouflage and surveillance techniques. In addition, survival and warfare in desert, mountain and Arctic conditions, unarmed combat, sabotage and explosives, prisoner interrogation and prisoner-of-war rescue, language training, parachuting techniques including HAHO (High Altitude High Opening) and HALO (High Altitude Low Opening), heliborne-insertion, combat swimming and counter-insurgency operations all form important parts of SPETSNAZ training. Weapons used include the 9mm Izhmekh PMM-12 pistol which began replacing the 9mm Izhmekh PM Makarov as standard army pistol in 1994. For use against foes in body-armour, the 9mm Tzniitochmash SR-1 Gyurza pistol was adopted. The 9mm Izhmekh PB sound-suppressed pistol is used for assassination and sentry removal, as is the 7.62mm Tzniitochmash PSS Vul silent pistol. 5.45mm PRI automatic pistols and such specialist weapons as the NR2, a combined combat knife with a blade that incorporates a short 7.62mm barrel fired by clipping the scabbard and knife together to give some stability. The 5.45mm Izhmash AK-105 assault carbine was adopted to replace the 5.45mm Tulamash AKS-74U, but it is unclear if it was acquired in any numbers. The 5.45mm Tulamash AKS-74UB assault carbine is a sound-suppressed version of the AKS-74U. All these are in the process of replacement by the 7.62mm KBP OTs-14 Groza assault carbine. The standard 5.45mm Izhmash AKS-74 airborne assault rifle with folding stock is still in the inventory. The 9mm Tzniitochmash ASS Val suppressed assault rifle was adopted in 1992, as was the 9mm Tzniitochmash VSS Vintorez suppressed sniper rifle. The 7.62mmR Izhmash SVDS sniper rifle is a SVD-variant with short barrel and folding stock. The 5.45mm Tulamash RPKS-74 light machine gun with folding stock is used for suppressive fire. The 40mm KBP BP-30 underbarrel grenade launcher will mount under the AKS-74U, AKS-74 and AK-105. The OTs-14 mounts a modified version of it. Portable anti-tank weapons include the 40mm Kovrov RPG-7D launcher.

NAVY

NAVAL SPETSNAZ continue to serve in the Northern, Baltic, Black Sea and Pacific fleets. Most of these are subordinate to the Fleet commanders, but some are under the direct control of the Naval Commander-in-Chief in Moscow. Again, their manning levels are not known and it may be that, like other areas in the Russian armed forces, they are seriously under strength. Russian naval special-designation forces, or SPETSNAZ, have been less visible in the wake of the USSR's dissolution. The Russian navy's commander in chief, Admiral Kuroyedov, has reaffirmed that naval Special-Operations units, which have a long, active history in the Soviet armed forces, remain assigned to the main Russian fleets. Although the admiral provided few specifics on the size and capabilities of the units, he did indicate that they were elite, that they were equipped with special weapons (including small submarines), and that they were comparable to US Navy SEALs or the Israeli Navy's 13th Flotilla. Stating that these units have no special name beyond their 'combat swimmer' or 'Naval SPET-SNAZ' designations, the admiral indicated that most of the units are directly subordinate to their respective fleet commander. Of particular note, Kuroyedov said that he retains Naval SPETSNAZ sub-units under his direct control as well, 'for resolving fleet tasks and rendering assistance'. Naval SPETSNAZ must, in addition to normal special warfare training, learn combat swimmer techniques, the use of underwater weapons, canoeing, arrival and exit over beaches, exit and entry to submerged submarines. Naval SPETSNAZ also use the 4.5×39mm Tzniitochmash SPP-1M underwater dart pistol and 5.66×39mm Tzniitochmash APS underwater dart assault rifle.

Delfin (Dolphin) First created in 1957, it was not until 1969 that a proper structure was finally developed within the structure of the main fleets: Baltic, Black Sea, Northern and Pacific for this small highly specialised team. In 1970 the main intelligence service of the General staff (GRU) created the reconnaissance–sabotage group 'Delfin' (Dolphin) in the style of the SBS-SEALs. Recruits are mainly from the Marine Corps and undergo some 26 weeks of extensive training in most Special Warfare skills from parachuting to SCUBA, with sabotage, demolitions, EOD, combat swimming and marksmanship high priorities. They use a wide variety of weapons and equipment, including standard SPETSNAZ arms, specialised underwater weapons such as the SPP1I and the APS55 pistol, towed nuclear demolition devices of 27kg and 70kg, 'Ida' closed cycle respiratory devices, 'Piranha' supersmall covert intelligence submarines with six combat swimmers and crew, 'Siren' two-man torpedoes and the 'Triton' and 'Akula' electrical towers for SCUBA divers.

CIVILIAN SPECIAL FORCES

Al'fa or 'Special group A' this dedicated Counter-Terrorist and Hostage Rescue force was set up originally in 1974 by the then KGB's seventh directorate and was inspired by the British SAS and the US Delta Force. It is this force that attacked the Dar-ul-Aman Palace in Kabul and murdered the Afghan President Hafizullah Amin and his family on 27 December 1979 right at the start of the Soviet invasion. Currently the Al'fa group is controlled by the FSB or Federal Security Service which replaced the KGB in 1992. It has its headquarters and one operational group in Moscow and three groups in St Petersburg, Murmansk and Vladivostok. It is without doubt the Russian unit nearest in technical ability and organisation to the specialist Counter-Terrorist groups currently operated by the major Western nations. KGB Chairman Yuri Andropov authorised the formation of group Al'fa on 28 July 1974 via a unique, hand-written letter. Officially designated Group A, the media came to refer to the unit as 'Alfa' after 1991. This unit has taken part in virtually all hostage rescue operations in Russia since its formation. The group is made up of FSB personnel, with priority given to those who excelled at certain types of sports. Those selected are trained in defensive driving techniques (from automobiles to armoured cars) and in the use of all types of firearms, sniping and combat shooting. Alfa also includes a subdivision for underwater demolition and combat swimming; indeed some members of this unit have trained with the Baltic Fleet and in Cuba. Alfa includes among its support staff, experts in negotiating, an analytical centre and psychologists.

Ministerstvo Vnutrennikh Del (MVD – Ministry of Internal Affairs)

OMON – Otriad Militsiya Osobogo Nasnacheniya – Militia Special Operations Detachment This organisation concentrates on internal security and controlling civil disorder, but has limited Special Forces capability. It is mainly for use against small-scale insurgency and organised crime.

Since the 1970s the weapons used by the internal security troops have been the 5.45mm Izhmekh PSM. The new standard sidearm appears to be the 9mm Tzniitochmash SR-1 Gyurza pistol. In recent years, a number of revolvers have been adopted, among them the big 12.3mmR Tzniitochmash UDAR revolver, which can fire ball, plastic baton and tear-gas rounds. Several compact machine pistols are in the inventory, including the 5.45mm KBP OTs-23 Drotik, 9mm KBP OTs-27 Berdysh, 9mm KBP OTs-33 Pernad and 9mm Zlatoust PP-91 KEDR machine pistol. The primary weapon of shock troops is the 5.45mm Tulamash AKS-74U assault carbine, which is in the process of being replaced by the 9mm KBP OTs-14 Groza assault carbine. The 9mm Tzniitochmash ASS Val suppressed assault rifle and 9mm Tzniitochmash VSS Vintorez suppressed sniper rifle are both in use. Other sniper rifles include the 7.62×54mmR

Izhmash SVD and 7.62mmR KBP SVU. The 23mmR KS-23 pump-action shotgun is also in use. Portable anti-tank weapons include the 40mm Kovrov RPG-7V rocket launcher.

RV

Rendezvous.

RWANDA

MILITARY SPECIAL FORCES

Three Special Forces Anti-Terrorist Companies. The chronic internal insurgency situation resulting from a civil war in which perhaps as many as one million civilians were slaughtered has created an urgent need for a genuine Special Forces capability. However, the economic situation prevents re-equipment and the creation of improved training facilities. The three units that exist are tainted by the extreme brutality of their actions in the fighting between the Tutsi and Hutu populations and their operational capability is strictly limited.

SABOTAGE

Both the British SOE and US OSS carried out widescale sabotage operations and developed a wide range of equipment and advanced training techniques during the Second World War. Much of this knowledge was passed on to Allied resistance forces, and to many others who later developed those selfsame techniques for the use of international terrorist groups. Explosive Bread Flour containing RDX which could in fact be made into cakes and cookies and was known as 'Aunt Jemima', a coal kit that could be mixed with the genuine fuel and would explode when placed on the fire, explosive filled baked bean or 'Coke' cans, 'Lacrima Tojo' a liquid explosive disguised as lubricating oil, exploding light bulbs, fountain pens, 'Odometer', a special fuse switch designed to ignite an explosive charge after a train had travelled a preset distance, and a hundred other sabotage or booby traps designed to kill, maim or terrorise the unwary were indeed the stock-in-trade of the saboteur from SOE following Churchill's call to 'Set Europe Ablaze'. Clam-mines, limpet-mines, thermite bombs, pencil delay fuses, barometric fuses that only detonated a bomb placed in an aircraft when it flew above a certain height all owe their origin to an earlier 'Q' and to 'Winston Churchill's Toyshop', the nickname given to one of the laboratories developing weapons for the clandestine war against the Axis countries. The Special Forces and Covert Action teams in 2002 have at their disposal some 60 years of experience and expertise. The advanced designs today can range from coin sized 'Plastique' (PE – Plastic Explosives) high explosive booby-trap devices, to a suitcase-sized SADM or Special Atomic Demolition

Munitions that could destroy important military targets or, of course, the centre of a big city, killing 50,000–100,000 civilians.

SADM

Special Atomic Demolition Munitions. Relatively small, man-portable but powerful nuclear bombs to be used by Special Forces in the opening stages of a major Cold War conflict to destroy high-value targets deep inside the Soviet Union and Eastern Europe. The US B54 Special Atomic Demolition Munitions had a mechanical timer with delays available from five minutes to 24 hours. It was available to US Army ADM platoons, Special Forces and US Navy SEALs from August 1964 to the mid-1980s. In addition to heavy security in storage areas, a mechanical Permissive Action Link was used to prevent unauthorised detonation. The SADM was a gun-type weapon with two sub-critical masses of U-238, one of the sub-critical components being a precisely machined 'doughnut' of uranium. Detonation occurred when the other sub-critical mass was fired into the doughnut.

The design required miniaturisation and machining to extremely fine tolerances, as well as a firing sequence timed in milliseconds, something the Soviets were incapable of on their own at the time of the Vietnam War, but apparently achieved later. Detonation could occur by timer or by radio transmission. The yield was between half a kiloton and one kiloton. The device could be carried by a man, since it weighed only about 70lb (33kg). The thinking behind the SADM was that there would inevitably be targets that the US Air Force could not reach, and which would also be out of the range of the other army weapons. Deployment was decided at the theatre level, though in certain instances the decision could be made at corps level. Targets might be command-and-control centres, dams, tunnels, passes or critical road junctions. Planning considerations had to include the fact that, since this weapon would have to be placed and detonated at ground level, soil contamination and fallout, with ensuing casualties, would inevitably result from its use. Special Forces troops, who would, in the event of full-scale conflict, be infiltrated deep behind enemy lines were recognised as a viable means for the infiltration and potential use of this device. Certain A-teams were trained in its use, since the SADM mission was regarded as something that could be added on to the normal duties of the team members. During the Vietnam War various scenarios were explored where it might be possible to use the device, particularly in the event of Chinese intervention which, given the experience in Korea, was always to be feared. The Soviet/Russian equivalent weapon system was available for use by both the Army Special Forces (GRU SPETSNAZ) and the Naval Special Operations forces (GRU Naval SPETSNAZ) known as the Delfin (Dolphin) group. There were at least two types, one weighing 59.4lb (27kg) and the other 154lb (70kg). The Chinese People's Liberation Army has shown an increasing interest in Special

Forces to deliver nuclear weapons and are believed to have a small number of SADMs now available.

SANGAR

A protective wall. Usually curved or even circular, built of sandbags or stone. Often used to refer to a fortified observation post built in a short time, usually at night and in complete silence.

SAR

Search and Rescue. Helicopters or specially modified search aircraft used to find and rescue downed aircrew or similar, but not under combat conditions (see CSAR).

SARBE

Search and Rescue Beacon, small enough to be carried by Special Forces on clandestine operations, and allowing Combat Search and Rescue (CSAR) to find and rescue a patrol in need of early exfiltration (see separate entry). It has some drawbacks in that it is obviously aimed at ground-to-air contact and its signal is terrain dependent. In some circumstances, therefore, the search aircraft may need to be virtually dead overhead to receive the signal, which would otherwise be blocked by surrounding high ground.

SAS

Special Air Service. British Special Forces 22nd (Regulars), 21st, and 23rd (TA -Reserve) Regiments.

The British Army formed what was to eventually become the role model for much of the world's Special Forces. Known originally as 'L Detachment', the new unit grew to 390 men in 1942 and was redesignated 1st Special Air Service Regiment (1 SAS). After various reorganisations and a period of further growth, an SAS brigade was formed in Scotland in January 1944, consisting of two British regiments (1 and 2 SAS), two French regiments (3 and 4 SAS), a Belgian squadron (later 5 SAS) and a signal squadron. Although the idea was temporarily abandoned for regular service in 1946, the changing nature of conflict was to quickly prove the value of such highly specialised forces. During the Malayan Emergency (1948–60) the 'Malayan Scouts (Special Air Service)' quickly built up to regimental size. Based on the operational skills developed by the SAS units, Force-136 and the Chindits in the Second World War, the 22nd proved itself supreme in operations against the communist terrorists. In 1952, the Malayan Scouts were formed and redesignated the 22nd Special Air Service Regiment (22 SAS), thus marking the official return of the SAS to the regular army's order of battle, though eventually with only two squadrons. A and D Squadrons were to be involved in suppressing an insurgency against the Sultan of Oman in 1958–59 and a successful campaign culminated in the outstanding assault on a heavily defended rebel mountain during the Battle for Jebel Akhdar in 1958. The continued need of Special Forces units in British territories around the world soon became apparent and the Far East soon beckoned again with the 'Confrontation Campaign' in Borneo, and a squadron of SAS arrived there in January 1963. Their success led to more demands for the SAS and the third squadron was re-formed in mid-1963. All three squadrons were to be involved in campaigns in Borneo and Aden during 1964–66 in a period known in the regiment as the 'happy time'. By 1967, these two wars were over and the SAS had a short period of consolidation and retraining. In 1969 the situation in Northern Ireland exploded and the SAS began a long and difficult relationship with the province. Renewed problems in Oman led to a return there and in 1972 they became involved in the Battle for Mirbat when a small 8-man BATT or British Army Training Team of SAS Troopers held off a day-long assault by 250 Communist insurgents or 'Adoo' until the arrival of SAS and Omani Army reinforcements. The SAS remained in Oman for many more years and in August 1983 it was disclosed that the SAS was training a similar unit for the Sultan of Oman as his own 'Special Force'.

The anti-guerrilla campaigns conducted between 1950 and 1975 were succeeded by a new role in which the SAS quickly built up an unrivalled expertise such as counter-terrorist actions. Influenced by operations in Northern Ireland against the Provisional Irish Republican Army (PIRA) and Irish National Liberation Army (INLA) the SAS has developed techniques which are now copied throughout the Western world. This has led to the SAS not only being consulted by overseas governments and Special Forces, but also being directly involved on some 'foreign' operations. Thus, in October 1977, two SAS men were with the West German GSG-9 unit at the attack to recapture a hijacked German airliner at Mogadishu, and SAS members were also involved in the earlier Dutch operation against the Moluccan terrorists who had taken over a trainload of hostages. High-visibility operations such as the successful storming, in May 1980, of the Iranian embassy in London, to free 90 hostages held by a group of anti-government rebels and conducted in the full glare of the world's television cameras have ensured the SAS lasting and largely unwanted fame. In 1982 the SAS were faced with a more traditional warfare scenario when the Falklands Islands were invaded by Argentinian forces. The SAS were immediately involved spearheading the return to South Georgia Island, although the first reconnaissance landing in helicopters had to be aborted in truly appalling weather on a glacier, with nearly disastrous consequences to the team involved. The second landing was by inflatable boats and most men got ashore. However, one boat broke down and the soldiers refused to compromise the operation by calling for help on the radio and were blown rapidly eastwards, only to be rescued much later by a RN helicopter. Meanwhile, at Grytviken, the squadron headquarters and one troop of D Squadron took advantage of the crippling of the Argentine submarine *Santa Fe* to quickly overwhelm the garrison and recapture South Georgia. The first soldiers of D Squadron were ashore on East Falklands by 1 May and remained undetected, in close proximity to the enemy and in foul weather, for some 30 days. They provided vital intelligence on troop movements and deployments, and also targeted enemy aircraft and naval gunfire support. On 14 May the SAS raided Pebble Island and blew up eleven Argentine combat aircraft. Their final role in the Falklands was to carry out a noisy and valuable diversionary attack on the eastern end of Wireless Ridge on the day before the Argentine surrender.

The SAS were to be involved in many further clandestine operations, often in support of foreign governments, during the next ten years. However, some operations, that were ultimately to prove unsuccessful during the Gulf War of 1991, failed mainly due to a woeful lack of sufficient and, at times, even basic equipment available to the operational squadrons deployed to Saudi Arabia. Considerable efforts have been made to ensure that the SAS is bettered funded and equipped for large-scale operations in future. The 22nd SAS has carried out innumerable anti-terrorist operations since, as well as in the Balkan conflict from 1994–2000. It is reported that SAS teams operated behind Serb lines in Bosnia, providing intelligence reports and calling down air strikes on Serb armour, artillery and anti-aircraft positions.

There is some concern that the effectiveness of the 22nd SAS has been somewhat reduced by the high level of public interest in this unit. The cohesiveness of the regiment has been undermined too, by the willingness of even senior ex-members of the regiment to write publicly about their experiences and, finally, the recruitment of so many Parachute Regiment personnel at the expense of the traditional and more technically orientated volunteers from the Engineers, Signals, Intelligence and elite Infantry corps. However, despite certain doubts about the direction the regiment was taking, the SAS were to be quickly deployed in covert intelligence gathering operations in Afghanistan within a few weeks of the attacks on the USA in September 2001. Several squadrons were deployed in identifying targets for later US bombing raids and went on to lead many of the operations in the Tora Bora mountains in particular. Extraordinarily dangerous firefights took place in well-defended cave complexes in the search for Osama Bin Laden and his Al Qa'ida senior commanders. In the on going War on Terrorism, the SAS are sure to be called upon to play a leading role and it is to be hoped that the British government will ensure that the regular 22nd and the two TA Regiments are equipped with the very best equipment available, and in sufficient quantities.

SATCOM

Satellite Communications. Of vital importance in today's information-rich combat environment. Mobile SatCom equipment has revolutionised command, control and intelligence on the modern battlefield. Individual Micro-SatCom receivers will eventually allow whole units, particularly valuable on Special Operations, to each receive information or orders simultaneously or instructions for individual action, threat warnings and much more.

SAUDI ARABIA

MILITARY SPECIAL FORCES

The Special Security Force was established in 1971 and gained its counter-terrorist and hostage rescue role in 1979. The SSF has some 3,500 personnel organised into two battalions and three to four independent company-sized units and receives regular training from the French GIGN and German GSG-9. However, the best such unit in Saudi Arabia is probably the 100-man Special Warfare unit made up entirely of volunteers from within the National Guard, armed with 5.56mm M16A1 automatic rifles, 9mm MP5 sub-machine guns and M700 sniper rifles. They were given special training by the French GIGN before launching the successful operation to retake the Great Mosque in Mecca, seized by radical Muslim terrorists in 1979. The Airborne Brigade controls a further three dedicated Special Force Companies. These units are made up of volunteers, who are fully trained parachutists. Their initial training period includes six months of basic fitness and combat skills, then a further six months developing a range of advanced techniques in all aspects of Special Operations. Parachute training include HALO and HAHO, heliborne insertion, combat shooting, desert survival and warfare, close-quarters battle, hostage rescue, long-range reconnaissance and patrol or LRRP. Specialist explosive disposal training is also given in dealing with potential sabotage within the petro-chemical industry. These units regularly train with US Delta Force and SEAL personnel and are posted abroad on courses with the German GSG-9 and French GIGN. There is very close co-operation with the CIA and US Special Forces based in Saudi Arabia. Since the end of the Gulf War with Iraq, US military bases have been the target of numerous terrorist attacks by, among others, Osama Bin Laden's group, and prevention of further such outrages is high on the list of priorities for the Saudi Special Forces. The threat of extremist Islamic terrorist activities spreading both to the migrant worker community, and to the indigenous population, is of continuing grave concern to the authorities, and the security and Special Forces in particular. The weapons available for use by these units are the pick of the world's arms, and a wide range has been purchased, but the most popular are the 5.56mm M16A1 automatic rifles, Steyr AUG automatic rifles and 9mm H&K MP5 sub-machine guns, PSG-1 sniper rifles, Remington 700 sniper rifles and the M203 grenade launchers. A number of specially converted UH60 helicopters are available for Special Forces use, and have been of considerable value in operations along the disputed desert frontiers to the south and in the north along the border with Iraq.

Airborne Brigade in Riyadh with the 1st Airborne Battalion, 2nd Airborne Battalion, 1st Special Forces Company, 2nd Special Forces Company, 3rd Special Forces Company, 1st and 2nd Attack Helicopter Battalion at Hafr al-Batin.

SBS

Special Boat Service/Squadron/Section. British Royal Marine Special Forces unit. This elite unit has a rather complicated history and though the unit today considers itself a direct descendant of the Royal Marines Boom Patrol Detachment, this was only one of the many maritime Special Operations units in the Second World War. These include the original Special Boat Section, formed in 1940, which later became part of 1st SAS Regiment, but regained its independence as the Special Boat Squadron, redesignated late in 1944 as the Special Boat Service; it continued to wear the SAS beret and wings throughout its short life. The RMBPD was raised specifically for raids on shipping; the Landing Craft Obstruction Clearance Units, the closest equivalent to the US Underwater Demolition Teams and other small units variously manned by the Army, RN and RM. At the end of the Second World War, members of the Royal Navy and Royal Marines returning from service with the Small Operations Group in the Far East were concentrated at Fremington in North Devon, where they helped form the new School of Combined Operations Beach and Boat Section. The RMBPD was kept in being, as in future all small-boat operations would be conducted by the Marines. In 1947 both these two organisations were moved to a new Amphibious School Royal Marines being formed at the major naval base in Portsmouth, Hampshire. They were combined to form the Small Raids Wing and in 1950 this became the Special Boat Wing with 1st Special Boat Section (SBS). They were soon to see combat as these swimmer-canoeists, as the members of this unit were known from the start, were among those who volunteered for No.41 Independent Commando, the RM unit which served in Korea in 1950–51 where it was employed mainly on coastal raids and also fought as regular infantry at the Chosin Reservoir alongside the US 1st Marine Division. 2nd and 3rd SB Sections were formed in 1950–51 for service with the RN Rhine Squadron in Germany and trained to destroy bridges and other targets along the Rhine and its tributaries if Allied forces were forced to retreat by a Soviet invasion, while 4th and 5th SBS were manned by members of the Royal Marines Forces Volunteer Reserve. When the 3rd Commando Brigade moved from Malaya to Malta in the mid-1950s, 6th SBS was established to serve with them. In 1958, with six sections now in existence, the SBW became the Special Boat Company and independent of the Amphibious School, now in new facilities at Poole in Dorset.

Britain's 'confrontation' with Indonesia began with the Brunei revolt in December 1962, which was soon followed by guerrilla warfare and regular Indonesian troops being infiltrated across the border into the Malaysian part of Borneo. British, Commonwealth and local forces became involved in a long drawn out counter-insurgency campaign and 2nd SBS, based in Singapore with 3rd Commando Brigade, was already in the area in 1961. Joined later by 1st SBS they operated mainly in the coastal areas and also across the border on recce missions and supplying larger jungle patrols by SAS and Gurkhas from the sea. A peace treaty signed in August 1966 ended the confrontation, but only after Indonesia had suffered severe casualties, mainly at the hands of the British Special Forces. Though the British withdrawal from Aden was completed in 1967, this was not the end of SBS service in the Middle East, as from 1970 to 1976 the SAS was involved in fighting communist insurgents in pro-Western Oman, and were supported by the SBS based in Bahrain. During the early stages of this campaign they were involved initially in bringing in SAS in small boats, but later joined ambushes and patrols inland. By 1971 the withdrawal from Malaysia and Singapore was complete and the Special Boat Company was concentrated at Poole and began to concentrate on becoming an elite anti-terrorist force. In May 1972 a four-man team was parachuted into the North Atlantic to look for bombs aboard the *QE2* in response to what turned out to be an unsubstantiated terrorist threat. The SBS sent teams to Northern Ireland for boat patrols on the coast and waterways to counter gun-running, and also supplied volunteers for what was to become known as 14 Intelligence and Security Company. The SB Company was redesignated the Special Boat Squadron in 1975 and the 1st SBS was dedicated to the maritime CT role, with the emphasis placed on protection of the oil rigs in the North Sea. This unit would later be replaced by the 5th SBS which operated as an integral part of the Royal Marines Commachio Company, established in 1980 and based in northern Scotland.

When Argentina invaded the Falkland Islands in April 1982, 2nd, 3rd and 6th SB Sections were soon heading south with a small tactical headquarters, 84 men in all. 2nd SBS was part of the small task force sent to successfully re-take South Georgia and a group of islands also invaded by Argentina. They also took part in a large-scale covert surveillance operation that established observation posts all over East and West Falkland, a full three weeks before the main landings. The SBS surveyed suitable landing beaches and guided ashore the marine commandos and paratroopers at San Carlos Bay on 21 May. The SBS carried out aggressive patrols behind enemy lines, inserted by helicopter or submarine, or sometimes by small craft launched directly from the task force, and during a raid to knock out an enemy OP one SBS team inadvertently strayed into an area being patrolled by the SAS. Sergeant 'Kiwi' Hunt was killed in the 'blue on blue' (Friendly Fire) incident and became the only member of the SBS to die in the South Atlantic conflict.

Since the early 1980s, the SBS has become ever more closely linked with the SAS in a growing CT role and through the creation of the Special Forces Group in 1987, where a senior SBS officer serves as the deputy to a Director drawn from the SAS. SBS also now became the Special Boat Service with its integral units known as SB Squadrons. Two rifle troops from the RM Commachio Company were put under command of the SBS and 1st and 5th SBS combined as the main counter-terrorist force as M Squadron based at Poole and fully manned by swimmer-canoeists. One squadron of the SBS was deployed to the Gulf in 1990–91 as part of the Desert Shield/Desert Storm operations, where during the night of 23 January 1991 some twenty swimmer-canoeists, with three US Army Special Forces personnel and one US Air Force combat controller, were flown by helicopters to within 65km of Baghdad. Their mission, ultimately unsuccessful, led by an SBS lieutenant was to destroy a fibre-optic cable believed to be part of Iraq's Scud missile command system. The SBS also secured the British embassy in Kuwait City at the end of the war. A small number of SBS teams were deployed in Bosnia in 1993 and a complete squadron in 1995–96. The SBS were also involved in both Kosova and Macedonia. Thirty SBS were among the first troops to land at Dili airport, East Timor, in 1999, along with elements of the Australian and New Zealand SAS. Since the events of 9–11 and the declaration of a War on Terrorism the special talents of the SBS have been in even greater demand, personnel having been deployed on numerous anti-terrorist operations both in the UK, Europe, the Middle East and in Afghanistan. The motto of the SBS 'Not By Strength, By Guile' still applies to their dedication to covert anti-terrorist operations, and it appears on the unofficial insignia of crossed canoe paddles with a frog on top of them and parachute wings above, which originated on a Christmas card in 1946.

SBU

Special Boat Unit – US Marine Corps.

SCHOOL OF THE AMERICAS

Renamed the Western Hemisphere Institute for Security Co-operation in 2001.

The US Army School of the Americas (SOA) has long enjoyed a reputation as a military training institution responsible for some of the worst human rights abuses in the Western hemisphere. The SOA, along with the Central Intelligence Agency, continues to be the primary ideological and tactical lynchpins of US counter-insurgency operations throughout the hemisphere. While the collapse of the Soviet Union and the restoration of capitalism in Russia and Eastern Europe presumably ended the Cold War, the militant opposition to Latin American socialism which grew out of Washington's relentless campaign against communism remains firmly in place. The SOA, located at Fort Benning in Columbus, Georgia, is the US Army's Spanish-language training facility for Latin American military personnel and, along with the US Air Force's Inter-American Air Forces Academy, attracts the largest number of Latin American military students. Since its creation in 1946, some 60,000 Latin American military officers have graduated from the school, variously known as the 'School of Assassins' and the 'School of Coups'. Courses in Special Forces, counter-insurgency strategies and tactics, psychological operations, torture and assassination have long figured highly in the SOA's curriculum. It therefore came as little surprise to human rights activists when the Pentagon released a report on 20 September 1996 largely confirming these allegations, though the Pentagon's initial findings were made in 1992 and had remained a closely guarded secret for more than four years.

The Pentagon's spokesman admitted that between 1982–91 the SOA had used seven US Army Spanish language intelligence training manuals that advocated secret executions, torture, selective assassination, blackmail and extortion against dissidents and their families. The first Bush administration is reported to have moved swiftly to revise the training manuals when it was discovered in 1992 that some aspects of the course curriculum constituted 'a serious violation of the policies that were in place in the United States at that time'. However, there is some speculation that all that effectively happened was that a serious attempt was made to more successfully hide the activities and curriculum of the school, just cosmetic changes to try to avoid further difficult public revelations. The truth remains that this US military institution has trained several generations of foreign Special Forces and Intelligence personnel in acts the government in Washington would forcefully condemn elsewhere in the world. Many who have taken part in the numerous Latin American death squads and those who later became assassins, coup leaders and torturers were graduates of the School of the Americas. Indeed many US Special Forces personnel have served as advisers with Latin American units and have reportedly become involved in a number of their activities. The doctrine and training methods of the SOA have been questioned for many years, as it trained many military personnel before and during the years of the 'national security doctrine' in which Latin American military regimes ruled or had disproportionate government influence and committed serious human rights violations. Training manuals used at the SOA and elsewhere from the early 1980s through 1991 promoted techniques that violated human rights and democratic standards. SOA graduates continue to surface in news reports regarding both current human rights cases and new reports on past cases. Defenders of the school, however, argue that they do not actually teach abuse and that the present curriculum includes human rights as a component of every class, with new rules codifying an existing school policy which requires that each student receive at least eight hours of instruction in 'human rights, the rule of law, due process, civilian control of the military, and the role of the military in a democratic society'. They also argue that no school should be held accountable for the actions of only some of its graduates.

Although the SOA was renamed the Western Hemisphere Institute for Security Co-operation in 2001, the official purpose remained 'to provide professional education and training to eligible personnel of nations of the Western Hemisphere within the context of the democratic principles set forth in the Charter of the Organization of American States ... while fostering mutual knowledge, transparency, confidence, and co-operation among the participating nations and promoting democratic values, respect for human rights, and knowledge and understanding of United States customs and traditions.' In other words no change, and the US will continue to be responsible for training another generation of politically motivated Latin American officers, sanctified by their determination to support the United States in the War on Terrorism, and safe in the knowledge that their own abuses will be ignored in return.

SCUBA

Self-Contained Underwater Breathing Apparatus, a technique developed by Jacques Cousteau in occupied France during the Second World War.

SDV

SEAL Delivery Vehicle, a minisub SEALs use to covertly insert over long distances under water.

SEAL

Sea Air Land Team – USN Special Forces Unit.

SELECTION

Four-week SAS course held at Hereford Regimental Depot and in the Welsh mountains (such as the Brecon Beacons) which all prospective recruits must pass before acceptance for the CONTINUATION course.

SELOUS SCOUTS – RHODESIA

The original Selous Scouts was an armoured unit in the former Central African Federation Army.

The later Selous Scouts were formed from the Tracker Combat Units in 1972. The Scouts were formed for one main reason, the ongoing war in Rhodesia was not going well. The terrorists (in this case the ZANLA and ZIRPA guerrillas headed by Mugabe and Nkomo) were striking the Rhodesians and fading back into the bush. The terrorists struck both military and civilian targets, in some cases targeting missionaries. Small groups of soldiers and policemen were pioneering the counter-insurgency task by occasionally succeeding in tracking the terrorists back to their bases and then neutralising them by either capturing or killing them. The Rhodesian Government turned to Captain Ron Reid Daly to form and train this new unit. Daly had served with the British Special Air Service, before returning to Rhodesia to serve in the Rhodesian Light Infantry (RLI). The Selous Scouts was an integrated unit, with a ratio of 90 per cent African and 10 per cent European. The unit also had both black and white officers. The purpose of the Scouts was to be able to track the terrorists back to a 'base' where the Scouts could then surprise them. The Scouts also found targets for the Fire Forces (the RLI) to assault. The Rhodesian government stated that 85 per cent of the terrorist casualties were from the Scouts, while the Scouts themselves only suffered some 40 per cent casualties. After the former terrorist leader Robert Mugabe became the Prime Minister of Zimbabwe (Rhodesia) the Selous Scouts were disbanded in 1980. The Rhodesian Army units were to become the backbone of the new Zimbabwe Army, with the Selous Scouts becoming the 1st Parachute Battalion. However a small number, perhaps 50–60, left for South Africa to join the Recce Commandos. The Selous Scouts formed 7th Recce Commando, which was later changed to 3rd Recce Commando, and then later to 5th Recce Commando.

SENEGAL

MILITARY SPECIAL FORCES

One Commando and one Airborne Special Forces Battalions. This latter unit has received training from the US 1st Battalion, 3rd Special Forces Group in recent years.

SEPS (SEPS)

Surrendered Enemy Personnel – future POW (Prisoners of War).

SERBIA (SEE YUGOSLAVIA)

SERE

Survival, Escape, Resistance and Evasion. The basic building blocks of Special Forces 'good practice'.

SF

Special Forces.

SFTG

Special Forces Training Group.

SHOOT-TO-KILL, THE SAS AND NORTHERN IRELAND

In 1975 the decision to play the military response to the conflict in Northern Ireland 'long', so 'long' in fact that attrition and despair would wear down the Provisional IRA in particular, had been taken by senior British commanders; however, not all military opinion was in favour of such gradualism. One senior SAS officer, who later described the killing of three unarmed IRA members as the 'Gibraltar cull' held a view which was repeated by another senior officer who admitted to *Time* magazine that 'a majority of officers are now strongly backing a shoot-to-kill policy as the principle method of defeating the IRA'. The evidence that the British authorities had finally resorted to a hard-line policy against the Provisional IRA in the mid-1980s appeared clear after a number of SAS and Security Force operations in which all the terrorists involved were killed. Eight IRA gunmen and a passer-by died in an SAS ambush when the Provisionals attacked an RUC station in Loughgall, Co Armagh, in 1987. Police shot two other unarmed IRA men in separate incidents in Lurgan, Co Armagh, in 1982, and Belfast in 1992, and loyalist terrorists of the UVF/UFF said to be acting in collusion with the RUC, killed a Sinn Fein official in Co Tyrone in 1991. This too seemed to fit smoothly into a pattern established by the 'execution' of five out of six gunmen during the assault on the Iranian Embassy in 1980, the sixth having to be arrested by one of the released hostages, Police Constable Lock, to prevent his killing by the SAS and seemingly confirmed later by the killing of three unarmed IRA members Sean Savage, Mairead Farrell and Daniel McCann, in Gibraltar in 1988.

The SAS and later the Protestant killers of the UVF and IFF have also targeted particular individuals for assassination usually after long periods of surveillance. A member of a British military anti-terrorist unit has told how killing Republican paramilitaries would be celebrated with a drinking session and a commemorative cake; a rather damning admission in light of continued allegations of collusion between the army, police and the Protestant death squads. The Stalker enquiry, named after the Assistant Chief Constable of the Greater Manchester Police, was called to investigate allegations that the Security Forces were not only killing rather than arresting suspects but were targeting Catholics for execution by Protestant gunmen. The refusal by John Stalker to countenance a 'whitewash' led to his removal on trumped-up allegations of dubious financial behaviour back in Manchester. Though the subsequent enquiry failed to pursue the matter, and indeed exonerated both the SAS and Ulster authorities, fresh evidence has surfaced in 2002 that has largely confirmed the involvement of the British Army and local Police Force (RUC, now the PFNI) in passing information relating to suspected Catholic members of the IRA or Nationalist movements to the Protestant death squads. It is also notable that as the number of Republicans killed by the SAS decreased, so the number murdered by Loyalist death squads increased, giving the distinct impression that the British government – aware of the potential political fallout from the policy of 'shoot-to-kill' – had decided to 'contract out' the work to the UVF/UFF terrorists. In 2001 the UK was actually convicted of human rights violations over ten IRA men shot dead by British troops and the Royal Ulster Constabulary in Northern Ireland. In four separate cases considered by the European Court of Human Rights in Strasbourg, involving a total of twelve deaths, a violation of Article 2 of the Human Rights Convention concerning a failure to conduct proper investigation into circumstances surrounding the deaths was proven.

SIERRA LEONE – OPERATION BARRAS 2000 – SAS

A hostage situation in Sierra Leone was successfully resolved on the morning of 10 September 2000 as a force of 150 British paratroopers, led and directed by SAS soldiers, assaulted the West Side Boys' camp where eleven British and one Sierra Leonean hostages were being held. On 25 August 2000, the eleven soldiers from the Royal Irish Regiment, along with their military liaison from Sierra Leone, were taken hostage by a 'renegade militia', known as the West Side Boys, who are said to be perpetually drunk and drugged. The soldiers were in Sierra Leone as part of a 200-strong force training the government army in the country. British forces in the country launched an immediate search operation, but helicopter overflights proved useless, and failed to locate the missing patrol. At this time, reports surfaced that a twelve-man Special Air Service (SAS) team was sent to the country to attempt a rescue. That same day, 27 August, the West Side Boys demanded the release of their leader, General Papa, from prison, along with food and medicine, in exchange for the British troops. Two days later, on 29 August, one of the captured soldiers was allowed to meet with a hostage negotiating team, and assured them that the soldiers were being treated well, and that no one was injured. Around this time, the British government admitted that the captured patrol might have been deep inside rebel territory, rather than on the main highway. The situation improved on Wednesday 30 August, when five of the eleven British soldiers were released, in exchange for a satellite phone and medical supplies. The other soldiers would not be released until the other demands were met. As negotiations continued, 5 September saw the arrival of over 100 elite British paratroopers from the 1st Battalion Parachute Regiment in Senegal in preparation for a possible military resolution to the crisis. The SAS had been on the ground for several days before the eventual assault, conducting reconnaissance among the swamps of Occra hills where the hostages were held. Supposedly, the hostages were lined up in front of firing squads for mock executions. The SAS had learned with the help of eavesdropping devices that the West Side Boys were discussing moving the hostages to higher hills. When the order for the rescue operation was given, the SAS operators moved to their final vantage point to guide in the paras. As dawn broke on Sunday 11 September the order to move was issued. At 06.16 three Chinook helicopters and two Westland Lynx gunships took off from Freetown airport. Flying at 200 miles per hour, they headed towards Rokel creek, the site of the rebel camp. At 06.30, the assault began as the lead Lynx helicopter began strafing the banks of the river. One Chinook landed near the huts, as soldiers disembarked from it and immediately shot the guards. This task most certainly fell to the SAS soldiers due to their expertise in hostage rescue. A firefight ensued, as the West End Boys opened up on the rescue force with a heavy machine gun, killing one paratrooper. A second force of SAS and paras, moving in through a valley from the south, soon overwhelmed them, as more of the rescue team took casualties. The hostages were hustled into the helicopter and, 20 minutes after the start of the operation, were safely airborne. The hostages were removed to a waiting ship off the coast of Freetown, the *Sir Percival*. During this time two other Chinooks landed at a secondary camp south of the first position, and the paras, with the second Lynx gunship providing cover, engaged in a vicious firefight with the West Siders. Fighting on this side of the creek took up to an hour and a half, the British forces using mortars. The last of the rescue force were airlifted around 16.00, after a mopping-up operation, which saw the capture of the West Side Boys' leader, Foday Kallay. The British forces suffered one death, one serious injury, and eleven 'light injuries'. The West Side Boys lost 25 fighters, along with eighteen captured.

SILENCED WEAPONS

While silenced weapons have usually been considered to be mainly used by spies and Intelligence officers, they have in fact found wide acceptance among the world's Special Forces. During the Second World War sub-machine guns like the US M3AI and British sten gun were fitted with silencers, but though the overall sound was greatly reduced it was not possible to eliminate the sound of the bolt. Therefore highly specialised and virtually silent weapons were developed. The 'Sleeve Gun', which could be concealed while strapped to the arm, or the Mark-1 Hand Firing Device, otherwise known as the Welrod, were produced in both 7.65mm (.32 Colt) and 9mm. These weapons, issued to the British SOE and later to the United States OSS and widely used by both the Special Forces and Resistance movements throughout Europe, had both silenced mechanisms and silenced projectiles. Since that time, however, developments have continued along several lines, first the true silencer used with reduced velocity (sub-sonic) ammunition and secondly, noise suppressers such as those fitted to the Colt XM177E1/2. However, most major arms-producing countries have also developed specialist-silenced weapons and these are the most valuable for Special Forces and clandestine operations. China has the Type-64 7.65mm pistol and the Type-64 7.62mm SMG; Britain produced the Sterling Mk-5 & L34AI silenced SMG and one the best and most silent weapons ever produced, the .303 De Lisle Carbine (see separate entry) Germany its 9mm MP5SD series; the US Navy SEALs had the 9mm Mk-22 Mod O silenced pistol. Firing special green-tipped ammunition, these weapons were known as 'Hush Puppies' and were used for eliminating Vietcong 'lookouts' and assassinating 'political undesirables' in Vietnam, while the Special Forces also had an M21 sniper rifle with a Sionics noise suppresser. Israel has several extremely quiet weapons developed for Mossad and the Sayeret Matkal, including a sound-suppressed Uzi SMG. The Soviet Union/Russia possessed a wide range of such specialist weapons including the 4.5mm SPP-1M underwater pistol; 5.66mm APS underwater assault rifle; 7.62mm PSS silenced pistol and the 9mm VSS silenced pistol, while the SVD sniper's rifle reputably can have a very effective silencer fitted.

Silencers work on the principle that when a bullet is fired from a gun, gunpowder is ignited behind the bullet creating a high-pressure pulse of hot gas. The pressure of the gas forces the bullet down the barrel of the gun. When the bullet exits the end of the barrel, it is like uncorking a bottle. The pressure behind the bullet is immense, however, around 3,000 pounds per square inch (psi) hence the loud explosive noise. The silencer screwed on to the end of the barrel has a huge volume, usually in the order of 20 or 30 times that of the barrel. With the silencer in place, the pressurised gas behind the bullet has a bigger space to expand into, so the pressure of the hot gas decreases significantly. When the bullet finally exits through the hole in the silencer, the pressure being released is significantly lower, often around only 60psi, with a consequently much reduced sound signature. However, no externally fitted silencer can compete with a purpose-built weapon with integral silencer and sound-suppressed bolt.

SILENT KILLING

Techniques developed over the centuries to dispose of sentries, guards or for assassinations. Can involve unarmed combat and martial arts skills, use of a garrotte, crossbows and blade-weapons. A whole range of specialist knifes have been developed for hand combat use, throwing or, in the case of the Russian NR-2 'silent-fire', actually launching a blade at the target over a distance of some 17m (50ft).

SINGAPORE

MILITARY SPECIAL FORCES

1st Commando Battalion The Singapore Armed Forces Commandos are an elite organisation that has a Command Headquarters with the School of Commandos within it, a Reserve Battalion, an Active Battalion and the Special Operation Force. The active unit is the 1st Battalion and currently comprises five companies with an additional Headquarters Company. Trains regularly with GSG-9, ASAS, Sayeret Matkal and both the Indian and Taiwanese Special Forces. The Commando Training Centre (CTC) is the Centre for Operationally Ready National Servicemen (NSmen) as they return for their annual in-camp training (ICT). The School of Commandos (SOC) is one of the premier training institutions of the SAF. It is responsible for all specialist commando training, as well as junior leadership training within the Formation. The SOC comprises two sections, the Parachute Training Wing and the Commando Training Wing. Each wing is responsible for specific areas of essential commando training.

Special Operation Force (SOF) is a unit within the Commando Formation that is specially trained for Counter-Terrorist actions. Members of this unit are specially selected and have to undergo a long period of Counter-Terrorist training before they can be accepted as troopers. It also serves as a national hostage rescue unit and proved its worth when five minutes was all the four Pakistani terrorists who hijacked Singapore Airlines SQ117 would give the authorities on Tuesday 26 March 1991 to meet their demands. Failing that, they would start killing one hostage every ten minutes. But barely had three of those minutes elapsed when the order was given for the SOF to storm the plane. Commandos went in at 06.50. The operation was over in 30 seconds with the four hijackers dead and none of the 123 hostages hurt. For their bravery and skill, HQ Commando was awarded the Medal of Valor and a Unit citation. 7th Elite Guards Brigade (Airmobile/Special Forces), 1st Guards Battalion (Rapid reaction unit), 2nd and 3rd Guards Battalion.

CIVILIAN SPECIAL FORCES

Singapore Police Force SOC was created in 1992 to gather all police tactical units under one central command. The command maintains three units: the Police Dog Unit, which is the Singapore Police Force K-9 unit; the Police Task Force, which is a specially trained riot control force; and the Special Tactical and Rescue Unit, or STAR, which acts as a national SWAT/HRU force.

The Special Tactical and Rescue (STAR) Unit was formed in 1993 with a 100–120 full-time force of officers to provide the Singapore Police Force with a 24-hour tactical armed-response capability. Organised along GSG-9 lines, it is a dedicated unit highly trained and equipped to respond to any incidents such as armed criminals and hostage situations. The STAR team is tasked with handling incidents that may require the use of specialised weapons, or when a situation arises where the use of their tactical skills will bring a rapid resolution to the crisis. This unit specialise in conducting K-9 operations, SWAT operations, riot control, CT and HRU operations. Team members are trained in conducting assaults on aircraft and buses, demolition techniques for conducting explosive or 'dynamic entry', precision shooting, close-quarters combat (CQB) techniques, heliborne operations such as rappelling and fast roping, firing from moving vehicles, operating motorcycles and all terrain vehicles, defensive driving and VIP protection techniques. The STAR team has also received training from the Israeli Border Guard's Ya'ma'm CT unit, Germany's GSG-9, and the ASAS. Weapons in use include the 9mm Glock 19 pistol, 9mm IMI Model 941 Jericho pistol, 9mm H&K MP5A3 sub-machine gun, 9mm IMI Model 46 Mini-Uzi sub-machine gun, the 7.62mm H&K PSG1 sniper rifle and 18.5mmR (12-gauge) H&K HK512 semi-automatic shotgun.

SKORZENY, OTTO

SS-Sturmbannführer Otto Skorzeny was the most colourful and the most famous Waffen SS commander during the Second World War. His daring rescue of Mussolini from Gran Sasso made him world famous and his subsequent missions during the Ardennes Offensive and in Hungary during Operation Panzerfaust gave him the the title among the Allies of 'The Most Dangerous Man in Europe'. His extraordinary wartime career was one of high risk and adventure . . . Otto Skorzeny was born on 12 June 1908, to a typical middle-class Viennese family. He attended the University of Vienna to study engineering. He joined the Nazi Party in the 1920s and signed up with the SS. During the Second World War he proved himself to be a superior soldier and was quickly promoted from ordinary soldier to non-commissioned officer and finally to officer. Skorzeny participated in the invasion of Holland and France, the invasion of the Balkans, and finally in the invasion of Russia, where he was wounded in late 1941 and returned home to convalesce. But Otto Skorzeny proved his worth – in 1942 he was awarded the Iron Cross, and in April 1943 he was promoted to captain and named 'Chief of Germany's Special Troops, Existing or to be Created in the Future'. When Hitler's ally Benito Mussolini was overthrown and imprisoned in Italy at Gran Sasso in 1943, it was Skorzeny who successfully planned and led the daring rescue, winning the Knight's Cross and promotion as a result. Hitler intended to put Mussolini back on the seat of a puppet government in the part of Italy still occupied by the Germans and he personally ordered Otto Skorzeny to rescue Mussolini. Skorzeny tracked Mussolini across half of Italy for a month and a half until he finally found him at the Hotel Campo, a resort high in the Gran Sasso mountains. On 8 September, the Germans intercepted a coded message by the Italians confirming the presence of Mussolini on the Gran Sasso. Skorzeny took a contingent of his troops in gliders and crashed-landed them on the steep rocky slopes surrounding the hotel. The Germans quickly stormed the hotel, capturing the place without a shot. Mussolini was found and promptly loaded onto an aircraft that landed after the assault was over and flown to Vienna. On the arrival at the Hotel Continental, where a suite had been prepared, they received a hero's welcome and Hitler telephoned to congratulate him personally.

Skorzeny's talents were brought into play again when he was sent to Budapest to prevent the Hungarian regent Admiral Horthy signing a separate peace with Stalin in 1944. His reputation thus enhanced, he was promoted again and awarded the German Cross in Gold. A few months later he took a critical role in the Ardennes Offensive, with a controversial plan to raise an armoured brigade disguised as Americans, using captured Sherman tanks, to spread chaos and confusion. Ten days after the war's end Skorzeny gave himself up to the US Forces who had launched a massive search for 'The Most Dangerous Man in Europe'. He was put on trial and held a prisoner until 27 July 1948. It was on this day that in true commando fashion he escaped. His whereabouts after his escape remained a mystery as US Intelligence officers, Soviet agents and Jewish organisations hunted for him all over Europe, but the ex-commando was not in Europe. In fact he had fled to Argentina where he became close to Juan and Eva Peron. Otto Skorzeny organised the Argentinian Security Police into one of the most brutal in South America and also acted as Eva Peron's bodyguard, foiling at least one attempt on her life. His other post-war activities included his service as an adviser to Colonel Nasser, the President of Egypt. Skorzeny eventually settled in Spain and became a successful engineering consultant for several years. His later years were all spent on helping his SS comrades to escape justice. He founded a secret organisation, which helped some 500 former SS members escape the hunt for Nazi war criminals. One of the better known people the organisation is said to have helped was Adolf Eichmann. Otto Skorzeny laid the groundwork for many of the Special Forces techniques used today. He died in Madrid in July 1975 and remained, to the end, a dedicated and unrepentant Nazi.

SLICK

A troop transport helicopter. US Special Forces nickname.

SLOVAK REPUBLIC

MILITARY SPECIAL FORCES
The Slovak 5th SF Regiment (5 Pluk Specialneho Urcenia or 5th PSU)   Established on 1 November 1994, this unit was officially designated the 5th PSU. The unit is directly attached to the Armed Forces General Staff but works for the Operational Reconnaissance Bureau. The unit's official strength is 400 personnel organised into six companies. There are four special reconnaissance companies, one signal company and one support company. Each special reconnaissance company has four ten-man reconnaissance teams. Each has one of the following technical specialities: communications, medical and demolitions/weapons. These parallel the specialities found in US Army Special Forces A-Teams. The soldier with the highest level of training on the Slovak reconnaissance team, however, is the demolition/weapons sergeant, a practice based on former Soviet SPETSNAZ (SF) doctrine, which focused on the ability to disrupt key Western facilities in advance of a Soviet invasion. The Slovak demolitions sergeant is trained in diving and underwater demolition techniques. The basic diving training takes place at the Slovak army's engineer base at Banska Bystrica. It begins with mastering techniques in a pool and then moves on to dives in local lakes. The demolition specialist then returns to Zilina for training in combat swimming techniques, deep water diving, and underwater demolition techniques. This unit regularly trains with Western Special Operations units, including the US Army's 10th SF Group. This was held in the Slovak Republic and simulated joint participation in a peace-keeping operation. In 1995, the 1st Marine Parachute Infantry Regiment (1er RPIMa) conducted a demonstration of high-altitude, high-opening (HAHO) parachuting techniques in the Slovak Republic. The 5th PSU has increasingly adopted Western Special Forces techniques and equipment, and since 9–11 has become an enthusiastic partner in the War on Terrorism.

CIVILIAN SPECIAL FORCES

OUO (Hostage Rescue Unit)   This anti-terrorist and hostage rescue unit uses the following weapons including the 9mm CZ75 pistol, 9mm H&K MP5A5 sub-machine gun and 5.56mm SIG-Sauer SSG3000 bolt-action sniper rifle.

SLOVENIA

MILITARY SPECIAL FORCES

Special Operations Command
32nd Mountain (Special Forces) 'Moris' Bde HQ Bohinjska Bola, with the 1st Mountain (SF) Battalion. Mountain and Special Forces School HQ Srednja.

ODRED ZA SPECIALNO DELOVANJE (ODSD) – Special Operations Detachment   The ODSD is a small, highly skilled anti-terrorist unit whose members are trained in Close-Quarters Battle (CQB), free-falling, alpine warfare and SCUBA diving. The unit is tasked with hostage rescue, long-range patrols (LRRP), demolitions and intelligence-gathering. Some instructors from the ODSD have been trained by foreign Special Operations Forces and apparently have close ties with the US Navy SEALs, Green Berets and several European Special Operations Forces. In 2001 the Slovenian Special Forces were training with the British Special Air Service (SAS) for 'snatch' operations aiming to apprehend alleged war criminals such as Radovan Karadzic.

CIVILIAN SPECIAL FORCES

MINISTRSTVO ZA NOTRANJE ZADEVE (MNZ) – Ministry of the Interior
SPECIALNA ENOTA – General Police Directorate Special Unit   Specialna Enota is Slovenia's counter-terrorist unit and comes under the Ministry of the Interior and was established in 1990. Its origins date back to 1972 when, in the wake of the Munich Massacre, the first operational unit was established in 1973. Specialna Enota is tasked with countering terrorism, counter-insurgency operations, guarding important facilities, VIP protection as well as hostage rescue. The unit is also responsible for training other police units and offices. Specialna Enota consists of a command detachment, a counter-insurgency unit, Operative Units A and B, a mechanised unit and a logistics unit. During Slovenia's ten-day war for independence in June/July 1991, Specialna Enota was employed as a military unit and was involved in limited fighting against the Federal Yugoslav forces. A small unit was tasked with securing the Ljubljana Airport, but after a skirmish with Federal troops, they were forced to withdraw from their positions. During the retreat of the Federal forces from Slovenia, Enota members supervised departures of Yugoslav People's Army (JNA) officers from army installations. The mechanised unit was disbanded in 1994 and there was some shuffling of

responsibilities within the unit to reduce its paramilitary side in favour of a counter-terrorist capability. Specialna Enota uses a wide variety of weapons, including the Beretta M92 and M-8000 handguns. The unit also uses M-70 assault rifles, Heckler & Koch MP5 and Beretta M-59/66 semi-automatic rifles. During the war for independence, Slovenian special police units were armed with weapons purchased on the black market, and M-16s and Steyr SSG-69 sniper rifles. The Specialna Enota has co-operated and trained with Austria's GEK Cobra and similar German, British and Hungarian units.

URAD ZA VARNOST IN ZASCITO – Security and Protection Bureau

The Security and Protection Bureau is in charge of protecting top representatives of the Slovenian state, foreign dignitaries visiting Slovenia, top representatives of foreign diplomatic missions, visiting VIPs such as Pope John Paul II (1996, 1999) and the visit of US President Bill Clinton (1999) and consular bodies in Slovenia and other entities defined by a special ordinance by the government.

SLOW MOVER

A propeller-driven aircraft.

SLR

Self-loading rifle. Odd British term for the L1A1 Semi-Automatic Rifle made by Belgium company FN, known throughout the rest of the world as the FAL.

SMG

Sub-machine gun. The Germans tended to call these weapons Maschine-Pistols, hence the MP in H&K MP5.

SNIPERS

Sniping has always been an integral part of the Special Forces and is the ultimate targeted anti-personnel warfare. Tactically the sniper is of paramount importance to the success of many hostage rescue situations; identification and tracking and the ability to 'kill' at long distance and unexpectedly whenever a hostage taker presents himself as a target, as most snipers are authorised in certain circumstances to 'shoot on sight', can present the assault team with the opportunity to launch their rescue operation. Snipers are selected for a range of characteristics such as stability, judgement, patience, calmness, eyesight, marksmanship and that vital ability to keep their concentration for long periods and still have instant reactions when a fleeting opportunity for a shot finally arrives.

Advances in materials and equipment since the end of the Second World War have given the sniper more lethal ammunition, greater range and astounding accuracy with a range of telescopic sights, image/light enhancers and laser target designators. Many sniper rifles have traditionally been modified standard service models or civilian hunting rifles, but the trend has been firmly towards specially designed weapons over the last 30 years. The Russian SVD 'Dragunov' 7.62mm weapon has a ten-round magazine and with its PSO-1 telescopic sight has proved extremely accurate at over 900yds (810m). The scope displays a graduated range-finding scale based on the average height of a man. By fitting the target into the grid, the sniper gets an accurate idea of the range and aims accordingly – a simple, quick and effective method. The PSO-1 also has an additional and unusual feature, incorporating an infrared detector element to enable it to be used as a passive night sight, although it is normally used in conjunction with an independent infrared target illuminator. The Russian equivalent of the long-range Barrett is the V94, which has been reported as being highly accurate at 1400m. The United States Armed Forces have used relatively straightforward sniper rifles such as the 7.62mm M21, a variation of the M14, while the US Marine Corps preferred the 7.62mm M40 (Remington-700). However, with the advent of such systems as Barrett M82A1/2 12.7mm (.5 Browning) in the 1980s there has been a move, in particular among the Special Forces, to develop new sniping techniques to allow them to benefit from the extended killing ranges of well over 1100yds (1km). The United States has also become one of the world leaders in advanced image and light enhancing scopes, making a lethal combination with the new long-range weapons and allowing targeted assassination and sniping to become an ever more useful part of clandestine warfare. Britain's SAS use a wide variety of sniper's rifles, including the Accuracy International L96A1 single shot long-range model. The weapon itself has an aluminium chassis clothed in a plastic outer casing to save weight, while many other nations such as France, Belgium, Germany and Austria produce superb specialist rifles. However, the fact that such state-of-the-art designs as the 'space age' Iver Johnson Model-300 7.62mm/8.58mm multi-calibre rifle claimed to have a range of over 1600yds (1.5km) or the Steyr IWS2000 anti-material/sniper's rifle can put a 15mm tungsten dart through 40mm of armour at 1100yds (1km) suggests that the next generation of Special Forces snipers will have truly frightening machines under their trigger fingers. (See separate entries for some of these weapons.)

SOCOM

Special Operations Command – USA. The controlling organisation for all US Special Forces units with the exception of those provided by the US Marine Corps.

SOE – SPECIAL OPERATIONS EXECUTIVE

British Second World War Subversion and Sabotage agency disbanded in 1946, but important elements were absorbed by SIS (MI6). The clandestine warfare techniques, training methods and specialist weapons they developed between 1941 and 1945 have significantly influenced later Special Operations throughout the world.

SOF

Special Operations Forces – Generic US.

SOG

Acronym: Special Operations Group for 'Special Projects'.

SOLOMON ISLANDS

CIVILIAN SPECIAL FORCES
A small squad-sized National Reconnaissance and Surveillance Force.

SON TAY – OPERATION IVORY COAST

This operation had first been considered in May, but was delayed until 21 November 1970, just one month before the bulk of US Special Forces were due to withdraw from Vietnam. Son Tay prison lay only 23 miles outside Hanoi, North Vietnam. Son Tay had been thought to house American POWs, (Prisoners Of War), and indeed Intelligence would later confirm that 55 American POWs were being held at the camp until a week or so before the raid. The POWs, using their laundry, had spelt out the letters 'SAR' on the ground for reconnaissance aircraft to see. A plan was put into action for a mixed group of US Air Force pilots and Army Special Forces to attempt to rescue the POWs. Training took place at Eglin Air Force Base, where the CIA built an exact replica of the prison. Three helicopters, two CH/HH3s, codenamed 'Apple 1' and 'Apple 2', and one HH-53 codenamed 'Apple 3' would be used in the operation and 56 Special Forces soldiers would perform the rescue. Colonel Arthur 'Bull' Simons was put in charge of the operation. Under him were Lieutenant Colonel Elliot P. 'Bud' Sydnor, Captain Richard Meadows, and Captain Udo Walther. On the night of 20/21 November 1970 the helicopters took off from Udorn, Thailand. The US Navy launched sea and air strikes on North Vietnam to divert attention away from the raid. The HH-53 went into a hover over Son Tay and provided cover for the main assault force with fast-firing Mini-guns. The HH3 that was carrying Meadows wasn't as lucky. To allow the rescue team to get into the compound faster, the pilot threw the helicopter onto the ground, almost crashing it. The assault team piled out and entered the building. The soldiers yelled for the prisoners to stay down and keep calm, but didn't receive an answer. The fourteen men cut down several NVA guards before realising that there were no prisoners. 'Apple 2' landed just south of the camp's outer wall. This helicopter was carrying 'Bull' Simons and as soon as it touched the assault team set up a roadblock about 100 metres away from the camp to stop anyone attempting to enter or leave the camp. By the end of the operation the NVA had lost 50 soldiers killed in firefights with no losses to the raiders. However 'Apple 1' had, by mistake, landed almost 500 metres away from the camp. Not knowing this the soldiers exited the helicopter and entered the main building, a barracks, housing over 100 Chinese and Russian advisers and NVA regulars. All of them died in under five minutes as the US Special Forces simply kicked open every door and fired their CAR-15s and combat shotguns into the sleeping soldiers. 'Apple 1' eventually linked up with the rest of the raiding force and, from the time the first helicopter touched down until the last one pulled out, the whole operation took about 25 minutes. Although no prisoners were found, almost 150 enemy soldiers lay dead without a single loss to the Son Tay Raiders. It has been argued that some US and Allied POWs received better treatment after this attack.

SOP

Acronym: Standing Operating Procedures.

SOPAG

Acronym: Special Operations Advisory Group.

SOUTH AFRICA

MILITARY SPECIAL FORCES

Special Forces Brigade On 1 October 1972, the 1st Reconnaissance Commando was established at Oudtshoorn, South Africa. It was relocated a few years later to Durban, South Africa, and was the first genuine South African Special Forces unit. In 1975, during the move of 1st RC to Durban, 4th Reconnaissance Commando was established in Langebaan, South Africa, this unit being set up to perform maritime operations. 5th Reconnaissance Commando 'Recces' had been set up at the Duku-Duku camp in Northern Natal and was later moved to Phalaborwa. In 1981, the Special Forces became an independent structure no longer under control of the army, answering only to the Ministry of Defence (Defence Forces). In 1991 the Headquarters unit of the Special Forces was disbanded and a Directorate of Reconnaissance was formed directly under the Chief of the Army. The organisation underwent a further change in 1993 when it became 45th Parachute Brigade. As a result of this, 1 Reconnaissance Regiment was now re-named 452 Parachute Battalion, while 4 and 5 Reconnaissance Regiment became 453 and 451 Parachute Battalion respectively. In 1996 the organisation changed yet again and is currently known as the Special Forces Brigade. It presently consists of 4th and 5th Special Forces Regiments.

The South African 'Recces' were deployed to many local hot spots during the late 1970s and early 1980s, particularly Angola. The main enemy then was a terrorist group known as SWAPO (South West Africa's People's Organization). It was an all-black guerrilla organisation fighting for an independent Namibia and SWAPO proved to be a formidable enemy. One of the Recces' most effective operations came in 1982. Operation Mebos penetrated deep into Angola and destroyed the SWAPO Headquarters. In Operation Askari, in the winter of 1994, the Recces cut off almost all supply lines to and from the SWAPO in Angola. The Ultimate Challenge, as SA SF Selection is often called, is one of the toughest selection courses in the world. A soldier must meet very high requirements to actually attend SF selection. However, he has to be in excellent shape to make it through. Pre-Selection Training: this includes all aspects of psychological and physical tests. For the psychological tests, soldiers will be given written tests and oral interviews with SF NCOs. A soldier must be self-controlled and mature. Any hints of a soldier being unbalanced and he is off the course. There is no room for 'nuts' in this business. The Physical Test included 40 continuous push ups, 67 sit ups in two minutes, fireman lift, three-kilometre run in full gear in eighteen minutes, a rope climb (to show upper body strength), 40 shuttle runs in 95 seconds and wall scaling. A student must scale a ten-foot high wall, complete a fifteen-kilometre march in less than 150 minutes and perform 120 shuttle kicks. The Parachute Selection Course–Basic Parachute school is one of the most demanding. All SF candidates who aren't parachute-qualified will have to attend this course. Special Force Orientation Course: this is a time when a student will learn what Special Forces are and what they do. He will be told about what to look forward to in training. He is made to PT every day to get into shape for the toughest part of Selection yet – Special Forces Selection. It has been a rough road for a Special Force Candidate, but it is not over yet. Not much is known about Selection. However, it is believed to be one of the toughest in the world. The Cycle: once past the Selection process, he will be placed on a training cycle to acquire the skills required. These include: air co-operation, water orientation, obstacle crossing, bushcraft, tracking and survival, demolitions and tactics in urban as well as rural areas. Advanced Airborne Training: a recruit will be taught about military free-fall such as

HALO (High Altitude Low Opening) and HAHO (High Altitude High Opening). They will also learn about helicopter operations – how to rappel fast down a rope out of helicopters. STABO extraction is also taught, along with learning how to set up a LZ (or Landing Zone). Land Training consists of many things: including sniping, demolitions and reconnaissance. Bushcraft and survival is also taught. Climbing and photography are taught to new recruits. Urban and rural combat is perhaps the newest training. Developed quite recently, this training provided SA with a new CT force. Medical and communications training is also given to those who wish to become qualified. Maritime training consists of the use of small boats, underwater demolitions, swimming, diving, beach recons and navigation. In all the maritime training given to Special Forces soldiers is extremely good. It is thought that it is based on the SBS training.

CIVILIAN SPECIAL FORCES
South African Police Special Task Force   Working directly under the Special Branch this is the premier national HRU. Established in 1977, this unit is parachute qualified and trained in fairly sophisticated CQB, assault tactics and other hostage rescue skills.

SP

Special Projects – US Special Forces/CIA Covert action teams.
Special Project (SP)Teams – SAS anti-terrorist units.

SPAIN

MILITARY SPECIAL FORCES
Special Operations Command Rabasa (Alicante),
HQ Company/Experience Unit,
III 'Valencia' Special Operations Group Alicante,
IV 'Ampurdan' Tercio Barcelona and the
XIX 'C.C. Maderal Oleago'
Legion Special Operations Bandera Ronda (Malaga)

The GOE-11 (Grupo Operaciones Especiales) was formed in 1978 and is based just outside Madrid. It is an effective Special Forces formation, largely based on the British SAS, and is a highly trained unit that covers most of the techniques common to similar units, such as HALO (High Altitude Low Opening), airborne insertion, mountain and desert warfare and survival techniques. In addition, combat swimming, combat shooting, marksmanship, hostage rescue, anti-hijacking, prisoner interrogation, prisoner-of-war rescue, intelligence and clandestine operations behind enemy lines play a part in their overall operational capability. While not as well known as its British or US counterparts, the Spanish GEO is a first-rate counter-terrorist unit. It took the opportunity to prove its quality when, in May 1981, 60 members of the GEO assaulted the Central Bank in Barcelona where 24 right-wing terrorists had taken more than 200 hostages. The operation was so skilfully handled that only one hostage was wounded, while one terrorist was killed and ten captured, the others managing to escape among the large number of hostages involved. The GOE has access to a wide range of domestic and foreign weapons, including Israeli 9mm Mini Uzi, German 9mm MP5 sub-machine guns, PSG1 sniper rifles, 5.56mm M16A1 automatic rifles as well as those of standard army issue. A ready action squad is kept on a 30-minute alert at all times. This regular unit is further supported by the GOE-111 and 1V, which are both reserve units and play a similar role to that of the British SAS 21st and 23rd Territorial Regiments to the Regular 22nd. Weapons used include the 9mmR (.357 Magnum) Manurhin MR-73 revolver or the 9mm H&K P9S pistol, but the latter was replaced by the 9mm SIG-Sauer P226 pistol in 2000. They also have the 9mm MP5A3 sub-machine gun, 9mm MP5A5 sub-machine gun, 5.56mm H&K HK53A3 assault carbine, 5.56mm SIG SG552 commando assault carbine (adopted 1999), 5.56mm H&K HK33A2 assault rifle, 5.56mm H&K G41 assault rifle, 5.56mm Santa Bárbara CETME L assault rifle, 7.62mm H&K PSG1 sniper rifle, 7.62mm Sako TRG-21 bolt-action sniper rifle, 7.62mm SIG-Sauer SSG2000 bolt-action sniper rifle, 8.6mm (.338 Lapua Magnum) Sako TRG-41 bolt-action sniper rifle and 12.7mm (.50 BMG) Barrett Model 82A1 sniper rifle.

Spanish Legion – Tercio de Extranjeros The 'Special Operations' role is carried out by the 4th Tercio Alejandro Farnesio (or the 4th Alexander Farnesio Regiment), based in Ronda. It has two Banderas, one a Parachute Element, and another the BOEL or Bandera de Operaciones.

BOEL (Bandera de Operaciones Especiales de la Legion). The battalion consists of about 500 men and is trained and equipped to the highest standards expected of the Spanish Legion. It would operate in wartime in a long-range reconnaissance and patrol (LRRP) role. In addition this unit has specialist training in several different areas: SCUBA/maritime warfare, Arctic and mountain warfare, sabotage and demolitions (BOEL demo experts are very highly regarded), parachute and HALO techniques, long-range reconnaissance, counter-terrorism and CQB (only a very small amount of training is focused on this), vehicle insertion, sniping and SERE. Basic military skills are taught, and forced marches are the norm – which are supposed to make or break a soldier. The assault course is one of the most difficult in the world, with live ammunition used to shoot at a recruit's feet and over their heads while they are trying to complete the course. Recruits who undergo E&E training, usually BOEL soldiers, should expect punishment as this particular course has a reputation for toughness. The men are subjected to brutal beatings and other means of 'torture' and, while no recruit has been killed during this phase, it must be said that it is probably very close to the real thing. The basic weapons used by the BOEL are the same as used by the Legion. These include the 5.56 CETME rifle, the 7.62 Ameli machine gun, the Star 9mm sub-machine gun and pistol, and 40mm grenade launchers. The Spanish Legion has the same camouflage as the rest of the Spanish Army. BRIPAC Recco/Sadda Platoons (Pathfinder/recon) and BRILEG (Brigada Legionaria) – 5th Banderas – 6th Banderas – 10th Banderas are based at Almeria, near Granada in southern Spain.

Marines (Infanteria de Marina)
The *Unidad de Operaciones Especiales, or UOE* is an integral part of the Infanteria de Marina's Tercio de Armada (TEAR), the Spanish Marines' equivalent to the USMC's Fleet Marine Force (FMF), and operates under the direct control of the Spanish admiralty.

The unit was originally formed in 1952 as the Amphibious Climbing Company, an all volunteer force tasked with acting as a first strike amphibious shock force capable of assaulting any coastal target. In 1967, using the US Navy SEALs and British Special Boat Section (SBS) as its guides, the unit was issued a new mandate that included underwater demolition, airborne insertions, and direct action sabotage strikes. The unit's first operational deployment occurred in 1969 when they spearheaded evacuation of Spanish citizens from the former Spanish colony of Equatorial Guinea. In 1985 the unit was redesignated the Comando Anfibio Especial (COMANFES), but it reverted back to its original designation in the early 1990s.

UOE has seen extensive action against Basque ETA terrorists operating inside Spain. They have also been deployed to the former Yugoslavia as part of the Spanish contingent of IFOR and SFOR, providing invaluable assistance to both Spanish and allied commanders. Based in San Fernando, Spain, the unit is currently composed of 169 men.

The unit is outfitted with a wide range of equipment in addition to having access to Spanish military ships, aircraft and submarines, and maintains a small number of Zodiac inflatable boats and Klepper two-man kayaks. Radio communications are provided through the use of UHF, VHF and burst transmission radios. The unit has also acquired a large number of Magellan and Slugger GPS units. Unit divers are equipped with both standard wet and dry diving suits. The unit is also equipped with laser target designators to mark targets for Spanish naval aircraft. The UOE weapons include Llama 82B 9mm with laser aiming devices and sound suppressers. Rifles include the CETME Model L 5.56mm assault rifle, but the HK G-36 5.56mm rifle will soon replace it. Sub-machine-guns consist of the sound-suppressed 9mm Patchett/Sterling Mk. 5 which is usually modified to accept a laser aiming device. Sniper rifles consist of the Mauser SP 66 7.62mm rifle. Machine-guns consist of the locally produced Ameli 5.56mm light machine gun and the US M-60 7.62mm GPMG. The unit has also contracted a local company to produce a specially designed 'commando' dagger to meet its many needs.

CIVILIAN SPECIAL FORCES

GEOS (Grupos Especiales de Operaciones – Counter-Terrorism)   Established in November 1977, with an HQ in Guadalajara, this first-class unit is an exceptionally well-trained and organised anti-terrorist and hostage rescue formation of the National Police and has provided special instructors to similar units in Algeria, Egypt, Ecuador, Guinea, Honduras and Mexico. They operate both within Spain, against such groups as the Basque separatists of ETA, and overseas providing diplomatic security. They have been involved in a number of hostage rescue operations, including the Central Bank of Barcelona siege in May 1981 and the rescue of the singer Julio Inglesias' father from kidnappers. The main operational units are the three OAG (Operational Action Groups) each 30-strong, six five-man commandos of two snipers, one breacher, one diver and one special systems expert. Their weapons include H & K P9S pistol, 7.62mm Mauser 66T and G3SG/1 sniper rifles, H & K MP5K/SD with Sure-Fire flashlights SMG, SIG 5.56mm assault rifles and SIG P226 automatic pistols with laser-sights and built-in flashlights.

UEI (Unidad Especial de Intervencion)   This unit was created on 13 February 1982. Their equipment is the most modern and sophisticated in the Guardia Civil and weapons in use include MP5A3, MP5K and MP5SD, Rugger 44 rifle, UZI SMG, Mauser 66SP and Winchester sniper rifles. They wear the usual black uniform, to blend in with the night missions they perform. The Special Training Centre was created on 6 August 1980 for the selection of the personnel to special courses and their instruction and experimentation with the most advanced equipment, techniques and resources. Only some two per cent of recruits complete the selection process and those that do are then assigned to the headquarters team, one of the ten assault teams or to the specialised hostage negotiation, communications, surveillance, intelligence or technical support teams. UEI has a countrywide responsibility for hostage rescue, kidnappings, aircraft hijackings, prison riots and VIP protection.

SPECIAL FORCES DIRECTORATE – UK

The Special Forces Directorate (Group) was established in 1982 and is in overall command of the SAS, SBS and 14th Intelligence Company along with

Army, Naval and Air Force Special Forces support units, and has its headquarters in the Duke of York Barracks, on Lower Sloane Street, in fashionable Chelsea, Central London.

SPECIAL FORCES – INTO THE 21ST CENTURY

The extraordinary worldwide upsurge of interest in the Special Forces has not been matched by an objective review, or indeed overview, of their actual capabilities. While Special Operations have encouraged the publication of countless books and acres of newsprint, it would be quite fair to say that most of what has been written over the last 25 years has been ill-informed at best, and downright misleading at worst. Former Special Forces soldiers have written their memoirs or given glorified accounts of their combat experiences for profit, irrespective of their historical accuracy. Little attention has been paid to the excellent Special Forces units in countries other than the USA, Britain, Russia and Israel, promoting the perception that only the SAS, Delta Force and the Sayeret Matkal are worthy of the title. However, the truth is somewhat different, as there are units of great ability elsewhere around the world, and indeed centres of excellence from the leading jungle warfare complex in Brazil to the long-range reconnaissance school in Germany that play a highly important role in the development of Special Forces techniques and provide advanced specialist training.

Elite forces, whether true Special Operations formations or highly trained commando units from the US Marines, Royal Marines, French Foreign Legion and the like, will be the first combat units to be committed in any war and in many cases the only such units to see actual fighting. Counter-terrorist, counter-revolutionary warfare, counter-insurgency, counter-narcotics operations and destabilisation campaigns aimed at the internal overthrow of a hostile regime are unsuitable battlefields for heavily equipped conventional forces. The further development of Special Forces with high-technology in the form of missile armed UAVs, real-time satellite surveillance, secure communications, improved mapping and an ever increasing range of specially adapted or designed Stealth helicopters and fixed wing support aircraft, are creating an alternative branch of the armed forces, a virtually independent new service to rank alongside the Army, Air Force and Navy.

Still treated with a degree of suspicion by military traditionalists, the Special Forces, long considered a useful oddity to carry out the operations no other unit wanted to handle, are now a fully fledged and important asset in their own right. They combine the vital flexibility of a small war fighting and clandestine operations capability with a strategic role in a major

291

conventional conflict. They are not, however, supermen nor do they achieve the levels of proficiency and success that Hollywood and the more lurid books would have us believe. The operations that tend to make the news headlines are either spectacular successes or horrendous failures; however, it would be true to say that many Special Operations are limited failures. Rarely do they go to plan, and indeed this is hardly surprising considering the very nature of the tasks and targets involved. Special Forces, their training, weapons and operations are likely to attract increasing attention over the next few months as anti-terrorist campaigns continue or are developed in Afghanistan, the Philippines, Yemen, Somalia, Kashmir, Colombia and the Middle East. The possibility that a future war against Iraq will be heavily dependent on the success of Special Forces operating with Kurdish rebels in a determined attempt to destabilise the Baghdad regime will further highlight the crucial role these elite soldiers are now being called upon to play.

As part of this growing interest in Special Forces operations and capabilities, the range of equipment being developed for their use is increasing in effectiveness and complexity. The very latest developments in optics and imaging require purpose-built headgear, providing not only secure communications with command and surveillance sections equipped with high value imaging sources, but also providing the individual soldier with something akin to a fighter pilot's cockpit or helmet-based HUD (Head Up Display). The soldier is thus able to rely on a threat display based on infrared heat sources and movement detectors, possibly even sound surveillance systems that monitor for noise as limited as the sound of breathing. The Special Forces soldier will be provided with a 360-degree possible threat warning potential; however, it is very doubtful whether there are many experienced personnel or future recruits that will cope well with combat stress along with the technological stress of the flood of information constantly appearing in his earpiece or reflected on the visor of his helmet. Particularly when cold, exhausted and quite rightly scared of making a mistake that may very possibly cost the life of a hostage, a colleague or even his own. Training and screening can only go so far and the Special Forces soldier of the future may find himself at a distinct disadvantage compared to the lightly equipped, fast-moving freedom of a 'warrior' in counter-insurgency and anti-terrorist operations.

An additional portent of the equipment that may be appearing in the early part of the 21st century is the attempt to produce a cross between a new version of the medieval knight and a *Star Wars* Jedi warrior. The US defence industry is developing an 'Exoskeleton' for battlefield soldiers. If the trials earmarked for 2005–06 are successful, it will be the first appearance of full battlefield armour since the seventeenth century. The exoskeleton is a frame that fits over the body. Designed to be strong with increased unit survivability and lethality, the obvious intention is to help the wearer move faster and further with heavier loads and larger weaponry. It wasn't until the First World War that the protective helmet was revived to provide some protection from weather, shrapnel and the occasional glancing bullet. Since then, keeping soldiers light, dry and comfortable has been more vital than loading them up with bulky armour that usually doesn't work. More recently, studies have found that soldiers tend to dump heavy equipment before marching long distances. Currently, soldiers carry about a third of their body weight, one of the main issues for the exoskeleton's designers. The exoskeleton's power plant not only must run for at least a 24-hour stretch, it also must be light, as must be the material that forms the exoskeleton itself. Weight is a deciding factor in whether the exoskeleton ever sees real combat situations. It is unlikely to be a cost-effective use of resources except for limited Special Forces use. An extensive standard equipment list for the exoskeletons has been compiled, and includes a visor that expands the field of vision, as well as devices to provide information about battlefield conditions, co-ordinate other soldiers and decrease friendly-fire casualties. Other possibilities are systems to monitor a soldier's health and wireless communications networks. Helping soldiers march, lift and leap to extraordinary heights and distances will be among the exoskeleton's main attributes. The exoskeleton would have to be physically intuitive, that is, to know when a soldier is walking or running, lifting or bending. One of the 'technological challenges' posed is the development of haptic interfaces, which would allow the exoskeleton to respond to touch to avoid the soldier needing to remove part of the suit to press buttons or to operate small pieces of equipment. There's even a chance that exoskeletons – with their ability to increase carrying loads – could help integrate women into combat situations, in terms of marksmanship and other combat skills, 'Women have proven themselves very equal.' The prevailing argument against women in combat is that most can't meet the job's physical requirements. Exoskeletons could prove the ideal 'equaliser', thus enabling a 130-pound woman to lift, carry and be as effective as a 180-pound man. There are, however, elements in the US Army that want to ditch this enhancement programme, for any fighter in the field is trained not to trust technology as it has the habit of going wrong at vital moments and things break. Visors can block gun sights, the exoskeleton can run out of fuel or become damaged, rendering it little more than a heavy frame. Most battlefield technology must be something that the average high school graduate can operate and repair. The exoskeleton may be used primarily by Special Forces, at least at first. While infantry soldiers go into battle with plenty of support, Special Forces operatives are often on their own and could use the performance boost that powered body-armour would provide. In the end, the multitude of technologies within the system must not only be rugged and dependable, but also work together to assist and protect the human inside without over-stressing the wearer. The challenge will be for the exoskeleton's designers to produce wearable technology with the range of movements that match the human body.

Much of this and other advanced technology will be developed in centres of excellence such as the Massachusetts Institute of Technology research centre, which has been requested to create the uniform of the future. The centre, called the Institute for Soldier Nanotechnologies, will develop new materials that industrial research partners will integrate into futuristic battle suits. The US Special Forces are looking far ahead, perhaps ten to fifteen years, but many of the pieces are already being developed at MIT – including shape-memory alloys to enhance soldiers' strength, advanced sensors to improve their awareness, and microphotonic materials to change their appearance. The centre will combine research efforts from nine departments in the schools of engineering, science and architecture and planning. The centre's goal is to increase the 'protection and survivability' of US soldiers with new technologies. Research at the centre will target six priorities: threat detection, threat neutralisation, automated medical treatment, concealment, enhanced human performance and reduced logistical footprint.

The last priority is particularly important to Special Forces, who may carry up to 100kg. The aim is to ensure that the soldier feels like its only 20kg instead. The institute will give new focus to materials research already underway at the university, including bioengineering research into artificial muscles. The muscle, actually a polymer called polypyrrole, is activated by electricity: when a current is applied, the polymer's accordion-shaped molecules stretch out like human muscles; when the current stops, the polymer contracts. Incorporated into a battle suit, the material could store energy generated by walking, and release it in a super-leap or other feat of strength. And the suit will stop or at least slow bullets. Certain liquids called ferromagnetic fluids change properties, including density, in the presence of an electromagnetic field. A battle suit that contains a similar layer of ferromagnetic fluid capsules could harden into a temporary shield; the same technology could also harden regions of a wounded soldier's suit into a splint or compress.

SPECIAL OPTICS AND OTHER SIGHTING DEVICES

One of the first major problems encountered in a Special Forces operation will often be darkness or very restricted visibility. This can be caused by smoke, the power being cut at some point in an enclosed CQB, or simply by the time of day set for the operation. A wide range of advanced low-light or fast-acquisition optics are now available for use on weapons or attached to helmets or worn as goggles. Snipers may also have to cope with limited visibility or poor light and therefore the effectiveness of light enhancing optics can prove the difference between the success of the mission and indeed life or death for the soldiers and hostages – usually, however, it means only a quicker death for the terrorists involved. For use on assault weapons various Laser-Targeting Devices are used. Mounted on a weapon, when activated, they place a small red-dot on the target at the point where the bullet should strike. In theory this allows for a disabling shot to be fired, an option only usually available to the star of a Hollywood movie. However, in reality it merely allows the sniper or combat shooter to accurately place his first shot to 'take down' his target permanently. It has its uses in rapid-target acquisition scenarios and, indeed, except in bright light conditions, the laser spot can be seen out to ranges of 110yds (100m). With improvements in technology which will allow snipers' scopes to pick up the scatter effect of the laser designator, the range of these laser-aiming devices will increase greatly.

However, it has to be remembered that the laser only marks a target, it does not illuminate it, while Passive Intensifiers do. First Image Intensifiers are used on a variety of assault and snipers' weapons and work off a self-contained power source. These often-bulky devices take the light available and intensify it so that visibility is enhanced several thousand times, though not entirely distortion-free. Second Generation Image Intensifiers tend to be more compact and, while providing the same resolution, have largely solved the distortion problem. Both are known as *Third Generation Image Intensifiers* and can operate with virtually no available light at all.

The Infrared Nite-Site includes an infrared lamp that produces an illuminating beam that is then picked up for display on an integral viewer. Infrared technology measures fraction-of-a-degree differences of heat given off by objects. All living things and many objects, people, animals and recently used equipment, emit heat in the form of infrared radiation. Infrared radiation is a part of the electromagnetic spectrum just below the frequency of red light. Infrared devices read heat by absorbing infrared light, converting it into a grid of video signals and creating a picture the viewer can see. There are drawbacks with this type of device as it does not work well in the diffused light caused by smoke or gas grenades that might be used in a Special Operation or hostage rescue assault. However, these somewhat bulky devices are used regularly by snipers under other less confused conditions, and as they provide their own infrared light such scopes are known as Active Intensifiers. The relatively straightforward Night-Vision Scopes and Goggles are capable of providing accuracy in the range of one inch (25mm) at 220yds (200m) in starlit conditions and are used by every Special Forces or HRU of any competence. The most advanced night scopes/image intensifiers give a light gain in excess of 80,000 times. The light, which is made up of photons, is converted into electrical energy and then accelerated through a thin disk called a microchannel plate. As the converted photons strike a phosphorus screen as electrons, they are perceived through an eyepiece in shades of green.

It is often thought that infrared technology is more effective in winter since contrasts between body temperatures and the external temperatures will increase. However, contrast doesn't necessarily enhance infrared images, and once snow falls, the opposite is true. Infrared systems are very sensitive to white and the images can be compromised if there is snow everywhere. Infrared devices can prove useful to ground troops and pilots for vision, and they can also help detect recent footprints or tyre tracks that are still emitting heat. Even objects that have recently been touched, like a desk or door, can show traces of the recent activity. One of the latest tools now in the hands of Special Forces soldiers is the Lightweight Laser Designator Range-finder, which resembles a video camera and can pick out a target several miles away, day or night, with a variety of sensors, including infrared. It also has a laser that can guide an aircraft or other weapon to a target. Although only a small number have been made so far, hundreds more will be produced over the next year or so. Another combat device entering service with the US Special Forces is the Mini Eyesafe Laser Infrared Observation Set, or MELIOS, which resembles an overstuffed pair of binoculars and can tell the distance to a target from miles away, day or night.

SPECTRE – LOCKHEED AC-130U

The USAF's gunships are one of the most unique ground support platforms in the world. In the waning days of the Second World War, a conclusion was reached that a solution to the accuracy problems fighters and bombers had with delivering ordinance would be to have an aircraft circle the target and shoot at it from the side, rather than make a run and have to squeeze off a short burst at just the right time. It wasn't until the Vietnam War that this concept saw service, first with the AC-47 'Spooky' Gunship. The AC-47 was a converted C-47 (or DC-3) cargo plane with three 7.62mm gatling guns mounted on the left side. The Spooky could put out a phenomenal amount of bullets and looked like it was firing a solid stream of fire, which was as demoralising to the Vietnamese as it was effective at routing their attacks through sheer destruction of forces. The AC-47 had some limitations, however, and the Air Force upgraded the concept by utilising the C-130 airframe and bigger guns. The AC-130A took the Vietnamese skies with two 7.62mm gatling guns, two 20mm vulcan cannons, and two 40mm cannons. Eventually the 7.62mm guns were dropped and one of the 40mms exchanged for a 105mm anti-tank gun, culminating in the AC-130E Spooky II. The AC-130E was a very accurate platform and sported an impressive array of sensors, including LLLTV (Low-Light Level TV) FLIR, and Black

Crow sensor, which could track Soviet-built trucks by the signals given off by their unshielded ignition coils. The AC-130E quickly became king of the night time sky, interdicting trucks and traffic on the famed Ho Chi Minh Trail and defending outposts from massed attacks by Vietnamese and Viet Cong forces. Upgraded again to the AC-130H (newer, more powerful engines and the capability for in-flight refuelling), the Spookys continued to serve the armed forces after the war, taking part in almost every major military action since the Vietnam War, including Grenada, Panama, and the Gulf War. In addition, gunships have been deployed with US forces to such hot spots as Somalia, Haiti and the Balkans. In each case they have been very popular with NATO forces and the US.

Late in the 1980s, however, the Air Force decided that it needed to upgrade the capacities of the AC-130, and the AC-130U project was begun. The weapons were changed somewhat, with the twin 20mm vulcan cannons being dropped in favour of a GAU-12 25mm rotating cannon. At one point it was planned to add the capacity to add hellfire missiles but this was never adopted. However, the biggest change to the AC-130 airframe was in its electronics and avionics. AN AN/APG-180 radar (derived from the same ground and air radar that the Air Force's F-15E uses) was added to allow tracking of targets and rounds for adjustment, as was an ALLTV (All Light Level TV) for operations at night or daytime, when the crew wants to keep their radars off to avoid alerting enemy forces or giving anti-radar missiles a target to home in on. Over 600,000 lines of computer code were written to tie all the weapons systems and sensors together, making the AC-130U second only to the new F-22 fighter in terms of complex airborne weapons systems. With these systems, the AC-130U can operate at night and in bad weather, engaging multiple targets simultaneously. The AN/APG radar allows the targeting crew in the control booth to follow rounds all the way to the ground and make live corrections without having to wait for ground troops to spot and report back. The larger 25mm gun has a longer range and more power, allowing the AC-130U to stay higher and further away from the target and any possible enemy ground fire.

SPECWAR

Special Warfare. Generic term for all forms of Special Warfare operations.

SRI LANKA

MILITARY SPECIAL FORCES

Special Forces Brigade Within each of the two Army Commando Regiments there is a 140-man counter-terrorist unit that provide the primary CT response for Sri Lanka. These units were created in 1980 and are based in Ganemulla, a suburb of Colombo. The units used twenty-man teams, which are split into four five-man assault units. They have received training from Great Britain, India, Israel and Pakistan. Approximately 40 per cent of the regiments are airborne-qualified either in India or in Sri Lanka itself. The two Commando Regiments and two Special Forces Regiments are grouped into the Independent SF Brigade under the command of a brigadier general. It operates in conjunction with the little-known Sri Lankan Special Boat Service, which operates mainly against Tamil Tiger coastal positions and gun-running operations.

Special Task Force   The Special Task Force (STF) was formed in 1983 to operate as a counter-insurgency force in the Batticaloa region. It later assumed the CT mission and, as the most highly trained police organisation, would be the lead unit whenever law enforcement forces react against terrorists. The STF has a strength of over 1,000 men that is split into units in Batticaloa and Amparia Districts, with an additional unit based in Colombo. They have received training from the British SAS as well as the security forces of India.

STABO

Stabilised Tactical Airborne Body Operations. To overcome the length of time taken to extract Special Forces by lowering a ladder from a hovering helicopter when it was impossible for it to land, the US Military Assistance Command Vietnam (MACV) Recondo School, tasked with training soldiers for LRRP missions, sought to overcome the problem with the STABO Rig. A Special Forces Team in danger of being overrun would have little time for a complicated harness, and instead the Recondo School replaced the standard issue webbing on the soldiers' load-bearing equipment or the yoke and belt that carry ammunition pouches. The STABO Rig was therefore worn throughout the mission and was easily snapped onto the suspension rope dropped from the helicopter, using two D-rings sewn onto the shoulders of the rig. Once each soldier was connected to his individual suspension rope the pilot of the helicopter would gain height as rapidly as possible, to pull his 'passengers' out of the jungle canopy before attempting to move forward. The soldiers would stretch out their arms to counteract the natural tendency to spin while waiting to be winched aboard.

STAG

Guard duty.

STANLEYVILLE 1964 – BELGIAN PARA COMMANDOS

Operation Dragon Rouge was one of the most dramatic military missions undertaken during the Cold War. It involved a flight of more than 4,000 miles by USAF C-130s carrying paratroopers of the crack Belgian 1st Para-Commando to rescue hostages who had been held for more than three months in the Congolese city of Stanleyville. The former Belgian colony of Congo, now known as Zaire, was granted independence in 1960. In early 1964, Congolese rebels calling themselves 'Simba' rebelled against the government. The Congolese government turned to the United States for help. In response, the US Strike Command sent JTF LEO, a task force made up of a detachment of C-130s, communications personnel and 82nd Airborne security team, to Leopoldville. By early August 1964, the Congolese, with the help of the LEO force and a group of white mercenaries led by Major Mike Hoare, was making headway against the Simbas. In retaliation, the Simbas began taking white hostages in the areas under their control. They took them to Stanleyville and placed them under guard in the Victoria Hotel. While the situation deteriorated the United States and Belgium worked on a rescue plan. In mid-November the C-130Es and crews of the Tactical Air Command rotational squadron from Pope AFB, NC, were called back to their temporary duty base at Evreux-Fauville AB, France, from missions throughout Europe. On Tuesday evening, 17 November, the crews were told to report to the operations room on the *Margarite* where the aircraft were deployed. The crews were told to rig seats and, just before take-off, each navigator was given an envelope and instructed not to open it until their aircraft had reached 2,000 feet. The instructions these contained required flying to Klinebrogel, a Belgian military airfield outside Brussels. There each aircraft embarked paratroopers wearing red berets, then took off again after being handed another envelope. This time it told them to head south for Moron AB, on the Spanish Mediterranean. At Moron the navigators went into Base Operations where they were given maps and instructions for the next leg of their flight, to Ascension Island in the South Atlantic, where they arrived eighteen hours after leaving France. Leaving Ascension the C-130s on flew across the Atlantic and much of Africa to Kamina, an airfield in the southern Congo.

Operation Dragon Rouge was launched in the early hours of 23 November 1964, when five C-130s took off from Kamina, each with 64 Belgian Red Berets in full combat gear seated on the red nylon troop seats in its cargo compartment. Behind the assault force came seven more Hercules aircraft, with Chalk 12 configured as a hospital ship. The C-130s flew north at high altitude, then dropped down to treetop altitudes to follow the Congo River as they neared the city of Stanleyville. As the sun rose over the horizon a CIA A-26 Invader flown by a Cuban mercenary pilot made a strafing pass over the Stanleyville Sabenas airport. Right behind the A-26 the first C-130 roared low over the runway. As the aircraft came over the field, paratroopers led by Colonel Charles Laurent spilled from the doors on either side of the aircraft. Within seconds, 310 para-troopers were in the air, then landing on the strip of grass alongside the runway. The five jump planes came around for another pass to drop the jumpmasters and bundles of equipment. Forty-five minutes after he jumped, Colonel Laurent reported that the airfield was secure. Five other C-130s roared in for assault landings from their orbit point near Stanleyville. Each aircraft discharged troops and vehicles to join the para-troopers on the ground, then took off again and headed to Stanleyville. Meanwhile, Chalk Six joined Chalk Twelve, the hospital plane on the runway at Stanleyville, to wait until the Belgian para-commandos returned to the airport with the hostages. After leaving the airport, the Belgian rescue team made haste to reach the Victoria Hotel before the Simbas carried out their threats to kill the hostages if a rescue was attempted. Several blocks from the hotel a paratrooper rounded a corner just in time to prevent the Simbas from firing a second volley of shots into the assem-bled hostages, who had evidently been walking towards the airport. Some of the hostages later said they thought the Simba officers intended to turn them over to the Belgians unharmed, but some of the Simbas, who had been drinking and smoking hemp all night the night before, decided to take matters into their own hands. They shot their own officers, then turned their guns on the hostages. They had fired one volley, picking women and children as their targets, and were preparing to fire another when the Red Berets showed up on the scene. At the sight of the Belgians, the Simbas quickly retreated. After more than an hour on the ground at Stanleyville, the C-130 crew finally saw the first hostages coming towards them – they were the most badly injured who had been driven to the airport. For the rest of the day, C-130s and other transports shuttled between Stanleyville and Leopoldville while more than 2,000 people were airlifted out of the city. Several times during the day the field was mortared, and every aircraft was hit by ground fire during their landings and takeoffs. One was hit in a wing fuel tank. The aircraft crew chief whittled a plug from a broom handle and wrapped it with a rag and used it to plug the leak. The airlift continued the next day, but late in the day the Belgians were finally pulled out of the city and flown to Leopoldville. Early the next morning a smaller scale mission designated as Dragon Noir/Black Dragon, freed hostages held at Paulis, a town 225 miles north-west of Stanleyville. The hostages at Paulis had also been roughly treated by the Simbas and an American missionary had been beaten to death during torture.

STAR (PROJECT TALON)

Surface To Air Recovery. The Fulton STAR system or 'Skyhook' allows a Special Forces Team to board a specially modified Project Talon C-130 Hercules transport aircraft as it passes overhead at around 130 knots. On the approach flight two waterproof bags are dropped containing the STAR equipment. This includes a balloon, 500 feet of tubular nylon lift-line, two fibreglass bottles filled with 650 cubic feet of helium gas, helmets, overalls, self-adjusting harnesses and protective hoods for head and neck. The inflated balloon is connected via the lift-line to the soldiers' harness and as the balloon rises to the correct height the first soldier sits down facing the approaching aircraft. As the Talon C-130 makes its run, a wide Y-shaped fork on its nose is deployed and at an altitude of between 370ft (120m) and 430ft (140m) the fork makes contact with the line just below the balloon and locks tight. The soldier is pulled into the air and quickly winched aboard. This uncomfortable and frightening procedure is repeated until the team has been extracted. A soldier can be lifted out of a clearing only 10ft (3m) in diameter surrounded by 50ft (18m) high trees, or longer heavy-duty lift-lines can accommodate multiple pick-ups.

STEN GUN

The classic simple solution to a major problem: how to rearm quickly and cheaply a shattered British Army following the hurried evacuation at Dunkirk in 1940 and in the middle of a major German bombing campaign. Variously known as the 'Woolworth gun' and the 'plumbers' delight', the early Sten guns – the name derived from the initial letters of the designers names, R. V. Shepperd and H. J. Turpin and the first two letters of the Enfield plant where it was developed – certainly had their faults when they first entered service in 1941. However, by the end of the Second World War many millions of Sten sub-machine guns had been built and were widely used by both Special Forces and by virtually every Resistance movement in Europe and the Far East. It was also built in Canada and copied by Germany, China, Argentina, Belgium and Indonesia. The Sten was indeed a triumph, for though shoddy and crude, it worked. It could stand up to more ill-treatment than practically any other weapon of its type. The Sten would still work after being dropped in mud or stamped on. It could be taken to pieces in seconds and the various parts fitted into a handbag or distributed among several pockets and indeed served the Resistance fighters of Europe very well. Chambered for 9mm, it had a 32-round box magazine and a cyclic rate of 540–575rpm. The most deadly variant for clandestine work was the Mk11S, designed for the Special Forces and fitted with a silencer so effective that the only sound heard was the clicking of the bolt. It was unlikely to attract attention beyond a range of 20yds (19m), but was only used on semi-automatic to avoid burning out the silencer. Late models of the Sten are still in use in 2002, although not with any of the major Armed Forces.

STINGERS – MANPORTABLE AIR DEFENCE

This US-made Surface to Air, shoulder-launched or light-vehicle-mounted missile is infrared homing (heat-seeking). Widely used around the world by leading Special Forces, it was also supplied by the United States to its Afghan allies during the Soviet invasion. Some of these missiles are believed to have fallen into Al Qa'ida's hands and then been passed on to other international terrorist groups. It is a highly capable weapon and fine example of a second generation missile, now being replaced by more advanced third and even fourth generation systems. The Hughes FIM-92 Stinger is 35.5lbs (15.66kg) fully armed, with a length of 5.5ft (1.5m), a range of up to five miles (1 to 8km) and an altitude of 10,000ft (3.046km) at supersonic speeds. The Fire and Forget passive Infrared Seeker (homes in on the heat from the engine) has been improved to allow head-on interception and this lethal little weapon can be reloaded and fired every three to seven seconds.

STIRLING, DAVID – THE PHANTOM MAJOR

When the Second World War started, Stirling joined the Scots Guards as a subaltern, but soon volunteered for 8 Commando or 'Layforce', named after its commander Captain Robert Laycock. At this time all Special Forces elements were viewed by the military establishment as, at best, of limited value. 'Private Armies', as they were disdainfully known, were given little support in quality men and material, and were undertrained and overcriticised. David Stirling got his first taste of this in Layforce, which was dismantled in all but name, prior to arriving in North Africa. Fortunately for the British army, David Stirling saw the real possibilities for Special Operations behind enemy lines. He firmly believed that a group of highly trained, highly motivated soldiers could wreak havoc on enemy supply lines, bases and morale. He joined forces with Australian Jock Lewes, an officer with the Welsh Guards, and this meeting would prove to be the nucleus of the Special Air Service Regiment. Lewes, an amazing adapter and improviser, had scrounged a supply of 50 parachutes, which at first seemed to be the best mode of delivery for troops to get behind the lines. He and Stirling started to jump immediately, and the result was at once disastrous and fortuitous. Disaster struck when Stirling jumped from the old Valentia aircraft, which was most unsuited for the job, and his parachute snagged on the tail of the aircraft. Stirling was injured in the fall, and ended up spending two months in the hospital. While uncomfortable, he was now able to devote his time to planning the new unit, and upon his release from the hospital Stirling headed straight for the High Command where he persuaded the Deputy Commander Middle East, General Ritchie, to consider his plan. Ritchie read Stirling's pencil-written notes and eventually presented the plans to the C-in-C Auchinlek. Both generals saw the opportunity to use the new unit immediately, as an offensive was planned for the near future. The new unit was to consist of 66 men from Layforce, including seven officers and many NCOs. This independent command was to be called L Detachment, Special Air Service Brigade. This was done to make the Germans think it was larger than it actually was. Stirling's dream had become reality.

Thus began an unparalleled adventure in North Africa. Rommel's Afrika Korps had arrived, Britain's forces were being pushed back to Egypt by the Desert Fox, and supplies to the Allies were running short as Malta lay under siege. The first mission for the SAS (17 November 1942) was to jump behind enemy lines and gather intelligence, as well as harassing and tying up German forces while the British mounted the offensive. It was a disaster. Because morale was high and the troops well trained, Stirling decided to jump despite terrible conditions. Many men never made it back, for of the 66 who went only 22 returned. While disastrous, Stirling and his officers Lewes and Paddy Mayne learned much from the experience. One of the most important innovations came from Jock Lewes, who was challenged to devise a bomb small enough to be carried which would both explode and ignite when detonated, to put a plane out of action. The Lewes bomb was created out of oil and thermite. It would explode on top of a wing and ignite the fuel within. It weighed one pound, and one man could carry enough to decimate a squadron of planes. The focus now changed from aircraft insertion to overland. The Long-Range Desert Group, a motorised reconnaissance unit, would pick up the SAS raiders, circle south and west then north to enemy territory, drop off their cargo and rendezvous at a specified point at a predetermined time. The SAS would walk to their destination, usually an airfield, carrying minimal weapons and supplies. They moved mostly at night and lay up during the day to avoid German and Italian air and foot patrols. The most successful of all the raiders was Paddy Mayne, an Irish rugby player whose fierce determination and courage accounted for dozens of planes blown on the tarmac. At one point, out of Lewes bombs, he ripped out an aircraft control panel with his bare hands. He is a legend in the regiment today, embodying the rugged individualism sought when recruiting Special Forces personnel. As the SAS successes mounted, and dozens of aircraft were destroyed on the ground, the Germans started to take notice. Their activities caused Hitler to issue a shoot to kill order in which he stated 'These men are dangerous.' Accordingly, the German army stepped up security and patrols in order to intercept the Raiders. This caused a change in tactics – along with the acquisition of several Jeeps. The SAS could now mount their own mobile operations. The Jeeps were equipped with twin Vickers K machine guns, and became a formidable weapon, perfect for the long, rugged journeys they encountered. The Jeeps, which formed the nucleus for mounted raids on enemy airfields would enter onto the tarmac, fan out and throw a sustained series of fire, consisting of tracers, at the aircraft, causing them to be torn to shreds and ignite. This caused so much confusion that casualties for the SAS tended to be light, and they could slip away back into the desert. These operations lost quite a few Jeeps due to enemy fire or breakdowns, but the cost was insignificant compared to the amount of damage inflicted. Eventually, disaster struck when David Stirling was captured and imprisoned at Colditz Castle POW camp, where he was to spend the rest of the war. His brother Bill ended up commanding 2 SAS, while Paddy Mayne took over Stirling's position as commander of 1 SAS. The war in North Africa ended, and Allied attention turned to Europe. SAS units became useful for establishing bases in France, far behind enemy lines. They were dropped in the standard squads of four men with limited supplies. Often they would contact Resistance groups and arrange for drops of supplies, weapons and communications equipment. The SAS teams would implement training and carry out raids on German supply depots, rail-lines and strategic positions. Reconnaissance was the most important function as the Allies prepared for Operation Overlord, the D-Day Invasion. The SAS succeeded in tying up thousands of German troops who otherwise would have been used against the Allies in Normandy. These actions were perilous for the men involved and on one occasion two dozen SAS were rounded up and, the evidence suggests, tortured and executed in a particularly unpleasant fashion. The SAS remained in Europe until the end of the war, taking part in the hunt for SS and Gestapo who tried to hide or slip away in the chaos. Though the SAS was disbanded after the war, a reserve unit was maintained and a regular unit reformed in 1952.

STIRLING LINES

The SAS Depot in Hereford, named after Colonel David Stirling founder of the Special Air Service.

STORMTROOPERS

The innovative new German stormtrooper tactics of 1918 were very successful and foreshadowed the many Special Forces and Commando techniques and tactics of the Second World War, but their very success contributed to German defeat. The stalemate on the Western Front was based on the growing invulnerability of the trench system reinforced with mines, barbed wire and machine gun strongpoints backed by mass artillery.

The British defence system was based on a captured German manual. The British, however, copied the letter and not the spirit of the German system. The British believed the machine gun supported the infantry, while the Germans more realistically believed the infantry supported the machine gun. The new defence system had a Forward Zone manned by one-third of the troops. Two to three miles back was the Battle Zone, of a depth of 2,000 to 3,000 yards. One-third of the troops and two-thirds of the artillery was stationed here. The Rear Zone was four to eight miles behind the Battle Zone. This system failed to be as efficient as the German system, which used two-thirds of the troops for counter-attacks. France was at the end of its manpower, so the artillery was their most important arm, and was protected by the infantry. The French wisely held their front lightly and kept most troops in the main position out of artillery range. The new German Stormtroopers (Stosstrupp) or Sturmabteilung (SA) were part of the Hutier or Infiltration Tactics of 1918. They had in fact first been used experimentally in 1915, but tactics were still primitive and their use abandoned. Now groups of three, one with a large shield, and two on either side, would toss grenades to spearhead attacks adopting General Oskar von Hutier's tactics of massed artillery and infiltration at Riga in Russia. For the new offensives in France, the rigid chain of command was made more flexible. Army commanders could direct the actions of battalions, thereby making corps and brigades used only for reinforcement and supply. Because of the loss of non-commissioned officers in 1917, all divisions were not converted into assault divisions. Divisions were categorised as assault or trench divisions and given different priorities of supply. Assault divisions were given Stormtroopers and four weeks' training in mobile warfare. The elite Stormtroopers were in top condition and were commanded by non-aristocrats, thereby increasing their camaraderie. Each offensive was preceded by the concentration of vast numbers of troops. In Operation Michael, 69 German divisions were massed against 32 British divisions, and in some places the British were outnumbered four to one. In the Lys Offensive, nine German divisions attacked three British divisions. Twenty-two divisions were massed against five in the Second Battle of the Marne. Artillery was massed in levels never before seen. In 1915 at Loos, artillery pieces averaged one per 60 yards. In Operation Michael, one gun was placed on average every twelve yards. Artillery bombardments were brief and shocking. The enemy artillery was first eliminated with shells and poison gas. Enemy headquarters, communication centres and supply depots were targeted. Forward trenches were then devastated, machine gun posts being prime targets. Trenches of the Battle Zone were then bombarded. The British had massed 30 per cent of their troops on the front line. Instead of the desired effect of stopping the attack with overwhelming firepower, the troops were annihilated with artillery fire. In the sector of the XVIII Corps, only 50 of 10,000 front line troops survived the bombardment and subsequent attack. The Stormtroopers attacked immediately after the bombardment. Wire cutters and explosives engineers created gaps in the barbed wire belts. Grenade throwers, flame throwers, machine gunners and mortar crews infiltrated enemy positions. Three or four waves of infantry followed. The attacking troops had no fixed objectives and left pockets of resistance for supporting troops to deal with. The Stormtroopers carried with them the first widely used sub-machine gun, the MP-18. The new sub-machine gun was light and easy to handle, and had much greater firepower than a rifle. Infiltrating troops often advanced beyond artillery range and left their flanks vulnerable. Most artillery was too bulky to be brought forward in the attack, so light trench mortars and machine gunners protected the flanks. The great German offensives were also supported by air power. In Operation Michael, 730 German planes were massed against 579 Allied planes. Operation Michael was a great success and indeed formed the basis of the Blitzkrieg tactics of some twenty years later. The Germans penetrated 40 miles, took 975 guns, and inflicted 300,000 casualties. However, the Allies eventually found antidotes to the new tactics.

On 15 July 1918, the French Fourth Army was attacked by three German armies. The front was held lightly and the main resistance was met two to three miles back. The French kept their command posts and ammunition depots beyond enemy artillery range. The night before the attack, the German assembly points were bombarded. The French totally defeated a major German offensive by the clever use of improved tactics, and the sagging morale of the German troops was made worse after the ferocious counter-attack of 8 August 1918. The Allied advance did not stop until 11 November 1918 when the Armistice was signed. However, the principle of the Stormtrooper had firmly established the techniques that would later form the basis of many Special Forces operations, and the spirit of the Stormtrooper mentality was to provide Adolf Hitler with his first paramilitary force, the SA or 'Brownshirts', until 1934 when in the 'night of the long knives' its growing power was destroyed by Hitler as he had now begun to see it as a challenge to his authority.

STRAPHANG

To operate with a team other than one's own.

STROBE GUN

A divisionary device occasionally used by Special Forces, and though it has a severe disorientating effect usually causing the target to turn away, the effects are only temporary.

STUN GRENADE/MUNITIONS

Widely used by Hostage Rescue Units/Teams (HRU/T) replacing the old 'Thunderflash' and made famous during the GSG-9 operation in Mogadishu and by the SAS in the Iranian Embassy siege, the modern 'Flash-Bang' was actually developed by the SAS. These all-important weapons are now standard SAS issue when deployed on Counter-Terrorist duties. Upon detonation they attack the senses with an extraordinarily loud single 'Bang' or multiple detonations of 200+ decibels and an intense and a blinding white flash of over 2 million candle power; they may also continue to burn brightly for up to fifteen seconds or more. The effect upon the unprepared target is to disorientate, deafen and temporarily blind, providing just enough opportunity for the assault unit or hostage rescue team to force an entry and fire enough rounds to disable or kill the terrorists. The important advantage of the 'Flash-Bang' is the absence of fragmentation, which is potentially lethal to the hostages and the assault team in the enclosed conditions so often associated with this type of operation. The latest of these 'diversionary' devices also now produces much less smoke.

SUDAN

MILITARY SPECIAL FORCES

144th Counter-Terrorist Unit (CTU) – 9th Airborne Brigade This is the prime national HRU capability. Established in 1980 it has received assistance and training from the SAS, Egyptian and US Special Forces in basic hostage rescue, CQB, assault, explosive entry, sniping and other skills. Their weapons include MP5 SMG and both G3 and AK assault rifles. The G3A3ZF is the unit's sniper rifle.

Special Forces Company – 9th Airborne Brigade This unit has a limited anti-terrorist role and is considered to be reasonably proficient. The unit successfully carried out the rescue of four white missionaries from the South Sudanese Liberation Front rebels on 8 July 1983, but has proved notably less successful in dealing with anti-government insurgency and Islamic terrorist groups. The US has expressed impatience at the Special Forces inability to seriously disrupt Al Qa'ida groups reportedly operating in the Sudan following the attacks of 11 September 2001.

SURINAM

MILITARY SPECIAL FORCES

One small Military Police/HRU Company. Trained by the Dutch Special Forces and would receive their active support in a hostage rescue crisis.

SURVEILLANCE – OPERATIONAL TERMINOLOGY

For clarity and rapid dissemination of relevant intelligence over a radio net, Special Forces surveillance teams around the world use the same or similar terminology as the examples listed here and commonly used by both the SAS and 14th Intelligence Company of the British Army.

ALPHA (Location), BRAVO (Targeted individual), CHARLIE (Vehicle); Often used as radio designations. As an example BRAVO-3, the target of surveillance, could arrive at ALPHA-4, a fellow terrorist's home, driving CHARLIE-1, a friend's vehicle as his own CHARLIE-3 vehicle had been left at the target's home or ALPHA-3. The use of such designations can avoid confusion, particularly if radio reception is poor.

DELTA through to ZULU. Reserved for call-signs for individual members of the surveillance operation whether on foot, in a vehicle or airborne. The exception is FOXTROT which is only used to describe an operative on foot, i.e. DELTA is Foxtrot towards BRAVO-3.

CLICK/DOUBLE-CLICK. If conditions do not permit normal conversation over the net, then a single CLICK for no or DOUBLE CLICK for yes can permit a reasonable level of communication.

COMPLETE. Meaning 'Inside'. BRAVO-3 is complete ALPHA-4 or even the surveillance operative may tell control as he gets into his vehicle 'I am complete.'

CONTACT. Visual contact with target, usually referring to an armed terrorist.

COLOUR CODE/TWO DIGIT NUMBER Used to designate particular topographical sites and roads/junctions within a target area for rapid description over the radio net. As an example: BRAVO-3 is mobile from BROWN One Four towards RED Six Two.

TO HAVE. To have visual contact with a target, i.e. DELTA has BRAVO-3.

INTENDING. Likely to make a turn to the left or right on foot or in a vehicle.

MOBILE. Travelling by vehicle.

OFF. Lost visual contact or having passed target on to another operator.

TWO UP, THREE UP. The number of targets in a vehicle.

DEFINITE/POSSIBLE/NEGATIVE. Refers to the probability that you have/have not acquired your designated target.

SHORTS/LONGS. Hand-guns/rifles.

TO STAKE OUT. Box surveillance of a target's likely routes in and out of a particular area.

STANDBY. Used to warn a surveillance team of a significant movement by the target.

ZERO. The radio call sign of the base station in any surveillance operation.

SWAT

Acronym: Special Weapons and Tactics. Police Special Forces Teams trained in combat shooting, anti-terrorist and hostage rescue techniques.

SWEDEN

MILITARY SPECIAL FORCES

Army Special Forces Corps
Formed in 1952 and comprised of both Intelligence and Special Operations units.

Fallskarmsjagare (Parachute Ranger Coy) (CADRE) The Swedish Army's Parachute Jaeger (Ranger) School (Armans fallskarmsjagare-FSJ) is the organisation responsible for training the elite airborne units (Fallskarmjagare) of the Swedish Army. The school's original cadre consisted of twelve officers who received airborne training at Fort Benning, Georgia, and RAF Brize Norton in England. Upon returning to Sweden the men established Sweden's first parachute training course at Karlsborg in February 1952. Soon after opening, the school's curriculum expanded to include Ranger and LRRP training for new recruits. Upon completion of their training the new Rangers will be posted to one of several independent Ranger platoons. Ranger platoons are divided into three separate six-man patrols. Within each patrol each man will have a speciality, such as demolitions, communications, sniping or intelligence. Patrols are armed with a variety of weapons including the AK5 5.56mm assault rifle, the AK5B (AK5 with scope), the AK5C (AK5 with M-203 40mm GL), the 5.56mm Belgian Minimi LMG.

Navy
Bassak-erhetskompaniet–Naval Counter SOF Attack (CADRE) Sweden's long, isolated coastline and harbours have long been a favourite target of Soviet, and now Russian, intelligence services. Throughout the Cold War, Soviet naval SPETSNAZ units, operating tracked midget submarines, routinely penetrated Swedish territorial waters. To counter the threat posed by these incursions, the Swedish Navy formed a new specially trained security unit in 1992. Known as Bassakerhetskompaniet, or Bassak (Naval Counter SOF Unit), the unit is tasked with defending Swedish naval installations, and protecting ships against attack by enemy SOF units. The Bassak company consists of 134 men and twelve dogs, which are subdivided into an HQ and support platoon, two SakJakt (Counter SOF Ranger) platoons, and two Sakbevakning (Counter SOF guard) platoons. SakJakt platoons are composed of six four-man squads. Each four-man squad will have one dog assigned to it. SakJakt teams are composed of the following: squad leader,

dog handler, support man (handles the squad's heavy weapons, and is cross trained as a boat coxswain), medic (also trained as the team's driver and marksman/sniper).

Attack Dykarna–Attack Divers (CADRE)   The Swedish Navy's Attack Divers are an elite unit of combat swimmers, similar in function to the US Navy SEALs or the British SBS. Attack Divers are tasked with performing intelligence-gathering missions, acting as forward observers for aircraft and naval gunfire, conducting direct action sabotage missions, and other Special Operations missions. Prospective Attack Divers are drawn from the ranks of the Swedish Navy's elite Kustjagare (Coastal Rangers) units. The training lasts approximately ten months. During training recruits will learn the use of open- and closed-circuit diving systems, small unit tactics, underwater demolition, sabotage, dive medicine, combat survival, and various other combat-related skills. Attack Divers are attached to the Recon platoon of each Amphibian Battalion HQ Company. The Divers are organised into an eighteen-man section, which is sub-divided into three six-man squads. Within each squad each diver will be assigned a specific task, such as commander, deputy commander, demolitions, sniper, signaller or small-boat coxswain. They have access to all standard Swedish military small arms and are extensively equipped with night vision equipment. For transport they use inflatable rubber boats, Klepper kayaks, speedboats and Swedish Naval aircraft. Due to the fact they operate in an extremely cold environment, Attack Dykarna are equipped with specially designed 'dry suits' to help them maintain their body temperature while in the water.

CIVILIAN SPECIAL FORCES

Ordningspolisens Nationella Insatsstyrka (ONI – National Security Police Task Force) (ACTIVE)   Based in Stockholm its personnel spend part of each year in ONI and part in the Stockhom SWAT team. ONI training includes assault tactics, counter-terrorism, hostage rescue and, in addition, they have a negotiation team that attempts to first gain the captives' release through peaceful means. It trains with the SAS, GSG-9 and Sayeret Matkal in particular, and receives additional training in parachuting, SCUBA, small boat operations and combat swimming. Transportation of ONI members is carried out by the Swedish Air Force, or by other branches of the Services. ONI has 48 members divided into five groups: two Assault Groups, one Intelligence/Liaison Group, one Sniper Support Group and one Command and Control Group. The assault groups are mainly armed with various HK MP5 models and Sig-Sauer P226s for personal defence. The sniper support group uses the PSG 90 7.62mm. Personal body-armour is mostly from indigenous Swedish origin and has been battle proven in Bosnia. Weapons used include the 9mm SIG-Sauer P228 pistol, 9mm H&K MP5A3 sub-machine gun, 5.56mm H&K HK53A2 assault carbine, 7.62mm Accuracy International AWP bolt-action sniper rifle, 7.62mm H&K PSG1 sniper rifle and 18.5mmR (12-gauge) Remington Model 870P pump-action shotgun.

Forsvarsmaktens Sarskilda SkvddsGrupp – SSG Special Protection Group (ACTIVE) The SSG is a small, hand-picked force formed in the early 1990s and organised to protect important buildings and act as bodyguards to the Supreme Commander and other important officers. The all-officer force is highly educated and trained in parachuting, diving, amphibious operations, advanced marksmanship and bodyguard service. They can be transported anywhere within Sweden to accomplish their mission and, if necessary, can rescue Swedish personnel caught behind enemy lines.

SSG is the Swedish equivalent of the US Delta or British SAS. In addition to the Ranger training that most unit members have already received, they will receive training in static line parachuting, HAHO and HALO parachuting, combat diving and small boat operations, explosives handling, advanced marksmanship, close quarters combat, sniping and VIP protection.

SWITZERLAND

MILITARY SPECIAL FORCES
Bundesheer (Federal Army)
Fernspah – Para-Grenadiers is an LRRP force established in 1972, FSK-17 (name changed from Fallschirm-Grenadiers in 1980). This is the main Swiss Special Forces unit and is formed from a company of the Parachute Grenadiers. Around 100-strong, it is divided into three sub-units of equal size and a small HQ ten-strong. They are trained to a very high degree of proficiency in combat shooting, anti-terrorist and hostage rescue techniques, HAHO/HALO parachuting and even pioneered the 'tactical diamond' technique where all four members of a tactical assault team exit the aircraft together and land as a team. Weapons used include the 9mm SIG P 75 pistol (P220), 9mm H&K MP5A3 sub-machine gun, 5.56mm SIG Stew 90 assault rifle (SG550) and 18.5mmR (12-gauge magnum) Remington Mzgw 91 pump-action shotgun (Model 870 Police Magnum).

CIVILIAN SPECIAL FORCES
Canton Tactical Units Switzerland does not field a national Counter-Terrorist unit. Instead, these duties are handled by the special tactical units (similar to SWAT teams found in US cities) from the local police forces of the various 'cantons'. These teams vary significantly in size, though manpower in the major Swiss units generally numbers approximately 40 to 50. It is assumed that one of the top two such units, the 'Stern' unit from Bern and the 'Enzian' unit from Zurich, might be called on to deal with a major terrorist incident.

This was borne out in 1984 when disguised members of the 'Stern' unit successfully rescued 62 hostages from a seized Air France 737. The unit from the Ticino canton is also regarded very highly, and shares close ties with the Italian NOCS. The training of Swiss Tactical Units involves about half of its time being devoted to basic CT and the rest to general police work. Weapons used include SIG P6 and P226 pistols, 9mm H&K MP5SD silenced SMG, 7.62mm H&K33 assault rifles and the Steyr SSG 7.62mm sniper rifle.

SYRIA

MILITARY SPECIAL FORCES

Special Units – Al-Wahdat al-Khassa The Counter-Terrorist capability is provided by one of the Special Forces Regiments, and believed to be known as Al Saiqa. This unit is trained in a whole range of Special Operation techniques, combat shooting, hostage rescue, anti-hijacking, intelligence-gathering, clandestine operations and long-range reconnaissance and patrol. In addition Al Saiqa has trained in recent years with the SPETSNAZ in Russia and is also believed to have a small number of ex-East Germans and non-Israeli Jews attached to its operations section. It is known to have operated covertly with some success within Lebanon, Jordan, the Palestinian areas on the West Bank of the Jordan and, on a very few occasions, within Israel itself. It has the pick of standard issue arms from the Syrian Army, but also has access to foreign weapons, often acquired on the black market, so that it is not unusual to see US 5.56mm M16A1 automatic rifles, Israeli 9mm Uzi, Italian 9mm Beretta BM12 and German MP5K silenced sub-machine guns being used for clandestine operations. The first attempt to create a viable Special Forces capability took place in 1958 when the 1st Parachute Battalion was raised. Interest in such units increased over the years until, in the opening moves of the 1973 Yom Kippur war with Israel, a daring helicopter-borne raid by the Syrian 82nd para-commando (Special Forces) battalion successfully captured the Israeli observation site on Mount Hermon overlooking the approaches to the Golan Heights. Syrian Special Forces had come of age and their usefulness was further confirmed during the Israeli invasion of Lebanon in 1982, when a Syrian commando battalion ambushed an IDF armoured unit at Sultan Yakoub and inflicted heavy casualties, both in men and tanks.

Special Forces Command with headquarters in Damascus that now controls a large number of units, including the 14th Special Forces Division (HQ Damascus, deployed near Golan, Mount Hermon and in the Lebanon) 35th, 46th, 54th and 55th Regiments largely tasked to ensure the safety of the regime both in peacetime and during any future conflict with Israel. Trained as both elite infantry and as commandos for Special Operations, these troops are heavily armed and have access to heavy armoured vehicles and modern missiles. In a more traditional role are ten Special Forces Regiments including the 41st, 44th, 53rd, 82nd and 804th. These are commando-trained and a number are permanently based in Lebanon where they have had some limited success against Israeli forces in the Beka'a valley. Other tasks include protection of Syria's long borders and the suppression of civil unrest throughout the country. The Syrians will continue to make considerable use of Special Forces and this is one of the areas that has seen the new strategic alliance between Syria and Iraq begin to take shape, with both nations beginning to share both training and intelligence.

TAIL (TAIL END CHARLIE)

The soldier who walks last in formation and covers the rear, or in SAS terms the soldier positioned at the rear of a four- or eight-man patrol as lookout.

TAIWAN

MILITARY SPECIAL FORCES
Airborne Special Operations HQ Pintung
62nd Airborne Special Force Brigade HQ Taoyuan (north)
71st Airborne Special Forces Brigade HQ Pingtung (south)
Four Special Forces (Raider) Groups (battalion-sized)
T'ai-chung Special Forces Airborne Warfare Training Centre (central)
These units are trained both in limited airborne operations, as elite infantry and finally in the assault commando role. However, each brigade also has a company trained for long-range reconnaissance and patrol or LRRP. These units would operate behind the lines of the landing zones of any communist Chinese airborne invasion, or the bridgehead of an amphibious invasion. They are also equipped with the pick of standard issue weapons and other equipment. In addition, these LRRP companies train on a regular basis with similar US Army units. The Taiwanese Special Forces were originally created in 1957 with the formation of the 1st SF Group, and are trained for the eventuality of clandestine intelligence operations on the mainland of China. In the event of a serious deterioration in relations between the two states it would be vitally important for the Taiwan forces to have a greater understanding of Chinese activities. Information on the overall capabilities and large-scale military movements can often be gathered successfully by either SIGINT (signals intelligence) or from satellite surveillance. However, the insertion of deep cover units from the offshore islands of Kinmen (Quemoy) or Matsu, or by the Taiwanese Navy, would certainly be within their known ability and would play a vital part in obtaining the sensitive information needed to predict Chinese intentions. Taiwanese Special Forces

are also known to have stocks of suitable documents, uniforms and standard Chinese weapons to equip such units, either to gather intelligence or to carry out a spoiling attack with sabotage operations against Chinese forces preparing for an assault on Taiwan or the offshore island garrisons.

In this context, it should be noted that the only other major Special Forces units are the *Long Range Amphibious Reconnaissance Commandos* trained for pathfinder operations, as para-commando, in underwater warfare and in the beach reconnaissance and sabotage role against enemy bridgeheads. This unit, though not strictly part of the army, is very similar to the USMC Recon (Reconnaissance) and receives regular training at USMC bases. The remaining Special Forces formation of note is the *Para-Frogman Assault Unit*. Very similar in training, equipment, organisation and operational techniques to the US SEALs. This unit can parachute into the sea in full SCUBA gear, and carry out underwater reconnaissance or sabotage missions against Chinese coastal positions or warships. Both these units also have a distinct anti-terrorist role. The Taiwanese Army has a relatively restricted Special Force capability, partly because there is only a limited scope for sabotage missions by the Communist Chinese, no domestic extremism and little interest from international terrorists. The small scale of potential insurgency from the native Taiwanese against the Nationalist Chinese who fled to the island in 1949 has yet to make any serious impact.

Marines
Special Operations Unit Around 100-strong and trained in combat swimming, SCUBA, airborne and intelligence operations.

CIVILIAN SPECIAL FORCES
Thunder Squad of the National Police The National Police 'Thunder Squad' are a highly trained SWAT-type unit established in 1985 to conduct high-risk arrests and other dangerous law enforcement duties. This 200 man group is organised into small, four-man elements, three of which make up an operating group.

TAJIKISTAN

MILITARY SPECIAL FORCES
One Special Forces Airborne Brigade, which still maintains close links with the Russian Army and the SPETSNAZ in particular.

One SF Anti-Terrorist and HRU detachment (battalion), this unit has received US equipment and weapons, and now co-operates closely with US Special Forces, particularly since Operation Enduring Freedom was launched against the Taliban in Afghanistan in late 2001.

TAKUR GHAR – AFGHANISTAN MAY 2002 – SEALs

The fog and friction of war ruled the day when seven American Special Operations forces died on 3–4 March 2002 on an isolated mountaintop in Afghanistan in an action now called the battle at Takur Ghar. It took place during Operation Anaconda, when US military command sent a Special Operations reconnaissance element to an area of key terrain. Reaching the 10,000-foot mountaintop, the team's assault helicopter took immediate ground fire. As it lifted out of the hot zone, a US Navy SEAL, Petty Officer 1st Class Neil Roberts, was lost out of the back. In the course of the next two hours, the Special Operations team went back to rescue their mate, who had continued to fight until his death. A more substantial rapid reaction force then went in and with the help of close-air support secured the ridge.

According to an executive summary of the battle, Takur Ghar was the most intense firefight American Special Operators have been involved in since 18 US Army Rangers were killed in Mogadishu, Somalia, in 1993. US commanders of Operation Anaconda wanted to insert Special Operators on the crest of the mountain. They reasoned the area would serve as a great observation point. 'Unfortunately, the enemy thought so too,' the battle report stated. Al Qa'ida had fighters perfectly positioned to fire on helicopters and troops operating in the valley below. An MH-47E helicopter with the call sign 'Razor 03' was to airlift SEALs and an air force combat controller to the mountaintop. As it neared landing, it took intense enemy fire. A rocket-propelled grenade struck the aircraft and machine-gun fire severed hydraulic and oil lines aboard it. The pilot immediately applied power to get out of the area. Petty Officer 1st Class Neil Roberts, a Navy SEAL, slipped on the fluid and fell five to ten feet onto the snow below the aircraft. The helicopter flew out of the area and crash-landed about seven kilometres away. Roberts was alone on top of the mountain. 'Based on forensic evidence subsequently gathered from the scene, we believe Roberts survived the short fall from the helicopter, likely activated his signalling device, and engaged the enemy with his squad automatic weapon. He was mortally wounded by gunfire as the (enemy) closed in on him,' the report said. Another helicopter – 'Razor 04' – picked up the SEALs and an air force top sergeant, John Chapman – a combat controller – and went in to save Roberts. The helicopter took fire but was able to deliver the team. The SEALs and Chapman approached the last known position of Roberts, but were fired upon. As they manoeuvred, they engaged the Al Qa'ida fighters and killed several. Chapman was killed and some of the SEALs were wounded. The SEALs decided to disengage. An Air Force AC-130 gunship provided covering fire as the SEALs moved down the mountain and requested immediate assistance. The mission fell to the US Army Ranger

Quick Reaction Force based in Gardez. The 23-man team loaded onto two MH-47E helicopters and headed to the area. Communications breakdowns, however, caused the Rangers to believe the SEALs were still atop the mountain, and that is where one helicopter went. As the chopper came in, Al Qa'ida fighters shot it down with RPGs and heavy machine-gun fire. Door gunner Army Sergeant Phil Svitak was killed and both pilots wounded. The MH-47E crashed and all aboard struggled to get out. Sergeant Brad Crose and Corporal Matt Commons survived the initial fire, but were killed as they exited the aircraft. Spc. (Specialist) Marc Anderson was hit and killed while still in the chopper. Even with the confusion, the Rangers, the Chinook crewmen and Air Force combat controllers moved to attack the enemy. Once it became apparent that the Al Qa'ida force on the mountain was too numerous, the group called in close-air support. The combat controllers called in 500-pound bombs within 50 metres of the special operator's position. In the meantime, the other helicopter, with the rest of the Quick Reaction Force, landed at another location. The Rangers climbed the 2,000 feet up the mountain to the original position and converged with their comrades at the scene around 10.30 a.m. The linked teams then assaulted the Al Qa'ida positions. 'As the Air Force (combat controller) called in a last air strike on the enemy bunkers and with two machine guns providing suppression fire, seven Rangers stormed the hill as quickly as they could in the knee-deep snow – shooting and throwing grenades. Within minutes, the Rangers took the hill, killing multiple Al Qa'ida,' the report said. The Rangers and airmen consolidated their position, but Al Qa'ida, on another ridgeline about 400 metres away, fired on the team's makeshift aid station. Air force para-rescueman Senior Airman Jason Cunnigham was hit and eventually died from his wounds. The group stayed on the top of Takur Ghar until nightfall as commanders decided the area was too hot for another daylight rescue attempt. Seven Americans died in the battle, and eleven were wounded.

TANZANIA

MILITARY SPECIAL FORCES
Two well-trained Special Forces Companies based in Dar-es-Salaam, one of which is being trained as a dedicated anti-terrorist and hostage rescue unit.

TEAR GAS

The irritating or harassing agents, which are more commonly described as vomiting or tear gas, are sensory irritants. Their action is usually rapid enough to be used as an incapacitating agent in hostage rescue situations. Their effects are usually comparatively brief though, in extremely high concentrations or in very confined spaces, they can be lethal. Some agents cause a temporary flow of tears and are known as lachrymators; some, known as sterutators, induce uncontrollable sneezing or coughing; some agents, known as orticants, cause severe itching or stinging to the skin; and others if swallowed or inhaled cause bouts of violent vomiting. Many of the wide range of agents now available were developed during the First World War and these include CN – Chloroacetophenone, the 'classical' tear gas, and DM-Adamsite which is slower acting than CN, but also caused severe headaches and nausea. The faster-acting and more effective CS named after its discoverers B. B. Corson and R. W. Stoughton, otherwise known as Orthochlorobenzylidene Malonbuitvise, dates from 1928, but was only really developed for military and police use in the mid-1950s by the British War Office (today's Ministry of Defence). CS in any concentration higher than two milligrams per cubic metre is likely to cause anything from a severe pricking sensation behind the eyes to an uncontrollable flow of tears, coughing, streaming nose, retching, vomiting and a gripping pain in the chest. In normal circumstances an individual is likely to be incapacitated within 20–40 seconds and to suffer the after-effects for up to ten minutes, even after exposure to fresh air. Although it is often described as an alternative to the use of a firearm, tear gas is still controversial because of the indiscriminate way it can effect innocent bystanders accidentally caught up in a riot or anti-terrorist emergency.

TERRITORIAL ARMY – SAS RESERVE REGIMENTS

The Territorial Army is the British Army's organised reserve, as opposed to the Regular Reserve, which provides individual members to regular units. The TA SAS dates from just after the Second World War and was originally conceived as a way of keeping the SAS concept alive after the original units were disbanded. Today the members of the primary TA units, 21 and 23 SAS, specialise in the area of long-range patrols. In wartime their role is to provide LRP support to the UK's Joint Rapid Deployment Force (JRDF) or the Allied Command Europe Rapid Reaction Corps (ARRC).

After 1st and 2nd SAS Regiments were disbanded in 1945, a campaign began to resurrect the SAS capabilities within the British Army. This was led by Lieutenant Colonel Brian Franks, a wartime commander of 2 SAS who was determined that the skills of the many SAS men now in civilian life should not go to waste. Through the newly formed Regimental Association Franks petitioned the War Office for the establishment of a reserve SAS unit, and eventually a compromise was reached and the SAS role was given to an old TA infantry battalion, the Artists' Rifles, which had served as an Officer Cadet Training Unit in the war. The new unit was to be called 21st Special Air Service

Regiment (Artists') and recruiting began in September 1947, initially mainly in London. Franks was the first Commanding Officer. In 1950 reservists volunteered for service in the jungles of Malaya, forming B Squadron of the Malayan Scouts, under Major Anthony Greville-Bell, a wartime 2 SAS squadron commander. After a quick course in jungle warfare B Squadron was soon hunting communist terrorists with the emphasis switched from large-scale conventional operations to small patrols, spending two or three months in the remote interior, often living among the local people and winning the battle for hearts and minds which was so important in a war like this, and without the support of the population the Chinese guerrillas were soon on the defensive. Most of the reservist members of B Squadron returned to 21st SAS after two or three years back in the army, being replaced by regular soldiers who had passed the new SAS selection course, as by this time the Malayan Scouts had been renamed 22nd Special Air Service Regiment. The Reserve Reconnaissance Unit had been originally known as Intelligence School No. 9 (d) and was descended from the MI9 escape and evasion organisation, a part of the wartime Intelligence Services. MI9's job had been to insert small groups of highly trained personnel covertly behind enemy lines to aid the return to safety of Allied evaders, whether they were downed aircrew or escaped prisoners of war. In 1959 the RRU became 23rd SAS, under the command of Lieutenant Colonel H. S. Gillies, and in the early 1960s came a further reorganisation of the TA SAS when Captain Peter de la Billiere, a regular officer and a future Director of Special Forces, became adjutant of 21st SAS and set about organising the regiments properly for war. He also concentrated on improving relations with the regular 22nd SAS, starting the process that would eventually lead to a seamless interchange of personnel between the various SAS units and the creation of an effective community. In 1963 former 21st SAS CO Jim Johnson was posted to Aden to oversee the British clandestine campaign to support the Yemen Royalists, and to lead the guerrilla campaign against the nationalist regime and the Egyptian Military Expeditionary force supporting them. Other reservist and former regular SAS personnel arrived to serve as instructors, along with a group of French mercenaries. For the next four years, 30–40 British and French 'advisers' operated in the Yemen at any one time, helping the Royalist forces and particularly running the more technical side of things such as heavy weapons and communications. However, by 1967 it was clear that the rebellion was doomed to failure, as more and more Egyptian troops arrived in the country, and the instructors were gradually withdrawn. Less laudable were the activities of a number of former SAS personnel who joined their former 'C' Squadron colleagues in supporting the racist regime in Rhodesia in the 1970s. In 2002 the 21st and 23rd TA SAS Regiments play a major role in supporting the regulars of the 22nd Regiment and must be considered to play a full part in the Special Forces Group. The TA SAS uses basically the same weapons as the 22nd Regiment.

TEUKGONG MUSUL

The fighters wear shoes rather than battle barefoot and their moves are determined by the opponent's proximity as they seamlessly combine traditional taekwondo kicks with jujitsu chokes, while at the same time wielding a knife. They are specialists in silent killing techniques. Anytime, anywhere, any weapon, anything you've got is the philosophy behind teukgong musul, a form of martial arts designed to meet the demands of Special Forces operations. In the late 1970s, President Park Chung Hee ordered the creation of a superior style of martial arts to counter the North Korean elite forces' 'Geuksul' style. The martial arts instructor and a senior officer with the 27th Anti-Terrorism unit were responsible for developing this new style of fighting, adapting many different forms of martial arts to meet the demands of the Special Forces. They performed a demonstration in June 1979 for President Park and the new techniques were accepted. Teukgong Musul is now taught to the Chong Wa Dae presidential bodyguards and units of the Korean Special Warfare Command Corps, as well as the Kuwaiti and some US Special Forces.

THAI HOSPITAL SIEGE – 2000

In January 2000 Thai Special Forces rescued 700 hostages from a besieged provincial hospital in a dawn strike, killing ten gunmen from a radical Myanmar guerrilla faction headed by twelve-year-old twins. 'All the hostages are safe,' Thai First Army Region Commander Lieutenant General Taweep Suwannasingh told a news conference. Authorities said about 700 had been held captive. Police said, at the end of the 24-hour siege, that all ten guerrillas from 'God's Army', a renegade faction of the ethnic Karen rebel movement, were killed. The battle had lasted about an hour. Hundreds of rounds were fired, then the shooting became sporadic and finally died away. A local radio reporter said he saw the bodies of ten guerrillas, all shot in the head, which were laid out in the hospital. Though the operation had been a qualified success, the suspicion remained that not only had some of the gunmen/terrorists escaped, but that those who remained had surrendered and been summarily executed by the Special Forces.

THAILAND

MILITARY SPECIAL FORCES
Special Warfare Command
Royal Thai Army 1st Division, 1st Regiment, 4th Battalion 'Royal Guard' Since the early 1980s, this unit, whose primary mission has been VIP protection, has held CT responsibilities for the Thai government. The 140-man unit has

a two-man command staff and six assault teams, each with 23 men. These teams are further divided into four assault, and two sniper, teams. Trained by GSG-9.

1st Royal Thai Special Forces (Airborne) Division with the 1st Special Forces (Airborne) Regiment and 2nd Special Forces (Airborne) Regiment.

2nd Royal Thai Special Forces (Airborne) Division with the 3rd Special Forces (Airborne) Regiment, 4th Special Forces (Airborne) Regiment and 5th Special Forces (Airborne) Regiment. PsyOps Battalion and LRRP Company.

Thailand maintains one of the largest and most effective Special Forces capabilities in Southern Asia; it is well trained, well equipped and very experienced. It also has a reputation for brutality and the wide-scale abuse of human rights in the large number of operations that have been carried out against revolutionary movements and ethnic rebels over the last 30 or so years.

Royal Thai Air Force Commando Company This 100-man unit, part of the Royal Thai Air Force's Special Combat Operations Squadron, has been in existence since the late 1970s. They are based near Don Muang Airport and provide anti-hijacking capabilities. They have three assault platoons, each divided into two smaller sections.

Royal Thai Navy SEALs In 1956 the Royal Thai Navy formed a small combat diver unit, based on the USN's UDTs. In 1965 the unit underwent a reorganisation, it was expanded and divided into two separate units, a USN Mobile Training Team (MTT) providing assistance. The first group was organised into a SEa, Air and Land, or SEAL, team. The second group formed an Underwater Demolition Team, or UDT. The SEAL team was assigned intelligence-gathering and reconnaissance missions. Maritime CT operations have also been added to the unit's primary tasks. The UDTs conduct salvage operations, underwater demolitions and obstacle clearance operations in support of RTMC amphibious operations. SEAL and UDT training is conducted at Sattahip. Training lasts for a period of six months and includes a Thai version of 'hell week'. Upon completion of their training Thai SEALs complete a basic airborne course at the RTMC airborne school also located at Sattahip. Additional training is conducted by other Thai armed forces or at foreign training courses. Both SEALs and UDTs have conducted joint training with USN SEALs, (A) SASR, and other Asian Special Operations units. The SEALs have been involved in a number of skirmishes along the Cambodian border, and in anti-piracy operations in the Gulf of Thailand. The UDTs have participated in salvage and rescue operations, and have supported RTMC training exercises. Currently the SEALs consist of approximately 144 men commanded by a Lieutenant commander, and are divided into SEAL teams One and Two. Each SEAL team is subdivided into four platoons. RTN SEALs are primarily equipped with US-manufactured weapons, due to their close relationship to the US. They also have access to the British owned H&K series of weapons, including the MP5.

Royal Thai Marine Corps Amphibious Recon Battalions   In 1965 the Royal Thai Marine Corps (RTMC) formed an amphibious reconnaissance company. The unit was tasked with conducting ground and amphibious recon missions, beach reconnaissance, obstacle clearance operations, and conducting Special Operations in support of RTMC operations.

In 1972 a small group of Thai Recon Marines deployed to Laos as part of a volunteer battalion, Commando 619. The group operated in the Plane de Jarres, conducting combat operations against the communist Pathet Lao guerrillas before being withdrawn. In November of 1978 the company was expanded to its current battalion size. Currently the battalion is based at Sattahip Naval Base. Commanded by a lieutenant colonel, the battalion is composed of four sub units: An HQ Company (with an attached war dog platoon), one amphibious recon company (which contains the battalion's combat divers), and two motorised recon companies (equipped with V-150 armoured cars). There is also a small counter-terrorism detachment assigned to the unit. The battalion's companies are attached to RTMC Regiments on an as-needed basis. In 1989 a RTMC task force was deployed along the border with Cambodia, and one recon company was attached to the unit while it conducted operations.

Prospective Thai Recon Marines are selected from the ranks of experienced marines. Candidates are required to complete a three-month-long amphibious recon course at the Sattahip Special Warfare Centre. The course provides instruction in long-range patrolling, amphibious operations, hydrographic surveys, and specialised ground combat tactics. Upon completion of the amphibious recon course, candidates then undertake a basic parachute course at the RTMC parachute school, collocated with the Special Warfare School at Sattahip. Recon marines are required to successfully make eight parachute jumps (including one at night, and two water jumps) before being awarded the Naval Parachute Qualification Badge. Selected battalion personnel receive training in HAHO and HALO parachute operations while others receive specialised training in CT techniques. The Recon Battalion routinely conducts training exercises along the Cambodian border and with USMC Reconnaissance units.

THOMPSON – 'THE CHICAGO PIANO'

Beloved by the gangsters in Chicago during the 1920s and 1930s the .45 Thompson M1921 and M1928 sub-machine gun found lasting fame in the hands of the Special Forces and commandos of the Second World War as the 'Tommy Gun' and in its use by the IRA terrorists in Ireland. Heavy and well built it could fire 40rpm in single shot or 120rpm in automatic mode. A maximum effective range of 220yds (200m) and a 30-round magazine made this weapon a favourite with generations of fighting men.

TIANANMEN SQUARE MASSACRE 1989

Though not normally associated with Special Forces, in fact the main formation used to put down the student demonstrations was closely linked to Chinese PLA elite and Special Operations units.

There was a difficult and dangerous period for the communist leadership during which the Beijing Garrison, the 38th Army, had only half-heartedly carried out the party's orders, partly caused by the fact that many of the students had only recently completed their military service with the 38th. This was then quickly followed by the near mutiny of the leading regiments of the 28th Group Army, when called upon to march on the capital. It was only brought to end when the 27th Group Army, a formation known as a sort of Praetorian Guard for the Chinese President Yang Shangkun, brutally intervened on 4 June. Over the next few days perhaps as many as 5,000 students were killed. Some reports suggest a much higher figure. The 27th Group Army included a number of assault regiments with Special Forces airborne companies, and it was these units that led the attack in Tiananmen Square. There, they were joined by another unit with a large Special Forces element, the 15th Airborne Corps. However, the use of such specialised units in putting down a popular protest that had the support of many moderates in the government seriously damaged the long-standing close relationship between the Chinese people and the PLA.

TOC

Acronym: Tactical Operations Centre. Cutting edge command of units in operational conditions. Involved closely enough to react to sudden changes in battlefield conditions. In theory at least!

TOGO

MILITARY SPECIAL FORCES
One Para-Commando and Presidential Guard Regiment with 3 SF-Airborne Companies trained and equipped by the French Special Forces.

TRACKING

The ability to track an enemy force or avoid being tracked successfully, has been a major part of 'light infantry' or insurgent skills for thousands of years.

Imperial European forces using locally raised scouts and trackers developed these techniques into a fine art. The British Army in India, the US Cavalry in countless small wars with Native American 'war parties', the French, Spanish and Portuguese colonialists in Africa all relied on these arcane skills for ultimate military success. Later the SAS during the Malayan Emergency, the US Green Berets and Rangers in Vietnam, the Selous Scouts in Rhodesia and the 'Recces' of the South African Army became famous for their abilities to track down communist guerrillas. Today these skills are still taught on countless Special Forces courses, and particularly in the British and Brazilian Jungle Warfare Schools. The ability to spot, confirm and correctly interpret small signs that would normally escape observation takes time and great patience to learn. A scuff on a tree from careless use of equipment; broken grass suggesting an enemy has taken a new path perhaps to avoid capture, perhaps to stage an ambush; the presence of human waste, state of decay, presence of insect eggs or larvae can all give an idea of time; rust can form on metal within twelve hours in the humid conditions of a jungle; paper bleaches and turns yellow in three days; even walking along a river bed to avoid tracking leaves marks that can be spotted by knowledgeable trackers at points of entry and exit. No amount of modern electronic gadgetry can probably ever hope to completely replace the practised eye of a well-trained tracker.

TRANSMISSION SECURITY – SF COMMUNICATIONS

This remains the most important element in preventing hostile electronic warfare (EW) specialists from discovering the timing and likely area of a covert mission and tracking it once under way. An operator using a 'continuous wave' or standard radio-telegraphic transmission will use a bi-directional aerial and the lowest possible setting, activating the set only at prescribed times or when absolutely necessary. Even then only a 'crack' or 'Q' code will be used to send short and simple messages, often in a pre-arranged form, which gives little idea to an enemy listening station of the true nature of its meaning. Though Morse has been discontinued officially, it is known that it is still being used occasionally in 'burst' or pulse transmissions and as so few operators now read Morse it is still surprisingly secure for a very old system. Modern DF (Direction Finding) equipment can, however, detect and intercept even ultra-short pulsed transmissions in seconds, and that alone will restrict its continued use.

By the early 1980s military 'frequency-hopping' sets were readily available and these sought to avoid hostile interception by switching frequencies rapidly during transmission, so that only a small fragment of any message would be broadcast on any particular frequency. The pre-arranged frequency

changes, with ten or more per second, would hopefully confuse enemy interception facilities. However, technology quickly met the challenge and produced 'hopper traps', which could detect a signal that remained for only three
milliseconds on any one frequency, and could cope with upwards of 1,000 frequency 'hops' per second. Paired with DF elements using the Doppler Effect,
which can use just a ten-second or less signal fragment to locate the transmitter, with a reported accuracy of one degree of the compass, even 'frequency-
hopping' failed to provide the Special Forces and covert operations with the
high degree of communications security they needed. The development of a
more secure covert communication system involved transmitting a highly
directional signal to an aerial platform, either an EW aircraft or a communications satellite. Functional man-pack satellite communications (SATCOM) first
became available in the 1980s for Special Forces' use and now all messages
can be relayed instantly to a space platform and on to a line-of-sight ground
station thousands of miles away, or stored for later transmissions as the satellite orbits over a friendly country. Communications from a SF command base
are transmitted via satellite to the team operating in hostile territory using a
low-powered, highly directional pulsed signal that can only be received in the
small area occupied by the SF X-Band Special Applications Terminal (SAT). It
is almost impossible to intercept these signals, which are highly unlikely to
provide a usable DF trace for even an EW-sophisticated enemy.

TRINIDAD AND TOBAGO

MILITARY SPECIAL FORCES
One Anti-Terrorist and HRU detachment under HQ Staff command.

TUNIS RAID – SAYERET MATKAL

In 1988 the Israeli Intelligence services devised a plan to take their war against
terrorism direct to one of its leading advocates, Abu Jihad. The Palestinian
extremist was living in some comfort in the exclusive Sidi Bou Said suburb of
Tunis and on 15 April a small fleet of Israeli Sa'ar-IV Fast Missile Boats arrived in
the waters just off the coast of Tunis, while two specially adapted IAF electronic
warfare Boeing 707s on a civilian flight path blanketed Tunisian radar with an
effective ECM shield. Mossad agents then tapped into the local telephone
exchange to block any possible warning reaching Jihad. Special Forces from the
Sayeret Matkal came ashore in five Zodiac craft. These were loaded into two
rented vans and driven to Sidi Bou Said. At shortly after 01.00 on 16 April they
arrived outside Jihad's house and joined up with Mossad agents conducting the
surveillance side of the operation. The operation temporarily stalled as Jihad
was not at home; however, the Israeli Special Forces remained safely hidden and
at 01.30 Jihad and his bodyguards returned. However, the Israeli Special Forces

waited a further 60 minutes until the lights in Jihad's bedroom were out. The guards were then killed and the Israelis entered the house and finally burst into Abu Jihad's bedroom. The Palestinian leader died instantly in a hail of 75 bullets, Jihad's wife lying alongside him was unhurt. The Sayeret Matkal, after an operation that took just thirteen seconds from breaching the doors to evacuating the building, then retired to Ras Cathage beach and the waiting Zodiacs protected by commandos from the Israel S'13 Naval Special Forces. The Mossad agents, posing as tourists, left safely on commercial flights from Tunis Airport.

TUNISIA

MILITARY SPECIAL FORCES

A Special Forces Brigade Made up of two battalions this unit, though well trained and armed, does not have the many skills required to be genuinely Special Operations-capable. The Tunisian Army is, however, attempting to enhance the anti-terrorist and counter-insurgency aspects of the unit and are reported to be receiving assistance from the US and several European Special Forces.

CIVILIAN SPECIAL FORCES

'Unite Speciale' Garde Nationale (USGN) – National Guard Special Unit This 50-man force was established in the early 1980s and is broken down into two operational sections and a headquarters element. Based in Hammemet, they have responsibility for CT(Counter-Terrorist) operations at government and diplomatic buildings, aircraft hijackings and maritime situations.

The Groupment de Commando of the Garde National (National Guard's Commando Company – GCGN) The GCGN is a 150-man unit formed in 1982 as an anti-terrorist unit. GCG, sometimes known as GN Special Forces, recruits from both the military and police and has received extensive counter-terrorist training with the emphasis on airborne, SCUBA, CQB, assault tactics and a range of other HRU skills from the GIGN and US Special Forces. Based at National Guard Headquarters near Tunis Airport, they respond to high criminal threats and have operated on the Tunisia–Algeria border on numerous occasions. It is equipped with Beretta M12 SMG, FN FAL & Steyr AUG assault rifles, M21 sniper rifles, Winchester M1200 combat shotguns and FN MAG machine guns.

TURKEY

MILITARY SPECIAL FORCES

The Turkish Army has a tradition of using Special Forces going back to the days of Kamal Ataturk in the 1920s when elite units were used with devastating effect against the Greek army and against insurgents and rebellions by ethnic populations such as the Armenians and the Kurds. The present Special Forces can trace their direct roots back to the first parachute units whose training was initiated with US assistance in 1949. Today Turkey has a considerable Special Operations capability and for much the same operational reasons – Kurdish rebellion and a continuing confrontation with Greece. However, to that must be added the potential for conflict with both Iraq and Syria, in part over control of the head waters of the Tigris and Euphrates rivers, but increasingly because of the role Turkey will be expected to play in the War on Terrorism. Turkey may well find itself in the forefront of any campaign to overthrow the Iraqi regime of Saddam Hussein, playing host to its US allies. As an important partner of Israel, they also have a common hostility to Syria and Islamic extremism.

The Turkish Army's Special Warfare Operations Department   with headquarters in Ankara, has under its command four brigades each of four battalions.

1st Commando Brigade, with headquarters in Kayseri, south-east of Ankara. They have recently been deployed to various areas in the south-east Anatolia region against separatist terrorists. During these battles this brigade earned itself the 'Distinguished Courage Medal of the Turkish Armed Forces', the second time it has done so since 1974.

2nd Commando Brigade, with headquarters in Bolu, north-west of Ankara. They also were deployed to the south-eastern Anatolia region to fight terrorism. In addition to the 1st Brigade, they were awarded the 'Distinguished Courage Medal of the Turkish Armed Forces' for their efforts.

3rd Amphibious Marine Brigade, with headquarters in Foca/Izmir in Western Turkey on the Aegean coast. Their main mission is probably infiltration and sabotage/intelligence-gathering behind enemy lines. Possible targets in time of war would be island airfield and communications centres and they are tasked for amphibious operations in the eastern Aegean. In the event of a conflict with Greece it would attempt to seize the disputed offshore Aegean islands and probably attempt to sabotage communications, arms dumps and airfields on the Greek mainland. This amphibious 3rd brigade is also available to reinforce military operations in Cyprus.

4th Commando Brigade, with headquarters near Iskenderun, in south-east Turkey. This unit's main tasks would be to carry out Special Operations in northern Cyprus and along the Syrian border.

However, with the 1st and 2nd Brigades regularly deployed on counter-insurgency operations in south-eastern Anatolia against the Kurds, and both brigades having been involved in hot-pursuit operations across the border into the Kurdish areas of northern Anatolia, the 4th is sometimes used to reinforce them.

These units have a well-earned reputation for both toughness and for being highly effective in combat against well-armed and determined insurgents. They have also been accused of human rights abuse and of the brutal treatment of their Kurdish opponents in particular. Training for these units concentrates on assault commando techniques, and while heliborne insertion, combat shooting, mountain warfare and unarmed combat play a major part in combat training, some of the more advanced techniques, such as the HALO and HAHO skills, are less well covered. However, combat swimming is considered particularly important, with emphasis placed on two specific techniques: SAS (Su Alti Savunma, Water Under Defence) and SAT (Su Alti Taaruz, Water Under Attack). Weapons in use include 5.56mm M16AI automatic rifles, 9mm MP5 sub-machine guns and PSG1 sniper rifles and are among a wide range of standard army issue and specialist arms available. The Turkish military has no Special Operations aircraft permanently attached, but UH-60 Black Hawks and AS-90 Cougar helicopters are optimised for CSAR (Combat Search And Rescue) missions; these could easily be used for covert insertion extraction. The first Turkish Special Forces unit, the 1st Airborne Platoon of the Guards Regiment, was formed with US assistance in 1949.

CIVILIAN SPECIAL FORCES
OIKB Ozel Intihar Kommando Bolugu – National Police Jandarma Commandos
The main Counter-Terrorist unit is presently organised into three Special Force companies in Ankara, Izmir and Istanbul. They are trained in anti-terrorist operations, hostage rescue and anti-hijacking, as well as riot control. Members of this unit receive extensive training at the Jandarma Security establishment at Foca near Izmir from selected army instructors. Operational control in peacetime is with the Ministry of the Interior, but in wartime it passes to the control of the Turkish Military Intelligence. Its personnel have seen regular action against such extremist groups as the left-wing TPLA or Turkish Peoples Liberation Army, Armenian and Kurdish rebels. Weapons in use include 9mm H&K MP5 SMG, 5.56mm H&K33 assault rifles and 7.62mm H&K G3SG/1 sniper rifles.

TURKMENISTAN

MILITARY SPECIAL FORCES
One independent Special Forces Airborne Assault Battalion based in Ashgabat, it now has a small 20-strong hostage rescue unit trained by Western instructors.

UDT

Underwater Demolitions Teams. Precursor to the SEALS, the unit was deactivated in the early 1980s.

UGANDA
MILITARY SPECIAL FORCES
An attempt is being made to rebuild a limited Airborne Special Forces capability to deal with the serious terrorist and insurgency problems, particularly in the north of the country. Three companies are understood to be receiving training from foreign instructors.

UKRAINE
MILITARY SPECIAL FORCES
Special Operations Command (Ground Forces Command) Ukraine maintains a fairly diverse make-up of SOF units within its military and paramilitary organisations. SOF includes SPETSNAZ, airmobile and special-purpose military police units.

There is currently one airmobile division and three airmobile brigades, one SPETSNAZ brigade and one SPETSNAZ regiment, and a security brigade directly subordinate to the MOD. SOF units within the Ground Forces Command have the primary mission of reconnaissance and intelligence-gathering within the enemy rear area. The units within the MVS and National Guard, and those directly subordinate to the MOD, have missions that consist primarily of internal security and conducting anti-terrorism operations. While these units are considered the best-trained, best-equipped, and most capable force in the Ukraine military, the current economic situation does not provide for a sufficient budget to train and equip them with modern and serviceable equipment. Units use older, Soviet-era equipment that is in various states of disrepair. The Ukrainian airlift capability is hampered by poorly maintained aircraft, lack of spare parts and insufficient fuel to conduct frequent airborne/airdrop training. As a result, the amount and quality of airborne/airdrop training has declined.. Training encompasses direct action, reconnaissance, civil unrest and counter-terrorism. Ukrainian SOF units actively participate in training with Russia and other neighbouring countries. Units also participate in training with the United States through Partnership for Peace (PfP). PfP training has typically involved small SPETSNAZ units from the National Guard and has taken place both in Ukraine and the US SF.

CIVILIAN SPECIAL FORCES
Berkut (Golden Eagles) Following the collapse of the Soviet Union, the former republics were left on their own to develop counter-terrorist capabilities. This need has become more urgent in recent years as the rising problem of organised crime has taxed the internal security resources that would normally be sufficient to deal with domestic terrorism. Ukraine has

responded by creating the Berkut (Golden Eagle) detachments under the authority of the Ministry of Internal Affairs. These battalion-sized units were originally formed in January 1992 and were based heavily on the Warsaw Pact era Special Purpose Militsiia Detachments (OMON), which dealt successfully with many of the same problems now facing an independent Ukraine. The headquarters of the 5,000-man Berkut is located in Kiev, with battalion- and company-sized detachments based in the larger Ukranian cities.

The Panther Battalion is an anti-terrorist SPETSNAZ team operating under the Ministry of the Interior (MOI). This group was founded in 1994 and is based in Kiev. Since the break up of the Soviet Union in 1991, Ukraine's government has downsized and reorganised its military forces, while adding a new paramilitary unit, the National Guard, and new Special Operations forces (SOF) to those inherited from the Soviet era. This reflects a priority in Ukraine's perceptions of its security needs, and while still perceiving Russia as a long-term potential military threat to its independence, of more immediate concern is the country's internal political instability, terrorism and organised criminal activity.

The National Guard has a number of special-purpose units. One of these, called Scorpion, is a battalion-sized unit that was deployed in early 1998 to quell civil disturbances and establish law and order in the Crimea. Within the MVS (Internal Security) are a variety of special-purpose military police units, which have been established since 1988. The SBU (Intelligence Service), which was the KGB in Ukraine during the Soviet era, has SOF units known as Alpha which are a direct successor to a special group within the KGB, and composed of two kinds of combat units – 'storm' (assault teams) and protective (VIP security). Alpha units also specialise in hostage rescue operations, and are attached to all the oblast directorates of the SBU.

ULTIMATE TERRORISM – NUCLEAR NIGHTMARE

Much of the world is fully aware of the role that the Special Forces play in Counter-Terrorist operations or the elite hostage rescue units (HRU) in storming a hijacked airliner, but much less well known is the absolutely crucial part they play in combating the ultimate terrorism. Though the world has remained traumatised by the events of 9-11, the real nightmare that haunts governments and security services around the world is the threat of nerve gas, or a deadly virus or perhaps even a crude so-called 'dirty bomb' in the hands of an international terrorist group like Al Qa'ida. There are now a few highly trained Special Forces units in the United States equipped to be able to hunt down the bio-terrorist in co-operation with the

FBI's dedicated Hazardous Materials Teams, and with advanced detection and surveillance devices pinpoint both the location and nature of the threat. Special Forces assault teams in specially designed lightweight bio-hazard suits and armed with low-velocity weapons whose projectiles are designed to kill, but with a reduced chance of penetrating metal, glass or plastic containers holding possibly deadly gases or germs, will then 'take out' the terrorists, leaving other emergency teams to contain the area and secure the hazardous materials. Fine in theory, but the security forces are painfully aware that the first warning they are likely to get of a bio-terrorism weapon will be its actual use.

It could be the release of a deadly nerve agent in the subway/tube as has already happened in Tokyo in 1972, when the Aum Shinri Kyo religious fanatics used SARIN gas to kill twelve and injure 5,500 passengers and staff; a more determined and widespread use of biological warfare agents like anthrax, where the terrorist has finally developed an effective method of dispersing the virus over a wide area; or indeed the detonation of a 'dirty bomb' in the centre of a major city. This last-named threat, following the evidence discovered in mid-2002 that Al Qa'ida is making determined efforts to develop such weapons for use against Washington itself, is being taken as a 'critical threat' by intelligence analysts. It is yet another task that Special Forces Nuclear Emergency Response Teams must fear, for a 'dirty bomb' is no more than a conventional weapon made up of a fast-burning or ultra high explosive such as HMX, seeded with nuclear waste stolen from a hospital laboratory, university science department or even from certain food processing plants. A yet more deadly version would see the explosives sheathed in enriched uranium U235 or plutonium, thankfully somewhat more difficult for the terrorist to obtain unless large amounts of money or a 'friendly' government solves that problem for them. Either weapon, though providing only a relatively small explosion, would be capable of contaminating perhaps as much as 30 per cent of New York or London, depending on the prevailing climatic conditions being favourable, with radioactive particles – some of which may have half-lives of several hundred years. The catastrophic effects of just one successful attack on a major city and the long-term effect on the nation's morale are taken very seriously by the intelligence community, and the elite Special Forces units who would be required to cope with the incident and to prevent a recurrence. The United States is creating a Special Bio and Nuclear Terrorism Defence organisation within the proposed Homeland Security Department, and this will be made up of emergency teams from both the FBI and CIA Science and Technology Divisions, with assault and containment teams from Delta Force and in particular the United States Marine Corps Special Weapons Brigade, established in early 2002. This latter unit is in the forefront of the technological war against this new form of terrorism and is so far the only such large, dedicated Special Forces unit in the world. However, by the early part of 2003 many other countries are expected to have in place specialist nuclear, biological and chemical terrorism emergency response teams, virtually all of which will probably be based on a combination of Intelligence Agencies and Special Forces. France, Germany, Russia, Israel, Japan and to a lesser extent Britain have a limited containment ability already, but certainly nowhere near sufficient to avoid becoming quickly overwhelmed by the after-effects of the detonation of even a relatively small 'dirty bomb' in a major population centre. The Special Forces are also aware that this is not the final highpoint of terrorist ambitions, the acquisition by whatever means of a SADM (Special Atomic Demolitions Munitions) commonly known as a 'suitcase nuke' with a nuclear explosive yield equivalent to a Hiroshima bomb or 250,000 tons of TNT, but small enough to hide in the boot of a family car, produces a nightmare scenario of a city devastated without warning with perhaps several hundreds of thousands killed and millions more at risk of a slow death from injuries and cancer. For the Special Forces and their intelligence colleagues, combating this threat will be their greatest test and, for the foreseeable future, they are likely to remain the final defence between the civilian population and the fanatic or terrorist with a weapon of mass destruction.

UNARMED COMBAT

As land wars have become composed of 'mini battles', insurgencies and terrorism, the growth of interest in the uses of Special Forces has quite naturally led to a serious re-assessment of guerrilla tactics, unconventional warfare and increases in alternative methods of killing. It became apparent that knives, bows and arrows, stalking techniques and all the other specialities of individual human combat were to become more important than ever. The only heroes of the Vietnam War were the US 'guerrilla-style forces', the Green Berets. US Special Forces soldiers are now trained in ancient fighting techniques in such places as the Hwarangdo Hand-to-Hand Combat and Special Weapons School. This Special Forces camp is located at John F. Kennedy Centre for Military Assistance, Fort Bragg, North Carolina. Instructors teach the age-old arts utilised by guerrilla fighters the world over, and particularly the Orient. Though hwarangdo is of Korean origin, its roots and ties are shared by other Asian nations such as China and Japan. And, in fact, the most celebrated guerrilla fighters of history were the 'invisible assassins', the ninja, who were employed as spies, kidnappers, killers and special surprise and shock attack forces during Japan's pre-Meiji Restoration period. The full range of fighting techniques are employed by hwarangdo experts. The art itself is a comprehensive amalgam of all forms of personal unarmed combat. Training includes the use of hand weapons, revival techniques, joint-breaking tech-

niques and stalking techniques. Techniques adopted from other martial arts including judo, aikido, jujitsu, karate, tang soo do, Korean kwon pup or kempo, are regularly utilised. Students at the special training camp learn the standard martial arts punching, blocking and kicking techniques. Beyond that, finger pressure points, joint breaking and throwing techniques are taught. There is a full week's instruction in such areas as knife fighting, knife throwing, short stick fighting, garrottes, crossbows and handgun reaction, blowguns and bayonet training. Special Forces are taught Korean Eun Shin Bop, or making oneself invisible. Trainees are taught to conceal themselves in front of others, utilising such techniques as conforming to the terrain and moving in light shadow. Sentry stalking, silent killing and prisoner-of-war snatches all figure prominently in the instruction. The training is designed to teach instructors in the basics of operational hand-to-hand warfare and the use of special weapons as taught by the hwarangdo method. Instructors then report back to their units and teach their staffs. The Green Berets, Rangers and SEALs in particular value highly the improvement in unarmed combat techniques this brings. One of the primary reasons, then, for training elite troops in martial arts, is to give them a decided mental and physical edge. The actual techniques themselves will most likely not even be used. The modern Special Forces soldier is heavily armed with a vast array of weapons specific to his mission. Sometimes he will engage the enemy only as a last alternative, especially if his mission is to gather intelligence without leaving any trace of him having been there. The SF soldier will use martial arts only as a last resort, when all his other weapons fail, or when he has no other weapons – for example during an escape and evasion attempt. If martial arts are his weapon of choice to be used in situations like trying to escape and evade, then the techniques taught to him must take into account his probable physical condition – hungry and nearing exhaustion. He cannot rely on techniques which require considerable strenuous activity. They must be quick, easy and efficient. Martial arts training for elite soldiers must be mission-specific, which generally means causing disabling injury or death. The soldier who will use martial arts in an escape and evasion situation, or whose other weapons have failed, will have no need of restraining techniques. If he must fight, he will not capture the enemy, he will kill him. Martial arts techniques must be maintainable with a minimum of effort and time, and the typical Special Forces soldier therefore spends the majority of his service either keeping his own skills polished, or teaching his skills to others.
(see also KRAV MAGA, TEUKGONG MUSUL).

UNCONVENTIONAL WARFARE

Non-traditional actions against enemy forces. Guerrilla warfare or psychological ops.

UNDERWATER SPECIAL OPERATIONS

This can refer to a very varied range of missions involving mini-Submarines and chariots (human torpedoes) to those requiring combat swimming techniques. Such operations can be used for covert reconnaissance, surveillance and intelligence-gathering on enemy harbours, beach defences or warships. Combat swimming also includes attacking enemy facilities and warships with magnetic limpet mines or specialist explosives designed to cut pipe-lines, underwater communications cables or destroy underwater surveillance devices. A total swim of at least 1 mile (1.1km) is considered practical for combat missions using closed SCUBA systems. These will often be made from small raiding craft or a submarine. Other skills developed include insertion by helicopter or parachuting with full SCUBA gear, particularly useful on anti-terrorist or hostage rescue missions involving merchant vessels on the high seas.

UNITED ARAB EMIRATES – UAE

(see entries for ABU DHABI and DUBAI).

UK

MILITARY SPECIAL FORCES

Special Forces Directorate (Special Forces Group) formed in 1987 and is directly in control of the SAS and SBS from its headquarters at the Duke of York Barracks in West London. The Director of the SAS, an Army brigadier, is also the Director Special Forces, while the deputy is a Royal Marines (SBS) colonel. It maintains close contact with both the Intelligence Service (SIS/MI6) and Security organisation (MI5) and with similar foreign SpecOps Commands, in particular USSOCOM.

The 22nd Regiment Special Air Service remains one of the prime anti-terrorist and hostage rescue units in the world. It also has its headquarters at the Duke of York Barracks in West London while the main training base and depot has recently moved to new accommodation at Credenhill just to the north-west of the city of Hereford in the West Midlands of England. It is presently organised into five operational units: four Sabre Squadrons each with four operations squads of sixteen men each, again in turn divided into four four-man specialist units known as the Boat, Air, Mountain and Mobility Troops and the fifth unit being its own communications support in the form of the 264th (SAS) Signals Squadron, which provides for secure links for operations worldwide.

Squadron Troops: 1 (Boat), 2 (Air), 3 (Mobility) and 4 (Mountain). Formed from local British Army volunteers in Malaya, 1950. Active service includes Malaya 1950–58; Oman, Jan–Feb 1959; first squadron in Borneo, Jan–April 1963; first squadron in Aden/Radfan, April–May 1964; thereafter served in Aden, like other squadrons, for a few weeks at a time during retraining during Borneo tours; Borneo June–Oct 1964 and May–Oct 1965; Oman 1970–76, on four-month tours as part of British Army Training Team (BATT); Northern Ireland since 1976; Gulf 1990–91, provided two half-squadron motorised raiding groups for work behind Iraqi lines and the Balkans since 1993.

B Squadron Troops: 6 (Boat), 7 (Air), 8 (Mobility) and 9 (Mountain). Formed from volunteers from 21SAS and other ex-SAS reservists who agreed to return to regular service for three years, Malaya 1950. Active service: includes Malaya 1950–59; disbanded 1959; reformed for service in Borneo, 1963; Borneo Nov 1964–Feb 1965 and Nov 1965–Feb 1966; Aden at various times, including providing teams for undercover work in the city itself; Radfan 1966; Oman (Musandam Peninsula) 1970, including first operational free-fall jump by 22SAS; Oman (Dhofar) 1970–76; Battle of Mirbat, 18 July 1972; like other squadrons did several four-month tours; Prince's Gate, London, 5 May 1980 (Operation Nimrod); Falklands War 1982 – proposed operations at Port Stanley and on Argentine mainland cancelled; Gulf 1991, provided three road watch patrols, including Bravo Two Zero; also provided reinforcements to A and D Squadrons;. Balkans since 1992; Afghanistan and Middle East since 2001.

D Squadron Troops: 16 (Air), 17 (Boat), 18 (Mobility) and 19 (Mountain). Formed in Malaya 1951.
Active service includes Malaya 1951–58; Oman (Jebel Akhdar) Nov 1958–Feb 1959; Borneo April–Aug 1963, Dec 1963–April 1964, Feb–May 1965, July–Sept 1966; Aden at various times in between Borneo tours; Northern Ireland as a rifle company, Sept–Nov 1969; Oman 1971–76, four-month tours; provided first troop for patrol/ambush work in Northern Ireland, Jan 1976; Falklands War 1982 – formed a squadron-strength strike force; part of task force to retake South Georgia (Operation Paraquat), late April; Pebble Island raid (Operation Prelim), 13 May; Darwin/Goose Green raid on night of main landings, 21 May; seizure of Mount Kent area, 24 May–1 June; later relieved some G Squadron patrols; two troops on raid on seaward side of Wireless Ridge, 13/14 June; Gulf 1990–91, operated as a motorised raiding force behind Iraqi lines, Feb–April, troops coming together for certain operations; Balkans since 1992; Afghanistan and Middle East since 2001.

G Squadron Troops: 21 (Mobility), 22 (Mountain), 23 (Boat) and 24 (Air). Formed from a troop-sized cadre from the Guards Independent Parachute

Company January 1967. Active service includes Oman 1970–76, including the Battle of Mirbat, one of the few times when two SAS squadrons were present in Dhofar; Northern Ireland from 1976; Falklands War 1982, ten four-man patrols inserted on East and West Falkland from 10 May; one troop on Wireless Ridge raid; Gulf 1990, became the first squadron deployed, but later returned to UK to take over CRW duties; and Balkans since 1993. This Squadron was established to replace the disbanded C Squadron formed from 100 Rhodesian soldiers, originally known as Far East Volunteer Unit, Southern Rhodesia 1950. This saw active service in Malaya 1951–53; disbanded on return to Southern Rhodesia; reformed 1961 and participated in several exercises in the Middle East, 1962–63; became the basis of the Rhodesian SAS in 1964; formal links with Britain cut after Unilateral Declaration of Independence by Rhodesia, 1965; participated in the Zimbabwe/Rhodesia civil war, 1966–80, especially external operations in Zambia and Mozambique; expanded to become 1st SAS Regiment in 1978 and finally disbanded 1980.

The main anti-terrorist capability is known as the CRW (Counter Revolutionary Warfare) or usually within the SAS as the SP (Special Projects) Team and is drawn from whichever of the four Sabre Squadrons is on stand-by. Each squadron takes it in turn for a six-month period to act as the 'crisis alert unit'. The SP team is normally made up of approximately 80 personnel who are divided into four troops of sixteen men, and while the SP operates similarly to the other squadrons during periods of training, the picture changes significantly when a terrorist incident occurs. The alert troop is broken down into a surveillance/sniper unit, while the remaining soldiers form the assault group. In addition, a Royal Air Force C-130 remains on standby at RAF Lyneham at all times should the SP Team require immediate long-range transportation. Unlike most special operations groups, the SAS rotates all of its squadrons through CRW/SP duty. Because of this, all SAS personnel are considered counter-terrorist qualified and refresher training is constant. Organisationally, the Special Projects unit is broken down into Red and Blue Teams, each with snipers and EOD-trained experts.

A major contributing factor to the continuing success of the SAS is the Operations Research Unit, which develops unique equipment for use by the SP team. It is this unit that developed the highly effective and now-widely used stun ('Flash-Bang') grenade. Other equipment included specialised ladders for train and aircraft assaults, night vision goggles, and audio/video equipment. While the SAS Training Directorate ensures that proficiency in firearms is constantly refined for close-quarters battle (CQB) in the 'killing house' at the Hereford Training Depot. The basic CQB course is six weeks, during which troopers may fire in excess of 2,000 rounds. This skill is further enhanced during a squadron's SP duty. Adding an element of realism to the training is the use of live personnel as hostages during room-clearing operations. SAS counter-terrorist and hostage rescue training is further facilitated by the inclusion of high-ranking members of the UK government, many of whom (including the Prime Minister) take part in actual training exercises. 22nd SAS demands an extraordinary level of physical fitness, stamina and technical ability from its personnel. They are trained in combat shooting and combat swimming, explosives and EOD, sabotage, sniping, heliborne-insertion, desert, mountain, Arctic and jungle warfare and survival, languages, camouflage, parachuting using paravanes, HALO (High Altitude Low Opening) and HAHO (High Altitude High Opening), hostage rescue, defensive driving, as VIP bodyguards and much more. The SAS Armoury has at their disposal a huge range of British and foreign weapons and explosives, including many used by the world's terrorists, including 9mm SIG-Sauer L105A1 (P226), often used with the optional 20-round magazine. A custom-made variant of this, the 9mm SIG-Sauer L106A1 (P226K), has a shortened slide. The compact 9mm SIG-Sauer L107A1 pistol (P228) since 1992. For close-quarter assault, the 9mm H&K L80A1 sub-machine gun (MP5K), 9mm H&K L90A1 sub-machine gun (MP5KA1), 9mm H&K L92A1 sub-machine gun (MP5A3) and 9mm H&K L91A1 suppressed sub-machine gun (MP5SD3), which have been partly replaced by the 5.56mm H&K L101A1 assault carbine (HK53A3). In more conventional military operations, the 5.56mm Colt AR-15A2 Model 705 assault rifle is preferred, along with the 7.62mm H&K L100A1 battle rifle (G3K), 5.56mm FN L108A1 MINIMI and 5.56mm FN L110A1 MINIMI-Para light machine gun, 7.62mm Enfield L7A2 general-purpose machine gun and 40mmSR Colt M203 underbarrel grenade launcher (under AR-15A2 Model 702). Sniper rifles include the 7.62mm H&K PSG1 rifle, 7.62mm Accuracy International L96A1 bolt-action rifle, 7.62mm Accuracy International AWS suppressed bolt-action rifle, 8.6mm (.338 Lapua Magnum) Accuracy International L115A1 bolt-action rifle and 12.7mm (.50 BMG) Barrett L82A1 sniper rifle (Model 82A1). Since 2001 a number of 5.56mm Diemaco C8SFW carbines have been delivered (Canadian-built variants of the Colt CAR-15A3). These will mount a 40mmSR H&K AG36 underbarrel grenade launcher. The 18.5mmR (12-gauge) Benelli M1 Super 90 semi-automatic shotgun is also used in 'house-clearing'. The 5.56mm Enfield L85A1 standard assault rifle of the British Army is only used by Territorial Army SAS units and when the 22nd SAS wish to pass as conventional soldiers. Vehicles include Land Rover 110 Defender utility vehicles armed with L7A2 machine guns. The 8th Flight of the Army Air Corps provides four Agusta A109A helicopters for use with the SAS, while the RAF's 7th Squadron supplies Boeing Chinook HC.3 helicopters (equivalent to CH-47D/E) with 7.62mm General Electric M134 mini-guns.

The operational composition is such that the squadron is the largest force normally used to conduct a single operation, though in most cases the standard combat unit will be one or more patrols of four men. However, operations of smaller size will usually require the squadron HQ to run a forward mounting base or to directly command troops in the field. If more than one squadron is 'in-theatre' a regimental tactical headquarters will be deployed to take command. Sometimes even if a squadron or less is involved, the CO of the regiment will be present though Squadron commanders are usually the highest-ranking SAS members to take part in actual operations. A full-strength squadron would have six officers and 78 other ranks, divided into a Headquarters and four Troops. The Officer Commanding (OC) is a major, with a captain as his Second in Command (2IC) and operations officer. Also in the HQ are the squadron sergeant major (SSM), a warrant officer class 2, the squadron quartermaster sergeant (SQMS), a staff sergeant, and a few clerks, storemen and armourers.

Each of the operational Troops, whether it specialises in mountain warfare, boating and diving, free-fall parachuting or vehicles, is authorised a captain and fifteen other ranks, further split into four four-man patrols. In practice a squadron is almost never up to strength. Because of the shortage of 'badged' officers, the SSM with up to fifteen years of SAS experience, will often act as 2IC. Many sixteen-man Troops will not have officers and in these cases a staff sergeant, otherwise the troop 2IC, will be in command. The squadrons are rotated every six months to carry out different duties; these include squadron training in the UK or overseas, especially in the United States, Middle East and Brunei, training foreign Special Forces and so-called 'Strip Alert' or Crisis Response duty, ready for deployment anywhere in the world on very short notice, and counter-terrorist duty, during which a squadron will come under the direction of the regiment's Counter Revolutionary Warfare (CRW) Wing.

Territorial SAS The 21st (Artists') Regiment SAS with its HQ Squadron (Greater London); A Squadron (Greater London); B Squadron (Wales) and C Squadron (East Anglia and Eastern Wessex). This is actually the oldest SAS unit, having been established in 1946 as a reserve unit, and which currently recruits highly trained personnel in southern England. It acts as a mirror unit for the 22nd SAS, as well as emphasising intelligence-gathering. The second territorial unit is the 23rd Regiment SAS with its HQ Squadron (West Midlands), A Squadron (Scotland), B Squadron (Yorkshire and Humberside) and C Squadron (North and North West of England) and which recruits largely in the north of England and Scotland. This unit keeps alive the skills developed by the highly secretive Second World War organisation, MI9, and carries out combat rescue, escape and evasion, prisoner of war rescue or interrogation and clandestine intelligence-gathering. There is also an additional communications unit the 63 (SAS) Signal Squadron Royal Corps of Signals which is based in the south-east and west of England, this squadron's four troops, authorised 31 men each, provide communications

support to 21 and 23 SAS. All TA SAS squadrons are authorised 79 men of
all ranks each. With a total of eight squadrons the two regiments have a
combined establishment of 632. The Sabre squadrons operate in the normal
four-man patrols, building up to sixteen-man troops.

The UK's Joint Rapid Deployment Force (JRDF) capability is provided by
the 10,000 strong 16th Air Assault Brigade based in Colchester, north-east of
London. It comprises two out of the Parachute Regiment's three elite
battalions (1st, 2nd or 3rd); one airmobile trained Infantry battalion; the 7th
Para, RHA with 18 105mm light guns; the 21st Defence Battery, RA, with
Javelin SAM and an air support component that will eventually have 18
CH47 Chinooks and 18 Pumas. However, in the light of the growing
demands made on the armed forces since 9-11 the helicopter element is
likely to be increased to give even greater mobility, and enhanced with a
dedicated gunship capability in due course. The brigade does contain one
genuine Special Forces unit in the form of Pathfinder Platoon of the
Parachute Regiment, which has a very effective LRRP capability and is similar
in many respects to the SAS.

Marines
Royal Marines Special Boat Service (SBS) HQ Hamworthy, Poole, Dorset, UK
The SBS is a part of Britain's Special Forces Group. It has operated all over
the world in its primary amphibious warfare role, as well as performing
many other tasks. SBS has variously stood for Special Boat Section and
Special Boat Squadron; since 1987 it has stood for SB Service. Before its
reorganisation in 1987, the then Special Boat Squadron was about 150-
strong, with about 50 reservists. Since then it has been expanded, but to
what extent is not exactly clear. According to a Ministry of Defence statement
on force structure, there are four squadrons (1 Reservist) in the Special Boat
Service.

M Squadron, the counter-terrorist force, consists of Black, Gold and
Purple Troops. Sixteen-man operational troops are used, at least in the
traditional swimmer-canoeist role, as they can be split into eight canoe pairs,
four four-man patrols or two boat-loads. Inflatable and rigid-inflatable boats
are operated by the SBS themselves, as are SDVs. The Rigid Raiders of 539
Assault Squadron RM, as well as the various landing craft used by this and
other squadrons, provide further support. Air support would come from
RAF Special Forces Flights, using Hercules aircraft and Chinook helicopters,
and from the RN's Naval Air Commando squadrons, with Sea King
helicopters.

Recruits must be Royal Marines Commandos with at least three years'
service. They will have started off their careers with the 30-week initial stint
at the Commando Training Centre or the fifteen-month Young Officers
Course, mostly at the same establishment. Later they may have had further

training in signals, heavy weapons, sniping etc. Those wishing to join the SBS must first go through a two-week aptitude test, which consists of the following: Boating Week – Candidates must pass a combat fitness test and pass the SBS swimming test, which demands 600m in fifteen minutes, 50m clothed with weapon and belt kit, and 25m underwater. Complete all canoe trials, including a 5km march with Bergen and canoe and 30km canoe paddle. Diving Week – Complete a number of dives, generally show confidence and willingness to dive. Those successful will go on to the joint SAS/SBS selection course Brecon Beacons phase (three weeks) – land navigation marches with Bergen and weapon, culminating in 'long drag'. The majority who drop out will do so in this phase. Pre-jungle training (two weeks) – working in four-man patrols. Jungle training, Brunei (six weeks). Officer week/signals training (one week). Support Weapons Training (one week). Army Combat Survival Instructor Course (two weeks) – survival, evasion, resistance and escape is well known for its harsh Resistance to Interrogation training, and the last phase where many will be failed ('Binned'). Continuation training takes place mainly at Hereford. Demolitions (two weeks), Observation Post Training (one week), CQB Course (two weeks), Individual Skills Courses (eight weeks) – during this time men will undergo training as Special Forces medics or signallers, or further demolitions training. Officers attend language training and a Special Forces commander's course, Static Line Parachute Course (three weeks) – for those who are not qualified paratroopers. SBS students go on to their own eight-week boating and diving course, including underwater navigation and demolition, negotiating surf zones and navigating a 55km course in the Klepper canoe, and infiltration via submarine. Following this Marines are rated as Swimmer Canoeist Class 3, and entitled to wear the badge of this specialist qualification on the left cuff of their blue and green dress uniforms, 'SC' over a wreath. This and the parachute wings worn on the upper right sleeve are their only distinctions; they wear the same green beret and capbadge as all Royal Marines, or white cap in blues. RM officers do not wear qualification badges, so they have just the parachute wings. For marines to be promoted to corporal they must qualify as SC2, and to sergeant SC3. These advanced training courses emphasise operational planning and training supervision. Promotion to sergeant also requires passing the Senior Command Course at the CTC, Lympstone in East Devon. Newly-qualified swimmer-canoeists will then join an operational troop, but of course training never ceases. They may go through further training in combat medicine, communications, counter-terrorist operations, foreign languages, SDV 'driving' and many other skills. Exercises are conducted with friendly nations' units, the closest relations being with the SEALs and Dutch SBS.

Weapons used include specialist and foreign weapons likely to be found on the battlefield or in the hands of a terrorist group, and include the silenced Sterling sub-machine gun, designated the L34A1 and the M16A2, a popular weapon among British Special Forces and often has the M203 40mm grenade launcher attached. Other weapons include the MP5 series of sub-machine guns, particularly the MP5SD which has now largely taken over the silenced SMG role, while the Browning Hi-Power remains the main pistol. The Royal Marines have a long sniping tradition, the Accuracy International L96A1 being the weapon used today. Support weapons include the 7.62mm GPMG ('Jimpy' or MAG), 66mm Light anti-tank weapon and 51mm mortar, the last even fired from specially modified canoes. Two-man kayak-type canoes are used by the SBS due to their stealth capability, portability and reliability. The latest model known to be in service is the Klepper Aeres Mark 13. Other craft are the Gemini inflatable and Avon Searider rigid-inflatable boats; these are always used with twin engines in case of failure on operations. The SBS started experiments with two-man Swimmer Delivery Vehicles in the late 1960s. Descendants of these prototypes are in service today, along with American-built four/six-man types. The Draeger LAR-V closed-circuit system is the most commonly used SCUBA gear today. On operations this will be worn with a dry suit over the combat uniform. Communications are, of course, of paramount importance to men on long-range patrols, and the PRC-319 and PRC-320 radios are known to be in service.

RM Mountain Leaders (Mountain and Arctic Warfare Cadre) The MLTC originated in the early 1950s as the Cliff Assault Wing. As the name suggests, the main mission in those days was to get troops and equipment up coastal cliffs. However, Cliff Leaders, as the members were known, also carried out exercises to improve their own climbing, originally in Wales and Scotland, but later also in Austria, Norway, Canada and the Alps. In 1962 the wing was renamed the Cliff Assault Troop, by which time it had begun training in general winter warfare techniques. Thus the CLs were called upon to prepare the men of No. 43 Commando for the first Norwegian exercise carried out by the Royal Marines in October 1962. Several years later it was decided to increase the troop's expertise by putting all members through a reconnaissance course run by the Platoon Weapons Branch at the Commando Training Centre Royal Marines (CTCRM), Lympstone, in East Devon. This was done in 1965 and the unit now became known as the Reconnaissance Leader Troop.

In 1970 the RL Troop became the Mountain and Arctic Warfare Cadre and moved to its present location at Stonehouse Barracks, Plymouth, in south-west Devon. The following year 3rd Commando Brigade returned to the UK after several years in the Far East. The brigade's main mission now was to be on NATO's northern flank and annual exercises were to be conducted in Norway, usually in the winter and in the far north of the country. The

M&AW Cadre had a big role to play in preparing the commando units for these exercises and mountain leaders were attached to all units in the brigade. 3rd Commando Brigade is among the world's leading exponents of cold weather warfare, thanks mainly to a small group of specialists who had been developing the necessary expertise for many years. The cadre was also given the wartime role of long-range foot and ski reconnaissance for the brigade. In the Falklands War of 1982 the twenty members of the cadre and twenty men undergoing training as MLs accompanied 3rd Commando Brigade 'down south'. Their war began immediately after the landings of 21 May. Four-man patrols were inserted all over the brigade's area of operations, in some cases relieving patrols of the SAS and SBS, and also mounting operations in co-operation with the latter. On 31 May a patrol spotted Argentine commandos (Buzo Tactico) landing by helicopter near Top Malo House, in the far north of East Falkland and just south of the proposed British route to Port Stanley. A request for an air strike on the Argentinians now setting up base in the house was denied; instead nineteen more MLs under their commander, Captain Rod Boswell, were flown in an hour after dawn. After landing one group opened fire on the Argentines with 66mm rockets and light machine guns, setting the house on fire, while the others began the assault on the enemy. In the subsequent 40-minute battle four MLs were wounded; of the 17 Buzo Tactico, eight were killed and nine captured. The M&AW Cadre operated in the mountains of northern Iraq in 1991, during Operation Haven, the Allied effort to bring aid to the Kurdish separatists then under heavy attack from the Iraqis. MLs worked in co-operation with US Army Special Forces and also the other elements of 3rd Commando Brigade in the area.

Marine Recce Troop (LRRP)   In 1992, during a period of reorganisation in 3 Commando Brigade, it was decided that a permanent Medium-Range Reconnaissance Troop (LRRP) would be formed. Usually referred to as Recce Troop, it was to form part of the Headquarters and Signal Squadron. Initially there were four six-man patrols, each with an ML sergeant, two ML corporals and three General Duties Marines, men drawn from a commando. In command was an ML lieutenant. By 2002 there were six four-man patrols.

All members have gone through the sniper course at Lympstone, lasting six weeks, and a three-week static line parachute course at RAF Brize Norton. Those who have not yet qualified as ML2s will have been trained by the Mountain Leaders to Reconnaissance Leader (RL) standard. Recce Troop concentrates on training in the same disciplines as the cadre: in climbing and cliff assault, cold-weather survival, long-range patrolling on ski and foot, long-range communications, high-altitude mountaineering, snow and ice climbing, target and route reconnaissance, primary interrogation and resistance to interrogation, and sabotage. In addition many members will have gone through the Army's Jungle Long-Range Patrol Course, run in Brunei. Some also train as specialists in desert warfare, for the Royal Marines must be ready to deploy almost anywhere in the world. Later members may go through advanced training as divers and/or free-fall (HALO) parachutists.

RM Commachio Group An RM unit based in Arbroath in north-eastern Scotland and charged with the anti-terrorist responsibility for Britain's North Sea oil rigs in particular, and certain other strategic assets in general. It is around 350-strong and contains a large contingent of combat swimmer-canoeists from the SBS. They train to carry out assaults on rigs from helicopters, small raider craft and underwater from submarines or by parachute-SCUBA insertions.

3rd Commando Brigade The Royal Marines also provides a major component of Britain's JRDF in the form of the this brigade with its HQ in Plymouth, Devon, which has under its command 40, 42 and 45 commando, battalion-sized combat units in addition to a range of support units that make this a very efficient and self-sufficient elite rapid reaction force.

CIVILIAN SPECIAL FORCES
D-11 of the Metropolitan Police   This is the nearest that the British Civilian Police have to a SWAT-style response unit, and though most police forces in the UK have increased the numbers of armed officers, none have chosen to create a genuine paramilitary capability as yet. D11 is based on the Metropolitan Police firearms instructors, with the unit being primarily trained for containment and as snipers. Several small teams are, however, trained for assaults in situations where it should not prove necessary to request SAS assistance. They also handle most non-political hostage rescue situations. Weapons in use include the 9mm H&K MP5 7.62mm L39A, Enfield Enforcer and Parker-Hale sniper rifles, and a range of other automatic rifles and side-arms.

USA

MILITARY SPECIAL FORCES
The US Special Operations Command or USSOCOM   has been in existence in one form or another since 1980, but was only formally established as a unified combat command at MacDill AFB, Florida, on 16 April 1987. It has been pushed to the forefront of US military activity and thinking by the rise in the number of small or unconventional wars and in particular terrorism. The events of 9-11 and the response of the United States government in declaring a 'War on Terrorism' which, according to some in the Bush administration, is likely to last a generation, has ensured that Special Forces

will play a pivotal role in US operations in the future. The need to minimise 'friendly' casualties and the difficulties caused by international terrorist groups such as Islamic Jihad and Al Qa'ida, with no permanent base or country to which they owe allegiance, makes the use of conventional military force increasingly difficult. The initial campaign 'Operation Enduring Freedom', and a predicated operation to overthrow the Iraqi regime of Saddam Hussein, can prove misleading, as they give the appearance of being traditional military operations. In fact one of the most significant innovations in Operation Enduring Freedom in Afghanistan during 2001–02 was the initial employment of US Special Operations Command (USSOCOM) as the principal operational command, rather than the Central Command (CENTCOM), which is strategically responsible for the area. By using a functional, rather than a geographic, command to plan the Afghan campaign, the US President and Secretary of Defence engaged in a radical and highly successful test of the 'capabilities-based' concept that is central to the current Department of Defence transformation. Indeed Iraq will be the target of a considerable Special Forces operation, and only if that fails to undermine the regime will a conventional attack be launched. USSOCOM will become the cutting edge of US military power with an increasing independent and vital role to play in the 21st century.

Though the USSOCOM has a total strength in access of 46,000, there are probably less than 10,000 troops actually available within the main combat units and by late 2002 there were distinct signs that its capability was becoming overstretched with its many serious military commitments throughout the world. It is organised into the US Army Special Operations Command (USASOC) with the 1st SFOD (Delta Force); five Special Forces Groups (Green Berets), one Ranger Regiment (the 75th); one Special Operations Aviation Regiment (Nightstalkers); one Psychological Operations Group, one Special Operations Support Command with a SpecOps Signal Battalion (112th), a SpecOps Support Battalion (528th) and six SpecOps Theatre Support elements, two Chemical Reconnaissance Detachments (CRD), a Civil Affairs (CA) battalion and the John F. Kennedy Special Warfare Center and School. The Naval Special Warfare Command (NAVSPECWARCOM) with a Naval Special Warfare Centre, two Naval Special Warfare Groups, five Naval Special Warfare Units, a Naval Special Warfare Development Group (DEVGRU), six SEAL Teams, two SEAL Delivery Vehicle Teams, two Special Boat Squadrons and three Special Boat Squadrons.

The Air Force Special Operations Command (AFSOC) with the 16th Special Operations Wing (SOW) with eight squadrons with five fixed wing, one rotary, one foreign aid and one training with a variety of aircraft including AC130H/U, MC13OE/H/F/P, MH60G, MH53J & TH53A. Two SpecOps Groups (the 352nd in the UK and the 353rd in Japan) and the 720th Special Tactics Group.

Reserves include two additional ARNG Special Forces Groups, four CA Commands, seven CA Brigades and 24 CA Battalions, two Psyop Groups, nine Naval Special Warfare detachments, five SEAL detachments, four Special Boat units. The 919th USAFR SpecOps Wing (two fixed wing Squadrons) and 193rd ANG SpecOps Wing (one fixed wing squadron).

While the United States Marine Corps is not an established part of USSOCOM, it takes its orders from the same source and co-operates fully with the overall Special Forces planning and operational requirements laid out by the Department of Defence (DoD). This elite force of some 175,000 provides additional Special Forces with three Marine Force Reconnaissance ('recon') units, three Marine Long-Range Reconnaissance Battalions (LRRP). They also provide Regimental Search and Target acquisition Platoons, two Fleet Radio Reconnaissance Platoons, Air-Naval Gunfire Liaison Companies (ANGLICO) and Fleet Anti-Terrorist Security Teams.

USASOC

1st SFOD – The Delta Force   For some years the US Army lagged behind many of the other leading armies in not having a dedicated anti-terrorist force and although the 'Blue Light', a small Counter Revolutionary Warfare or CRW unit drawn from 5th Special Forces Group (Airborne), was assigned an anti-terrorist role, it was not until the formation of Delta Force that the US Army finally had a genuine anti-terrorist capability. The Ist Special Forces Operational Detachment, otherwise known as Delta Force, is the United States' first dedicated national intervention, counter revolutionary warfare and aggressive Special Operations unit. It was activated in November 1977, and was largely the brainchild of Lieutenant Colonel Charles 'Charlie' Beckwith, an experienced Special Forces officer who had served with the British 22nd Regiment Special Air Service during the 1960s. Organised and indeed trained along SAS lines, Delta Force soon developed a very distinct ethos and character of its own, with the initial intake being from the 10th Special Forces Group (Airborne) at Camp Dawson, WVa. To this were soon to be added a sprinkling of volunteers from the US Army Rangers and other Special Forces Groups, and in May 1978 the first 73 trainees were accepted into the newly operational force. Delta's first major operation was the failed attempt to rescue the hostages held by Iranian militants in the occupied US embassy in Tehran on 25 April 1979. Delta Force then took part in Operation Urgent Fury, Grenada 1983, and Operation Just Cause in Panama in December 1989, where they successfully carried out Operation Acid Gambit, the rescue of the US citizen Kurt Muse, being held hostage in the Carcel Modelo Prison. In the Gulf War 1990–91 they covertly hunted SCUD missile launchers inside Iraq and were part of Task Force Ranger in Somalia during 1992–93. Delta Force has also seen service in the recent Balkan wars of 1992–2000, particularly in tracking down suspected war criminals. However, after the events of 9-11 the important part that Special Operations are likely to play in future warfare has been further highlighted. New technologies, new methods and a decade of practical experience have established the US Special Forces and their CIA covert action colleagues as important players in the global-security arena.

The Delta Forces headquarters are at Fort Bragg, NC, and its training is of the very highest standard, providing its personnel with extraordinary levels of physical fitness, mental toughness and motivation. All aspects of modern Special Forces techniques are practised regularly until they become instinctive: combat shooting, sniping, the 'House of Horror', Delta's own version of the SAS 'killing house', hostage rescue, anti-hijacking, VIP protection, heliborne insertion, HAHO (High Altitude High Opening) and HALO (High Altitude Low Opening) parachuting, unarmed combat, combat swimming, demolition and sabotage, and training to survive and operate effectively in all combat environments – jungle, desert, Arctic, mountain, riverine, urban and built-up city areas. It trains and operates regularly with other similar units from around the world, in particular the British SAS, German GSG-9 and the French GIGN. With the Middle East conflicts in mind, increased training has been undertaken in desert and mountain warfare and this has involved building an even closer relationship with the highly secretive Israeli Sayeret Matkal and the Turkish Para-Commando Brigades. It has access to a huge range of high-technology surveillance, electronic warfare, communications and intelligence equipment ranging from personal night-vision goggles and thermal viewers to detect hidden objects by a generated heat pattern, to near real-time information on an enemy transmitted directly from Intelligence Satellites, while GPS (Global Positioning System) allows almost inch-perfect positioning anywhere in the world. The US military provides a range of electronic warfare and surveillance, transport and logistic support, including low-observable or stealth helicopters for covert operations, while Delta Force's close links to the CIA and other Federal agencies ensures access to high-grade intelligence. The Delta Force has access to an amazing range of personal equipment, ranging from specialist uniforms, Kevlar bullet-proof vests, CBW respirators to a complete arsenal of US and Foreign weapons and explosives. Those in current use include the 7.65mm PPK, 9mm P7 and Browning HP automatic pistols, 9mm MP5, particularly the MP5SD3 with a collapsing stock and integral silencer. The bolt noise is absorbed by rubber buffers and, when used with subsonic ammunition, this weapon is virtually silent from only fifteen feet away. Also in use are the Israeli 9mm Uzi sub-machine guns, 5.56mm M16A1 automatic rifles and the CAR-15 carbine version; Remington 40XB sniper rifles, .5 Barrett M82 long-range sniper rifles, H&K 21 machine guns, 7.62mm M60 machine guns, 40mm M79/M203 grenade launchers and an eye-opening array of unusual and exotic weaponry.

The Delta Force provides the United States with a first-rate national intervention anti-terrorist force.

The Special Forces Groups (The Green Berets). The role of the US Special Forces Groups are best expressed in the words of its founding officer, Colonel Aaron Bank, a wartime veteran of the OSS. Against vehement opposition from both the traditionalists in the US Army and the CIA, which considered the covert action role to be its prerogative particularly after it finally absorbed the OPC with its clandestine warfare capabilities, Bank pushed through the formation of a new Special Warfare School at Fort Bragg in North Carolina. Here volunteers would be trained to 'infiltrate by land, sea or air, deep into enemy-occupied territory and organise the resistance/guerrilla potential to conduct Special Forces operations with the emphasis on guerrilla warfare'. Bank must certainly be considered an important visionary and one of the first to see the future revolution in major conflicts where unconventional warfare conducted by nationalist, racialist, religious or politically motivated groups would be a predominant factor. The importance of training foreign Special Forces, or civic actions, what the British were to call 'winning hearts and minds', has been a major factor in the Green Berets' workload over the last 50 years. Banks also wanted the Special Forces soldier to be a linguist and to be able to relate to different environments and peoples of different cultures. Indeed the Green Berets became a sort of American Foreign Legion with a good response from European, Asiatic and Hispanic expatriates keen to gain US citizenship through service in the armed forces. General Bank was a staunch admirer of the British commandos and considered the wearing of a Green Beret an appropriate symbol for the new US Special Forces. The accusations of 'elitism' from senior officers put an end to this until President Kennedy, on a visit to Fort Bragg, ordered its reinstatement. In 1964 the Green Berets introduced the Studies and Observation Group or SOG, basically a cover name for clandestine intelligence-gathering teams that would operate for long periods deep behind enemy lines. The SOGs also include additional personnel drawn from the SEALs and USMC Recon teams. The Special Forces provide highly effective elite commandos, more in the style of the French Foreign Legion's specialist 2nd Regiment than that of the British SAS or, of course, the US Army's own Delta Force. Their often little known operations and specialist foreign training activities have taken them regularly to virtually every corner of the world. In the aftermath of 9-11 the calls upon their services have grown to a point that a reassessment of their numbers and organisation cannot be long delayed, along with a serious rethink about the deployment of so many skilled Special Forces on training missions to areas unaffected by the War on Terrorism, which is very much on the cards. The US Army can currently call upon five front-line Special Forces Groups each with an establishment of three battalions;

1st headquarters at Fort Lewis, Wa (Pacific and Eastern Asia) with 1st battalion in Okinawa and Detachment K – S Korea

3rd headquarters at Fort Bragg, NC (Caribbean and Western Africa)

5th headquarters at Fort Campbell, Ky (South-west Asia and North-eastern Africa)

7th headquarters at Fort Benning, Ga (Central and South America) C Company 3/7th Special Forces Group – Panama

10th headquarters at Fort Devens, Ma (Europe and Western Asia) 1st battalion at Bad Tolz, near Stuttgart, Germany

11th SFG Reserve – Fort Meade, Maryland

12th SFG Reserve – Arlington Height – Illinois

19th SFG NG, Draper – Utah

20th SFG NG, Birmingham – Alabama

The 75th Ranger Regiment The Rangers of the Second World War and Korea had been designed as light-infantry shock troops; their mission was to hit hard, hit fast, then get out so larger and more heavily armed units could follow through, much the same as the modern Ranger force. Reactivated as 'The Rangers' at Fort Benning, Georgia, in 1975 with two battalions, a third being raised in 1984 when the official title of the '75th' was actually given. This unit will play a major role in the 'War on Terrorism' as it is superbly trained in light infantry and counter-insurgency tactics and is quickly deployable for operations in such areas as the Philippines and Somalia. When the 1st and 2nd Ranger battalions were re-activated in 1974, General Abrams wanted the battalions to be 'the best light infantry unit in the world' and a 'standard bearer for the rest of the Army'. After Operation Urgent Fury (Grenada, 1983), the requirement for more Rangers and a better-suited command structure resulted in the formation of the 3rd Ranger Battalion and the Regimental Headquarters in 1984. The 75th Ranger Regiment plans and conducts special military operations in support of US policy and objectives and its specially organised, equipped and trained soldiers provide the National Command Authority (NCA) with the capability to rapidly deploy a credible military force to any region of the world. The cornerstone of Ranger missions is that of direct action, more specifically the Rangers are the premier airfield seizure and raid unit in the US Army. In order to remain proficient in all light infantry skills, Ranger units also focus on 'mission essential tasks' that include mobility, ambush, reconnaissance, airborne and air assaults and improvised actions. A typical Ranger battalion or regiment mission could involve seizing an airfield for use by follow-on more heavily armed ground forces, and conducting raids on key targets of tactical or strategic importance. Once secured, follow-on airmobile or airborne forces are introduced into the theatre of operation and relieve the Ranger force, so that it may withdraw for future SOF operations elsewhere.

Rangers rely heavily on external fire support and the fire support personnel train extensively on the employment of CAS, attack helicopters, Naval Gunfire (NGF), AC-130 gunship and artillery. The close working relationships with units that usually support the force is intended to ensure that the Rangers should have the required assets needed to carry out their mission. The 75th Ranger Regiment, headquartered at Fort Benning, Georgia, is composed of three Ranger battalions and is without doubt still the premier light-infantry unit of the United States Army. The three Ranger battalions that comprise the 75th Ranger Regiment are geographically dispersed; 1st Battalion, Hunter Army Airfield, Georgia; 2nd Battalion, Fort Lewis, Washington and 3rd Battalion, Fort Benning, Georgia. Regimental Headquarters consists of a Command Group, normal staff positions (S-1 through S-5), a sophisticated and highly mobile communications detachment, a fire support element, a reconnaissance detachment of three six-man teams, a cadre for the Ranger Training Detachment (RTD) and a Company Headquarters. Additionally, the regiment has the capability of deploying a planning team consisting of experienced Ranger operations, intelligence, fire support, communications and logistics planners. The team can deploy on short notice with USASOC approval, to theatre SOCs to carry out operations during a crisis.

Each of the three Ranger battalions is identical in organisation. Each battalion consists of three rifle companies and a Headquarters and Headquarters Company. Each battalion is authorised 580 Rangers. However, the battalions may be up to fifteen per cent overmanned to make allowances for schools and TDYs. The flexibility of the Ranger Force requires it to perform under various command structures. The force can work unilaterally under a Corps, as a part of JSOTF, as an ARSOTF, or as an Army component in a JTF. The US Army maintains the regiment at a high level of readiness. Each battalion can deploy anywhere in the world with eighteen hours' notice. Because of the importance the Army places on the 75th Ranger Regiment, it has a number of capabilities, including infiltrating and exfiltrating by land, sea and air, conducting direct action operations, conducting raids, recovery of personnel and special equipment and conducting conventional or special light-infantry operations. On any given day, one Ranger battalion is on Ready Reaction Force (RRF) 1 with the requirement to be ready to go within eighteen hours of notification. Additionally, one rifle company with battalion command and control can deploy in nine hours. The Regimental Headquarters remains on RRF1 at all times. RRF1 rotates between the three battalions, normally in thirteen-week periods. While on RRF1, the designated battalion is prohibited from conducting any off-post training, deployments for training (DFTs), etc., as they would be unable to meet the required deployment time standards. The Ranger Regiment can deploy in any number of ways, including directly from home station to the area of operations. More often, the force deploys to an Intermediate Staging Base (ISB) to link-up with attachments before conducting operations.

The USAF Special Operations Aviation Command and the 160th Special Operations Aviation Regiment in particular. Shortly after the failed hostage rescue mission, Desert One, in Iran in 1979, the Army formed a special aviation unit. The 160th provides a modern night fighting aviation capability with advanced night flight techniques and the use of Stealth technology. Established on 16 October 1981, when it was formally designated as the 160th Aviation Battalion or Task Force 160, it has since become known as the 'Night Stalkers', because of its capability to strike undetected during darkness. This is often performed in the most demanding of environmental flight conditions, including habitually operating at only thirty feet above the water, at night or in bad weather, using night vision goggles and forward looking infrared devices. The unit has continued to grow and was officially activated as the 160th Special Operations Aviation Regiment (Airborne) on 16 May 1990. Responding to an increased demand for elite highly trained Special Operations aviation assets, the regiment activated three battalions, an additional separate detachment, and incorporated one National Guard battalion. It operates a number of low-observable or Stealth helicopters, including the specially modified Black Hawk known as HH-60G 'Pave Hawk'; the AH-6G 'Little Bird' and the advanced RAH-66 Commanche. The 'Night Stalkers' have already seen service in Grenada, Panama, Somalia and Afghanistan and will take a leading role in any future conflict with Iraq and the worldwide War on Terrorism. The 160th SOAR (A) is based at Fort Campbell, KY, and is composed of four active duty battalions and one forward-deployed company. Its battalions include the 1/160, which flies the AH-6, MH-6, MH-60K and MH-60L DAP, 2/160 which flies the MH-47E and 4/160 Special Operations Aviation Support battalion all based at Fort Campbell, KY. The 3/160 which flies the MH-60L and MH-47D is based at Hunter Army Airfield, Savannah, GA, and also controls the D/160 which consists of five MH-60Ls based at Ft. Kobbe, Panama. Although all army aviation units have an inherent capability to support Special Operations, the units of the 160th SOAR (A) have been specifically designated by the Secretary of Defence to be prepared, trained and task organised for Special Operations mission support.

4th PSYOP Group. One of USASOC's least well-known units is the Psychological Warfare Group based at Fort Bragg with four battalions – one of which saw widespread use in Afghanistan, often broadcasting anti-Taliban propaganda from specially modified C-130 aircraft. It has an important role to play in undermining local support for hostile regimes or terrorist groups.

Reserve units are the 2nd PSYOP, Parma Cleveland – Ohio, 5th PSYOP, Washington DC, and the 7th PSYOP Group, San Francisco, California.

Navy

US Naval Special Warfare Groups – SEALs and DEVGRU The SEAL (SEA-AIR-LAND) teams are similar to their British equivalents the SBS and SAS Boat Sections, and regularly train with them both in the UK and the USA. They are generally recognised as the most highly skilled and trained combat units in the US armed forces. They can trace their history back to the UDT (Underwater Demolition Teams) formed in 1943 to assist in the dangerous task of beach reconnaissance and clearing safe lanes through German waterline defences for the waves of landing craft that would be used in the Normandy invasion in 1944. Additional UDT would do sterling work at Guam, Iwo Jima and Okinawa. During the Korean War they proved hugely successful in preparing the way for the major amphibious landing at Inchon. In 1960 a US Navy review suggested that there was a real need for an even more specialised unit to conduct deep penetration, reconnaissance, sabotage and counter-terrorist operations. In 1962 President Kennedy authorised the establishment of the first two SEAL teams. Recruited at first principally from the UDT, the SEALs performed well in the Vietnam War. Their reputation for being 'go anywhere soldiers' has been enhanced by their ability to operate in jungle, desert, mountain and Arctic zones with only marginal preparation. Combat teams are each made up of 27 officers and 156 enlisted men, and were eventually to be formed and based at their Pacific headquarters at Coronado naval base at San Diego, California, and the Atlantic headquarters at Norfolk naval base, Virginia. SEAL Team 6, however, was formed and acted as a dedicated anti-terrorist and hostage rescue force. The SEALs are trained in every conceivable Special Forces technique and tactic from HALO/HAHO to combat swimming. They use a wide variety of advanced helicopters, and fast surface raiding craft to SDV (Swimmer Delivery Vehicles) maintained and operated by specialist SDV teams. Indeed the US Navy has a number of advanced mini-subs with specially modified fleet submarines for clandestine insertion for Special Operations. Much of what DEVGRU, or the Naval Special Warfare Development Group, is and does remains classified and unknown. It was formed in the mid-1990s after SEAL Team 6, the Navy's counter-terrorism group, was disbanded. DEVGRU was created after Richard Marcinko, the original commander of ST6, published a series of books that outlined the history and purpose of the original Team. According to the US Navy, DEVGRU was formed to create, test, and evaluate new tactics, weapons and equipment. However, with the disbanding of ST6, the Navy was left without a maritime CT unit. DEVGRU is actually a CT unit created to replace ST6. While under the command of NAVSPECWARGRU, Navy Special Warfare Group, DEVGRU is also a component of JSOC, with other units such as the US Army's Delta Force and 160th Special Operations Aviation Regiment, both units that list counter-terrorism in their primary activities. Weapons most commonly used include the following: the H&K MP5 is used mainly in CQB and the Colt M4 is the primary assault weapon. The SOCOM pistol has been issued but it is reported that the Sig-Sauer P-228 is preferred for personal defence. DEVGRU is thought to consist of around 400 combat and support personnel, divided into four combat teams and one training team. The combat assault teams are Red, Gold and Blue, with Gold being the premier assault team. Gray team is the transportation unit containing the SDV and boats used to transport the assault teams. Green Team consists of the new operators who have just joined DEVGRU and are in training. Each operator inside the Teams has a speciality, but all are experts in underwater and HALO insertion. DEVGRU has a small number of dedicated MH/HH60 helicopters available for clandestine operations.

The US Naval Special Warfare Command is based at the Naval Amphibious Base at Coronado, situated on Silver Strand across the bay from the city of San Diego in California, along with SEAL Teams 1, 3 and 5, Special Boat Unit 12 and a host of development and training establishments. The major Naval Amphibious Base at Little Creek, on Hampton Roads in Virginia on the East Coast is home to SEAL Teams 2, 4 and 8, along with Special Boat Squadron 2 and Special Boat Unit 20. SEAL Teams have been based in many parts of the world including the west coast of Scotland at RAF Machrihanish and now elements of SEAL Team 3 are deployed at Manama, Bahrain, in the Persian Gulf.

Marines

Recon Units (LRRP)   Among the many elite units provided by the USMC, the Recons have probably most deserved their outstanding reputation for toughness, skill and battlefield success. In the aftermath of 9-11 it is likely that the USMC will often be the first into combat in many future campaigns and there will be an increased use made of their expertise as Special Forces in the ongoing War on Terrorism. In the 1980s the USMC made two of their Marine Expeditionary Units Special Operations capable (MEU-SOC) and prepared them for a range of missions such as amphibious raids, anti-terrorist and hostage rescue operations.

Marine Anti-Terror Unit 2001   The marines established an anti-terrorism brigade on 10 October 2001 at Camp Lejeune, NC and it became fully operational as the 4th Marine Expeditionary Brigade on 1 December. The brigade has 4,800 marines and sailors assigned and will merge existing anti-terrorism capabilities. These are the Marine Security Force battalion, the Marine Security Guard Battalion and the Chemical and Biological Incident Response Force. The units' individual missions are similar, and working closely together is intended to create a synergy that will be helpful to the overall anti-terrorist effort. The unit will also have a fourth element: an anti-terrorism battalion. The new battalion will evolve from the 1st Battalion, 8th Marines, the unit terrorists hit in Lebanon in 1983, killing 241 US service members.

The Chemical, Biological Incident Response Force was established in 1996 following the sarin gas attack in Tokyo the year before. Headquartered in Indian Head, Md., the force is ready to back up local, state and other federal agencies at a moment's notice.

CIVILIAN SPECIAL FORCES

The FBI have a range of specialist response teams including:

HRT or Hostage Rescue Teams

NEST or Nuclear Emergency Search Team

However, since the events of 9-11 the FBI are under increasing pressure to establish a genuine rapid response anti-terrorist capability.

Phoenix Police have the SAU-Special Assignments Unit,

Atlanta Police the SOS-Special Operations Section and the

NYPD have the ESU-Emergency Service Unit.

All are SWAT and hostage rescue teams and, in the case of the ESU, some 400-strong.

URUGUAY

MILITARY SPECIAL FORCES

Batallón de Infantería Paracaidista No. 14 – 14th Para Battalion – Toledo, Canelones, one parachute company (compañía paracaidista 'Fantasma'), one commando company (compañía de comandos 'General Artigas') and the CEAT (compañía especial antiterrorista) 'Escorpión' – Anti-terrorist company.

Uruguay has had a long-term insurgency problem, but the brutal tactics of the Security and Special Forces have so far managed to keep these at a fairly low intensity. However, the huge abuse of human rights has ensured that these units are hated by whole sectors of the population, which in turn has seriously affected their operational efficiency.

UZBEKISTAN

MILITARY SPECIAL FORCES

One Airborne Brigade with a single Special Forces Battalion based in Tashkent. Based on a typical SPETSNAZ unit, it is now slowly receiving more modern Western weapons and equipment. The threat from the growing number of Islamic insurgencies in the region is likely to see the creation of at least one additional Special Forces Battalion by 2003, and a dedicated hostage rescue capability.

UZI

Designed by Lieutenant Uziel Galil in 1952 to replace the motley collection of sub-machine guns used by the Israelis in the 1948 War of Independence, the Uzi has gone on to become one of the best known and most widely used automatic weapons in the world. Many of these, however, were to be made later under licence both in Belgium by FN (Fabrique Nationale) and Germany. Made of relatively inexpensive stamped steel pressings simply spot-welded together, with only the barrel, breech and magazine receiver being machined components. Chambered in 9mm, the 25- or 32-round box magazines are inserted through the pistol grip, which is of considerable help when having to reload particularly quickly or in the dark. Fitted with either a fixed wooden stock or a folding tubular stock, the Uzi is also fitted with internal dust and sand grooves which usually prevent the weapon from being jammed or clogged by loose particles. Weighing just 9lb (4kg) fully-loaded, it has a cyclic rate of fire of 600rpm and an effective range of up to 110yds (100m). The standard weapon has been followed by the Mini-Uzi with a shorter barrel for covert operations, and though range has naturally suffered this is normally of little importance in enclosed situations or in hostage rescue operations. An even smaller variant has appeared in recent years. Known as the 'Micro' or Micro-Uzi this powerful little weapon is capable of literally being hidden in a largish coat pocket.

VENEZUELA

MILITARY SPECIAL FORCES
Army Special Forces Command HQ Caracas
(72nd) Ranger Special Forces Brigade
73rd Ranger Special Forces Brigade – HQ Maturin
23rd Special Forces Brigade (Brigada Especial de Seguridad y Desarollo) – Fort Tavacare, Barinas
232nd Bn. de Cazadores CNEL. VICENTE CAMPO ELIAS (SF Battalion)
233rd Bn. de Cazadores CNEL. JUAN JOSE RONDON(SF Battalion)

Special Intervention Brigade   Formerly the main anti-terrorist unit it assumed responsibility for HRU duties in 1978. Trained and re-organised by the GSG-9, it later received assistance from Israeli Special Forces advisers. In addition to Special Operations and hostage rescue training, emphasis is placed on CQB, combat shooting, rappelling, breaching and other specialist skills. Weapons used include H & K MP5, Ingram and Uzi SMGs, FN FAL and M16 assault rifles. Because of the importance of the oil industry this unit is particularly well equipped and indeed trained in handling terrorist incidents within the highly vulnerable oil production fields and facilities. The unit has been deployed abroad on several occasions, notably to El Salvador in 1979 to rescue the Venezuelan Ambassador, though in this case negotiations proved successful. In July 1984 the SIB successfully assault a hijacked airliner on the island of Aruba in the Caribbean. All 79 passengers were rescued and the hijackers were killed. However, this apparently outstanding operation was marred by the persistent rumour that the hijackers had in fact been disaffected Venezuelan intelligence personnel, trying to exhort payment for their covert services from the authorities in Caracas. Not surprisingly the Venezuelan government of the time were apparently highly relieved that none of the hijackers survived to face the press or stand trial in what could have been a very difficult and politically embarrassing event. Since the failed coup against the Venezuelan President in April 2002 considerable steps have been taken to ensure the loyalty of the Special Forces as a protection against the largely hostile army staging another attempt. Better pay, conditions and new equipment have been promised, and a serious effort made to place loyal officers in vital command positions. The Special Forces have had their communications removed from the Army Command net for added security.

VIETNAM

MILITARY SPECIAL FORCES

Special Forces Command
One Airborne-Commando Brigade,
Two Sabotage and Assault Regiments (LRRP).
Much of the still large Vietnamese Army was trained in jungle warfare and unconventional operations, but the creation of a genuine Special Forces was neglected. However, as there are signs of growing unrest among some of the ethnic peoples of central Vietnam, the authorities in Hanoi have created an Airborne-Commando unit with a dedicated anti-terrorist capability. This unit is also probably responsible for providing a hostage rescue unit.

VNUKOVO AIRLINES HIJACKING 2001

Thirty minutes after taking off from Istanbul in Turkey on the afternoon of Thursday 15 March 2001, a Moscow-bound Russian Tupolev-154 passenger jet carrying 174 passengers was hijacked by three men armed with knives. The Russian Federal Security Service, the FSB, immediately started putting together a team to take down the aircraft if the opportunity arose. The hijackers, however, diverted the aircraft to Saudi Arabia, and forced it to land at the airport in Medina. The aircraft was isolated from the rest of the airport, sitting by itself away from the main airport area. Meanwhile, FSB negotiators attempted to establish a dialogue with the terrorists, suspected to be Chechen separatists. In conflicting reports, the Russians reported that they were in direct contact with the pilots, who had managed to barricade themselves in the cockpit. Saudi officials received the hijackers' demand, an end to the Russian counter-terrorist campaign in Chechnya. Initially, a Chechen rebel spokesman denied involvement in the incident, but the rebels later identified the hijackers as a former Chechen Interior Minister, Aslambek Arsayev, and his brother. On 16 March negotiators succeeded in securing the release of 47 hostages, mainly women and children, and a steward who was stabbed during the initial minutes of the hijack. Negotiations resumed to gain the release of the 100 plus hostages still on board the Tu-154. Later that day negotiations broke down and Saudi officials, with the approval of the Russians, decided to storm the aircraft, but only after the hijackers finally threatened to blow up the aircraft if it was not refuelled for a suspected flight to Afghanistan. Saudi commandos dressed in camouflage fatigues and tactical vests and helmets, stormed the aircraft and secured the aircraft and the hostages, but at the cost of the deaths of two hostages, a female flight attendant and a Turkish passenger, and one of the hijackers. Despite the successful storming of the Vnukovo Airways aircraft the Russian government has accused both Turkey and Saudi Arabia of co-operating with the Chechen rebels.

WALK POINT (POINT)

The first soldier in a patrol, responsible for finding mines or enemy soldiers.

WELROD

Built during the Second World War for the British SOE and for Special Forces covert action, the Welrod was designed as a single-shot silent killing/assassination weapon. Chambered in 9mm, it is very easy to conceal, reliable and accurate up to 55yds (50m) in daylight or perhaps 22yds (20m) on a starlit night. The Welrod, though probably in an updated version, is still available to the SAS in 2002.

Other variations developed during the Second World War at the Welwyn Experimental Laboratories for SOE were the Wel-Wand, a .25 calibre 'Sleeve-Gun', a silenced single-shot device hidden in the sleeve of the assassin's overcoat; the Welfag, a .22 calibre firing device concealed within a cigarette; the Welpen, a firing device concealed within a fountain pen and the Welpipe, a .22 calibre firing device concealed within a smoking pipe.

WILLIE PETE

WP, a white phosphorus round or grenade.

WOMEN'S ROLE IN SPECIAL FORCES

Women, though playing an ever more important role in the world's Intelligence and Security agencies, are not usually considered to feature prominently in Special Forces operations, but this is in fact quite far from the truth. Soviet elite para-commando units in the Second World War were regularly made up of ten to fifteen per cent female soldiers and this has continued to the present day, when Russian SPETSNAZ companies have female personnel at most levels, even in potential combat roles, as well as the covert surveillance and reconnaissance teams. While no women are officially posted to the 22nd SAS Regiment, a number of highly trained female personnel have regularly played important roles in many SAS undercover operations, particularly in Northern Ireland, usually on secondment for limited periods from the Intelligence Corps, Royal Military Police and in particular the secretive 14th Intelligence company.

However, female personnel have traditionally been ever present in the front line with the Israel Defence Forces, and in particular the numerous Special Operations conducted within Europe and the United States. In fact women had valuable full combat status in both the Jewish underground prior to the creation of Israel and in the Army during the 1948 War of Independence. From 1948 to the late 1990s women officially had no combat role to play, although many were armed and were indeed called upon to fight. They remained vitally important within the Special Forces and Intelligence services, particularly in clandestine operations and close surveillance. Volunteers have apparently been called upon to use certain female attributes in intelligence operations, both to obtain information not normally available by any other manner and on occasions to set up a target for capture or assassination.

However, by the late 1990s the shortage of male recruits was to force the IDF to accept a more visible combat status for female soldiers and indeed a disproportionate number now serve with Special Forces units such as the Sayeret Matkal, the Sachlav Military Police stationed in the Occupied Territories, MAGAV–SAMAG, a highly specialised patrol unit and other similar Special Forces formations such as the Unit YAMAG; Unit 669 serving as airborne paramedics and on helicopter operations behind enemy lines to rescue downed aircrew; and Unit YABAN as defence divers and Unit OKET'Z as canine handlers or those attached to regular military units. Women officers and NCOs were to take over almost all of the field instructing positions in the IDF where, having undergone a tough selection course, they are then selected for individual specialised areas and can be currently found as instructors in physical fitness, explosives and demolition, close combat shooting skills, mortars, sniping, missile warfare, diving, parachuting and driving (APC, Jeeps and ATV). However, their most important role within the Special Forces remains in the dangerous but highly important areas of clandestine operations, surveillance and intelligence-gathering, both within the occupied Palestinian lands and abroad. Israel and many other countries will see the growth of female participation in combat roles over the next few years as male interest in military service appears to wane. Without a shadow of doubt women have proved themselves both mentally and emotionally tough soldiers, with a highly respected role to play in undercover and intelligence Special Operations, and it cannot be too long before full combat status will be granted to women by many of the world's most elite units.

YEMEN

MILITARY SPECIAL FORCES
Two Airborne-Commando Brigades each with a Special Forces Anti-Terrorist Company. With the reported presence of Islamic terrorist groups linked to Al Qa'ida in the country, these Yemeni units are now receiving considerable assistance from the US Special Forces, with new weapons, surveillance and intelligence equipment and improved training. Covert US anti-terrorist teams have also been conducting joint patrols with the Yemeni forces in search operations for terrorist camps in the months following 9-11.

YUGOSLAVIA

MILITARY SPECIAL FORCES
The 63rd Paratroop Brigade is stationed at Nis. The unit uses night parachute jumps to gain the advantage of surprise prior to attacking an objective. Several units were stationed in Bosnia during 1993 and 1994 without being properly deployed in action. Although it is called a brigade and should therefore have a strength of some 4,000 paratroops, the strength in peacetime is a rather less.

72nd Special Brigade – Specijalna Brigada The 72nd Special Brigade was created in the early 1990s and is tasked with various missions that include direct actions, reconnaissance, special warfare and counter-terrorism. During the early 1990s, the 72nd Special Brigade was placed under the control of the Special Forces Corps, but after its disbandment, the brigade was subordinated back to the 3rd Army. Recruits participate in a three-month selection course, where their knowledge of military tactics, various skills, physical condition and the ability to make decisions is tested. In the second month of selection, the first 30km march is conducted and in the third month a 40km march with 25kg of equipment. Only 20–30 per cent of applicants pass the selection course. Those who succeed are sent off for specialised tactics training that will last eight months, after which they may take specialised courses in parachuting, alpine operations (winter and summer), survival, skiing, hand-to-hand combat, field medicine, demolition, high-speed driving, use of special equipment and others. Total training lasts about two years. Weapons used include Yugoslavian-produced assault rifles, sub-machine guns and machine guns, M-76, M91, M93 (7.9mm) and M93 (12.7mm) sniper rifles. Other weapons include 60mm light mortars, 30mm automatic grenade launchers, 40mm underbarrel grenade launchers, all variants of the H&K MP5 sub-machine gun, South African R-4 rifles, CZ-99 .357cal pistols, Zastava and Franchi SPAS shotguns, silenced Ingram and Skorpion machine pistols and crossbows. In their arsenal, the 72nd Brigade also has M-16s, SIG Sauer sniper rifles, H&K G3, .50cal Barrett sniper rifles and other Western firearms.

Kobre (Cobras) – counter-terrorist unit Highly trained in anti-terrorist actions, the Cobras, and a similar unit, Sokolovi (Falcons/Hawks), are equipped and armed with a variety of sophisticated gear, including optic-electronic devices for night operations. The Cobra unit consists of two platoons and a total strength of 60, who are trained for activities with unconventional weapons such as crossbows. Created in 1978.

CIVILIAN SPECIAL FORCES
The Special Antiterrorist Force – Specijalna Antiteroristicka Jedinica – SAJ Created in 1995. There are two SAJ units, one in Vojvodina, the other in Kosovo. Now some 500-strong, they use the Paklenik training centre in Goc, where there is a 'model' town for CQB and urban warfare training. Weapons used include the 9mm Heckler-Koch MP-5 and 7.62mm Heckler-Koch G-3 SSG sniper rifles. They were involved in various operations in Bosnia and Kosovo, which resulted in gross abuses of human rights and ethnic cleansing. The SAJ were also involved in the arming and training of various paramilitary Serbian nationalist death squads responsible for mass rape, torture and murder of ethnic minorities throughout the Balkan conflict from the mid-1990s onwards.

ZAMBIA

MILITARY SPECIAL FORCES
A small Special Forces security detachment is attached to each of the three brigade HQs.

They are reported to provide the sole national anti-terrorist and hostage rescue capability.

ZIMBABWE

MILITARY SPECIAL FORCES
Special Forces Command
1st Parachute Battalion (formerly the 'Selous Scouts' – Rhodesian SF unit)

and the 1st Commando Battalion are both based at the former KGVI (King George 5th) Barracks in the capital city, Harare.

These units are effectively President Robert Mugabe's private army and are dedicated to keeping him in power. Their actions have been brutal and the widespread human rights abuse of all ethnic backgrounds by these Special Forces units has become increasingly widespread in recent years.

BIBLIOGRAPHY

Our own AFI Research Files provided the vast majority of the information contained in this book, backed-up with thirty years of newspaper cuttings and thousands of metres of video tape in our archives and indeed countless meetings with former and serving Special Forces personnel.

The Internet, though very largely full of misinformation or downright rubbish, can still turn up the odd gem or two.

In particular Special Operations (www.specialoperations.com) and Special Warfare (www.specwarnet.com).

Among the hundreds of books that have been published on this subject, we found the most interesting included:

Airborne: A Guided Tour of an Airborne Task Force, Tom Clancy, Berkley Pub Group 2000

Airborne Rangers, Alan Landau, Frieda Landau, 1992

Air Commando Fighters of World War II, Edward Young, Specialty Pr 2000

Air Commando: 50 Years of the USAF Air Commando and Special Operations Forces, 1944–1994, Philip D. Chinnery, Harry C. Aderholt, 1997

Air Commando One: Heinie Aderholt And America's Secret Air Wars Warren A. Trest, Smithsonian Institution Press 2000

Ambush: the War Between the SAS and the IRA, Adams, Morgan & Bambridge, Pan, 1988

Any Place, Any Time, Any Where: The 1st Air Commandos in WWII (Schiffer Military/Aviation History), R. D. Van Wagner, Schiffer Publishing Ltd 1988

At the Hurricane's Eye: US Special Forces from Vietnam to Desert Storm, Greg Walker, 1994

Big Boys Rules, Mark Urban, Faber 1992

The Black Devil Brigade: The True Story of the First Special Service Force in World War II, Joseph A. Springer, Pacifica Pr 2001

Clandestine Warfare, Ladd, Melton & Mason, Blanford 1988

The Commandos: The Inside Story of America's Secret Soldiers Douglas C. Waller, Dell Pub Co 1995

Delta Force: The Army's Elite Counterterrorist Unit, Charlie A. Beckwith, Donald Knox, Mass Market 2000

Delta: America's Elite Counterterrorist Force, Terry Griswold et al, 1992

Elite Fighting Units, David Eshel, Arms & Armour 1984

Elite Warriors: 300 Years of America's Best Fighting Troops, Lance Q. Zedric, Michael F. Dilley, 1996

Ghost Force: The Secret History of the SAS, Ken Connor, Orion 2000

Guards Without Frontiers, Samuel M. Katz, Arms & Armour 1990

Guerrillas and Terrorists, Prof. Richard Clutterbuck, Faber 1977

The History of the SAS Regiment, John Strawson, Grafton 1986

In Search of the Warrior Spirit, Richard Strozzi Heckler, 1992

In the Combat Zone: Special Forces Since 1945, Robin Neillands, 1998

March or Die, Tony Geraghty, Arms & Armour 1986

Military Elites, Roger Beaumont, Robert Hale 1976

Mobile Guerrilla Force: With the Special Forces in War Zone D, James C. Donahue, 1997

Once Upon a Wartime: A Canadian Who Survived the Devil's Brigade, Peter L. Cottingham

Perilous Options: Special Operations As an Instrument of US Foreign Policy, Lucien S. Vandenbroucke 1993

The Quiet Operator: Special Forces Signaller Extraordinary, Simpson and Adkin 1977

SAS in Action, Peter Macdonald, Pan 1990

The SAS, Savage Wars of Peace, Anthony Kemp, John Murray 1994

SBS – The Invisible Raiders, James Ladd, Fontana 1984

Secret Armies, James Adams, Hutchinson 1987

Secret Forces of World War II, Philip Warner, Scarborough House 1991

Secret Warfare, Adrian Weale, Hodder 1997

Secret Warriors, Steven Emerson, Putnam 1978

Special Forces, Bruce Quarrie, Guild 1990

The Supercommandos: First Special Service Force, 1942–1944 An Illustrated History, Robert Todd Ross

Unconventional Warfare: Rebuilding U.S. Special Operations Forces (The Rediscovering Government Series), Susan L. Marquis, The Brookings Institution 1997

US Elite Counter-Terrorist Forces, Stephen F. Tomajczyk 1997

US Special Forces: Airborne Rangers, Landau, Landau and Halberstadt, Motorbooks International 1999

Who Dares Wins, Tony Geraghty, Little Brown 1992

However, dozens of other books and magazines were consulted and snippets used here and there, but as with all matters as subjective as unconventional warfare the opinions remain mine alone and therefore I happily accept the criticism of those I may offend.

INDEX